ONE THOUSAND LANGUAGES

Living, Endangered, and Lost

ONE THOUSAND LANGUAGES

Edited by **Peter K. Austin**

University of California Press
Berkeley   Los Angeles

University of California Press, one of the most distinguished
university presses in the United States, enriches lives around
the world by advancing scholarship in the humanities,
social sciences, and natural sciences. Its activities are
supported by the UC Press Foundation and by philanthropic
contributions from individuals and institutions.
For more information, visit www.ucpress.edu.

University of California Press
Berkeley and Los Angeles, California

Library of Congress Cataloging-in-Publication Data

One thousand languages : living, endangered, and lost /
edited by Peter K. Austin.
p.cm.
Includes bibliographical references and index.
ISBN 978-0-520-25560-9 (cloth : alk. paper)
1. Language and languages. I. Austin, Peter K.
II. Title: 1000 languages.

P371.O56 2008
417'.7—dc22   2008006958

Manufactured in China

17 16 15 14 13 12 11 10 09 08
10 9 8 7 6 5 4 3 2 1

This book was conceived, designed,
and produced by **Ivy Press**

Creative Director Peter Bridgewater
Publisher Jason Hook
Editorial Director Caroline Earle
Art Director Clare Harris
Senior Project Editor Mary Todd
Senior Art Editor Sarah Howerd
Design JC Lanaway
Cover Design Alan Osbahr
Map Creation Lyndsey Harwood
Picture Researchers Katie Greenwood,
Shelley Noronha, Sarah Skeate

CONTENTS

INTRODUCTION

There are an estimated 6,900 languages spoken in the world today. They range in size from very large, with hundreds of millions of speakers, to very small with as few as one or two speakers. This book aims to give an overview of the languages of the world, organized by broad geographical regions.

The languages of the world are unevenly distributed both geographically and across speaker populations. Just 4 percent of all languages (around 275) are spoken by 96 percent of the world's population or, in other words, just 4 percent of the world's population speaks 96 percent of its languages. The largest eight languages alone have over 150 million speakers each and together account for 40 percent of the world's population. These are the "major languages" discussed in the World Languages chapter (pages 10–35). More than half of all languages today have fewer than 10,000 speakers; more than a quarter have fewer than 1,000 speakers. In some cases of highly endangered languages in Australia or the Americas, there are just one or two elderly people who speak them. Geographic distribution of languages is also very uneven. The largest numbers of languages are spoken in Africa and Asia, and much smaller numbers elsewhere. Papua New Guinea stands out as a single island with 820 languages. Vanuatu, with 120 languages among its 100,000 population, has the highest language density of any country in the world. Each chapter of this book covers a different geographical region and presents a number of feature languages with shorter discussions of other selected languages. The chapters cover such topics as history and origins of languages, numbers of speakers, writing systems, special features, and basic vocabulary items.

Distribution of languages by area of origin

Continent	Living languages		Number of speakers	
	Count	Percent of total	Count	Percent of total
Africa	2,092	30.3	675,887,158	11.8
Americas	1,002	14.5	47,559,381	0.8
Asia	2,269	32.8	3,489,897,147	61.0
Europe	239	3.5	1,504,393,183	26.3
Pacific	1,310	19.0	6,124,341	0.1
Totals	6,912	100.0	5,723,861,210	100.0

From Gordon, Raymond G., (ed.) 1995 *Ethnologue. Languages of the World.* Fifteenth Edition. Dallas, TX: SIL International.

So what is a language? In ordinary speech we often use the terms "dialect" and "language," however it is very difficult to distinguish these terms clearly. People often think that a language is written, while a dialect is spoken. However, only about one-third of the world's languages have a form of writing, and most exist in spoken form only. Alternatively, dialects are thought of as rural and highly variable while languages are

Above and Left This book covers the sheer diversity of the written and spoken word all over the world—820 languages are spoken in Papua New Guinea

Russian and Polish descend from an ancestor proto-Slavonic, and so on). Linguists arrive at sub-group and family classifications through careful comparison of vocabulary and grammatical structure between languages that share features in common. Some classifications, such as the Indo-European family that covers most of the languages of Europe, Iran, Afghanistan, and northern South Asia are well worked out and have been deeply studied, others are more tentative and require further work. Throughout this book you will find references to language classifications and families but remember that some of these are less established than others. Note also that languages can share words and features in common for another reason, namely contact between the peoples speaking them. For example, English and French share many words in common, however, a large number of these arose from English borrowing words for French beginning during the Norman Conquest (1066) and continuing until today. English has borrowed words from hundreds of languages (think of *kangaroo* from Guugu Yimidhirr in Australia or *sushi* from Japanese, for example) and today contributes vocabulary to a great deal of languages via its influence as the language of global communication. A few languages, like Chinese and Icelandic, resist borrowing but most of the world's languages show evidence of borrowed vocabulary arising from historical patterns of contact.

The normal situation throughout the world and throughout human history is multilingualism, that is, people regularly speaking two or more languages. Communities that are monolingual, speaking just one language, are extremely rare. Most typically, multilingual communities use different languages for different purposes (one language for trade, another for education, a third for ordinary conversation, for example, or one language for writing and formal situations and another for speaking and informal contexts), or for different people (one language for in-group communication and another for speaking to outsiders, for example). Multilingualism allows people flexibility in communication and language use that is absent for monolingual societies. Sometimes we can distinguish between a language learned in childhood as a "first language" and one learned later as a "second language." In many of the chapters in this book multilingualism will be highlighted and the use of particular tongues as first or second languages will be mentioned.

Sometimes contact between communities speaking different languages results in the rise of a "lingua franca," a common tongue that serves as a neutral vehicle for both sides. These lingua francas have existed throughout human history, and frequently have very wide geographical coverage. Thus, Swahili is a lingua franca over a wide area of eastern Africa, used for trade between people speaking a huge range of different languages. Ex-colonial languages like French serve a similar function in parts of west Africa. Occasionally special contact languages are developed called "pidgins" that are simplified mixtures that are noone's native language. If such languages are learned as a first language they expand their vocabulary and grammar to become a full language called a "creole."

Examples are *Tok Pisin* in Papua New Guinea or *Krio* from Sierra Leone. Today, English has become a global lingua franca as the vehicle of everything from air traffic control to computer technology and popular music.

As mentioned above, roughly a third of the world's languages are written, and the majority of languages with writing systems have acquired them relatively recently, often as a result of education introduced during the nineteenth or twentieth centuries. Most written languages have taken their writing systems from a neighboring language, just as the Romans borrowed writing from the Etruscans who borrowed it from the Phoenecians and so on. Writing is a human invention that has developed independently only a few times in human history. In the chapters of this book the writing systems of different languages and groups will be illustrated, and patterns of borrowing and change identified.

Even if a language is not written, it will have an oral literature comprising the myths, tales, stories, and songs that encapsulate the culture and history of the people who speak it. All human societies have oral literature, and indeed much written literature originates in oral storytelling, such as the *Odyssey* written down by Homer or the fairytales like *Cinderella* collected by the Grimm Brothers in nineteenth-century Germany. Similarly, all languages have rich vocabularies to describe the environment, actions, thoughts, and feelings of the people who speak them, and complex grammatical systems to express relationships between words and sentences. There is no such thing as a "primitive language," and indeed most minority languages have grammars as complicated and difficult as any large standardized written language. The complexity and beauty of all human language is exemplified in the pages that follow.

We hope that you enjoy exploring the diversity, structure, relationships, and history of the many languages of the world displayed in the following pages.

PROFESSOR PETER K. AUSTIN
Linguistics Department, School of Oriental
and African Languages, London.
February 2008

Above and Left
Language is a unique human gift, enabling us to communicate concepts, emotions, or to inspire and entertain.

WORLD LANGUAGES

WORLD LANGUAGES

What is a world language? Above all, it is a language that is used well beyond its place of origin, so that it gives its users access to a far wider public. There is not the space to feature all such languages of wider communication in the world, but the restriction here—in this chapter's comprehensive survey of world languages—is to those with truly global speaker populations, in numbers above 100 million, or 1.5 percent of the world population. These then are not only world languages, but the top eleven by population, too.

Left *With populations increasingly dispersed throughout the world, it is often necessary to trade in multiple languages, as this store window shows.*

Above right *Children read the Bible at a missionary orphanage in Ivory Coast—part of French-speaking West Africa.*

World languages are not a new phenomenon. The Spanish scholar and grammarian Antonio de Nebrija remarked in 1492 to Queen Isabella that language had always been the companion of empire. Certainly empires on a continental scale have always required some common means of communication for administrators: Akkadian and later Aramaic for Babylon and Assyria; Aramaic and later Pahlavi for Persia; Greek for Alexander the Great of Macedon; Latin and later Greek for Rome and Byzantium; Prakrit for the Mauryas and Guptas of India; Persian for the Mughals in India too; Nahuatl for the Aztecs in Mexico; and Quechua for the Incas of Peru. The list could go on, but all these languages, great in the past, are missing from our modern list. Sometimes imperial languages are not taken up by the people; sometimes new imperial languages replace old ones. This is true of Arabic, Chinese, English, French, Hindi, Spanish, Portuguese, and Russian in our listing. Will their predominance prove any more lasting?

Trade networks have also been important in creating global languages: Phoenician and Greek in the ancient Mediterranean; Sogdian along the Silk Road from central China to the eastern Mediterranean; Arabic, Malay, and Portuguese around the coasts of the Indian Ocean; and Swahili in East Africa. English and French, too, have grown and changed from use in international business. But trade links, it seems, create weaker language allegiance than do imperial takeovers.

To establish permanent linguistic links, religion is usually more effective. Of our eleven languages here, four (Arabic, Spanish, Portuguese, and Russian) were spread with active missionary support, and another two (English and French) were taken to the Pacific by missions. Everywhere missionaries have had a major impact on language education and literacy. But perhaps the most reliable means to achieve world-language status is stability, when a speaker population grows within and from a permanent heartland: Bengali, Chinese, German, and Hindi owe most of their considerable influence to this simple process.

The languages covered in the following pages are: Arabic, Bengali, Chinese (Mandarin), English, French, German, Hindi, Japanese, Portuguese, Russian, and Spanish.

CHINESE MANDARIN

1,055 million speakers

Chinese is—linguistically—a family of languages spoken widely across the People's Republic of China (with greatest diversity in the southeast), and also in some other parts of East and Southeast Asia. Politically and culturally, however, it is a single language, as it has been for well over two millennia. Chinese is a Sino-Tibetan language, with its closest relatives in Tibet. All the historical and archeological evidence suggests that it spread from the valley of the Yellow River southward, and much later eastward, to cover the area now known as China or zhōngguó (中国) meaning "central kingdom." Yet this history presents a paradox to linguists.

Above *The major non-standard Chinese dialects are concentrated in the southeast of the country, south of the Yangtze valley.*

The area of greatest linguistic diversity—usually a sign of a language's original home—lies, however, in the southeast, south of the valley of the Yangtze, where the major non-standard dialects are concentrated. To associate them with major centers, these dialects are **Wú** (Shanghai), **Gàn** (Ganzhou), **Xiāng** (Hunan), **Mǐn** (Fujian), and **Yuè**, better known as Cantonese (Guangzhou and Hong Kong). The Hakka dialect exists in scattered communities across the southeast. They range in population from 90 million (**Wú**) to 20 million (**Gàn**), the others being about 50 million. They probably arose as different groups of non-Chinese speakers assimilated to the incoming Chinese farmers, from the fifth century BCE to the eleventh century CE. In fact, more than 200 other non-Chinese languages are still spoken by various minorities within China.

Elsewhere, the form of Chinese spoken (by more than 70 percent of the total number of speakers) is the standardized dialect of the northeast, known as Mandarin (after the Western term for Chinese administrators), or **guóyǔ** 國語 literally, "national language." Standard Chinese is now usually known as **pǔtōnghuà** 普通话 (common speech) or more generally as **zhōngguóhuà** 中国话 (Chinese speech).

Overseas, there are communities all over the coasts of the South China Sea. They largely speak **Mǐn**, with significant communities in Singapore, Malaysia, Thailand, and the

Loanwords

The constraining Chinese sound system has resisted much loan vocabulary: new foreign concepts are taken over as loan translations: e.g. **wànwéiwǎng** 万维网 (www, literally "10,000 connections net"). Chinese has exported to the West its own cultural concepts: e.g. feng-shui (風水 fēngshuǐ = wind-water). Sometimes they have arrived as loan translations: "Triads" translates as 三合会 **sān-hé-huì** (literally "three unite society").

Count to 10

Character		Pinyin	Phonetic
一	1	yī	yī
二	2	èr	èr
三	3	sān	sān
四	4	sì	sẓ
五	5	wǔ	wǔ
六	6	liù	lyòw
七	7	qī	čʰī
八	8	bā	pā
九	9	jiǔ	čyǒw
十	10	shí	šṛ

The accents show tone; the underposed circles mean the letter above is pronounced as a vowel. This shows something of the idiosyncrasies of Chinese phonetics.

Philippines. The Indonesian Chinese have largely lost their own language. The island of Hainan is **Mĭn**-speaking, as was (the Chinese community in) Taiwan before the mass incursion of Mandarin-speakers under Chiang Kai Shek in 1949: but there are still three **Mĭn**-speakers for every Mandarin. The Chinese spoken in Kyrgyzstan and Kazakhstan is known as Dungan—and like most ex-Soviet languages, it is written in Cyrillic; however, this community is extremely tiny—perhaps 50,000 speakers.

Chinese is an "isolating" language, each sentence a string of immutable monosyllables. Chinese writing represents this atomized structure directly. The syllables are rather simple, especially so in modern Mandarin. They begin with at most one consonant (there are twenty-two of these in total) and then one of thirty-three combinations of vowels + "n" or "ng." Mandarin distinguishes four tones (ā, á, ǎ, or à) on these monosyllables, for example, **mā** (mother), **má** (hemp), **mǎ** (horse, number), **mà** (blame). But of the resulting 3,036 possible syllables in the whole language, only 1,620 actually occur.

China's indigenous writing system is called **hànzì** (漢字) meaning "Han letters." Each character represents a syllable pronounced with a given tone and a meaning, in fact more like a word than a letter. The forms of characters were standardized under the Qin emperor in 221–210 BCE; but the first great literary classics (including the works of Confucius, Mencius, and Lao-tse) go back to 770–476 BCE. This form of the language, known as **Wényán** (文言), or Classical Chinese, continued in use until the early twentieth century, regardless of any changes in spoken Chinese. But in the 1920s and 1930s, under the new Chinese Republic (1911), it was officially replaced by the colloquial form **Bái huà** (白話) meaning "white speech"—as used in Beijing—which had long been the language of popular literature.

The forms of the characters were somewhat simplified in 1956 and 1964; for example, 國語 became 国语, 漢字 became 汉字. But these changes were not followed outside the People's Republic: Taiwan and Chinese communities in Southeast Asia keep the old forms, and Japan has simplified its characters rather less, but differently.

15

ENGLISH 👄   **760 million speakers**

English is now the most widely used language in the world, although only 400 years ago it was hardly known outside its home in the British Isles, with approximately 7 million speakers, or about 1.5 percent of the world population at that time. It now has some 330 million native speakers (5 percent of the world population), but if users of English as a second language or as a business lingua franca are included then that figure rises to 760 million (12 percent). This makes English the second most populous language in the world, behind Chinese, which has more than 875 million native speakers (15 percent of the world population), and perhaps 1,055 million users (17 percent of the world population).

Below *American English is familiar throughout the world as a result of its dominance in movies, television, and popular music.*

English is that rare phenomenon, a language that appears to have arisen at a determinate date. In the fifth to sixth centuries CE, Germanic raiders, speaking various Low German dialects (including Saxon and Frisian) settled in eastern Britain, from Kent to Lothian. English developed in these areas, a highly inflected language comparable in complexity to Latin. In the ninth to tenth centuries it was influenced by Norse invaders from Scandinavia; the resulting mixture of Germanic languages probably effaced inflexions marking case in nouns and person in verbs.

After 1066, the Saxon ruling class was replaced by French-speaking Normans; English became exclusively a commoners' language for two centuries. This also affected English vocabulary; by 1450, half the words recorded in English were of French origin (e.g. curtain, chair, towel, dance, music, squirrel, forest, park). But political links with France were gradually lost, and in the fourteenth century the Black Death, especially devastating in cities, told against the French-speaking classes; English re-emerged as the common language of England.

By the tenth century, English had produced some of the earliest vernacular (that is, post-Latin) literature in Europe: King Alfred was one major writer. Vernacular English literature enjoyed a new vogue in the fourteenth to fifteenth centuries, led by Geoffrey Chaucer (c.1343–1400), and authors used many different dialects. Two generations after Chaucer, printing was introduced by William Caxton (d.1492): a standard for English was established, based on the language of London, Oxford, and Cambridge. The great flowering of English literature then came at the turn of the seventeenth century, the age of Shakespeare and the King James Authorized Translation of the "Bible," and a rich harvest of words was further borrowed from Latin (e.g. education, protest, attempt, maturity).

For its first 1,000 years English was restricted to the British Isles. Only in the past four centuries, beginning with Sir Walter Raleigh's failed 1586 colony in Virginia, has English spread around the world. In North America, English farming settlements grew and crowded out both native peoples and competing Europeans, such as the French and Dutch. It then took a mere century for the coastal strip claimed for the thirteen American Colonies in 1750 to be expanded westward to cover the whole breadth of North America. North America was soon filled with immigrants who spoke other languages.

The USA (through Noah Webster's *Dictionary*, 1828) has asserted its own standard for the language, though the written differences from British English are slight: the main spoken difference (key to "an American accent") is a thoroughgoing nasalization of vowels. "General American" is now familiar worldwide through the US dominance of broadcast media, especially news coverage, film, television, and pop music. Other English-speaking territories, such as Australia and New Zealand, South Africa, Nigeria, and the Caribbean islands have evolved their own spoken norms, but have been less able to project them worldwide.

The UK discouraged English settlement in its next major colony, India, being determined to maintain it as a trading dependency. Missionary concerns, however, ensured that English, as well as trade, would follow the flag in the nineteenth century, and all colonies either acquired a majority of white (English-speaking) settlers, or at least spread English to elites among local populations.

By 1897, the year of Queen Victoria's Diamond Jubilee, the language was being used across a quarter of the world's surface. British political control disappeared in the twentieth century, but the use of English persisted and even grew, very much reinforced by the business and cultural expansion of the USA after the Second World War.

Count to 10

Modern English		Middle English thirteenth to fifteenth century (showing varying dialects)	Old English tenth century (West Saxon standard)
one	1	on(e), oon(e), ane, oo, o	ān
two	2	twey(e), tweyne, tuo, twa	twēgen
three	3	thre(e), þreo, þrinne	þrīe
four	4	four, fowr	fēower
five	5	fyve	fīf
six	6	syxe	siex
seven	7	sevyn, seve, sovene	seofon
eight	8	æchte, eachte, eyghte	eahta
nine	9	nighe, nyghe, neyghe, nie, niene	nigon
ten	10	ten(e)	tīen

Above *A twelfth-century Lewis chess piece, evidence of Norse settlements in Britain.*

HINDI

490 million speakers

Officially, and by the number of native speakers, Hindi is the leading language of India. The word "Hindi" is derived from Persian and means simply "Indian," though nowadays the terms are by no means synonymous: Hindi refers to a specific group of languages rather than all of the many languages that are spoken in India. Originating in Aryan dialects from the area around Delhi, Hindi was spread by Muslim powers that dominated northern and central India from the thirteenth century, and it was promoted further during the time of the British Raj. Since 1947 it has aspired to be a language for all India, but it has not yet transcended the perception that its use favors the north over the south.

Above *The Mughal Empire ruled India from the early sixteenth to the mid-nineteenth centuries, and was instrumental in spreading the Hindi language.*

Below *Hindi is spoken natively in northern and central areas of India, a region that has become known as the "Hindi belt."*

Hindi has official status throughout the country, and is spoken natively in most of northern and central India, which is the so-called "Hindi belt," comprising the regions of Bihar in the east to Rajasthan in the west. The central dialects are Braj (northwestern) and Awadhi, which is more highly inflected (southeastern); but speakers of variants such as Rajasthani in the east, Bhojpuri and Maithili in the west, Chattisgarhi in the south, and even Panjabi in the north, often see themselves as part of the Hindi community. Dialect boundaries are not fixed, nor even well understood.

Under the British Raj, many Indians moved as indentured laborers to other colonies, notably Mauritius, South Africa, the Caribbean, and Fiji. Their communities (and language) persist, self-identified as Hindi, although it seems that most came from the Bhojpuri area. This diaspora only numbers about 1 million speakers in all, half a percent of the speaker population in India. Twentieth-century emigrants, largely to the UK and USA, are also relatively few, but are now distinguished among Indian migrant communities as mostly highly qualified (as against, for example, speakers of Panjabi, Gujarati, or Bengali).

Hindi is first recognizable around the thirteenth century as **Khaṛī Bolī** (standing speech), a term still used for the standard, which is closest to Braj. Its literature was mostly devotional, and in verse, until the nineteenth century. In some cases, dialect diversity translates to religious affiliation: among Hindus, Krishna is praised in Braj, but Rama in Awadhi. The most famous poem in Hindi is Tulsi Das's *Rāmcaritmānas*, an epic about Rama narrated in Baiswari, a dialect close to Awadhi. Hindi was then heavily influenced by Persian, the official language of a series of Muslim conquerors, especially the last, the Mughals, who arrived in India in the early sixteenth century; known as Hindustani, this dialect spread as a lingua franca to most parts of India under Muslim rule. Finding it a convenient medium of communication, the

British colonial rulers promoted Hindustani further, moderating the use of loans from Persian, as did national leaders such as Mahatma Gandhi who sought unity rather than partition for the country after Independence in 1947.

At this time, however, Hindustani was notionally divided as Urdu for Muslims, written in Persian/Arabic script, and Hindi for everyone else, written in Devanagari. With its high prestige, Urdu was then recognized as the official language of Pakistan, although it had not previously been much spoken in any of its territories, either to the east or west.

When spoken, Urdu and Hindi are identical, if speakers stick to basic vocabulary; but Hindi is consciously developed with loans from Sanskrit, whereas Urdu still draws on Persian and Arabic. Such contrasting words are more common in abstract, technical, or euphemistic vocabulary: hence "freedom" in Urdu is āzādī but in Hindi is swatantratā; "visibility" in Urdu is namūdār, in Hindi driśyatā; "lavatory" in Urdu is pāχānā, in Hindi shauchālay. Nonetheless, the shared basic vocabulary has words from both sources: for example, ādmī (man) from Persian, but laṛkā (boy) and laṛkī (girl) from Aryan dārik-. Words borrowed directly from Sanskrit are called **tatsama** (that-same), those inherited (often with vast sound changes) are called **tadbhāva** (that-origin): so "village" (Sanskrit **grāmas**) turns up as both **grām** and **gãw**, "tiger" (Sanskrit **vyāgʰras**) as **vyāgʰr** and **bāgʰ**; the word "see" dekh-, is from dṛkṣ-, directly related to the root of "visibility" above.

Hindi is being promoted as a neutral national language in India, with pressure for it to replace English in all its roles. However, Hindi is still seen as a north Indian language by speakers of Dravidian languages in the south and withdrawal of English, originally scheduled for 1965, has been postponed indefinitely.

Count to 10

१	1	एक(ek)
२	2	दो (do)
३	3	तीन (tīn)
४	4	चार(čār)
५	5	पांच (pānč)
६	6	छै (čʰɛ)
७	7	सात(sāt)
८	8	आठ(āṭʰ)
९	9	नौ (nɔ)
१०	10	दस (das)

Hindi has its own variants of the numeral symbols.

Loanwords

Until the twentieth century, loans into Hindi came from Arabic and Persian: now they come from Sanskrit, but also from English (e.g. **ṭrafik**, **ṭænis**, **ṭāiṭs**). Loans from Hindi into English were legion during the two centuries of British Raj: for example, chintz, cot, loot, pyjama, thug, shampoo. There have also been cultural items—particularly clothes (dungarees, puttee, sola topi) and food (chutney, ghee, kedgeree)—and slang expressions: "take a dekko" (look), "in chokey" (jailed), "don't give a dam" (a brass farthing).

Left *Hindi is usually written in Devanagari script, while the Urdu alphabet is derived from Persian/Arabic script. When spoken, however, the two languages have many similarities.*

SPANISH

417 million speakers

Count to 10

uno	1
dos	2
tres	3
cuatro	4
cinco	5
seis	6
siete	7
ocho	8
nueve	9
diez	10

Spanish has its roots in Latin, because it evolved in the center of the Iberian Peninsula when under Roman influence. One dialect, Castilian, spread to become the official language of the whole of Spain in the fifteenth century, and shortly after it disseminated to the Americas. It is now one of the four most widely used languages in the world. Although Latin had been spoken throughout Spain since the Roman conquests of the second century BCE—replacing all the previous Iberian languages except Basque—the linguistic equilibrium was repeatedly shaken after the fall of the Roman Empire, by Germanic invaders in the fifth century CE, Byzantines in the sixth century, and Arabs and Berbers in the eighth century.

By 732 all but the northern strip of Asturias was in Muslim hands, and Arab rule was stable for the next three centuries, spreading Andalusi Arabic at the expense of Mozarabic Latin.

Modern Spanish originated during this early period in the central region of Castile (named for its castles). Yet in the first millennium CE, there seemed little prospect that this dialect would be especially influential. But Spain was to undergo yet another military reversal: Christians managed to reclaim Spain from the Arabs over the period from 1037 to 1492, and it was the spread of their language that became the true foundation of modern Spanish. Although all the different regions (but principally Galicia in the west, Aragon and Catalonia in the east) had their own regional languages, the political triumph of Castile meant that only Castilian was established as a contender as the national language for Spain. (The political independence of Portugal gave its form of Galician the chance to establish itself as another national language.)

Furthermore, it was Castile that produced the grammarian of genius Antonio de Nebrija, who understood that his language could be standardized with rules, on a par with Latin grammar: in 1492 he presented his Spanish grammar to Queen Isabella as a foundation for Spain's future imperial role, creating the world's first consciously national language. He was prescient: within two generations, Spanish was established, permanently, in the Americas—its main centers being in Mexico and Peru—whence it was carried across the Pacific to the Philippines.

Below *The conquest of a Moorish army base by John II of Castile, 1431. Castilian became the official language of Spain in the fifteenth century, providing the basis for modern Spanish.*

The golden age of Spanish literature was created largely in this same period, the sixteenth and early seventeenth centuries. Its masterwork is widely accepted as Miguel Cervantes' *El ingenioso hidalgo don Quixote de la Mancha*, an extended satire on the romantic fantasy literature of the age. Lope de Vega, a contemporary, is Spain's classic dramatist. Nowadays, the Spanish language is most famous for "magical realist" literature by such writers as Carlos Fuentes of Mexico, Mario Vargas Llosa of Peru, and Gabriel García Márquez of Colombia, and for its telenovelas (soap operas) such as *Yo soy Betty, la Fea* (*Ugly Betty*).

Spanish in the Americas is in mostly minor ways distinct from the Spanish of Spain. In Central and South America, "z" or "c" before "e" or "i" is pronounced exactly like "s," much as it is in southern Spain: **cocer** (cook), and **coser** (sew), are pronounced the same. Likewise "ll" (lʸ) and "y" are often pronounced as "ž" (French "j"), though in modern Spanish there are few if any words that are distinguished by them. In some parts of the Americas, especially Argentina and

Central America, **vós** instead of **tú**, is used for the informal "you." And there are differences in vocabulary between Spanish of the Americas and that of Spain—**amarrar** for **atar** (to tie up), **botar** for **echar** (to throw)—some due to the influence of English, for example, **educación** for **pedagogía**, **lonche** (lunch) for **almuerzo**.

Spanish flourished in almost all regions of the Spanish Empire, even after the liberation wars of the 1820s; only in the Philippines, which Spain lost to the USA in 1898, was it replaced as the official non-native language by English. Spanish now benefits from massive population growth in Latin America, and from large numbers of immigrants into the USA, especially to the traditional Spanish-speaking regions (these being California, Arizona, and New Mexico) that were annexed in the Mexican-American War of 1846–48. Chicano Spanish (short for Mexicano) remains significant in these regions as well. By population Spanish is now among the top four most widely used languages of the world, comparable with English and Hindi, though of course far behind Chinese.

Above *A mural with Spanish text adorns this school wall in Caracas, Venezuela. The language has continued to flourish in former Spanish colonies.*

Loanwords

The Arabic influence on Spanish, exercised over seven centuries of coexistence in the Iberian Peninsula, can be seen in a profusion of some 4,000 borrowed words, many beginning with *a-/al-/az-*, representing the Arabic definite article: **alcohol**, **ajedrez** (chess), **almacén** (emporium), **almohada** (cushion), **azúcar** (sugar), **berenjena** (aubergine), **fulano** (so-and-so), **jinete** (rider), **tambor** (drum) and even **usted** (you) if it was derived from **ustādh** (master) rather than, as usually claimed, **Vuestra Merced** (your grace).

RUSSIAN

277 million speakers

Count to 10

Cyrillic		Roman
один	1	odín
два	2	dva
три	3	tri
четыре	4	četir^{y}e
пять	5	p^{y}at^y
шесть	6	šest^y
семь	7	s^{y}em^y
восемь	8	vós^{y}em^y
девять	9	d^{y}év^{y}at^y
десять	10	d^{y}és^{y}at^y

Russian is the largest, and the farthest east, of the Slavic languages. Until 1917 it was the official language of the Russian Empire. Under Communist rule, individual republics were nominally permitted their own official languages, but Russian retained a superior status. As well as being used on the eastern plains of Europe, it is now spoken all over northern Asia, and is the world's fifth most spoken language. But the political setbacks that Russia faced at the end of the twentieth century, especially the dissolution of the Soviet Union in 1991, plus an aging Russian-speaking population, mean that Russian faces a more uncertain future than other world languages.

Below *St. Cyril and St. Methodius are widely credited for devising the Cyrillic alphabet. It is still used today in several languages, including Russian.*

Russian has been the lingua franca of eastern Europe, and northern and central Asia, the area of the Soviet Union that collapsed in 1991. Despite losses in peripheral states, it is holding its ground within the remaining domains of Russia, which still include much of the Caucasus and all of Siberia, an area of more than 6.6 million sq miles (17 million sq km), or 11.5 percent of the world's total landmass. The two neighboring languages to the west, Belarusian (or Belorussian) and Ukrainian, are linguistically very close to Russian, though often separated over the last 1,000 years by a national border.

The language community of eastern Slavs had probably migrated from the Baltic region in the fifth century CE, but had been converted to Orthodox Christianity, and learned to write, only in the tenth century. Russian, as the language of Moscow, began disseminating in 1240, when Kiev, previously the leading city of

Russia, and at that point speaking essentially the same language as that of Moscow, was destroyed by the Mongols and Turks of the Golden Horde. The Russian leadership passed from Kiev to the northern city of Moscow; but only 300 years later, with the campaigns of Ivan the Terrible in the mid-sixteenth century, did Russia turn the tables on the Golden Horde, and begin its expansion to the east, west, south, and north. One hundred years later the power of the tsar (Russian for *Caesar*) had reached the Pacific (and indeed Alaska, which remained Russian until 1860), and Russian, and the Orthodox Church, followed. Russia incorporated Belarus and Ukraine in the eighteenth century, the Caucasus and Central Asia in the nineteenth.

Russian dominated a vast linguistic range of more than eighty other languages, and this dominion was maintained after the monarchy was overthrown during the Russian Revolution in 1917 and during the seventy years of Communist rule in the twentieth century. Literacy rates increased from 28 percent in 1897 to 99.7 percent in 1970, and Russian was the first human language to be used in space, by astronaut Yuri Gagarin in 1960.

Russian has remained a highly inflected language. It has three genders, two numbers, and six cases of inflexion for nouns and adjectives. For verbs it has three persons, two numbers, but only three tenses: past, present, and future. Verbs, however, usually come in pairs, which differ in aspect: one aspect views the verb's action as a complete whole e.g. **uvíd^yel** (meaning saw, or espied), while the other looks at the verb's action as something ongoing, in other words, as a process or a custom e.g. **víd^yel** (could see, or used to see). One of the most difficult parts of the grammar is to explain fully and exactly when to choose which verb form in a given context.

The classic era for Russian literature was the nineteenth century. The leading Russian novelists such as Lev Tolstoy, Fyodor Dostoyevski, and Nikolay Gogol, and dramatists such as Anton Chekhov, gained a worldwide reputation. For Russians, though, the absolute master remains Aleksandr Pushkin (1799–1837), the poet, playwright (his most famous play being *Boris Godunov*), and novelist who died young in a duel. Poetry is also an extremely popular art form in Russia, and was often (as for Osip Mandelshtam and Olga Tsvetayeva) though not always (as for Yevgeny Yevtushenko) the focus of political disaffection during the Soviet era.

Russian is always written in the Cyrillic alphabet, **kirillitsa**, originally largely derived from Greek but probably supplemented with other alphabets, for example Ц, Ш from Hebrew צ "ts" and שׁ "sh." The alphabet's invention is credited to St. Cyril and St. Methodius, brother missionaries in Moravia (central Czech Republic) in the 860s. Cyrillic was adapted for Bulgarian in the late ninth century and Russian in the late tenth century.

Above *The 1917 Revolution led to wider education in many languages of Siberia and Central Asia, emphasizing literacy, but after 1939 the Cyrillic alphabet was imposed.*

Right *An illuminated page from Radoslav's Gospels, beautifully lettered in Cyrillic by the Serbian scribe in 1429.*

Russian literacy has maintained use of the Cyrillic alphabet. The Soviet government imposed the Cyrillic script on all the languages of East and Central Asia within the Soviet Union during the late 1930s. Hence, after the dissolution of the Soviet Union in 1991, many of the Turkic languages chose to reintroduce Roman script. Within one century, these languages have known four different scripts: Persian, Roman, Cyrillic, and back to Roman.

BENGALI

230 million speakers

Bengali, increasingly known by its local name Bangla, is the second largest of the Indo-Aryan languages derived from Sanskrit, prevalent in the state of West Bengal in India and neighboring Bangladesh. It breeds strong loyalties and has a long literary tradition. The people of Bangladesh have fought for this language, but it also provided the words for the national anthem of India. Bengali is spoken in a single area covering about 186,416 sq miles (300,000 sq km), or just 7 percent of the subcontinent. Nevertheless, it is on the lips of one person in seven (15 percent). It is one of the world's most populous languages, outranking French or German, but smaller than Hindi. The largest expatriate community, in the UK, numbers about 400,000.

Above *Bengali script is derived from the Brahmic family of scripts, the same family as the Devanagari script used for writing Hindi.*

Below *Despite the relatively small area in which it is spoken, Bengali is one of the world's most populous languages.*

Bengali is the official language of Bangladesh (formerly East Pakistan) and several Indian states; it is sole official in West Bengal and co-official in Tripura, Cachar (South Assam), and the Andaman and Nicobar Islands.

The name derives from **Vangāla**, country of the Vanga, who lived at the mouth of the Ganges. However, modern "Bengal" (the name filtered through Persian) extends northward to ancient **Gauḍa**, where the Brahmaputra river turns south to join the Ganges. Bangla is related to Sanskrit, and comes from Magadhi, a language which by the later first millennium BCE had spread over the whole eastern course of the Ganges: the Buddha and the emperor Ashoka, living in Patna, both spoke it. But in Sanskrit plays it is put into the mouths of lower-caste characters. The properties of Magadhi are still characteristic of Bengali and its neighbors: the prevalence of ɔ rather than "a" or "uh" as its basic vowel-sound; and various coalescences, "r" into "l," "v" into "b," and all Sanskrit's hissing sounds such as "s," "ś," "š" (compare: soon, huge, shoot) are merged into hushing "š." Bengali script comes from the Brahmi alphabet (used by the emperor Ashoka in the third century BCE for edicts across India). It began to diverge from Devanagari in the eleventh century CE but was not standardized in print until 1778.

Bengali itself has many dialects. Nowadays the main written variants center on the two capitals, Kolkata in East Bengal and Dhaka in Bangladesh. Dhaka is noted for dropping "h"s: Kolkata **čhobi hɔbe** versus Dhaka **čobi oibɛ**, (will be a picture). Sylheti in the northeast is often considered separate: it has "f" and "x" where standard Bengali has "ph" and "kh." Chittagong is also different, even tonal, like the (unrelated) languages to its east, Burmese and Arakanese. Eastern dialects also lack nasal vowels, characteristic of central India (and notable in Hindi): Kolkata **bãši** and Dhaka **baši**, meaning "flute" (compare Sanskrit **vãśa**).

CACHAR

WEST BENGAL

TRIPURA

Dhaka

ANDAMAN AND NICOBAR ISLANDS

BANGLADESH

In Bengali grammar—like its surrounding languages, Assamese and Oriya, but unlike central Indo-Aryan such as Hindi—nouns have no gender; verbs mark person (I/we, you, he/she/they) and honor (intimate, familiar, formal), but not number. The verb comes last. Copular sentences of the form "X is Y" can lack a verb altogether: **še šikkɔk** means "he (is a) teacher."

Written Bengali has six centuries of history, but since the nineteenth century a new standard has been asserted: **čolit-bhaša** (running language), with shorter inflected forms, for example, **tara jačče** instead of **tahara jaiteče**, meaning "they are going." Crucially, Bengal's greatest modern writer, Rabindranath Tagore (1861–1941) favored **čolit-bhaša**. India's West Bengal is now more literate than Bangladesh (70 percent versus 43 percent), all in **čolit-bhaša**. Two thousand titles are published in Bengali every year in India, about 10 percent of the national total, and only slightly fewer than Hindi. (English-language titles in India number about 7,000 per year.)

Bengali was the mother tongue of many of India's founding fathers: India's national anthem, written by Tagore, is actually in Bengali, though its usual pronunciation when sung makes it sound more like Hindi. Bengali has been even more significant in Bangladesh. At Independence in 1947 Urdu had been decreed the sole official language for Pakistan (though Bengali was more widely spoken in the east, and Panjabi in the west); after a bloody demonstration in Dhaka on February 21, 1952, Bengali was made a national language. The anniversary has become "Language Day" or **bhaša dibaš**, now endorsed internationally by UNESCO.

Count to 10

১	1	এক (ek / ek / ek),
২	2	দুই (dui / dui / dui)
৩	3	তিন (tin / tin / tin)
৪	4	চার (tʃa:r / čār / char)
৫	5	পাঁচ (pa:ntʃ / pānč / panch)
৬	6	ছয় (tʃhɔj / čhɔy / chhoy)
৭	7	সাত (ʃa:t / šāt / shat)
৮	8	আট (a:ʈ / āʈ / art)
৯	9	নয় (nɔj / nɔy / noy)
১০	10	দশ (dɔʃ / dɔš / dosh)

Bengali has its own variants of the numeral symbols.

Below *The vibrant flower market in Calcutta, West Bengal.*

ARABIC  **205 million speakers**

Arabic is spoken across western Asia and North Africa in many distinct dialects, often viewed as languages. A single form, Classical Arabic—fuṣḥā—is used as the religious language of Islam, and also for written and formal communication; dialects are seldom written or employed in the media. Arabic script has been used for other languages wherever Islam (and hence literacy in Arabic) has spread: Persian, Urdu, Pashto, and until recently Hausa, Swahili, and Malay. Arabic is a Semitic language and as such closely related to Hebrew; to Punic, the language of Rome's great adversary Carthage; and to Aramaic, spread in the ancient Near and Middle East by the Assyrian and Persian Empires.

Above *A miniature showing the battle of Karbala (Iraq) in 680 BCE. This is one of the most significant battles in the history of Islam.*

Arabic was almost unknown outside Arabia until the seventh century CE; but in the two generations after the death of the prophet Muhammad in 632, Arab conquests spread it as far as Afghanistan in the east and Iberia in the west. In the ninth century cultural and social changes eliminated Arabic (outside the mosque) from central Asia and Iran. In the fourteenth century it died out in Spain and Portugal, the victim of Christian reconquests. Nevertheless, it became permanently established in the Middle East between Iraq and Morocco, where previously Aramaic and Punic had been widespread. Arabic was also disseminated south down the Nile into Sudan and westward south of the Sahara desert to Timbuktu. Strangely, the extensive use of the language by Arab traders around the Indian Ocean did not help its growth there significantly at all.

Arabic had already been a literary language before Muhammad received his prophecy in it (subsequently recorded in the Qur'an). Arabic soon became the staple of Islamic education, a world language in the making. Its spelling was minutely analyzed and reformed to reconcile Muhammad's dialect with the norm: this had lacked the glottal stop and case endings, so these features, retained in Classical Arabic, are marked with accents. Its grammar too was minutely analyzed (notably by the Persian linguist Sibawayhi at the end of the eighth century), and hence standardized. The standardization developed at that time remains unchanged to this day, and is used in publishing, broadcasting, universities, politics, and business.

Count to 10

Numeral		Written	Classical	Iraqi	Moroccan
١	1	واحد	wāḥid	wāḥid	waḥed
٢	2	اثنين	iθnayni	iθnēn	žūž
٣	3	ثلاثة	θalāθah	θalāθe	tlata
٤	4	اربعة	arbaʕah	arbaʕa	arbaʕ
٥	5	خمسة	xamsah	xamse	xamsa
٦	6	تة	sittah	sitta	setta
٧	7	سبعة	sabʕah	sebʕa	sebʕa
٨	8	ثمانية	θamāniyah	θemāniye	tmenya
٩	9	تسعة	tisʕah	tisʕe	tesʕūd
١٠	10	عشرة	ʕašarah	ʕašere	ʕašra

Arabic's so-called "dialects" are not in general mutually intelligible, no doubt partly reflecting the earlier languages of these regions. These dialects are not used outside their home communities. They do, however, fall into more closely related groups: the east (and south), centered on the bloc bounded by Yemen, Iraq, Syria, and Egypt, but also including Sudan and Chad; and the west, which covers the remainder of North Africa as far as Mauritania, and Maltese, now usually considered a separate language. There are also some small outlying dialects, Kashkadarya and Tajiki eastward in Uzbekistan and Afghanistan, and Hassaniyya westward in Mauritiania and Mali; the verb system has been radically simplified in all of them.

Arabic has a wide range of consonants. It describes itself as **lugat aḍ ḍaḍ** (language of the ḍ), and there is a consciousness, and perhaps

pride, that Classical Arabic and most of its dialects have preserved, more fully than any other Semitic language, the range of "emphatic" consonant sounds, ṣ, ḍ, ṭ, ẓ, which are articulated with a certain tension (its essence still controversial among linguists); it also has pharyngealized consonants ḥ and ʕ, to be distinguished from "h," "x," and the glottal stop ʔ; uvular "q," distinct from velar "k"; and fricative θ, ð, distinct from "t," "d," as well as from "s" and "z."

Arabic has sisters in the south of Arabia—the Arabian languages, known from inscriptions since the eighth century BCE, including Sabaean, the Queen of Sheba's language. Nowadays, Arabian languages include Mehri, Shhawri, Harsusi, Bathari, and, offshore, Soqotri.

Above *Sheet from a tenth-century Qur'an manuscript written in the Kufic script, the oldest calligraphic form of the Arabic script.*

Below *An advertisement for wedding dresses in Alexandria, Egypt. Modern Standard Arabic is the language of the vast majority of written material in the Arabic-speaking world.*

Loanwords

The vast mass of learned vocabulary in Persian and Turkish, absorbed during the past millennium, comes from Arabic. Arabic also had a massive effect on the languages of western Europe in the eleventh to thirteenth centuries, when many Arabic-language scholarly works (especially in medicine, astronomy, and mathematics) were translated into Latin: hence alcohol, saffron, mummy, almanac, cipher, and zero.

PORTUGUESE  **191 million speakers**

Portuguese owes its worldwide dissemination ultimately to its pioneering naval explorations from the late fifteenth century, which created a trading empire (and a network of Catholic missions) around the Indian Ocean in the sixteenth and seventeenth centuries. But the most significant spread of Portuguese—to Brazil—came almost as an afterthought. Although Brazil was discovered by the Portuguese explorer and navigator Pedro Álvares Cabral in 1500 CE, a large-scale settlement for the mother country was not established until the early eighteenth century. Brazil remained a Portuguese colony until it achieved independence in 1822.

Above *Vasco da Gama's third journey to India, 1524. Gama is a key figure in Portugal's history, opening trade routes to Asia for the first time.*

Count to 10

um	1
dois	2
três	3
quatro	4
cinco	5
seis	6
sete	7
oito	8
nove	9
dez	10

Portuguese has its roots in Latin, as it evolved in the northwest of Iberia (the name for the area covered by modern-day Spain and Portugal when under Roman influence). Being associated with a kingdom independent since 1179 CE, Portuguese has achieved the status of a national language; yet Galician (Gallego), now considered a minority language of northwestern Spain, sounds very similar—with different spelling.

Portuguese was spread around the world by Portuguese mariners, the first to seize the potential of long-distance navigation. In 1497 Vasco da Gama had rounded the Cape of Good Hope—the southern tip of the African continent—and established the beginnings of the Portuguese trading network across the Indian Ocean, soon extended from Sofala in Mozambique through Goa in India to Macao in China. The Portuguese language followed this trade, and became a lingua franca of the Indian Ocean. By the seventeenth and eighteenth centuries it was being used in the British and Dutch colonies, too, also becoming associated with Christian missions.

Pedro Álvares Cabral discovered Brazil in 1500, en route to Asia. The colonies set up there were largely missionary outposts—and Tupinambá, an indigenous language, was the main medium, spoken between Jesuit missionaries and their converts. But the Jesuits—and the use of Tupinambá—were banned in 1759. More importantly for the Portuguese, gold and precious stones were discovered in Brazil in the late seventeenth and early eighteenth centuries, causing a rush of settlers from the old country. To them, as Portuguese speakers, were added the 3.6 million slaves brought in between 1526 and 1870. As a result, Brazil has become the largest Portuguese-speaking nation on earth, with seventeen speakers for every one in Portugal. Brazilian Portuguese is no more different from the European original than American is from British English. Certain vowels have a different quality, giving a distinctive Brazilian accent. Some words have developed variant senses: **virar**, which means "make a turning" in Portugal, can mean "change into" in Brazil; **função** which means "function" in Brazil, can also mean a "dance party" in Portugal.

Portuguese is widely spoken in creolized forms, especially in the Atlantic Islands of Cape Verde, São Tomé, Annobon, and Principe; on the western coast of India in the dialects of Daman and Diu; in Sri Lanka; in Malacca in Malaysia, where it is called Papiá Kristang from Portuguese **papear** (chatter), and **cristã** (Christian), and Macao (macauenho). There are Portuguese creoles in the Americas, for example, Papiamentu in the Dutch Antilles. The complex inflexions of Portuguese inherited from Latin are replaced by less involved structures. In Diu, "dog" may still be **cão** and "son" **filho**, but in the plural they become **cão-cão** and **fi-fi**, instead of **cães** and **filhos**. Verb forms are likewise made up of distinct parts, with person and tense markers separate: **eu tá vai** (I stand go = I am going); **eu já comeu**, (I already eat = I ate); **eu had vai**, (I have go = I shall go). These forms are instead of the standard (and irregular) **vou**, **comi**, **irei**.

Very recently, the numbers of Portuguese speakers have been increasing in the African colonies of Angola and Mozambique; these were originally centers of the slave trade, with a very small Portuguese-speaking elite. Portugal's tiny East Indian colony of East Timor, having undone the Indonesian invasion of 1975, voted in 2002 to restore Portuguese as one of its official languages. This seems a largely symbolic gesture, since there are few Portuguese speakers among young Timorese. The economic and demographic growth of Brazil in the twentieth and early twenty-first centuries suggests that the importance of Portuguese will continue to increase.

Above *The Monument to the Discoveries in Lisbon, Portugal, built in 1960.*

Below *Passersby browse a news stand in Brazil, which now has the largest population of Portuguese speakers in the world.*

FRENCH

128 million speakers

Count to 10

French		Occitan
un	1	un
deux	2	dous
trois	3	tres
quatre	4	quatre
cinq	5	cinq
six	6	sièis
sept	7	sèt
huit	8	vue
neuf	9	nòu
dix	10	dès

French is the language of the state of France, though native also to Belgium, Luxembourg, Monaco, and Switzerland. As France was a dominant power in Europe from the ninth to the nineteenth century, so French became Europe's most important language. Only after the First World War did French begin to yield its international role to English. As Roman consul in Gaul, Julius Caesar, in a single decade (59–49 BCE) extended Roman control from the Province (along the Mediterranean) to the area of modern France, and so laid the basis for French (which derives from Latin), as spoken in Gaul. This territory was Celtic-speaking before the Roman Conquest, and was invaded again by (Germanic) Franks and Burgundians in the fifth century CE.

Above *French-speaking Europe today: France (including Corsica), Luxembourg, Monaco, and parts of Belgium and Switzerland.*

Since then French has undergone considerable foreign influence in its development. There were many other Romance dialects spoken in France, but the language that has become "French" derives principally from the speech of the Île de France, the area that includes Paris, which has been the capital of the country ever since the reign of the Frankish king Clovis (late fifth century).

After the Norman Conquest of 1066, the Norman ruling classes disseminated French throughout England, and the language continued to dominate official discourse there until the Black Death ravaged English society in the late fourteenth century. The Crusades, beginning in the eleventh century and undertaken above all at the instigation of France and by French knights, also spread French to Palestine, though the French-speaking communities did not long outlast Muslim reconquest in the thirteenth century.

France itself was at last fully united under a Parisian king in 1453. In the next century Parisian French spread as the standard for the whole country after the Ordinance of Villers-Cotterêts of King François I in 1539: henceforth all official documents—at all levels down to the parish— were to be written *en langage* **maternel françois et non autrement** (in the French mother tongue and not otherwise). This gave French priority over Latin, as well as over other Romance varieties; hitherto, the main dialect of the south, Occitan (or Provençal), had developed as a distinct language, with its own literature.

French gathered prestige from the sixteenth to the nineteenth century, as France became the dominant military power and cultural leader in Europe. René Descartes, the French philosopher and mathematician, was the first European scholar to have a major work (*Discours de la Méthode*, 1637) published in a vernacular language. An Academy was founded in 1635 to regulate the language, and its influence can be felt to this day. French also benefited from the decline of Latin as the universal language of the

BRASSERIE LES PONCHETT

this time in North and Central Africa, and Indochina. French remains official in twenty-one African states, where it is still current among elites.

The Treaty of Versailles, in 1919, saw French begin to be replaced by English as the dominant language of international diplomacy. From the 1950s France, like all the other remaining European powers, started to withdraw from its colonies worldwide. But, with its self-appointed **mission civilisatrice** to the world at large, France has created an international organization of French-speaking countries and governments, **la Francophonie**, to sustain the use and influence of its language. As a matter of tactics, France has increasingly supported multilingualism, even though this goes against the traditional language policy in France (called **jacobinisme**), which is highly centralizing: even in 1992 France added to its constitution the stipulation that "the language of the Republic is French."

Left *A busy Paris street café. The French language derives mainly from the speech of the Île de France region, which includes the capital city.*

Below *A school for girls in Ouagadougou, Burkina Faso—part of French-speaking West Africa.*

European elites, and in the seventeenth century became the leading language in diplomacy. French literature, especially novels and plays, dominated eighteenth- and nineteenth-century European culture. In Russian high society it was the fashion to speak French instead of Russian.

French was also transplanted overseas: it was widely spoken in the sugar plantations of the Caribbean, and from the beginning of the seventeenth century it was the language of European settlers to Canada. It remains established in Quebec province, though defeat in the Seven Years' War with Britain (1756–63) and subsequent English immigration have undone its wider dominance in Canada. In the later nineteenth century a new French empire arose,

GERMAN

128 million speakers

German has formed the northern and eastern boundary to the Latin- (or Romance-) speaking world for more than two millennia. Largely unwritten until the eighth century, after the Protestant Reformation of the sixteenth century it became central to European civilization, competing in the eighteenth and nineteenth centuries with the leading language, French. The recent expansion of the European Union to the east may counteract the various reverses the language community sustained in the twentieth century.

Above *The title page from Martin Luther's translation of the New Testament (1522). In 1534, Luther published the Old and New Testaments together in German.*

Count to 10

High German		Low German
eins	1	een
zwei	2	twee
drei	3	dree
vier	4	veer
fünf	5	fiev
sechs	6	sos
sieben	7	söben
acht	8	acht
neun	9	negen
zehn	10	tein

German is the major language of Central Europe (**Mitteleuropa**), spoken in the areas between those of the Romance languages to the west and south, the Slavic languages to the east, and the Nordic languages to the north. Besides Germany itself, German is native to Austria, Luxembourg, and Liechtenstein, and parts of Switzerland and Belgium. Over the centuries, large numbers of German speakers have moved out of these areas: the Vandals, Suevi, Franks, and Saxons migrated to western Europe and north Africa in the fifth century; farmers settled across the Elbe toward Poland in the tenth, twelfth, and thirteenth centuries; the Teutonic knights moved into Prussia and the Baltic regions in the thirteenth and fourteenth centuries; more farmers were invited

by Catherine the Great of Russia to populate the Volga steppe in the eighteenth century, and their descendants moved on to Kazakhstan as a security measure in 1941. But the dissemination of the language has turned out ultimately to be rather limited: although there were German settlements scattered throughout eastern Europe until 1945, the resettlements following the defeat of Germany in 1945 and (latterly) the dissolution of the Soviet Union in 1991 have massively reduced or eliminated their populations.

Unlike other western European powers and because largely land-locked, Germany was not a significant overseas colonial power. Although it was Germany under Bismarck that initiated the "Scramble for Africa" in the nineteenth century, there was never more than a single generation of German schooling in any of its colonies, either in Africa or in Papua and Micronesia. Many Germans became colonists personally—especially in North America and southern Africa—but they lost their language in doing so. Nevertheless, there are still small communities of German speakers all over the world—notably

Characteristics

German word order is rigidly regular: the main or auxiliary verb comes second in a main clause, but at the end of subordinate clauses, while past participles and infinitives come last: for example, **Die Schrift, die gewisse Bedingungen berücksichtigen muss, soll aber unverändert erhalten bleiben** literally, "The writing, which certain conditions respect must, should however unchanged kept remain." In spelling, all nouns that begin with capital letters and compounds, however long, are written without breaks: for example, **Auseinandersetzungsunterbrechung** (breaking off an argument).

among the Amish of Pennsylvania (speaking "Pennsylvania Dutch," or **Deutsch**), in Texas in the USA, and in Chile, Argentina, and Brazil.

Though set back by the world wars of the twentieth century, German's great long-term advantage has been its contribution to education and culture. Germans invented and propagated printing, and hence vernacular publishing itself: Martin Luther's 1534 German "Bible" gave further impetus for the Reformation. After the thirteenth-century fragmentation of the Holy Roman Empire (with the exceptions of Switzerland and Austria), Germany was not united again politically until the nineteenth century, yet a standard language for the whole area had been achieved much earlier.

High German is based on the language of central Germany (Hanover) and Southern Germany (Bavaria), the language of medieval poets taken up by the Saxon Court (the Minnesinger courtly love poets, and the anonymous author of the "Nibelungenlied" epic), and it was standardized in Luther's 1534 "Bible." The Low German dialects of the north (Saxony)

differ mainly in keeping "p," "t," and "k" in words where the south has "f," "z," and "ch" (e.g. **Appel, dat, maken** versus **Apfel, dass, machen**). These dialects have never been accepted as a basis for a national standard—though in writing they have a tradition that goes back to the ninth century CE (*Heliand, Genesis* poems) and dominated medieval trade in the Baltic. One such dialect became Yiddish, spread within Jewish communities from the Rhine Valley out into eastern Europe (and thence to the USA). Dutch and English, too, which did define national standards, are closer to Low German than High German.

German is now one of the three principal languages of the European Union, particularly after the 2002 accession of many eastern European countries. In fact, it is the most populous language in the EU, since English and French find much of their global strength outside Europe.

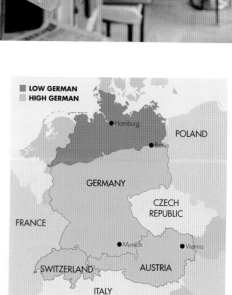

Above The distribution of German dialects, ranging from Low German in the north (Saxony) to High German in the south (Bavaria).

JAPANESE

122 million speakers

Count to 10

Native		Sino
hitotsu	1	ichi
hutatsu	2	ni
mitsu	3	san
yotsu	4	shi
itsutsu	5	go
mutsu	6	roku
nanatsu	7	shichi
yatsu	8	hachi
kokonotsu	9	kyū
tou	10	jū

Japanese is, in many ways, highly distinctive, even mysterious. It is one of the world's eleven most populous languages, yet spoken in one small island state. It is not proven to be related to any other languages (besides those to the south in the Ryukyu Islands). Its script, in use for more than a millennium, is actually a combination of four distinct systems (two of them uniquely Japanese), and hence is the most complicated in the world. Ninety-nine percent of Japanese speakers still live in Japan. Its home population vastly outnumbers the small speaker communities to be found in the USA—especially Hawaii (805,000)—and also Brazil (400,000), Canada (43,000), Mexico (35,000), Australia, and the UK (12,000 each).

Below *Japanese is spoken almost exclusively in Japan, but is still one of the world's eleven most populous languages.*

In trying to establish how Japanese relates to other languages, the problem is to reconcile clues that point in opposite directions. Is Japanese an Asian language originally learnt by Pacific Islanders, or vice versa? Its simple sound structure makes it seem like a language of the Pacific: for example, it has no consonant clusters, and all syllables end in a vowel or "n." But its word and sentence structure are more like Korean and neighboring languages on the Asian continent, such as Manchu and Mongolian. Words often end in strings of suffixes with clear meanings; an extreme example, **shi-nak-er-eba nara-nak-at-ta**, means "had not to do" (literally, do-not-being-if become-not-being-past). Verbs are rigorously placed at the ends of sentences, but adjectives and relative clauses precede their nouns: **kanojo-**ga eranda akai bōshi kare-ga suteta means, "he threw away the red hat that she had chosen," (literally, "she chose red hat he discarded"). To date, no one has found enough convincing cognate words between Japanese and any neighboring language to determine how one may have influenced the other. Japanese also has dozens of regional dialects, although Standard Japanese has become more prevalent due to media influences, better transport links, and social mobility.

The first Japanese on record is poetry (**Mān-yō-shū**, or 10,000 leaf collection) and mythology (**Ko-ji-ki**, or old-things-account) from the eighth century CE. The language was at first written in Chinese characters used as phonetic symbols to denote Japanese text; later—from the ninth century—it was increasingly written in a specially designed syllabary, the kana, often intermixed with Chinese characters that are now interpreted as words borrowed from Chinese, or just as shorthand for corresponding Japanese words. This system of some 50 kana with over 2,000 selected Chinese characters is still in use.

All early Japanese writing was created by aristocrats at the imperial court, and much of it—especially those examples that employ few Chinese characters—was written by women. (Women did not receive a classical Chinese education.) The greatest work of early Japanese literature, the extended psychological novel *Genji Monogatari* (*Tale of Genji*) from the eleventh century, was by a woman.

Japan embraced a form of Westernization in 1871, and has increasingly tolerated loanwords from Western languages, at first French and German, but later especially English. Text also began to be written left-to-right in lines across the page, as well as (traditionally) in columns right-to-left. The elaborate system of indicating courtesy

Characteristics

Japanese is highly allusive, especially in informal and colloquial registers, typically leaving unexpressed those pronouns that would express subject and object. Although traditionally this might be alleviated by the choice of honorific or deferential vocabulary, e.g. **meshiagaru**, "eat" (of a superior), **kuu**, "eat" (rough, masculine), **taberu**, "eat" (neutral, but polite), more and more such pronouns nowadays are simply left unspecified and neutral forms are used. Allusive expression is prized in Japanese conversation because, when successful, it builds a sense of solidarity and mutual understanding.

and politeness, and honorifics, became less rigorous, and indeed less widely understood, during the twentieth century, along with many formal features of Japanese style (e.g. in letter-writing). However, the use of Chinese loan vocabulary (in heavily Japanized pronunciation), and the traditional mixed script of kana with Chinese characters—now enriched here and there with foreign words in Roman script, too—has not diminished at all.

Above A seventeenth-century painting and poem entitled Dancer by Hinaya Ryuho. Note the traditional right-to-left columns of text.

Left Tametomo and the Demons by Katsushika Hokusai, 1811. The traditional mixture of kana syllables and Chinese characters is still in use today.

EUROPEAN LANGUAGES

EUROPEAN LANGUAGES

Depending on how one defines (i) Europe and (ii) a language (and precise definition of either term gives rise to considerable disagreement), and excluding immigrant languages, at least 107 languages are spoken in Europe, by populations ranging from several millions to a few dozen. Estimates of numbers of speakers are sometimes reliable but often are no more than educated guesses, if that.

Numerically, the most important group of European languages consists of the 47 members of the various subdivisions of the Indo-European family. These subdivisions are: **Slavic**—12 (Belorussian, Bulgarian, Cassubian, Czech, Macedonian, Polish, Russian, Serbo-Croat, Slovak, Slovene, Sorbian, and Ukrainian); **Romance**—(i.e. languages descended from Latin) 11 (Catalan, Corsican, French, Galician, Italian, Occitan, Portuguese, Raeto-Romance, Romanian, Sardinian, and Spanish); **Germanic**—10 (Danish, Dutch, English, Faroese, Frisian, German, Icelandic, Norwegian, Swedish, and Yiddish); **Celtic**—4 (Breton, Irish, Scottish Gaelic, and Welsh); **Iranian**—4 (Kurdish, Ossetic, Talishi, and Tat); **Baltic**—2 (Latvian and Lithuanian); and, each being the sole representative of its subdivision: Albanian, Armenian, Greek, and Romani.

Left A Kurdish man reads a Turkish newspaper. Prior to legislation in 2002 the Kurdish language was suppressed in Turkey, despite the presence of up to 15 million Kurds in the country.

Other linguistic families represented in Europe are as follows: Uralic (Estonian, Finnish, Hungarian, and nine others); Turkic (Azeri, Turkish, and ten others); Caucasian (Georgian and thirty others); Semitic (Assyrian and Maltese); and three others, each being the sole representative in Europe of its family, namely, Basque (which has no known relatives), Kalmyk (a Mongolian language), and Nenets (a Samoyedic language).

English, French, German, Portuguese, Russian, and Spanish are among the major world languages (see World Languages, pp. 10–35). Greek and Italian, too, are among the major historic literary languages of the world, and many of the others have ancient and still flourishing literary traditions. Some, though not the principal language of a nation-state, have official or quasi-official status within their own area. However, although in most cases these languages are not under immediate threat, they

come within the category of "lesser used languages." They include Western Frisian, Galician, and Welsh. The situation of yet others is more precarious and they can be considered as under threat; these include Breton, Cassubian, Eastern and Northern Frisian, Raeto-Romance, Scottish Gaelic, Sorbian, and many of the Caucasian and Turkic languages. Two Celtic languages that went out of use as day-to-day community languages, namely Cornish and Manx, are now being revived.

The languages covered in the following pages are:
(i) feature languages: Bulgarian, Catalan, Czech, Danish, Dutch, Finnish, Greek, Hungarian, Italian, Norwegian, Polish, Romanian, Serbo-Croatian, Swedish, Turkish, and Ukrainian; and (ii) others: these are Albanian, Armenian, Basque, Estonian, Frisian, Galician, Georgian, Icelandic, Latvian, Lithuanian, Macedonian, Occitan, Slovak, Slovene, Welsh, and Yiddish.

Above *Corsican men enjoy refreshments outside a cafe. Corsica is a territory of France and its official language is French, though its traditional language, Corsu, is similar to Italian.*

ITALIAN

56 million speakers

Below *Distribution of the major Italian dialects.*

Italian is a Romance language spoken in Italy (55 million); the Republic of San Marino (30,000); parts of Switzerland (principally in the canton of Ticino), where it is an official language (c. 300,000); Croatia, where it is an official language in Istria (around 70,000); Slovenia (4,000); and it is spoken by large immigrant communities in North America, Argentina, Brazil, and Australia. Until 1934, it was also an official language in Malta. In many respects, in relation both to pronunciation and to grammar, Italian has evolved less from its Latin origins than have its main sister languages: French, Spanish, Portuguese, and Romanian.

Below right *Italy is rightly famous for its food, and many Italian culinary terms have become well known worldwide.*

Count to 10

uno	1
due	2
tre	3
quattro	4
cinque	5
sei	6
sette	7
otto	8
nove	9
dieci	10

International words

Italian has contributed many words to international vocabulary in such fields as music and the arts. These include **aria**, **concerto**, **crescendo**, **fresco**, **libretto**, **opera**, **piano**, **solo**, **soprano**, and **stucco**.

Italy is one of the most dialectally diverse countries in Europe. In many countries local dialects are dying out, or have already disappeared, but in many parts of Italy they are, in relative terms at least, still flourishing. The main dialectal areas are: (northern) Piedmontese, Lombard, Venetian, Ligurian (Genoese), and Emilian-Romagnol; (central) Tuscan, Umbrian, and the dialects of the Marche and the Abruzzi; and (southern) Apulian, Campanian, Calabrian, and Sicilian.

Other Romance forms of speech within Italy that are sometimes considered as dialects of Italian are more usually classified as distinct languages. Friulian in the northeast, spoken by around 700,000 people (with large communities in Romania, North America, and elsewhere), and the two small Ladin-speaking communities in valleys of the Dolomites, numbering around 30,000 speakers in all, compose, together with the Romansh dialects of the Grisons canton in Switzerland, the Rhaeto-Romance subgroup of Romance languages. Sardinian, one of the most conservative of the Romance languages, is also divided into a number of dialects, and estimates of the total number of Sardinian speakers range from 1.2 to 2.5 million.

The first known text in Italian dates from the tenth century. Various dialects were written in succeeding centuries, but in the thirteenth and fourteenth centuries a literary language based on Florentine Tuscan was used by three of the main Italian writers of the time—Dante, Petrarch, and Boccaccio—and that form of Italian was adopted as the basis of the official language.

TURKISH

46.5 million speakers

The Turkic languages, spoken by about 130 million people from the Balkans to central Siberia, fall into four groups. Numerically, politically, and culturally, Turkish is the dominant member of the southwestern, or Oguz, group of closely related and, to some extent, mutually intelligible languages. Other members are Azeri, Gagauz, and Turkmen. Estimates are unreliable, but Turkish is probably spoken by some 45 million people in Turkey (mainly in the Asian regions, but including 7 million in the European areas); 120,000 in Cyprus (where it is an official language); 1 million in Bulgaria; and 200,000 in Greece, Macedonia, and Kosovo.

Above *The Latin alphabet was adopted by Atatürk, first President of the secular Republic of Turkey, as a move toward Westernization.*

Eighth-century Turkic inscriptions found in the area of the Orhon (or Orkhon) river in Mongolia, written in what have been called "Turkic runes" (the similarity to northern European runes is coincidental), could be claimed by all the Turkic languages as their earliest texts. These texts date from the period after the Seljuk Turks, who, having defeated the forces of the Byzantine Empire at the Battle of Manzikert in 1071, settled in Anatolia and adopted Islam. For several centuries, most poetry, and later prose, was inspired by Islam. It was not until the seventeenth century (much later than in Western countries) that books in Turkish were first printed.

Although early texts were written in a variety of other scripts, from the thirteenth century onward the medium of writing was the Arabic script. This remained the case until as recently as 1928 when, in line with his general policy of modernizing and Westernizing Turkey, Atatürk's linguistic reforms led to the imposition of the Latin alphabet. Simultaneously, large numbers of Arabic and Persian elements in the vocabulary were replaced with neologisms based on Turkish roots, or by words drawn from old Turkish texts or other Turkic languages. Atatürk also transferred the seat of government from Constantinople (renamed Istanbul) to Ankara, but Istanbul remains in practice the cultural capital of the country. While there are generally reckoned to be eight to ten dialects of Turkish, the modern standard language is based on the Istanbul dialect.

Count to 10

bir	1
iki	2
üç	3
dört	4
beş	5
altı	6
yedi	7
sekiz	8
dokuz	9
on	10

Loanwords

bomba	bomb
grev	strike; French **grève**
kompütür	computer
televizyon	television
tiyatro	theater

POLISH  **40 million speakers**

Polish is a member of the West Slavic subgroup of Indo-European languages. This subgroup also includes Czech, Slovak, Cassubian (spoken by around 150,000 people west of Gdansk and sometimes regarded as a dialect of Polish), Sorbian (also known as Wendish or Lusatian Serb, spoken in a small area of southeast Germany), and Polabian (once spoken in the Lüneburg Wendland in Germany, but dying out in the mid-eighteenth century). Polish is spoken by over 37 million people in Poland itself, by 1 million or more in neighboring countries, and by substantial numbers within immigrant communities in Western Europe, North America, and elsewhere.

Above *Modern, standardized Polish incorporates features from several different dialects.*

Below right *The Polish language can still be divided into four main dialects, though the differences between them are slight.*

Excluding the Cassubian area, there are four main dialects of Polish: (1) northwestern, known as Great Polish (in an area including Poznán); (2) northeastern, or Mazovian (in an area that includes Warsaw and Białystok); (3) southeastern, or Little Polish (in an area including Kraków and Lublin); and (4) Silesian (including Katowice).

The first written examples of Polish consist of place names and personal names in Latin documents dating from the ninth to the twelfth century. The first piece of connected text is a single sentence in a thirteenth-century Latin chronicle. Since much of the documentary production of the medieval period in Poland was in Latin, there is comparatively little by way of other medieval textual evidence for the Polish language, an important exception being a translation of a number of Old Testament books dating from the mid-fifteenth century.

In the sixteenth century, referred to as "the Golden Age of Polish literature," Polish finally emerged as a well-established literary language. In 1537 King Sigismund dictated that sermons should be preached and legal documents written in Polish. There emerged a number of Polish and Latin dictionaries (the first dating from 1526, the most important from 1564), and the first Polish grammar dates from 1568.

Also in the sixteenth century a more or less standardized language came into being, which formed the origins of the present-day literary standard. It is characterized by features drawn from different dialects, in particular those of the Great Polish and Little Polish areas.

Count to 10

jeden	1
dwa	2
trzy	3
cztery	4
pięć	5
sześć	6
siedem	7
osiem	8
dziewięć	9
dziesięć	10

UKRAINIAN

40 million speakers

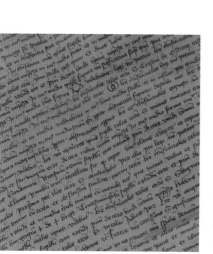

Ukrainian is one of the three languages that compose the East Slavic subgroup of Indo-European languages, the other two being Russian and Belorussian. Figures for numbers of speakers are unreliable, even for Ukraine itself and more so for Russia and other neighboring states, and within immigrant communities in Western Europe, North America, and elsewhere. Total estimates range from 37 million (31 million in Ukraine itself) to 52 million. Complicating factors are that, in Slavic-speaking regions, linguistic boundaries and international frontiers rarely coincide. Also, it is often not clear to which language dialects in border areas should be assigned.

Above *The Treaty of Thorn, 1411, was signed by the Grand Duchy of Lithuania, which incorporated the territory of modern Ukraine.*

Right *A man reads the facts on the back of an election poster in Kiev, the Ukranian capital.*

The language of some medieval texts in Old Church Slavonic is colored by Ukrainianisms, but, even though we have a Ukrainian grammar from 1595 and a dictionary from 1627, there is little Ukrainian literature until the eighteenth century. There are important texts in the nineteenth century, but until the early twentieth century Ukrainian writers often preferred to use Russian.

Although at various times and in various places there have been attempts to adopt the Latin alphabet, Ukrainian has nearly always been written in the Cyrillic alphabet in a form similar, but not identical, to that of Russian; currently, three characters not in the Russian alphabet are included, while four Russian characters are omitted. An official orthography was first adopted in 1936 and has been revised on several occasions since, most recently in 1990.

In the past, Ukrainian was often referred to either as Little Russian (to distinguish it from Great Russian, as Russian was formerly known) or as Ruthenian. Ruthenian, however, is best avoided: Ukrainian is the preferred name in the country itself, and the term Ruthenian has been used in a number of other senses. Historically, it refers to a form of West Slavic used in the sixteenth and seventeenth centuries in the Grand Duchy of Lithuania (which included much of contemporary Ukraine and Belorussia), from which both Ukrainian and Belorussian are descended. Ruthenian can also refer to two separate Ukrainian dialects, both otherwise known as Rusyn. One is spoken by about 25,000 people in the Vojvodina in Serbia, the other by 50,000 in northeastern Slovakia where, since 1995, it has been recognized as an official language.

Count to 10

один (odín)	1
два (dva)	2
три (tri)	3
чотири (chótiri)	4
п'ять (pyat')	5
шість (shist')	6
сім (sim)	7
вісім (vísim)	8
дев'ять (dévyat')	9
десять (désyat')	10

ROMANIAN

24 million speakers

Below *Distribution of the four main Romanian dialects.*

HUNGARY
• Budapest
ROMANIA
MOLDOVA
CROATIA
BOSNIA HERZEGOVINA
• Belgrade
• Sarajevo
SERBIA
• Bucharest
BULGARIA
• Sofia
MACEDONIA
ALBANIA
GREECE

■ DACO-ROMANIAN
■ ISTRO-ROMANIAN
■ AROMANIAN
■ MEGLENO-ROMANIAN

Romanian is a Romance language spoken by some 20 million people in Romania itself and 2.5 million in Moldova. There are also around 750,000 speakers in other parts of the Balkans, Ukraine, and Russia, and over 1 million émigré speakers around the world. In addition, three markedly different varieties are spoken outside Romania: Megleno-Romanian, with around 5,000 speakers in northern Greece and a few communities elsewhere in the Balkans; Aromanian, with around 500,000 speakers in communities throughout the Balkans; and the moribund Istro-Romanian, with a few hundred speakers in the Istrian peninsula in Croatia.

Below right *A Romanian girl walks past a billboard in Bucharest. Romanian has used the Latin alphabet since the mid-nineteenth century.*

Count to 10

unu	1
doi	2
trei	3
patru	4
cinci	5
şase	6
şapte	7
opt	8
nouă	9
zece	10

Loanwords

Romanian	from Latin
închide to close	includere
miere honey	mel
sat village	fossatum
spune to say	exponere

At the beginning of the first century CE, the Latin language was introduced in what was to become in 106 the province of Dacia, which included much of modern-day Romania. It seems that the indigenous population were Romanized and had abandoned their native language for Latin by the mid-third century. It is uncertain what happened to that population when Roman armies withdrew from the area in 271 or 272. Although it has been argued that the indigenous population withdrew south of the Danube river and did not cross it back into Transylvania for several centuries, the more plausible hypothesis is that most of them remained. After the occupation of what was later to become Yugoslavia by Slavs in the sixth century, these Romance speakers were cut off from the western Romance-speaking regions and their language developed along significantly different lines.

Although Romanian words occur in medieval Old Church Slavonic documents, the earliest extant Romanian text is a letter of 1521. Early literary works include sixteenth-century religious texts and seventeenth-century chronicles, written in Cyrillic.

However, it was not until the mid-nineteenth century that a modern, European-style literature arose and the Latin alphabet was adopted.

Because Romanians and their language were largely isolated from contact with the West for more than a thousand years, Romanian grammar developed differently from that of Western Romance languages in a number of important respects. The vocabulary has been profoundly influenced by Slavic languages, and to some extent by Hungarian, Greek, and Turkish.

DUTCH

21 million speakers

Below *Dutch signage is crystal clear—but an official body is still working to standardize the language's spelling and grammar.*

Below *A copper engraving, c. 1650, showing the arrival of the Dutch in West Africa. Dutch Guinea, as it was then known, is now part of Ghana.*

Dutch is a member of the West Germanic subgroup of Indo-European languages (other members being English, Frisian, and German) and is spoken principally in the Netherlands (15 million) and Belgium (6 million). Although it is often referred to as Flemish in Belgium, where it is also an official language, the official name there is Dutch (in Dutch it is nederlands, and in French néerlandais). Dutch is also spoken in parts of North Rhine-Westphalia in Germany, the extreme north of France (Hazebrouck), Surinam (the former Dutch Guiana), the Netherlands Antilles, and by immigrants to North America and Australia.

Count to 10

een	1
twee	2
drie	3
vier	4
vijf	5
zes	6
zeven	7
acht	8
negen	9
tien	10

Related words

These sets of related words show the similarities between Dutch, English, and German:

alleen	alone	allein
brood	bread	Brot
door	through	durch
jaar	year	Jahr
melk	milk	Milch
uit	out	aus
vis	fish	Fisch
woord	word	Wort

From the late seventeenth century Dutch was taken by settlers to South Africa, where it developed into what is now recognized as a different language, Afrikaans, spoken as a native language by some 6 million people.

As part of a westward movement of Germanic-speaking peoples, the Franks moved into the Netherlands from the fourth century onwards. Their language evolved and it is from one variety, West Low Franconian, that Dutch is descended. Two brief, West Low Franconian texts dating from around 1100 could be considered the earliest examples of Dutch. The twelfth-century poet Henric van Veldeke is claimed as the first Dutch poet (though, since he wrote in the dialect of what is now the Dutch-Belgian-German border, he is also claimed as an early Middle German writer).

Throughout the Middle Ages, a more or less standardized form of Dutch gradually emerged, particularly in the northern Netherlands. The first standardized orthography was officially adopted in the Netherlands (then under French rule) in 1804, and later in Belgium, but it was not popular, and a revised orthography was adopted in Belgium in 1864 and in the Netherlands in 1883. However, disagreements, reform proposals, and occasional divergences between the two countries continued until in 1982 the Nederlandse Taalunie (Dutch Language Union) was set up to decide on matters of orthography and grammar on behalf of both countries. In 1996, a number of its recommendations came into force and revisions were made in 2004. These have not all met with universal approval and the matter cannot yet be regarded as settled.

SERBO-CROAT

20 million speakers

"Serbo-Croat" is an umbrella term (officially used in the former Yugoslavia but now widely regarded as unacceptable) for the major speech varieties of Croatia (Croatian), Serbia (Serbian), Bosnia and Herzegovina (Bosnian, or Bosniak), and Montenegro (Serbian). It is one of the South Slavic group of languages, the others being Slovene, Macedonian, and Bulgarian. The main dialects are Štokavian (varieties of which are the basis of Croatian, Serbian, and Bosnian), Čakavian, and Kajkavian. Numbers of speakers are estimated at 6 million for Croatian, 8 million for Serbian (including Montenegrin), and 1.7 million for Bosnian.

Above *Distribution of the three main dialects—Štokavian, Čakavian, and Kajkavian.*

Below right *Croatian musicians in national costume. The Croatian variety of Serbo-Croat is written in the Latin alphabet.*

There are additional large numbers in immigrant communities elsewhere, especially in North America (principally Ontario and Illinois). Under the Yugoslav regime, only Croatian and Serbian were recognized as distinct varieties of Serbo-Croat. Bosnian was recognized as a distinct language under the Dayton Peace Accords of 1995 (which brought about the end of the civil war in Bosnia). The language of Montenegro is still officially termed Serbian but, particularly since the separation of Serbia and Montenegro in 2006, there have been moves to have it termed "Montenegrin"; as of 2007, the matter is undecided. Croatian and Bosnian are written in the Latin alphabet; Serbian in both Serbia and Bosnia is written in the Cyrillic alphabet. Both scripts are used for Serbian in Montenegro.

The South Slavs arrived in the Balkans in the sixth and seventh centuries and were converted to Christianity. After the schism between the Eastern (Greek Orthodox) and Western (Roman Catholic) Churches in 1054, the northwestern area, including Croatia, became Catholic and adopted the Latin alphabet, while the southeast adhered to the Orthodox Church and adopted the Cyrillic alphabet. In the fifteenth century, Bosnia and Herzegovina fell under the domination of the Ottoman Turks and many of the inhabitants became, as their descendants still are, Muslims.

The earliest texts, mainly in the now virtually obsolete Glagolitic alphabet, date from the eleventh to twelfth century. In the early nineteenth century, Serbian and Croatian were codified by **Vuk Karadžić** and **Ljudevit Gaj** respectively. The Vienna Accord of 1850 recognized that the two varieties formed one language.

Count to 10

Croatian		Serbian
jedan	1	један
dva	2	два
tri	3	три
četiri	4	четири
pet	5	пет
šest	6	шест
sedam	7	седам
osam	8	осам
devet	9	девет
deset	10	десет

HUNGARIAN

14 million speakers

Left *A twelfth-century religious text in Hungarian.*

Below *Hungarian is influenced by German and Latin as well as Slavic languages.*

Hungarian is a non-Indo-European language (known to its speakers as Magyar), spoken by more than 10 million in Hungary, some 3 million in neighboring countries (mainly Romania, Slovakia, Serbia, and Ukraine), and by around 1 million in immigrant communities in North America and elsewhere. It is a member of the Ugric, or Ugrian, subgroup of the Finno-Ugric languages and so is related, though only remotely, to Finnish and Estonian, which belong to the Balto-Finnic subgroup. Hungarian's closest relatives (not spoken in Europe) are the other two Ugrian languages, Ostyak (also known as Khanty) and Mansi (also known as Vogul).

Count to 10

egy	1
kettő	2
három	3
négy	4
öt	5
hat	6
hét	7
nyolc	8
kilenc	9
tíz	10

Non-Indo-European words

ember	man
fehér	white
fekete	black
folyó	river
híd	bridge
ír	to write
kenyér	bread
olvas	to read
szép	beautiful
víz	water

Ostyak and Mansi are spoken east of the Urals in western Siberia by about 12,000 and 3,000 people respectively. From their original Siberian homeland, which they may have left in about 1000 BCE, the Magyars gradually moved, or were driven, westwards and arrived in the Danubian area at the end of the ninth century CE. From non-Ugric words in the vocabulary of Hungarian, it can be deduced that during their wanderings the Hungarians came into contact with Turkic-speaking and Slavic-speaking peoples. Later, after they settled in central Europe, the language was further influenced by borrowings from Slavic languages and also from German and Latin, from which some 2,000 words, many relating to religious concepts, have been borrowed.

Latin charters and other documents from the eleventh to the thirteenth century contain many Hungarian place names and personal names, and occasional other words. The first text written in Hungarian is a translation of a Latin sermon and prayer dating from the 1190s, and the earliest literary text (also the earliest in any Finno-Ugric language) is the *Lamentation of Mary*, a loose adaptation of a Latin poem, dating from the mid-thirteenth century. Printing reached Hungary in the fifteenth century but at first it was in Latin; the first printed book in Hungarian was produced in Kraków, Poland, in 1527. The first book in Hungarian printed in Hungary was a New Testament translation in 1541. Many of the early printed books were religious works, including a Protestant translation of the complete Bible from 1590. After a period in which various dialects were written, by the mid-nineteenth century a unified literary language had been established.

CZECH

11.5 million speakers

Czech is a member of the West Slavic subgroup of the Indo-European languages, the principal other members being Slovak, Polish, and Sorbian (also known as Wendish, Lusatian, or Serb). Numbers of speakers are estimated at 10 million in the Czech Republic, and from 1 to 2 million elsewhere, including around 500,000 or more in neighboring states (mainly Slovakia) and 1 million in immigrant communities in North America.

Czech and Polish

These Czech words with their Polish equivalents illustrate their lexical closeness:

dén/dzień	day
dobrý/dobry	good
léto/lato	summer
noha/noga	leg
otec/osciec	father
pes/pies	dog
ulice/ulica	street
večer/wieczór	evening
velký/wielki	big

Count to 10

jeden	1
dva	2
tři	3
čtyři	4
pět	5
šest	6
sedm	7
osm	8
devět	9
deset	10

There are four main dialects: Bohemian, including the speech of Prague, the basis both of the dominant spoken language (Common Czech) and the standard written language, though the two are not the same; central Moravian; eastern Moravian, bordering Slovakia and considered transitional between Czech and Slovak (the two are largely mutually intelligible); and Silesian, spoken in the north, which is similar to Polish.

Czech names and occasional other words appear in tenth-century Latin texts, but the earliest pieces written in Czech are a complete sentence in a legal document, and a four-line hymn, both dating from the thirteenth century. The language was first extensively written in the fourteenth and fifteenth centuries, in a variety of compositions in many genres, both verse and prose. The real foundations of the modern literary language were laid at this time, in particular with the revision and codification of the orthography—which from the beginning had always used the Latin alphabet—by the religious reformer Jan Hus (1369–1415), who devised the original system (since modified) of diacritics that characterize modern Czech

Above *The city of Český Krumlov in the South Bohemian region of the Czech Republic.*

orthography. The first printed book, a prose chronicle, dates from 1468, the first grammar from 1533, and the first complete translation of the Bible from 1579–93. Despite the domination of cultural life by Germany during the long period of Austrian rule (1620–1918), an unbroken, if declining, literary tradition continued, with a revival in the nineteenth century. This tradition still flourishes, particularly since Czechoslovakia's independence in 1918. Josef Dobrovský's *Czech Grammar* (1809), in German, and Josef Jungmann's five-volume Czech–German dictionary (1835–1839) were both profoundly influential.

GREEK  11.5 million speakers

Greek is an Indo-European language, spoken by some 10 million people in Greece, 500,000 in Cyprus (where it is an official language), small communities in Albania and Turkey, and by large immigrant communities in Britain (mainly Cypriots), North America, and Australia. The language of the Linear B tablets from Crete and mainland Greece, dating from the fourteenth to the thirteenth century BCE, has been shown to be Greek, so Greek is therefore the earliest European language attested in writing. The earliest form of the Greek alphabet, which is still in use, was derived some 3,000 years ago from the Phoenician alphabet.

Above *The language used on the Linear B tablets is thought to be Mycenaean Greek.*

Count to 10

ένα (éna)	1
δυο (dhío)	2
τρία (tría)	3
τέσσερα (tésera)	4
πέντε (pénde)	5
έζι (éksi)	6
εφτά (eftá)	7
οχτώ (okhtó)	8
εννιά (enniá)	9
δέκα (dhéka)	10

International words

Words in international use deriving from Greek include:

aphrodisiac	photography
dynamic	poem
hypothesis	polygamy
osteopath	rhinoceros
philosophy	theater

The earliest known dialect, that reconstructed from the Linear B tablets, is Mycenaean Greek. Ancient Greek contained four or five other dialect groups, the most important being: (1) northwestern Greek and Doric (much of mainland Greece, Crete, Rhodes, and other islands); (2) Attic-Ionic (the area around Athens, parts of western Asia Minor, and many of the islands in between); and (3) Aeolic (Thessaly, Boeotia, Lesbos, and the neighboring coast of Asia Minor).

Attic emerged by the fourth century BCE as the standard language, or **koine**, from which all modern dialects developed, except the Tsakonian dialect in the southeastern Peloponnese, which is of Doric origin and so highly differentiated that it is sometimes considered a separate language.

The New Testament and most other early Christian texts were written in Greek. From the early fourth century CE, after Constantine adopted Christianity as the religion of the Roman Empire and transferred his capital to Constantinople, Greek remained a prestigious language until Constantinople fell to the Turks in 1453.

Above *A newsstand in contemporary Athens. Today's Greek is a mixture of both classical and colloquial, or demotic, language.*

The quest for a modern, standard written language led to a lengthy dispute between the partisans of a purist form, much influenced by Ancient Greek, and the advocates of a demotic form, based on contemporary speech. One or other was favored depending on the political color of the government of the day. However, the demotic form, incorporating elements from the classical language, finally triumphed in 1976 following the overthrow of the military regime.

BULGARIAN

9 million speakers

Bulgarian is a member of the South Slavic language subgroup, together with Slovene and Serbo-Croat, and is closely related to Macedonian (considered in Bulgaria to be a dialect of Bulgarian). It is spoken by about 9 million people, some 7.5 million in Bulgaria itself, with the remainder in neighboring countries and Moldova, or in immigrant communities in Western Europe, Israel, and North America. The original Bulgars were most probably a Turkic-speaking people who, in the seventh century CE, moved into the eastern Balkans and came into contact with a Slavic-speaking people who had settled there a century earlier, whose language they eventually adopted.

Above *Bulgarian is derived from Old Church Slavonic, a form of which is still used in the Russian Orthodox Church today.*

Below right *Bulgarians in traditional costume at the annual masquerade festival in the town of Pernik, near the capital Sofia.*

The first attestations of the Slavic speech of Bulgaria date from the tenth to the twelfth centuries, when a literary language, based on southern Bulgarian and Macedonian dialects, and designed primarily for ecclesiastical purposes, came into being. This language, known as Old Church Slavonic, came to have in some Orthodox churches a liturgical role not unlike that of Latin in the Catholic Church; a form of it is still in use in the Russian Orthodox Church today. It was also used as a literary language for religious and other texts. In certain areas, including Bulgaria, regional varieties developed. At first, Old Church Slavonic texts were written in the Glagolitic alphabet, said to have been devised by two Byzantine Greek brothers, Saints Cyril and Methodius, in the ninth century, and later by the Cyrillic script, which was derived in the tenth century from Glagolitic.

Although these Old Church Slavonic texts were produced in Bulgaria during what is known as the Old Bulgarian period, they could be claimed by other Slavic-speaking peoples as part of their heritage. The first specifically Bulgarian writings date from the Middle Bulgarian period (twelfth to sixteenth century) and the first printed book in Bulgarian dates from 1566. From both literary and linguistic points of view, the Modern Bulgarian period is considered to begin in the sixteenth century, but it was not until the nineteenth century that a truly modern literature, judged by European standards, evolved. Not until 1899 was an official codified form of the language adopted, based on northeastern dialects rather than on the western dialect of the capital, Sofia.

Count to 10

едно (ednó)	1
две (dve)	2
три (tri)	3
четири (chétiri)	4
пет (pet)	5
шест (shest)	6
седем (sédem)	7
осем (ósem)	8
девет (dévet)	9
десет (déset)	10

SWEDISH

8.5 million speakers

Below *The Swedish-speaking regions of Scandinavia: principally Sweden itself, but also some parts of Finland.*

Swedish is a member of the Scandinavian subgroup of the Germanic branch of Indo-European languages. It is spoken by around 8 million people in Sweden and by some 300,000 in Finland (including the Åland Islands), where it is an official language. There is a considerable degree of mutual intelligibility between Swedish, Danish, and Norwegian, but this does not apply to the other main member of the Scandinavian subgroup, Icelandic. Swedish has a great variety of highly differentiated and, in many cases, strictly localized and mainly rural dialects. Despite attracting considerable interest and a desire to preserve them, they are in decline.

Count to 10

en	1
två	2
tre	3
fyra	4
fem	5
sex	6
sju	7
åtta	8
nio	9
tio	10

Related words

Swedish shares many words with related forms in English and/or German:

Swedish	English	German
dotter	daughter	Tochter
hand	hand	Hand
tusen	thousand	Tausend
läsa	to read	lesen
rök	smoke	Rauch
slott	castle	Schloss
gammal	old	alt

Swedish has a lengthy written history, beginning with some 3,500 inscriptions written in the runic alphabet, mainly on standing stones dating from the ninth to the eleventh century. The Latin alphabet came into use in the twelfth century after the adoption of Christianity, principally in religious and legal texts. The language of the twelfth to fifteenth century, usually referred to as Old Swedish, is marked by grammatical simplification and, in vocabulary, by the influence of Danish.

The first printed book in Swedish was published in 1495, and the Modern Swedish period is usually reckoned to begin a little later with the translation of the New Testament (1526) and of the complete Bible (1541). These texts were to play an important role in the evolution of a standard written language. Efforts to develop a cultivated literary language were pursued through succeeding centuries. The vocabulary continued to be influenced by other languages, in particular German in the sixteenth and early seventeenth centuries, French in the seventeenth century, and English during the nineteenth and twentieth centuries.

The Swedish Academy, founded in 1786, has published the main Swedish dictionary and a four-volume grammar (1999). It plays an important role within the Swedish Language Council, which aims to further the development of the language in a number of ways, by acting in an advisory rather than a statutory capacity.

Above *The Karlevi runestone in Öland, Sweden.*

CATALAN

7.5 million speakers

Below *Catalan-speaking regions in Europe: Spain, Andorra, France, and Alghero in Sardinia—often known as "Little Barcelona."*

Catalan is a Romance language spoken principally in northeast Spain, but also north of the eastern Pyrenees in the Roussillon in France (principal town, Perpignan); in Andorra, where it is the official language; and in the town of Alghero in western Sardinia, where it was introduced in the fourteenth and fifteenth centuries when the island was ruled by Aragon. It is spoken by just under 7.5 million people, made up of more than 7.25 million in Spanish Catalonia (including the Balearic Islands and a fringe area in Aragon), 60,000 in Andorra, 145,000 in the Roussillon, and 17,000 in Alghero.

Count to 10

un	1
dos	2
tres	3
quatre	4
cinc	5
sis	6
set	7
vuit	8
nou	9
deu	10

Catalan and Spanish

These closely related words illustrate some of the principal similarities and differences between Catalan (placed first) and Spanish:

any/año	year
baix/bajo	low
canvi/cambio	change
clau/llave	key
mel/miel	honey
oblidar/olvidar	to forget
perill/peligro	danger
pluja/lluvia	rain

There are two main dialectal areas, each with subdivisions. The eastern area includes the northeast of mainland Catalonia (from the French frontier to well south of Barcelona), Andorra, the Roussillon, and Alghero. The western area covers the northwest, from the Pyrenees southwards and including the Catalan-speaking fringe in Aragon, and the provinces of Castellón, Valencia, and Alicante. In much of the southern area, centered on Valencia, there is an ardently held view that their speech is a distinct language from Catalan, referred to as Valencian.

The earliest literary text in Catalan, and indeed in any of the languages of the Iberian Peninsula, is a collection of sermons from Organyà (93 miles/ 150 km northwest of Barcelona), dating from the late twelfth or early thirteenth century, which are of linguistic rather than literary interest. From the thirteenth century, there is an extensive prose literature in Catalan. After a decline of some three centuries, there was a literary renaissance in the nineteenth century. Like other regional languages in Spain, Catalan labored under severe restrictions during the Franco dictatorship

(1936–75), but since the restoration of democracy and the establishment of the Autonomous Communities of Catalonia (1979), Valencia (1983), and the Balearic Islands (1984), there have been radical changes. The language is now actively encouraged in all three communities, particularly Catalonia where the teaching of Catalan is mandatory in schools (and in which it is often also the medium of instruction), and where the ultimate aim is that it should replace Spanish as the principal medium of communication.

Below *Chess players in Andorra La Vella, capital of the Catalan-speaking principality of Andorra.*

DANISH  **5.5 million speakers**

Danish is a member of the Scandinavian subgroup of the Germanic branch of Indo-European languages. It is spoken by about 5.2 million people in Denmark, by around 50,000 in Schleswig-Holstein (northernmost Germany), where it receives official recognition, and by immigrant communities in North and South America. It is an official language in Greenland, which is an autonomous state under the Danish Crown. Historically, some twenty dialects have been identified, but by now these have largely disappeared and most people speak standard Danish or a regional Danish based upon it.

Above A Danish sign warning drivers of children at play.

Right Denmark granted home rule to the Arctic island province of Greenland in 1978, but Danish remains an official language alongside Greenlandic.

During the lengthy period (1397–1814) when Norway was under Danish rule, Danish came to be used in Norway for a widespread range of official and social purposes and is the source of one of the two contemporary varieties of Norwegian, the **Bokmål** or "book language." However, though almost completely mutually comprehensible, in the course of time Danish and **Bokmål** have each evolved and there are now significant differences in pronunciation, grammar, and vocabulary between them.

The origins of Danish are to be found in Old Norse, which was the common language of all the Scandinavian countries in the eighth century CE, but which by about the year 1000 was already diversifying into two main branches: Eastern Old Norse, which later developed into Danish and Swedish, and Western Old Norse, which evolved in due course into the other variety of Norwegian, **Nynorsk**, or "New Norwegian," and into Icelandic and Faroese. This early, or Old Danish, period lasted until about 1100, and it is from this time that we have the earliest Danish inscriptions, written in runes before the Latin

alphabet was adopted after the introduction of Christianity in the twelfth century. The language of the next four centuries or so, referred to as Middle Danish, has left few literary texts, largely because religious works tended to be written in Latin. The Modern Danish period is reckoned to begin with the Protestant Reformation of 1536.

The Danish Language Council regulates the language, particularly its vocabulary (deciding which neologisms are acceptable) and spelling.

Count to 10

een	1
to	2
tre	3
fire	4
fem	5
seks	6
syv	7
otte	8
ni	9
ti	10

FINNISH

5 million speakers

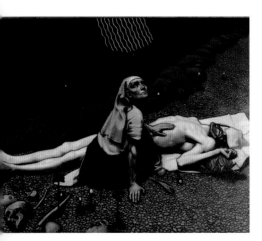

Finnish is a member of the Balto-Finnic subgroup of Finno-Ugrian languages, and therefore a remote relation of Hungarian (which belongs to another Finno-Ugrian subgroup, the Ugrian languages). The Balto-Finnic languages are also related to the Sámi (Lapp) language, which belongs to yet another Finno-Ugrian branch and which may have separated from the Balto-Finnic group in the second millennium BCE. The closest relatives of Finnish are Estonian, Karelian, and Veps, together with Ingrian and Livonian, and Votic (probably now extinct). It is spoken by nearly 5 million people in Finland, and by around 200,000 in Sweden.

Count to 10

yksi	1
kaksi	2
kolme	3
neljä	4
viisi	5
kuusi	6
seitsemän	7
kahdeksan	8
yhdeksän	9
kymmenen	10

Above *Depiction of a scene from the Finnish epic poem* Kalevala, *one of the language's finest literary works.*

Finnish and Estonian

These words illustrate some of the similarities between Finnish (placed first) and Estonian:

hyvä/hea	good
isä/isa	father
kaksi/kaks	two
kuum/kuum	good
lukea/lugeda	to read
musta/must	black
nuori/noor	young
päivä/päev	day
vanha/vana	old
vapa/vaba	free

Finnish is also spoken by smaller communities in Estonia and Russia, and by immigrant communities in North America (particularly around the Great Lakes), South America, and Australia.

The Finns have occupied their present area for at least 2,000 years and perhaps much longer. The Balto-Finnic languages contain many early Germanic, Baltic, and other Indo-European loanwords, indicating that the Finns must have been in prolonged contact with Indo-European speakers. More recently, many more words have been borrowed from Old Norse (later from Swedish) and from Old Slavonic (later from Russian).

The outstanding figure in the history of the creation of a standard Finnish language is a Lutheran Bishop, Mikael Agricola, whose *ABC* book, published in or around 1542, is the first known book in Finnish; however, he is especially remembered for his Finnish catechism, a prayer book, and a translation of the New Testament (1548). He has been called "the father of the written Finnish language." Other religious and secular writers followed, and a translation of the

complete Bible was published in 1642. In 1835, the first edition of the Finnish national epic, the *Kalevala*, was published, with a second, enlarged edition in 1849. Agricola's language was based on southwestern dialects, but in the mid-nineteenth century a standard literary language incorporating features of other dialects was adopted.

Below *Language distribution in Finland and its neighboring countries.*

NORWEGIAN

4.5 million speakers

There are two distinct though closely related Norwegian languages, both being forms of the Western Scandinavian subgroup of Germanic languages. Altogether, there are some 4.2 million speakers in Norway, with substantial numbers in neighboring countries and in immigrant communities, especially in North America. From 1397 to 1523, Norway was part of a union with Denmark and Sweden, in which Denmark was the dominant member. Thereafter, Norway remained under Danish rule until the turbulent year of 1814, when, after a brief bid for independence, Norway entered into a union with Sweden.

Count to 10

(Nynorsk) ein	1
(Bokmål) en	
to	2
tre	3
fire	4
fem	5
seks	6
sju	7
åtte	8
ni	9
ti	10

Above *A twelfth-century wood panel from a church in Setesdal, Norway, depicting the legend of Sigurd (Siegfried) from a Norse mythological poem.*

Right *A Norwegian newsstand. Two versions of the language—Nynorsk and Bokmål—have equal official status in Norway, but the latter is more widespread.*

One consequence of the lengthy period of Danish domination, referred to by Ibsen as "the 400-year night," was that the traditional dialects of Norway, derived from Old Norse, were completely overshadowed in official and written use by Danish, and in due course were abandoned as a written medium. The written language, and in some quarters (particularly the urban bourgeoisie) the spoken language, became a form of Danish with a Norwegian flavor, referred to as Dano-Norwegian.

From the seventeenth century, there were sporadic attempts to recreate an authentically Norwegian written language on the basis of the rural dialects, but these did not reach fruition until after the separation from Denmark in 1814. Norway was then politically united with Sweden until 1905. The outstanding figure in the revival movement was Ivar Aasen (1813–96), who codified a form of Norwegian based on the speech of the rural areas. This language, first known as **Landsmål** (national language) and later as **Nynorsk** (modern Norwegian), is therefore distinguished from Dano-Norwegian, which came to be known

as **Riksmål** (language of the realm) and later as Bokmål (book language). **Landsmål** was first recognized officially in 1885 and authorized for use in schools in 1892.

Since 1930, the two languages have shared equal official status and local authorities have the right to decide which is to be the medium of instruction in schools. In practice, over 85 percent of pupils are educated in **Bokmål**, which is also roughly the proportion of Norwegians who use it as their primary spoken language.

55

Left *A monument near Ashtarak dedicated to the thirty-eight letters of the Armenian alphabet.*

ALBANIAN

6 million speakers

Albanian is a Balkan Indo-European language, a separate branch of the Indo-European family, not closely related to any other language and having two main dialects, Gheg in the north and Tosk in the south. It is spoken by some 3 million people in Albania, probably more than 2.5 million in Kosovo, Macedonia, and other parts of the Balkans, and a substantial community in Italy (dating from medieval migrations). The earliest text (apart from a few fragments) is a missal of 1555. Various scripts were used until a literary standard, based on Gheg and using the Latin alphabet, was adopted in 1909. This was replaced by a Tosk-based standard in 1952.

SLOVAK

5.5 million speakers

Slovak is a Western Slavic language, closely related to Czech. There are some 5 million speakers in Slovakia, about 500,000 in the Czech Republic, and others in neighboring states and in immigrant communities in North America, Argentina, and elsewhere. Western dialects are mutually intelligible with Czech. Slovakisms sometimes occur in medieval and later texts written in Czech by Slovaks, but the first attempt to codify the language was made by Anton Bernolák, who produced a grammar (1790) and a dictionary (1825–27) based on western dialects. However, the modern standard language, codified in the mid-nineteenth century, is based on central dialects.

ARMENIAN

5 million speakers

Armenian is separate and independent of the Indo-European languages and has two main dialects. Eastern Armenian is spoken by some 3 million people in Armenia, and by substantial numbers in Iran and other parts of the Middle East. Some 2 million are claimed for Western Armenian, most of whose speakers, since the massacres of the late nineteenth and early twentieth centuries, are members of the Armenian diaspora in western Europe and North America. The language is written in its own alphabet of thirty-eight letters devised in 406 CE by St. Mesrop Mashtots. An extensive literature dates from the fifth century.

LITHUANIAN

3.5 million speakers

Lithuanian is one of only two surviving members of the Baltic branch of the Indo-European languages, the other being Latvian; extinct members include Old Prussian and other languages for which no records remain. Lithuanian is spoken by about 3 million people in Lithuania itself, and by others in neighboring states and emigrant communities. Various dialects are confirmed in writing from the sixteenth century, mainly in Protestant and Catholic religious texts. The first printed book, a Lutheran catechism, dates from 1547. The modern standard language emerged in the late nineteenth century and became established in the 1920s.

GEORGIAN

3.5 million speakers

Georgian is a member of the South Caucasian, or Kartvelian, family of languages, which also includes Mingrelian, Laz, and Svan, the last two being seriously endangered. Georgian is spoken by some 3 million people in Georgia, by substantial numbers in Russia, Iran, and Turkey, and by immigrant communities in western Europe and the United States. There are numerous dialects, the literary language being based on the central dialect of the capital, Tbilisi. The language has its own alphabet of thirty-three characters dating from the eleventh century, and an even earlier script used for ecclesiastical purposes. There is a long literary tradition going back to the fifth century.

YIDDISH

3 million speakers

Yiddish is basically a Germanic language, but one whose vocabulary in particular, and to some extent pronunciation and grammar, have been influenced by Hebrew, and by Polish, Russian, and other Slavic languages. Having originated among Ashkenazi Jews in German-speaking parts of central Europe in the Middle Ages, Yiddish was taken eastwards into Slavic-speaking areas by Jews fleeing from persecution. The beginnings of Yiddish literature date from the fourteenth century. Of the two main dialects, an Eastern one is the basis of the modern literary language, which is written in the Hebrew alphabet. Although millions of Jews perished in the Holocaust, there may still be 3 million speakers today.

GALICIAN

2.5 million speakers

Galician is a Romance language spoken in northwest Spain. It is closely related to Portuguese, and, in border areas, dialects of the two languages shade into one another. There are some 2.5 million speakers, representing around 60 percent of the population of the province of Galicia. There is little literature in Galician before the mid-nineteenth century and it was not until 1982 that agreement on a standardized orthography was reached. Like other regional languages in Spain, it suffered under severe restrictions during the Franco dictatorship (1936–75) but, since the establishment of the Autonomous Community of Galicia in 1981, it has been actively encouraged and given official status.

SLOVENE

2 million speakers

Slovene is a member of the South Slavic language group, which includes Serbo-Croat, Macedonian, and Bulgarian. Slovene has around 2 million speakers in Slovenia and contiguous parts of Austria, Italy, and Hungary, with others in immigrant communities in North America, Argentina, and elsewhere. There is considerable dialectal fragmentation. The earliest confirmations of the language date from the tenth or eleventh centuries, but the first major written works, mainly Protestant texts and a translation of the Bible (1584) using the Latin alphabet, are from the sixteenth century. By the eighteenth century, various different dialects were used in writing, but a standard literary language evolved in the nineteenth century.

Left *Tallinn, the capital city of Estonia. The country's northern dialect is based on the language spoken here.*

MACEDONIAN

2 million speakers

Macedonian is a South Slavic language closely related to Bulgarian, of which it has sometimes been considered (especially by Bulgarians) to be a dialect. It is spoken by around 2 million people, mainly in Macedonia itself, but including some speakers in neighboring states and in immigrant communities in North America and Australia. Although certain medieval and sixteenth-century texts from the area show Macedonian linguistic features, the earliest literary texts in the language date only from the mid-nineteenth century. Macedonian was not officially recognized as a distinct language until 1944, when it became the official language of the Yugoslav Republic of Macedonia.

OCCITAN

1.5 million speakers

Occitan is a Romance language spoken in southern France from the Alps to the Pyrenees. Estimates of the number of speakers range from 500,000 to 2 million. The principal dialects are Provençal, Languedocian, Gascon, and Northern Occitan (including Limousin and Auvergnat). Occitan has no official status. A rich medieval literature is represented principally by the poetry of the troubadours. Nowadays, there are two rival orthographies: that of the Félibrige (founded in 1854), based on French orthography and representing local dialectal features, and a more standardized system, the **graphie occitane**, based on the orthography of the troubadours and recognizing only major dialectal differences.

LATVIAN

1.5 million speakers

Latvian is one of only two surviving members of the Baltic branch of the Indo-European languages, the other being Lithuanian. It is spoken by about 1.5 million people in Latvia, by small communities in neighboring states, and by immigrant communities, particularly in North America and Australia. There is considerable dialectal variation. The literary tradition dates from the time of the Reformation, and the first printed book is a Catholic catechism of 1585, which was followed by other religious texts, mainly translations, both Protestant and Catholic. Moves toward the creation of a standard literary language began in the nineteenth century and came to fruition in the 1920s.

ESTONIAN

1.1 million speakers

Estonian is a non-Indo-European language belonging, like Finnish, to the Finno-Ugrian language family. It is spoken by about 1 million people in Estonia itself and neighboring countries, and by substantial immigrant communities, mainly in Sweden and America. There are two main dialects, one based on the speech of the capital, Tallinn (in the north), and a southern one based on the speech of the university city of Tartu. Apart from fragments, the earliest evidence for the language consists of a number of sixteenth-century printed religious books. For some centuries, both dialects were written, but a common literary language emerged in the nineteenth century. The vocabulary has been heavily influenced by German.

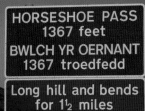

Left Road signs in Wales are written in both Welsh and English.

Left The Icelandic sagas dating from the tenth and eleventh centuries are the best-known examples of Icelandic literature.

WELSH

700,000 speakers

Welsh is one of the Brittonic subgroup of Celtic languages, which includes Cornish and Breton. It is spoken by more than 600,000 people in Wales and by 100,000 or more in England. It is the only Celtic language not seriously under threat. The language has long been used in religion and education, and laws dating from 1964 onwards now give it a position of equal validity to English in Wales. It figures prominently in public life, including the broadcasting media and the National Assembly, and is taught in all schools in Wales. A Welsh-speaking community of some 2,500, descended from nineteenth-century immigrants, survives in Patagonia, Argentina.

BASQUE

650,000 speakers

Basque is a language spoken on both sides of the western Pyrenees, with some 600,000 speakers in Spain and perhaps more than 50,000 in France. As far as can be proved, it is unrelated to any other language. After suffering severe restrictions under the Franco dictatorship (1936–75), Basque is now an official language and widely taught in schools in much of the Spanish Basque-speaking area. In France, it has no official recognition. There is little written evidence for Basque before the appearance of the first printed book in 1545. Dialectal fragmentation has made agreement on a standard literary language difficult, but considerable progress has been made in this direction since 1968.

FRISIAN

412,000 speakers

Frisian is a Germanic language, which, historically, is the one most closely related to English, although over time the two have diverged considerably. There are three distinct varieties. West Frisian, spoken by approximately 400,000 people in Friesland (the Netherlands), is an official language taught obligatorily in primary schools and in the first three years of secondary school; North Frisian—spoken by perhaps 10,000 on the west coast of Schleswig-Holstein (south of the Danish border) and on neighboring islands—and East Frisian, spoken by (at most) 2,000 in the Saterland area of Lower Saxony, are both under threat. An extensive literature, mainly in West Frisian, dates back to the thirteenth century.

ICELANDIC

300,000 speakers

Icelandic is a West Germanic language, descended from Old Norse and related to the modern Scandinavian languages, although considerably more archaic in its grammar. There are some 300,000 speakers, including communities in Denmark and North America. The language was probably taken to Iceland by Viking settlers in the late ninth century. The earliest writings date from the twelfth century and the Icelandic sagas are among the most important medieval European literary texts. The language never ceased to be written: the first printed book (a New Testament, printed in Denmark) dates from 1540, and there is a flourishing modern literature in various genres.

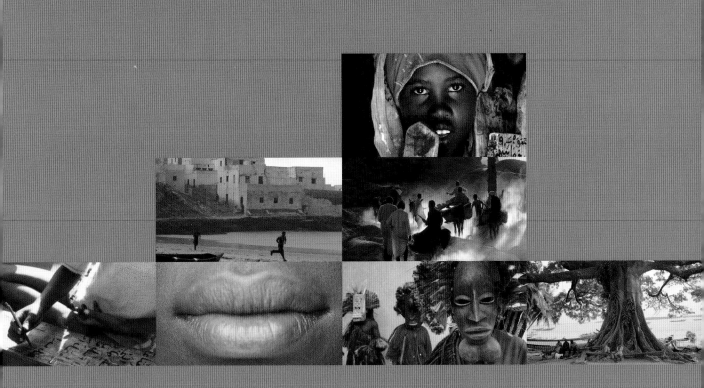

NORTH AND WEST AFRICAN LANGUAGES

NORTH AND WEST AFRICAN LANGUAGES

The complex problem of distinguishing languages and dialects, and counting their speakers, poses challenges for linguistic taxonomy and classification worldwide. It is especially an issue in wide areas of Africa. African languages defy easy categorization for several reasons. First, Africa is one of the world's hotspots of linguistic diversity, with an extremely high density of languages in some areas, among them the West African countries of Nigeria and Cameroon. Consequently, bilingualism and multilingualism are very widespread and have an impact on the structure of the languages spoken and written in the region.

Secondly, ethnic and linguistic identities are often not clear-cut. They overlap and can easily be modified or transformed in areas of high cultural convergence. As a consequence, denominations for ethnic groups and languages often originate in the attempts of colonial administrators to catalog the populations under their control, and do not truly reflect the hybrid nature of these groups.

Finally, linguistic knowledge about the majority of African languages—with the exception of some of the major languages featured below—is very limited, and demographic data, if they exist, are outdated or highly unreliable. Therefore, names for given languages can vary, and numbers of speakers are to be taken with caution.

The languages of North and West Africa belong to three of the four large language families of the African continent:

1. Afro-Asiatic languages (approximately 350) are spoken all over North Africa and extend well into sub-Saharan Africa (and Southwest Asia in the case of Semitic). They comprise the

branches Chadic, Berber, Ancient Egyptian, Semitic, Cushitic, and Omotic. They typically have complex noun plurals and common word formations. Chadic, Omotic, and many Cushitic languages are tonal.

2. The Nilo-Saharan family (close to 200) are so diverse that many linguists doubt their genetic unity. Typical features include the use of tone, in addition to case marking on nouns.

3. Niger-Congo languages, the largest language family, cover more than half of the African continent from around the equator to the Cape. These languages fall into a number of branches, of which several (Adamawa-Ubangi, Bantu, and Kordofanian) are discussed in Chapter 4 on Central, East, and Southern Africa (pp. 86–111). The branches used in North and West Africa are Atlantic, Mande, Gur, Kwa, and Benue-Congo. Most

Niger-Congo languages are tonal languages, have systems of nominal classification, and have an extensive set of verbal extensions (Mande being the exception). Many exhibit vowel harmony, a phenomenon in which the vowels in a word need to harmonize according to the position of the tongue.

The languages covered in this chapter are:
(i) Feature languages: Hausa, Yoruba, Igbo, Amharic, Oromo, Fulani, Somali, Akan, Tamazight/Tachelhit, Tigrinya, Manding, Kanuri, Ewe, Songhai;
(ii) Others: Moore, Wolof, Kabyle, Temne, Nigerian Pidgin, Senufo, Efik, Baule, Cameroonian Pidgin, Tarifit, Sidamo, Gbaya, Tiv, Beja, Mende, Ga, Igala, Nupe, Serer, Soninke, Soso, Dagbani, Dan, Dogon, Jola, Kisi, Krio, Bissa, Kabuverdiano, Vai, Bole, and Teda.

Left A market in southern Niger, where the Hausa language is used widely in commerce. Hausa is an Afro-Asiatic language.

Above Berbers in Tafilat, Morocco. The term "Berber" also applies to languages spoken in northern and Saharan Africa.

HASA 〰 **30 million speakers**

Below *A Hausa rider from southern Niger, where the Hausa language is spoken.*

Hausa is a Chadic (Afro-Asiatic) language spoken by an estimated 30 million or more first-language speakers (more than for any other language south of the Sahara), mainly ethnic Hausa and settled Fulani in northern Nigeria and southern Niger. As a major transnational language, Hausa is also spoken by diaspora groups of merchants, Muslim scholars, and immigrants in large urban centers in West Africa (e.g., Ibadan, Lagos, Accra), and also in the Blue Nile region of the Sudan. It is the most widespread West African language, and continues to spread (with creolized varieties), sometimes replacing smaller languages.

Above *A wooden board discovered in Nigeria, displaying the ajami script.*

Hausa dialects are roughly classifiable into three groups: Eastern Hausa (e.g., Kano State, which represents Standard Hausa), Western Hausa (e.g., Sokoto), and dialects in Niger (e.g., Ader).

Hausa is widely used in commerce, government, education, and in the mass media, and is one of three Nigerian languages with official status along with Igbo (see p. 65) and Yoruba (see p. 68). There are a number of Hausa language newspapers, and book publishing, television, and video production are thriving. Many radio stations, both African and international, broadcast programs in (mainly Standard Kano) Hausa, including the BBC World Service, Voice of America, Radio Deutsche Welle, and China Radio International. A number of universities in Nigeria and Niger teach undergraduate and postgraduate degree courses in Hausa, and there are also specialists in Hausa language and/or literature at universities in Nigeria/Niger, Europe, USA, Japan, China, and South Korea. Hausa has the best dictionaries and reference grammars of any African language.

The language was originally written in Arabic script (**ajami**), an orthographic system still used in Qur'anic schools and also by mainly non-Western educated Hausas for religious and literary purposes. Although most Hausas still learn the Arabic script as young children, ajami is gradually being replaced by a modified version of the Roman alphabet referred to as "boko" (probably from the English "book"). Boko was introduced by the British and French colonial authorities in the early twentieth century, and there is a growing body of modern Hausa literature written in this alphabet. Extensive borrowing from African languages such as Kanuri, Mande, and Yoruba has enlarged the Hausa lexicon.

Loanwords

Here is a comparison of some English loanwords incorporated into Nigerian Hausa with their French-derived counterparts incorporated into Niger Hausa to the north:

English	Nigerian Hausa	Niger Hausa	French
lawyer	lauya	aboka	avocat
license	lasin	parmi	permis
lorry	lori	kamyo	camion

IGBO

Below *The distribution of Igbo in relation to Hausa, Fulani, and Yoruba in Nigeria.*

- **IGBO**
- **HAUSA AND FULANI**
- **YORUBA**

With between 18 and 25 million first-language speakers, Igbo is one of the main languages of Nigeria and has official status. It is mainly spoken in the southeast of the country, in the area formerly known as Biafra. The Igbo were the main victims of the ethnic tensions leading to the secession of Biafra and culminating in the Nigerian Civil War, 1967–70, after which the area was reincorporated into Nigeria. Igbo-speaking communities are also found in neighboring Cameroon and in diasporas in other African and Western countries. The language belongs to the Benue-Congo branch of the Niger-Congo family.

Chinua Achebe

Chinua Achebe (b.1930) is one of the most acclaimed African writers. His poetry and fiction are deeply rooted in his native Igbo culture, although he has mainly published in English. Like fellow writer and Nobel laureate Wole Soyinka (see p. 68), his works reflect his political activism, not only surrounding the Biafra conflict where both writers took the side of the Biafrans, but also in the denouncement of racism. This is most noteworthy in his famous criticism of Joseph Conrad's novel *Heart of Darkness* in which Africa is depicted as a "metaphysical battlefield devoid of all recognizable humanity, into which the wandering European enters at his peril."

Above right *In 2002, Chinua Achebe received the Peace Prize of the Association of Publishers and Booksellers of Germany.*

Igbo has a number of dialects, and Standard Igbo is based on Central Igbo, which in turn draws on two dialects of the Ezinehite group, but tries to integrate words from other dialects in order to create a generally accepted norm. However, Standard Igbo and its orthography, created by missionaries and standardized in 1962, has been the subject of great controversy. The writer Chinua Achebe, one of the most famous African novelists, and author of *Things Fall Apart* (1958), the most widely read book in African literature, accused it of being a dogmatic imposition. He believed it did not do justice to the multitude of Igbo dialects, and was responsible for restraining the artistic and linguistic creativity of those writing in Igbo. The debate launched by Achebe sheds light on the problematic nature and limited acceptance of many standardized written forms of African languages.

The distinctive vowel sounds of Igbo can be grouped into two sets, based on vowels that can co-occur in the same word. The vowels of set A— "i," "e," "u," "o" in the Igbo orthography— are produced with an advanced tongue root, as in isi

(head), whereas those of set B—i̩, a, u̩, o̩—are uttered with a retracted tongue root; compare isi̩ (to tell). Since the vowels in a word need to harmonize according to the position of the tongue root, this phenomenon has been labeled "vowel harmony." It is a widespread occurence throughout West Africa.

AMHARIC

22 million speakers

Below *A copy of the Bible in Amharic.*

Amharic is an important Ethiopian Semitic language, spoken as a first language by approximately 17 million people, and with more than 5 million second-language speakers. Amharic, together with Oromo, is second only to Hausa, Igbo, Swahili, and Yoruba in terms of numbers of speakers of an African language. Among Semitic languages, only Arabic has more speakers. As a South Semitic language, Amharic derives from an earlier Semitic language that was introduced by migrants from southern Arabia and Yemen during the first millennium BCE.

Ethiopic syllabary

	h	l	s
A	ሀ	ለ	ሰ
AA	ሃ	ላ	ሳ
U	ሁ	ሉ	ሱ
I	ሂ	ሊ	ሲ
EE	ሄ	ሌ	ሴ
E	ህ	ል	ስ
O	ሆ	ሎ	ሶ
WA		ሏ	ሷ

Amharic is the "official" language of Ethiopia, and a nationally recognized language together with Oromo. The standard form spoken in the capital Addis Ababa (Shoa) is generally used in a wide range of social and official situations, such as government business, primary and secondary education, the courts, the military, and the media. Other dialects include Gondar Amharic and Gojam Amharic.

Amharic is widely used as a lingua franca in the area, and its prestige and distribution are partly due to the policy of "Amharization" imposed by earlier governments prior to the 1974 revolution. In addition, the rise of the Amhara people and the expansion of Ethiopian Christian rule has increased its use.

Another group of predominantly Amharic speakers are known as the Beta Israel, some of whom also speak a related language, Tigrinya. They are also known as Falasha (a pejorative term) and claim to be descended from Ethiopians who converted to Judaism, many of whom have migrated to Israel.

Amharic is written in the Ethiopic syllabary or **fidäl** (literally, letter)—a system of symbols representing whole (consonant + vowel) syllables—which evolved from the South Arabian consonant alphabet. The orthography was originally devised to write Ge'ez, or **abugida**, the classical language of the imperial court, which has been preserved as the liturgical language of the Ethiopian Orthodox Church. The earliest surviving Ge'ez inscriptions date back to the fifth or sixth century CE, and the earliest Amharic documentation (in the form of royal songs) is from the fourteenth century CE. This time span means that Amharic has one of the largest surviving outputs of literature in sub-Saharan Africa.

Over time, the language of Amharic has been heavily influenced by close contact with neighboring Cushitic languages such as Oromo and Qafar (Afar), especially in its lexicon. For example, the Amharic word **joro** (ear) probably derives from the Oromo word **gurra**, while the Amharic **ahayya** (donkey) may have come from the Qafar **okaalo**.

Below *Somali children practice their writing skills at the Quarn School in Bandera.*

Oromo is a major language of the Horn of Africa, spoken by more than 20 million people, mainly in Ethiopia (in Oromia State) but also in northeastern Kenya, Tanzania, and southern Somalia, and by 2 million or so people as a second language. Within Ethiopia, these numbers are therefore greater than the total for the "official" language of Amharic, and so Oromo ranks as one of the most used languages in sub-Saharan Africa. Oromo, like Somali, is a member of the Cushitic language family. There are three main dialect groups: West Central (the largest cluster, located in Ethiopia), Eastern, and Southern.

Until 1974, when the Ethiopian Revolution signaled the end of Emperor Haile Selassie's rule, the use of Oromo in schools and the media was forbidden (Amharic [see p. 66] and Tigrinya [see p. 74] were the only languages that were used in education and publishing). With the establishment of the Marxist regime, and subsequent to its replacement in 1991, Oromo eventually gained official recognition as one of fifteen indigenous languages to be used in literacy campaigns, and was designated as the national language of the Oromo-speaking region, where it has been increasingly used in elementary schools, administration, and the media.

Historically, Oromo was written in the so-called "Ethiopic syllabary" (see panel p. 66) system used to transcribe Ge'ez, the surviving classic written language of the court and the Orthodox Church, and also used to write Amharic and Tigrinya. Since the early 1990s, however, ethnic groups in Ethiopia have been free to choose either the syllabary model or the Roman alphabet for purposes of developing orthographies, and Oromo is written in a modified version of Roman script (known as "Qubee"). Standard Oromo is based mainly on the West Central variety, but a number of orthographic issues remain unresolved, for example, distinguishing between long and short vowels.

Over time, the Oromo language has borrowed extensively from other languages, specifically Arabic (see pp. 26–7), Somali (see p. 70), and Swahili (see p. 100). It also has an unusual case-marking system, which encodes the subject but not the object of a sentence, an asymmetry that is found in some other Cushitic languages (such as Somali) but is relatively rare outside Africa. For example, the base form **nama** (man) converts to **namni** when it is acting as subject (nominative), but remains **nama** when it is functioning as object (accusative). The basic word order is subject-object-verb, for example, **an gaala xiyyan arke** means "I saw my camel" (literally, I my camel saw).

Count to 10

tokko (m.), takka (f.)	1
lama	2
sadii	3
afur	4
shan	5
ja'a/jaha	6
torba	7
saddeet	8
sagal	9
kudhan	10

YORUBA

c. **20 million speakers**

Distributed mainly over Nigeria, Benin, Togo, and Ghana, with diasporas in other African countries as well as the UK and the USA, Yoruba (or Yorùbá in the tone-marking official orthography) is one of the most important African languages. No exact numbers of first- and second-language speakers are available, but estimates range between 19 and 22 million. Apart from being the first language of a large segment of the population in these areas, Yoruba is also used as a lingua franca in parts of southwestern Nigeria and, alongside Igbo and Hausa, is one of the three national languages of Nigeria with official status.

Above *Acclaimed Nigerian musician King Sunny Adé, whose 1998 collection of Yoruba songs,* Odu, *was nominated for a Grammy award.*

Below *A wooden Yoruba statue of a twin, which serves as a memorial to twins who have died.*

Yoruba belongs to the Benue-Congo branch of the Niger-Congo language family. It consists of a dialect continuum (see p. 126) comprising about fifteen different dialects, which are used in three different areas. A standard variety is used for interdialectal communication in the areas of education, the media, and writing. The traditional Yoruba-speaking area, also termed Yoruba-land or Ìlẹ̀-Yorùbá, spans many present-day political boundaries and comprises areas in mid-eastern Ghana, Benin, and Togo. Apart from first-language speakers, many speakers of minority languages in these areas are also fluent in Yoruba. Yoruba has a well-known and thriving oral literature. Although the written literary tradition does not predate the colonial period, since the inception of the Yoruba writing system the language has developed a flourishing body of fiction. Nobel Prize winner Wole Soyinka, despite mainly writing in English, draws on the Yoruba literary tradition.

Orishas

Orishas are the numerous spirits that are manifestations of God in the Yoruba belief system. Reminiscent of the Greek and Roman gods, they impersonate the forces of nature. In the wake of the slave trade, the cult of the **orisha** crossed the Atlantic, and variations of it are practiced in Brazil, Cuba, Puerto Rico, Guyana, Trinidad, Tobago, the US, Mexico, and Venezuela, making Aborisha the most influential religion of African origin.

The Yoruba orthography was developed by missionaries of the Central Mission Society who worked with the Akú (Yoruba-speaking, liberated slaves named after the first words of greetings in the language, Ẹ kú àárọ̀ "Good morning," and Ẹ kú alẹ "Good evening") in Sierra Leone. The modern Yoruba orthography marks the three tones of the language, and is based on the Roman alphabet, plus a number of additional diacritics, mainly from the International Phonetic Alphabet.

Count to 10

õkan, ení	1
méjì, éjì	2
êta mẽẽta	3
êêrinmêrin	4
árùn-únmárùn-ún	5
ẽfàmẽẽfà	6
méjè, eêje	7
çëjô	8
êsan, mêsàn	9
êwámẽẽwá	10

FULANI

15 million speakers

Below *Map showing the vast territory over which Fulani is spoken.*

Map legend:
- FULANI MOSTLY SPOKEN
- FULANI WIDESPREAD
- FULFULDE
- FUUTA JALON
- FUUTA TOORO

Fulani belongs to the Atlantic branch of the Niger-Congo language family, and the languages most closely related to it are spoken in present-day Senegal. Fulani-speaking areas cover a vast territory, comprising a belt along the entire Sahel from Mauritania to Sudan, and falling into two large dialect areas: Pulaar in the western areas, with the Fuuta Tooro dialect spoken in Senegal and the Gambia, the Fuuta Jalon dialect spoken in Guinea, and Fulfulde in the central and eastern language areas. There are important regional varieties that are situated in Mali (Massina), Niger, Nigeria, and Cameroon (Adamawa).

Count to 10

gooto	1
ɗiɗi	2
tati	3
na'i	4
jowi	5
jeego	6
jeeɗiɗi	7
jeetati	8
jeena'i	9
sappo	10

Noun class system

All dialects of Fulani group nouns in one of a maximum of twenty-five classes. Some of these have clear semantic motivations, for instance class 1 and its plural are used for human beings, e.g., **laamɗo** (chief) and **laambe** (chiefs), as well as dimensional classes, such as **laamngel** (petty chief), and **laamngum** (insignificant little chiefling).

Fulani-speaking pastoralists probably settled first on the Atlantic coast, before migrating eastward and gradually occupying the entire Sahel where they found pastures for their cattle, which were safe from tsetse flies. Popular theories often ascribe an Egyptian origin to the Fulani. Presently, their nomadic lifestyle is in regression and more and more Fulani have become sedentary.

Fulani were involved in a number of Islamic Jihad state foundations, most notably the Adamawa empire in Cameroon, the Massina empire in Mali, the Sokoto empire in northern Nigeria, and the Fuuta Jalon empire in Guinea. Since they were one of the first sub-Saharan ethnic groups to be Islamicized, many of these empires were theocratic in nature, and they were key to the spread of Islam throughout the Sahel.

Among other African languages, Arabic as the language of religion has had a major impact on Fulani, evident in numerous borrowings, but also in a writing system still employed today that uses modified Arabic characters (**ajami**). Although a Roman orthography was created in colonial times

Above *The mountainous northern region of Mali where a regional variety of Fulani is spoken.*

and is in limited use, the **ajami** writing system survives in formal (mainly religious) as well as informal contexts.

With the exception of Guinea and the Gambia, where the Fulani are in the majority and tend to be monolingual, Fulani is a minority language in other countries.

SOMALI

10–15 million speakers

Somali is a major Cushitic (Afro-Asiatic) language, spoken principally in Somalia, where it is the official language, and in neighboring regions of Djibouti, Ethiopia, and Kenya. As a result of internal instability, there are also significant diaspora communities in Europe, North America, and Australia. Somalia is sometimes cited as an example of an essentially monolingual country, which is unusual in Africa. However, there are some Bantu languages spoken in the south. It has also been shown that some of the so-called "dialects" of Somali are in fact not mutually intelligible, and so are more accurately described as distinct languages.

Above *A young Somali girl attends a religious ceremony in southern Somalia.*

Below *The port city of Merca, situated 62 miles (100 km) south of Mogadishu, the Somali capital.*

As the language of a traditional Islamic society, Somali has borrowed a substantial number of loanwords from Arabic, relating to such fields as religion, law, and education, and many Somalis also speak Arabic. There are also many loanwords from English and Italian, deriving from the colonial era (British Somaliland and Italian Somaliland merged to form Somalia in 1960). In pre-colonial times, Somali was written in a form of Arabic script known as "Osmania," but a Roman-based system was finally introduced in 1972, after years of bitter wrangling.

Loanwords

On the left are some Somali words with the original Arabic words on the far right.

fecrád	idea	fikrat
kúrsi	chair	kursii
maktabád	library	maktabat
márkab	ship	markab
qálin	pen	qalam

together with Hausa (see p. 64) and Swahili (see p. 100), is also one of the three sub-Saharan languages broadcast on the BBC World Service.

Somali ihas a rich literary history, beginning with traditional Islamic poetry, for example in praise of the Prophet Muhammad, and prose texts, in addition to traditional folktales. More recently, following the introduction of the Roman script, there has been a growing body of literature, including plays, some dealing with political issues as in the works of Mohamed Hashi Dhama Gaarriye and Cismaan Caligul. Somali,

Somali is usually analyzed as a tone language. For example, **êy** (with falling tone) means "dog," while **é** (with high tone) means "dogs," where tone distinguishes the singular from the plural. Like other East Cushitic languages, Somali also has a complex system of marking emphasis (focus) with particles, in addition to a special marker for subjects. The basic word order is subject-object-verb, for example, **ay ku keentay** means "she brought you" (literally, she you brought).

AKAN

Akan is the most important language of Ghana. It has two major dialects, Fante and Twi (which in turn incorporates the dialects Asante/Ashanti and Akuapem). Sometimes the term Twi is used to designate the language as a whole. Akan is also spoken in the eastern Ivory Coast, Togo, and Benin, and belongs to the Kwa group of the Niger-Congo language family. The Bight of Benin was a center of the slave trade, and therefore speakers of Akan were brought as slaves to the Americas, and a form of Akan is still spoken in the interior of Suriname. The Akan ethnic group is renowned for crafting bronze gold-weights.

Akan is an official literary language in Ghana, and serves as a lingua franca throughout the country. It is used for education at university level and as the medium of instruction for the first three grade levels of primary school in areas where it is the mother tongue.

Above A man printing Andinkra cloth showing some of the Andinkra symbols, with which the Akan language is closely associated.

Right Akan is also spoken in Ivory Coast, from where this sacred golden footstool originates.

Akan is closely associated with the development of Adinkra ideograms, a writing system that is made up of a limited number of symbols. A standard Roman-based spelling system was developed in 1975. Pronunciation is quite complex and involves a system of nasal as well as oral vowels. Tone also plays a significant role in the grammar of the language. For example, a verb like **da** can take the grammatical aspectual low tone to mean "to be in a lying position," or alternatively the high tone which means "habitually enters a lying posture." Akan nouns are grouped into classes indicated by a prefix added to the root; for example, **a-baa** (stick), **m-baa** (sticks). Word order is subject-verb-object, as in English.

Akan names

Children in the Akan culture and related groups (e.g., the Gbe) often receive names that specify the name of the day of the week on which they were born (e.g., "Friday" for the Secretary-General of the United Nations, Kofi Annan), or the order of birth related to their siblings. A selection of names is as follows:

Female name	Male name	Meaning
Adjwoa	Kwadwo	born on Monday
Afua	Kofi	born on Friday
Ataa	Ata	first born of twins

TAMAZIGHT & TACHELHIT

Tamazight (3 million speakers)
Tachelhit (8 million speakers)

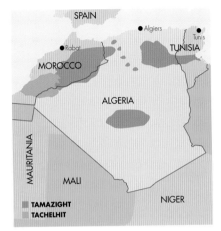

TAMAZIGHT
TACHELHIT

Tamazight (or Tamashek, Tamahaq, etc) and Tachelhit (or Tashelhit, Tashlhiyt, etc) are important Berber languages spoken across wide areas of Morocco and Algeria. Shilha is the Arabic designation for Moroccan Berber varieties. They are closely related to each other as well as to Judeo-Berber, the variety formerly spoken by Jewish communities in Morocco. "Berber" is a generic term describing a number of ethnic groups that have several customs and practices in common. As a linguistic term, it applies to between twenty and thirty languages or dialect clusters spoken in northern and sub-Saharan Africa (some of them under threat).

Above *The general distribution of the Tamazight and Tachelhit languages.*

Below *A Berber village in the Atlas Mountains, Morocco. Most speakers of Tamazight are located in the Middle and High Atlas Mountains.*

Berber is a branch of the Afro-Asiatic family, so Tamazight and Tachelhit are related to such languages as Arabic and Amharic (Semitic), Hausa (Chadic), and Somali (Cushitic). Tamazight is one of the northern Berber languages, spoken by more than 3 million people located mainly in the Middle Atlas Mountains and eastern High Atlas Mountains in Morocco, but also across northern Algeria and into Libya. There are also large diaspora communities in France. Historically, the designation "Tamazight" was used by various Berber communities to describe their language.

Tamazight was first written in the so-called "Tifinagh" consonantal alphabet still used by the Tuareg, particularly women, in southern parts of the Sahara (for example, Mali and Niger), due in part to their historically high status and social functions as poets and musicians. Tifinagh is an ancient Libyan script (possibly related to Latin Punica, or Punic) dating back more than two millennia, and formerly used across North Africa and on the Canary Islands (where the Guanche variety of Berber was spoken until the

advent of Spanish colonialism). Tamazight was later written in Arabic, and many Tamazight speakers use Arabic as a second language. During the twentieth century Roman script has increasingly been used, especially in Morocco, though a modified version of traditional Tifinagh has recently been made official and introduced into Moroccan primary schools.

Tachelhit is the most used and widespread northern Berber language, spoken mainly in the Sous valley of southwestern Morocco, but also in Algeria and by diaspora communities in France. Tachelhit has a rich and extensive oral literary tradition, and there are some important Tachelhit religious manuscripts in France and Holland. Like all Berber languages, Tachelhit has borrowed substantially from Arabic, for example, numerals and religious concepts.

Tifinagh alphabet sample

o	Θ	Χ	Χᵘ	Λ
a	b	g	gw	d

MANDING 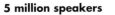 **5 million speakers**

Manding is a general term that covers a dialect continuum spoken in the West African countries of Senegal, Gambia, Guinea, Mali, Burkina Faso, and Ivory Coast. Linguistically, the dialects can be divided into two groups: eastern and western. The most prominent dialects are Bambara, or Bamana(n), the de facto national language of Mali; Mandinka, the main language of Gambia, also spoken in parts of Senegal; Maninka, or Malinké, a major language of Guinea; and Dioula (Dyula, Jula), located mainly in Ivory Coast and western Burkina Faso, and also used as a trade language.

Above *Young children learn traditional songs in the village of Songo, Mali. One of the most prominent Manding dialects, Bambara, is spoken in Mali.*

Below right *The broad areas in which different dialects of Manding are spoken.*

Count to 10

kilin	1
hùlàà	2
sàbà	3
nani	4
lulu	5
woro	6
worowùlà	7
seki	8
kononto	9
tan	10

The nomenclature for the different varieties is a mixture of colonial French and self-terms; while the self-terms designate the ethnic groups, they can be turned into language names by adding the suffix **kan** (tongue, language), for example, **maninka-kan** (Maninka language). Manding belongs to the Mande branch of the Niger-Congo family and constitutes its most debated subgrouping, because of the structural differences between the Mande languages and all other Niger-Congo languages. For instance, they are the only group without a system of nominal classification.

Manding spread over West Africa in the wake of a number of empires, most prominently the Mali empire led by its best-known ruler Sundjata Keita (c. 1217–55). He is said to have created and promulgated the caste system still widespread among Mande-speaking cultures and their neighbors. Caste membership is signaled through clan names, and creates an intricate system of so-called "joking relationships" between members of different castes, through which they owe each other loyalty and support.

Manding can be written in three different scripts. The oldest is an Arabic-based (or **ajami**) script still widely used. A competing Roman script devised during the colonial period also exists. It uses a number of characters drawn from the International Phonetic Alphabet and is employed in formal contexts. Their indigenous alphabetic system, N'ko, invented by the Guinean scholar Solomana Kante in 1949, is written from right to left, and has diacritics written above and below the characters. N'ko is an important symbol especially of Maninka cultural identity, but it is becoming influential in Mali and other parts of West Africa.

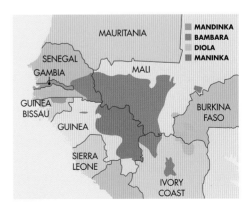

TIGRINYA

4–5 million speakers

Tigrinya, not to be confused with the related but distinct language Tigre, is, like Amharic, a northern Ethiopian Semitic language. It is spoken as a first language by an estimated 5 million people: some 2 million in the southern Eritrean highlands and cities (known as the Asmara dialect), and more than 3 million in the Tigray province of Ethiopia (the Tigray dialect). The Eritrean and Ethiopian varieties are mutually intelligible. As a Semitic language, Tigrinya is distantly related to Arabic and Hebrew, and both Tigrinya and Amharic are descended from an ancestral language introduced across the Red Sea from the southern Arabian Peninsula.

Above *The northern Tigray Province of Ethiopia, where more than 3 million Tigrinya speakers live.*

Below right *The distribution of Tigrinya dialects in Eritrea and Ethiopia.*

Tigrinya is also the first language of an estimated 10,000 Beta Israel migrants now living in Israel (see p. 66). It is the dominant language in Tigray province where it functions as a lingua franca and is classed as a "national" language. Until Eritrea gained independence from Ethiopia in 1991, the use of Tigrinya in education and government had been outlawed, and Amharic was used instead.

After Amharic and Oromo (see pp. 66 and 67), Tigrinya has the third most native speakers in Ethiopia, and it is the most widely spoken language in Eritrea, where it functions as the official language. Tigrinya is widely used in education, the mass media, government, and in schools (together with Arabic and English). There is also a growing body of modern literature in the language.

Like Amharic, Tigrinya uses a version of the Ethiopic syllabary, the Ge'ez script or **abugida**, for writing. In this system, which has more than 200 characters, each consonant symbol occurs in seven forms depending on the following vowel, and the symbol itself represents a consonant-plus-vowel sequence. The earliest known Tigrinya documents date from the thirteenth century CE. Tigrinya has borrowed many words from Arabic—for example, **bab** from **baab** (door), **səmmi** from **sam** (poison), and **shakwi** from **suk** (market)—as well as from Italian and English. Tigrinya has a rich set of rules for forming noun plurals. They include suffixes, for example, **säb/säb-at**, (man/men); internal changes, for example, **mänbär/mänabər** (seat/s); and combinations of these features, for example, **qamis/qämawəs** (shirt/s).

Count to 10

hadi	1	፩
kilitte	2	፪
siliste	3	፫
'arb'te	4	፬
hammushte	5	፭
shuddushte	6	፮
shob'atte	7	፯
shommonte	8	፰
tesh'atte	9	፱
'assirte	10	፲

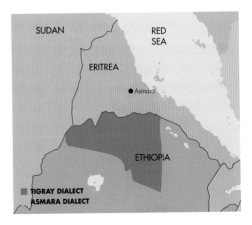

KANURI

Kanuri is a major Saharan language spoken in the Lake Chad Basin, in the Borno area of northeastern Nigeria, as well as in Niger, Cameroon, and Chad (where the variety is known as Kanembu), and by smaller communities in the Sudan. Together with Teda-Daza and Zaghawa, Kanuri constitutes the Western Saharan branch of the Nilo-Saharan family, though scholars differ in their opinions as to whether Kanuri represents several distinct languages or a chain of internally diverse dialects. Kanuri is one of the official languages of Nigeria, and Standard Kanuri is spoken in the city of Maiduguri, and used for broadcasting and publications.

Above Cattle are herded through the Sahel Desert, Lake Chad Basin, Niger, one of the main regions where Kanuri is spoken.

Historically, Kanuri was the language of the powerful Kanem-Bornu empire near (the fast disappearing) Lake Chad. Kanem-Bornu was one of the first states in the Sahel region to adopt Islam around the end of the first millennium CE, and as an empire it reached its zenith in the sixteenth century CE. As a result, a rich scholarly tradition of writing Kanuri in Arabic (**ajami**) script evolved, and it continues to be used alongside Roman script. Kanuri was also a major lingua franca in the region, and has influenced a number of nearby Chadic languages. There are still perhaps as many as 500,000 second-language speakers of Kanuri, but its influence has been eroded as a result of the expansion of Hausa (see p. 64; many Kanuri also speak Hausa and Arabic).

Kanuri has a subject-object-verb basic word order; for example, **Músà Kánòrò lèwónò** means "Musa traveled to Kano" (literally, Musa to Kano [he] traveled). It is unusual in allowing the subject of transitive verbs (but not of intransitive verbs) to be marked in certain situations; for example, the subject **sàndí-yè** (they) in **sàndí-yè shí-gà lèwàzánà**, meaning "they greeted him."

Tone plays an extremely important part in the language, and there are three distinct Kanuri tones—high, low, and falling. These are used to distinguish similar-sounding words. For example, words such as (low-falling tone) **kàrê** (hyena) versus (high-high tone) **káré** (draughts) versus (high-low tone) **kárè** (goods).

Kanuri in Arabic script (ajami)

Some of the major languages of sub-Saharan Africa (spoken by predominantly Muslim communities) have a long and rich history of writing in Arabic script, known as **ajami**. The earliest known records of a fully developed sub-Saharan African **ajami** are found in Qur'anic commentaries written in an archaic variety of Kanuri, and these manuscripts date back (at least) to the sixteenth and seventeenth centuries CE. Kanuri **ajami** was used in a variety of genres, including chronicles of rulers and religious poetry.

EWE

3 million speakers

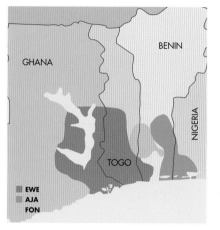

The Ewe language extends over southeastern Ghana, Togo, and Benin. Its speakers call the language Eʋegbe. Ewe belongs to the Kwa branch of the Niger-Congo family, and forms part of the Gbe cluster, which comprises about twenty closely related languages. Ewe has a large number of dialects, falling into two major groups: the coastal dialects Aŋlɔ, Tɔŋú Avenor, Dzodze, and Watsyi; and the inland dialects called Ewedomegbe and comprising Ho, Kpedze, Hohoe, Peki, Kpando, Fódome, Danyi, and Kpele. The varieties in Ghana and Togo are in contact with two different official languages that exert different influences on them.

Verb sequences

Below are two very simple examples of the construction of sentences in the Ewe language that require two verbs, and their translations.

Wo da fufu du
They cook fufu eat
(They cooked fufu and ate it.)

Me nya devi-ɛ dzo
I chase child leave
(I chased the child away.)

Above *The distribution of Ewe and the closely related Fon and Aja languages of the Gbe cluster.*

Right *Ewe is taught as an official subject in Ghanaian schools.*

Ewe has a long history of linguistic research, which began in the 1840s with the pioneering work of German missionaries, the most prominent of whom was Diedrich Westermann (1875–1956), who wrote the first reference grammar of the language. A number of Ghanaian and Togolese scholars are continuing this important research today. Ewe is taught as an official subject in Ghanaian schools, and is also widely used in the media, as well as forming part of adult literacy campaigns in Ghana and Togo.

Like most Niger-Congo languages, Ewe is a tonal language with simple and complex (rising and falling) tones. Tone is not generally marked in the orthography. Serial verb constructions are a widespread feature of Niger-Congo languages.

Ewe uses these constructions involving sequences of two or more verbs (hence the term "serial verbs") that share the same subject and temporal frame but can be marked independently for aspect to express complex events. Two examples are shown in the panel on the left.

Loanwords

The varieties of Ewe in Ghana and Togo are in contact with two different official languages, and hence exhibit different borrowings. For instance, Ghana Ewe has loans from English like **konset** (concert) and **flawas** (flowers), and Togo Ewe borrows words from French like **vatwi** (car; from **voiture**) and **ladjo** (radio; from **radio**).

SONGHAI

3 million speakers

Above *The Djingareiber Mosque in Timbuktu, which was famous for its centers of Islamic learning and great mosques. Most speakers of Songhai are Muslims.*

Varieties of Songhai (Songay/Songhay) are spoken in southeastern Mali, as well as in Niger and Burkina Faso in the Sahel zone of West Africa, as well as a cluster of dialects spoken near the great bend of the Niger river. The Korandje language, spoken 700 miles (1,000 km) north of the Niger river at Tabelbala in Algeria, belongs to the Songhai group. There are an estimated 3 million Songhai speakers. The most widely spoken variety is Zarma (Djerma) with about 2 million speakers, used largely in southwestern Niger in and around the capital city Niamey, where it is an official language. Songhai and its varieties are widely used as a lingua franca.

Linguists differ on the question of whether Songhai represents a single language with many dialects or a cluster of distinct but closely related languages. In terms of its genetic affiliation, most scholars consider Songhai to be a separate branch within the Nilo-Saharan family, but its inclusion is disputed by some. This is mainly because of its geographical separation from (other) Nilo-Saharan languages, and also the numerous lexical and grammatical similarities with Mande languages (Niger-Congo family); for example, the third-person pronouns (singular **a**), demonstratives (**wo** "this"), and a causative form of the verb (**-(e)ndi**). These cannot be due to chance. Songhai has a basic subject-object-verb word order. There is also a number of alternative theories regarding its affiliation, for example, that it is a creole language with a Berber base. The Songhai language has certainly been influenced by Berber languages to the north, but the matter remains intriguingly unresolved.

The Senni variety of Songhai is one of the national languages of Mali, the language of instruction in many primary schools, and has a number of dictionaries and grammars. Songhai was originally written in Arabic script (most speakers are Muslims); the fabled city of Timbuktu was famous for its prestigious centers of Islamic learning and its great mosques, and was one of the main historical sources for the spread of Islam throughout the Sahel region. It was also located on a major trans-Saharan trading route for gold and salt.

Count to 10

foo	1
hinka	2
hinza	3
taachi	4
guu	5
iddu	6
iiye	7
yaaha	8
yagga	9
woy	10

Loanwords

There are numerous loanwords in the Songhai language, many of them borrowed from Arabic (historically) or French:

alman	wealth	from Arabic **almaan**
waati	time	from Arabic **wakat**
poti	tankard	from French **potée**
kamsel	camisole	from French **camisole**
tappii	carpet	from French **tapis**

Malian varieties in particular have borrowed from Fulani, e.g.:

bilta	be rescued

MOORE

5 million speakers

Moore is the language of the Mossi people, the largest ethnic group of Burkina Faso, where they constitute about 40 percent of the population. Moore is also spoken in the nearby countries Benin, Ivory Coast, Ghana, Mali, and Togo. The language belongs to the Gur branch of the Niger-Congo language family. The name of the country Burkina Faso (Upper Volta was the colonial name) is composed of the Moore word **burkina**, roughly meaning "men of integrity," and the Dioula word **faso**, "father's house" or "country" to mean "the country of men of integrity." The people of Burkina Faso call themselves Burkinabé.

WOLOF

4 million speakers

Spoken on the coast of Senegal and in Gambia, Wolof is the most widely used language of Senegal, where it is spoken by about 40 percent of the population as a first language, and by about 80 percent as a second language. Wolof and its closest relatives, Sereer and Pulaar (Fulani), belong to the Atlantic group of Niger-Congo. Some types of Wolof, most notably the variety spoken in the capital Dakar, exhibit a number of simplified structural traits compared to rural varieties. The noun class system, for instance, differentiating up to ten noun classes in other dialects, is breaking down in Dakar Wolof, where only noun class marked by **bi** survives and is used with all nouns, replacing the other nine classes. Wolof uses an Arabic script called Wolofal, mainly adopted by the Mourides Sufi brotherhood.

KABYLE

3–7 million speakers

Kabyle is a Northern Berber (Afro-Asiatic) language with several dialects, spoken in Algeria. There are also sizable diaspora populations in Belgium and France. Estimates of the total number of native speakers range from 2 to 5 million in Algeria and 3 to 7 million worldwide. Arabic is the official national language of Algeria, and Kabyle (as well as other Berber languages) does not have any recognized status, a situation that has created much hostility and resentment over the years. Kabyle has borrowed many loanwords (mainly) from Arabic and French, both of which are widely used as second languages. Kabyle is written using the Roman-based Berber alphabet (Tifinagh).

TEMNE

3.5 million speakers

Temne is one of the most important languages of Sierra Leone, where it is mainly spoken in the Northern Province and the Western Area in and around the capital Freetown. Temne belongs to the Atlantic branch of the Niger-Congo language family; its closest neighbors are Sherbro and Gola. The Temne chiefdoms are renowned for their secret societies, the male Poro and female Bondo associations. The Temne were involved in the long-distance trade of kolanuts from early on, and the English word "cola" (as in Coca-Cola) is taken to originate in the Temne word **aŋ-kola**. The language is tonal and has borrowed from English, for example, **biskit** (biscuit), **polis** (police), **swit** (candy, sweet).

Left A Senufo ritual dance being enacted in Ivory Coast.

Left A striking Baule mask, part of this people's rich artistic culture.

NIGERIAN PIDGIN

3 million speakers

Nigerian Pidgin is a pidgin on the verge of becoming a creole language, continually expanding and acquiring a sizable number of native speakers. It is spoken all over Nigeria (less so in the north) for communication across language borders, but also by a growing first-language population, which is crucial for identifying it as a creole. While it is based on English, it has been influenced by Nigerian languages as well, most notably Hausa (see p. 64), Igbo (see p. 65), and Yoruba (see p. 68). Nigerian Pidgin English belongs to the family of Atlantic Creoles, originating in the wake of the slave trade and developing into creoles on both sides of the Atlantic.

SENUFO

2.7 million speakers

The Senufo (Senoufo) are an ethnolinguistic group speaking about fifteen related languages in southern Mali, western Burkina Faso, large areas of Ivory Coast, and eastern Ghana. Senufo is a member of the Gur group of the Niger-Congo family. Senufo languages exhibit many influences from Mande languages, due to longstanding contact. The languages fall into three large dialect groups: Northern Senufe comprising Suppire, Sicite, and Minyanka, among others; Central Senufo containing Karaboro, Senari, and Kpalaga; and Southern Senufo containing Tagwana and Nafaanra. Senufo languages have a suffixal noun-class system, and verbs are marked for aspect. There are three distinctive tones (high, mid, low). Word order is subject-verb-object.

EFIK

2 million speakers

A language of the Benue-Congo branch of the Niger-Congo language family, Efik is spoken in southeastern Nigeria. Settling on the coast, the Efik served from early on as middlemen between white traders and inland populations of the Cross River and Calabar areas. The Efik are known for their secret society, the Ekpe or Egbo, based on the cult of a spirit, Ekp. The (exclusively male) members of the society serve as messengers of the ancestors. Members of the Ekpe society devised an ideographic script, **Nsibidi**, that uses symbols derived from objects, and whose characters are not linked to the sound structure of the language.

BAULE

2 million speakers

Baule (**Baoulé**) belongs to the Akan group of languages, spoken in the center of Ivory Coast by 20 percent of the country's population. According to oral tradition, the name of the language means "the child is dead," and it refers to an important event in the history of the people: when they were fleeing from the Ashanti, their queen, Pokou, had to throw her child into the water in order to save her people from the pursuers. Baule belongs to the Kwa branch of the Niger-Congo language family. The Baule are famed for their art, and their language reflects this.

Left *School children in the Central African Republic, where Gbaya is spoken by over 2 million people.*

CAMEROONIAN PIDGIN

2 million speakers

Cameroonian Pidgin (Wes Cos, Kamtok) is a creole language of Cameroon. Due to the huge linguistic diversity of the country, which contains approximately 300 national and two official languages (French and English), this Atlantic Pidgin based on English and a number of Cameroonian languages has now evolved into a creole. About 5 percent of the Cameroonian population speaks it as a first language; another 50 percent uses it for communication in the most diverse linguistic arenas, for example, in church, speaking across the official language barriers, and as a lingua franca.

TARIFIT

2 million speakers

Tarifit is a Northern Berber (Afro-Asiatic) language used by around 2 million speakers, located mainly in northern coastal parts of Morocco, a region known as the Moroccan Rif, and also in Algeria. There are also substantial diaspora communities in Spain, France, Belgium, Germany, and the Netherlands. Tarifit is also known as Rifi and Rifia (the latter is the Arabic name for the language). It uses several orthographic systems, including the alphabetic Roman-based script used by Berber-speaking peoples (known as **Tifinagh**), in addition to Arabic, and has also been heavily influenced by Arabic, for example, in the forms of negation in some varieties.

SIDAMO

2 million speakers

Sidamo is an East Highland Cushitic (Afro-Asiatic) language spoken by several million speakers (the people are known as the Sidama) in the mountainous regions of central southern Ethiopia, including the Rift Valley and the River Omo area. The Sidama people have a history of close contact with the dominant Amhara (Amharic-speaking) and Oromo peoples. There are a number of vernacular publications in Roman script (health manuals, primers, dictionaries, etc), in addition to scholarly publications (grammars, dictionaries, in English and Italian).

GBAYA

2 million speakers

Gbaya is a member of the Adamawa-Ubangi branch of the Niger-Congo language family. It is spoken by more than 2 million people, mainly in western regions of the Central African Republic, in addition to communities of speakers in the Democratic Republic of Congo, and a few groups in eastern Cameroon and Nigeria. It is an important regional language with many dialects, and has a number of second-language speakers. It has an orthography and is used as the language of instruction in some primary schools. There is a Gbaya-French dictionary and a grammar written in French.

Left *A Beja man in Sudan. The Beja language is mostly spoken along the Red Sea coastline.*

Left *A market in Accra, the capital of Ghana. Ga is spoken in and around Accra by 3 percent of the population.*

TIV

2 million speakers

Tiv is spoken by a large population mainly in Benue State, Nigeria, and surrounding areas, but also by a few speakers in neighboring Cameroon. The language is a member of the Benue-Congo branch of the Niger-Congo language family. Tiv chiefs use a variety of musical instruments, including drums carved from tree trunks, and cow horns, in order to communicate with their people. Specific instruments and messages of this drumming language are associated with, for example, the news of harvest celebrations such as yam festivals, or socially important events like the death of an elder, or the announcement of the birth of a child of the king.

BEJA

1.5 million speakers

Beja (also known as Bedawi) is a North Cushitic (Afro-Asiatic) language spoken by more than 1 million nomadic, mainly Muslim, people located mainly along the Red Sea coastline of Sudan in the Horn of Africa. There are also communities of Beja speakers in Eritrea and southeastern parts of Egypt. The language and its speakers have been strongly influenced by Arabic (Beja is written in Arabic script), and many Beja people speak Arabic and Tigré. The lexicon differs so markedly from other Cushitic languages that some linguists consider Beja to be an independent branch of the family.

MENDE

1.5 million speakers

Mende is one of the major languages of Sierra Leone, where it is spoken by about 30 percent of the population, and serves as a lingua franca, stretching into neighboring Liberia. Most Mende populate the Southern Province of Sierra Leone. The language belongs to the Mande group of the Niger-Congo language family. In the 1920s, a syllabic script (in which every character stands for an entire syllable) was created for Mende, probably under the influence of the existing Vai syllabary. This script was widely used for a time, but has been replaced by a competing Roman-based orthography. In the nineteenth century, many Mende speakers were captured and shipped as slaves to the USA, most notably those on board the schooner *Amistad*.

GA

600,000 speakers

Ga (or Gaa), a language of Ghana, is spoken by about 600,000 people corresponding to 3 percent of the population, in the coastal region in and around the capital Accra. The name of a Ga kingdom, Nkran, is supposedly the origin of the place name Accra. The language belongs to the Kwa branch of the Niger-Congo language family, with Adangme its closest relative. Most languages of the world do not distinguish more than two degrees of vowel length within the syllable. Unusually, Ga vowels have three distinctive lengths: short, long, and extra long. There are two tones, high and low. Ga was first written in about 1764. The orthography, which is Roman-based, has been revised a number of times, most recently in 1990.

Left *Léopold Sédar Senghor, the first president of Senegal, was a Serer speaker.*

IGALA

c. 1 million speakers

Igala, a language closely related to Yoruba and Nupe, is spoken by between 800,000 and 2 million speakers in the Kogi, Delta, and Edo states of Nigeria. Igala incorporates the Ebu, Idah, Ankpa, Ogugu, Ibaji, Ife, and Anyugba dialects. The language is a member of the Benue-Congo branch of the Niger-Congo family. Igala is taught in primary education, and in 2005 the Attah of Igala (President of the Kogi State Council of Chiefs) suggested that it be introduced at university level. Although their language is the one most closely related to Yoruba, Igala speakers have been in contact with Igbo for a long time.

NUPE

1 million speakers

The Nupe are an ethnic group settled mainly in northern Nigeria, where they are the dominant population in Niger State. They were converted to Islam by Mallam Dendo, a wandering preacher, and subsequently incorporated into the Jihad empire of Usman dan Fodio. Nupe belongs to the Benue-Congo branch of the Niger-Congo language family. The Nupe have a reputation for being very prudish, evidenced by a high number of verbal taboos on words denoting body parts etc, which are replaced in ordinary speech by loanwords from Arabic or euphemisms to avoid the taboo items.

SERER

1 million speakers

Serer (Sérère, Sereer) is the second most widely spoken language of Senegal, and it is also spoken in adjacent Gambia and Mauritania. The language is closely related to Wolof, and belongs to the Atlantic branch of the Niger-Congo family. The Serer are associated with two former kingdoms, Sine and Saloum, which also correspond to dialects of the language. The famous poet, philosopher, and first president of Senegal, Léopold Sédar Senghor (1906–2001; r. 1960–1980)—who developed Négritude, a philosophy drawing on African cultural traits—and the poets, philosophers, and activists Aimé Césaire and Léon Damas, were all Serer. Serer has an orthography standardized by Senegalese government decree in 1975.

SONINKE

1 million speakers

Soninke, a language of the Mande branch of the Niger-Congo language family, is spoken mainly in Mali, but also by populations in Senegal, Mauritania, Gambia, Guinea, Guinea-Bissau, Burkina Faso, and Ivory Coast. The Soninke were the founders of the Ghanaian empire, and were among the earliest converts to Islam in the region. Their language manifests influences of the socio-religious traits of the society, for instance through the reservation of honorific lexical items for the prophet, marabouts (Muslim holy men or mystics), angels, etc, and their actions; compare **séerè** (the foot [of the prophet, a marabout]) with **tá** (the foot [neutral]). The closest related languages are the Bozo languages, spoken mainly in the Malian Niger delta.

Left *A Dan dancer wearing one of this people's famous masks.*

Left *Classic Dogon (mosque) architecture in the village of Teli, Mali.*

SOSO

1 million speakers

A language of the Mande branch of the Niger-Congo language family, Soso is mainly spoken on the coast of Guinea, and in the capital Conakry, stretching into Sierra Leone and Guinea Bissau. Soso (Susu, Soussou) is, together with varieties of Fulani and Manding, one of the three major languages of Guinea. Its closest relative is Yalunka (Diallonké, Jalonke). The Jalonke are believed to be the original inhabitants of the Fuuta Jalon area in Guinea, and are probably referred to in the place name. Since Soso and Jalonke developed independently and were in contact with different languages, they are shifting away from each other.

DAGBANI

800,000 speakers

Dagbani is a member of the geographically widespread Gur (Voltaic) branch of the Niger-Congo language family, and has an estimated 800,000 speakers (known as the Dagomba) located mainly in Ghana, where it is one of the national languages, and also in Togo. It is used as a trade language in northeastern Ghana, and is taught in schools. There are a number of linguistic publications on Dagbani (e.g., on its complex tonal system), including a grammar and dictionary. It uses a Roman-script-based orthography for producing vernacular texts. However, a standard writing system remains to be devised.

DAN

800,000 speakers

Dan (Yacouba, Yakuba, Gio, Gyo) is a language of the Mande branch of the Niger-Congo language family. It is spoken mainly in the western part of Ivory Coast, but it is also found in the adjoining countries of Liberia and Guinea. Like the overwhelming majority of Mande languages, Dan is a tonal language, and has a ten-vowel system. The Dan, who farm cocoa, rice, and manioc, are renowned for their numerous and varied masks and cults associated with them. Smaller versions of masks attached to certain families, also called "passport masks," used to be carried around and often received libations.

DOGON

800,000 speakers

Dogon is the designation of an ethnic group who speak about fifteen different languages in the central plateau of Mali. Their culture and one of their languages, the Toro So variety spoken in Sanga, are described in the work of the French anthropologist Marcel Griaule (1898–1956). The languages have been grouped in the Mande and Gur branches of Niger-Congo, or as constituting a separate branch in their own right, this being the most widely accepted view. The Dogon are known for their mythology, masks, and cults, as well as their architecture.

Left *The Casamance region in Senegal, where the Jola language is spoken.*

JOLA

500,000 speakers

Jola (Diola, Joola) is a term covering about twenty related but distinct languages spoken in the south of Senegal, in the Casamance area, in Gambia, and Guinea Bissau. The names for the different languages vary greatly, but the most widely spoken variety is Jola Fogny (Foñi, Foni, Fonyi), spoken in Ziguinchor, the capital of the Casamance, and used as a lingua franca. Jola languages exhibit vowel harmony and an intricate system of nominal classification, whose semantic motivations are poorly understood. Recent research points to culture-specific semantic motivations, such as rice cultivation as governing the distribution of nouns in classes.

KISI

500,000 speakers

The Kisi (Kissi, Gizi) are an ethnolinguistic group mainly situated in Guinea, but also in Sierra Leone and Liberia in unconnected areas. The closest relatives of this Atlantic language are Bulom and Krim, spoken on the coast. Kisi falls into two dialect groups: Northern Kisi, spoken in Guinea and Sierra Leone, and Southern Kisi, spoken in Sierra Leone and Liberia. The name of the town Kissidougou in Guinea is a Maninka term meaning "the village of the Kisi." Kisi has a large word class of ideophones, or words whose sounds imitate properties of their referent; for instance, **vwùm vwù** meaning "sound of heart beating rhythmically," and **fásékà-fásékà:**, meaning "quickly, in a rough manner."

KRIO

500,000 speakers

Krio, a creole language mainly spoken in Sierra Leone, was originally the language of liberated slaves "repatriated" from the Americas to Sierra Leone. The language dates back to the slave trade in the sixteenth and seventeenth centuries, when a pidgin based on English emerged in the course of coastal trade in the area. Now the native language of about 500,000 speakers, mainly centered in and around Freetown, the capital, Krio is spoken by up to 4 million second-language speakers as well, and is gaining importance among the younger urban generations. The lexicon of Krio is mainly based on English, but African languages, in particular Yoruba, have influenced its structure as well.

BISSA

500,000 speakers

Bissa (Bisa) is a member of the Eastern Mande branch of the great Niger-Congo family, spoken mainly in Burkina Faso, but also in neighboring Ivory Coast, northern Ghana, and Togo. It includes as dialects Barka, Lebir, and Lere. It has its own orthography, and there are a number of publications, for example, teaching and agricultural manuals, books of proverbs, etc. Many speakers also know Moore, and use French as the language of education and the wider world. Bissa are well known as peanut farmers.

Left *Cesaria Evora, a renowned Cape Verde musician, performs in Kabuverdiano.*

Left *Men from Tibesti Tubu in Chad. Teda is spoken mainly in the Tibesti region on the Chad–Libya border.*

KABUVERDIANO

400,000 speakers

Kabuverdiano, or Cape Verdian Creole (also called Kriolu), is the main language spoken on the Cape Verde archipelago off the coast of West Africa. The official language of the islands is Portuguese, yet this Portuguese-based creole is the first language of almost all the inhabitants. Two varieties, the Santiago and São Vincente dialects, have an important body of literature. Since varieties spoken on different islands remain very distinct from each other, there has been limited success in standardizing the language so far, with some researchers proposing two different standards, a North and a South standard, based on the São Vincente and Santiago dialects respectively. Cesaria Evora (b. 1941), Cape Verde's most famous musician, sings in Kabuverdiano.

BOLE

300,000 speakers

Bole (Bolanci) is an important West Chadic language related (with Hausa) to other Afro-Asiatic languages such as Arabic, Ancient Egyptian, and Somali. Bole is spoken in northeastern Nigeria by an estimated 300,000 people, making it second only in numbers of speakers to Hausa. There are a large number of published works on the language and people, in addition to some vernacular texts, and there is a website at the University of California, Los Angeles, that includes a dictionary, greetings, songs, and poetry in Bole. Historically, the Bole people have played a major part in Nigerian politics and education, and the Emir of Fika (the traditional capital located in Yobe State) is a prominent traditional ruler.

VAI

100,000 speakers

Vai, a language of the Mande branch of the Niger-Congo language family, is spoken mainly in Liberia, but it is also spoken by a small number of people in Sierra Leone. Vai is noteworthy for its syllabic writing system, in which one symbol corresponds to an entire syllable, as opposed to one sound. This writing system is one of very few indigenous African scripts. One hypothesis links the Vai script to the Cherokee syllabary of North America, known to a missionary who also worked with the Vai. The script was devised around 1833 by Momolu Duwalu Bukele, and inspired the development of several other syllabaries for related languages.

TEDA

50,000 speakers

Teda (also Tedaga) is a member of the Nilo-Saharan language family, closely related to Kanuri, spoken by an estimated 50,000 people, living mainly in the Tibesti area on the Chad-Libyan border, and also in Niger. It is very similar to Daza, which is spoken to the south, and so is sometimes referred to as Teda-Daza. Together they make up (part of) the Tubu (Toubou) ethnic group. The Teda people are Muslims, live in small communities, and are semi-nomadic, camel-herding pastoralists. They are also renowned for their warrior-like qualities, and historically they controlled much of the trans-Saharan trade in the area. They speak Arabic and usually prefer to write in it rather than in Teda.

CENTRAL, EAST,
AND SOUTHERN AFRICAN
LANGUAGES

CENTRAL, EAST, AND SOUTHERN AFRICA

The languages of Central, East, and Southern Africa are, like the cultures in which they are embedded, diverse, dynamic, and vibrant. They offer a wealth of exciting structural, sociolinguistic, and comparative material, which is a key to our understanding of the human capacity for language.

More than 500 languages are spoken in this vast area and the majority of countries covered have a high degree of multilingualism, because several languages are part of the public discourse and also because speakers smoothly manipulate different languages according to function and context. These circumstances allow for, and sometimes compel, the shifting of linguistic identities and allegiances, which are reflected in new linguistic structures and varieties due to contact and migration, as well as endangerment of many languages.

In terms of classification, all four African linguistic groups are represented in Central, East, and Southern Africa: Afro-Asiatic and Nilo-Saharan languages in northern East Africa; Khoisan languages in Southern Africa; and Niger-Congo (mainly Bantu) languages in the whole area. In addition, Afrikaans represents a Germanic language, and Malagasy belongs to the Austronesian family. The vast majority of languages in the whole region, however, are Bantu. Originating, as far as we can ascertain, from the Nigerian-Cameroonian borderland, Bantu languages have come to be used more widely during the last three millennia and are now spoken throughout the larger part of Central, East, and Southern Africa.

Bantu languages are structurally characterized by a complex noun class system according to which each noun is grouped into a specific class marked by a prefix which must agree with dependent elements. Most Bantu languages have between fifteen and twenty classes, including a number of singular-plural paired classes. In addition to noun classes, the study of Bantu tone, verb structure, agreement, and constructions involving the equivalent of English pronouns have contributed profoundly to developments in these areas in general linguistics.

Many, probably most of the languages of Central, East, and Southern Africa have not yet been comprehensively documented. More study would illustrate how much the languages from this part of the world can tell us about the cultures and histories of the region, and language in general.

The languages covered here are among the largest in terms of numbers of speakers. They include fourteen feature languages: Zulu, Shona, Malagasy, Nyanja, Kinyarwanda, Luba, Xhosa, Afrikaans, Kirundi, Gikuyu, Swahili, SeSotho, Tswana, and Kituba. In addition, there are thirty-two languages for which a shorter overview is provided: Northern Sotho, Luo, Runyakitara, Sukuma, Tsonga, Umbundu, Ganda, Luyia, Bemba, Lomwe, Kongo, Kimbundu, Makuwa, Kalenjin, Kamba, Lingala, Yao, Swati, Gusii, Ndebele, Chaga, Tumbuka, Wambo, Tonga, Makonde, Meru, Nyamwezi, Chokwe, Zande, Gogo, Nyakyusa, and Sena

Opposite Fishermen on Lake Victoria in East Africa. The lake is administered by Tanzania, Uganda, and Kenya. The vast majority of languages in this region are Bantu and multilingualism is common.

Above Cosmopolitan Durban, South Africa, capital of the KwaZulu-Natal province.

Below Children in the Democratic Republic of Congo, in traditional dress.

ZULU  **10.7 million speakers**

Zulu, or isiZulu, is a Bantu language spoken throughout South Africa. The majority of Zulu speakers live in South Africa's KwaZulu-Natal province, plus 1.9 million speakers in Gauteng province. Zulu is one of the eleven official languages of South Africa and is widely used in the media, the national and provincial parliaments, and daily life, as well as at all levels of education. It is also spoken in the neighboring countries of Botswana, Lesotho, Swaziland, and Mozambique, and is taught at universities and language schools throughout the world. Zulu is part of the Nguni group of Bantu languages and most closely related to Xhosa, Swati, and Ndebele.

Above *The main Zulu-speaking areas of South Africa, as well as the other countries where it is spoken.*

Zulu has a rich tradition of literature, both oral and, more recently, written. Traditional literature includes oral poetry, for example, praise songs (izibongo), which use a rich poetic language of metaphors and special grammatical constructions. Contemporary literature includes poetry, fiction, and drama. In addition, there are a number of Zulu newspapers and magazines, as well as radio and television programs.

The development of Zulu is closely linked to the political history of Southern Africa. At the beginning of the nineteenth century, Zulu was used by the small Zulu clan, who lived among a number of other Nguni-speaking groups in what is today KwaZulu-Natal. By the 1830s, a large number of these groups had been incorporated into the Zulu Empire of Emperor Shaka (1787–1828), and Zulu developed from a dialect spoken in a wide dialect continuum into the language of the expansive Zulu nation.

Hlonipha

Hlonipha is a special form of Zulu which is traditionally only spoken by married women. It is a so-called avoidance language, as women have to avoid using words that sound like the names of any of their close male relatives. As a result, hlonipha vocabulary may differ widely from the standard vocabulary, so that, for example, the word for "day," **umuhla**, becomes **umugca**. Forms of hlonipha are also found in related Nguni languages.

Clicks

When Nguni-speaking people first arrived in Southern Africa, they came into contact with Khoisan-speaking people, and during an extended period of contact, the Nguni speakers adopted the click sounds that are characteristic of Khoisan. Today, three click sounds are used in Zulu, represented in the orthography as "c," "q," and "x."

Right *Dancers celebrate in the province of KwaZulu-Natal, South Africa, where the majority of Zulu speakers live.*

SHONA

10.6 million speakers

Shona is a Bantu language spoken mainly in Zimbabwe with some speakers in southern Zambia, Mozambique, and Botswana. There are also an estimated 2 million second-language speakers of Shona in Zimbabwe. The main dialects are Kalanga, Karanga, Korekore, Manyika, Ndau, and Zezuru. The term "Shona" was first used by the South African linguist Clement Doke (1893–1980) in 1931 to consolidate the amalgamation of mutually intelligible dialects. The origins of the Shona can be traced back to the Monomotapa Empire—the first major civilization established in Zimbabwe about 1420 CE among the Karanga people at Great Zimbabwe.

Above *A Monomotapa chief. The origins of the Shona people can be traced back to this Empire.*

At the height of the Monomotapa civilization, Zimbabwe was part of a gold trade network that extended as far as China. Together with Ndebele and English, Shona is an official language of Zimbabwe spoken by 80 percent of the population. The orthography of Shona was codified in the early twenty-first century and it is taught in schools but not used as a medium of instruction. Although the Karanga and Zezuru dialects may be considered the basis of standard Shona, all dialects are equally acceptable in schools where they are taught locally. There is a strong genre of Shona literature, starting with the first novel written in the language in 1956, as well as good language resources, such as grammars and dictionaries.

Right *An example of Shona sculpture: Open Handed Man by Gedion Nyanhongo.*

Shona names

Names of people and places in Shona often consist of a full sentence describing an event around the time of birth or the significance of a place:

Domboramwari	God's stone
Harare	He doesn't sleep (there)
Zimbabwe	Stone house
Tafadzwa (common first name)	We are happy
Fungai (first name)	Think
Tatenda (first name)	We thank
Tapiwa (first name)	Gift
Tsitsi (first name)	Mercy
Takafakare (last name)	We are already dead!

Shona slang

Shona, particularly as used by groups of young people in Harare, incorporates many slang terms usually borrowed from English or Ndebele. Shona slang usually "nativizes" foreign borrowings to make them conform to the structure of Shona, but not always so. Some examples of English influence that mainly involve adding the consonant -z toward the end of the word are as follows:

bigaz	big	geliza	girl	boyz	boy
pini	pin	dhombi	dollar	monaz	morning
taimi	time	mafella	fellows	tolaz	tall
tonaz	town	dhawezi	down	Halemu	Harare
kulazi	cool	chilaz	chill	coldaz	cold

MALAGASY

10.4 million speakers

Malagasy is mainly spoken in Madagascar where it is the official and national language, but it is also used in other Indian Ocean islands including Reunion, Comoros, and Mayotte. Malagasy belongs to the Austronesian family; it is related to the Malayo-Polynesian languages of Indonesia, Malaysia, and the Philippines, and more closely to the southeastern Barito group of languages spoken in Borneo, particularly Maanyan. There are eighteen dialects of Malagasy. Merina (sometimes also called Houa or plateau Malagasy) is the standard. Malagasy is not related to the African languages spoken nearby.

Above *The Indian Ocean islands of Madagascar, Reunion, Comoros, and Mayotte, where Malagasy is spoken.*

Below right *A Madagascan woman takes a break with her daughter at a market in Ranohira.*

However, Malagasy contains words borrowed from Bantu languages, Arabic, and French, the former colonial language, which still enjoys official status, and also English, thanks mainly to the eighteenth-century pirates who made the island their base.

The language has a written literature dating back to the fifteenth century, and a rich tradition of oral and poetic histories and legends. Malagasy is broadcast on radio and television, and there are daily newspapers in Malagasy. In addition, the Ministere de l'information's monthly *Bulletin de Madagascar* contains Malagasy linguistic issues and studies.

From the fifteenth century to 1823, Malagasy had an Arabic-based transcription called **Sorabe**, used by a group called Antemoro, then replaced by a standardized, Latin-based orthography.

Malagasy word order

Malagasy has the unusual verb-object-subject word order typical of other Austronesian languages, such as Old Javanese and Fijian.

Mamaky	boky	ny	mpianatra
reads	book	the	student

The student is reading the book

Nividy	ronono	ho	an'ny	zaza	ny	vehivavy
bought	milk	for	the	child	the	woman

The woman bought milk for the child

Another somewhat unusual feature of Malagasy grammar is that demonstratives are repeated both before and after the noun so that, for example, "this book" is literally "this book this": **ity boky ity**.

NYANJA

9.3 million speakers

Nyanja (or Chinyanja/Cinyanja) is one of the major transnational languages of Central Africa, spoken in Malawi, eastern Zambia, northern Mozambique, and Zimbabwe. In Malawi, where the language is also known as Chichewa, it was the national language from 1968 until the early 2000s and is used in education, public discourse, and the media. In Zambia it is the lingua franca of the Eastern Province as well as one of the two main national languages of wider communication. It is spoken by about 20 percent of the population as a first language. In Mozambique it is the first language of about half the population of the northern Tete Province.

Word order

Bantu languages typically show elaborate marking on the verb (V), including subject (S) and object (O) markers. Consequently, the order of the subject and object in a sentence is very free, as the following Nyanja examples, taken from a classic article in Bantu syntax by Joan Bresnan and Sam Mchombo (1987), show:

Njûchi	zi-ná-wá-lum-a	a-lenje	(SVO)
bees	bite	hunters	

The bees bit the hunters

Zináwáluma alenje njûchi	(VOS)
Alenje zináwáluma njûchi	(OVS)
Zináwáluma njûchi alenje	(VSO)
Njûchi alenje zináwáluma	(SOV)
Alenje njûchi zináwáluma	(OSV)

The first Nyanja speakers came to present-day Malawi in the sixteenth century from their previous homelands in the lower Congo basin. They established the Maravi kingdom (the base of the modern name of the country) and spread their influence southward and eastward. During British colonial times, Nyanja was used by missionary societies in their fight against the slave trade. Partly due to the different ethnic names that local groups of Nyanja speakers adopted, the language became known by a variety of different names: Chinyanja, Chimang'anja, Chipeta, Chinyasa, or Chichewa (**chi-** is a Nyanja prefix meaning "language"). Chichewa was the name adopted in Malawi under the rule of Kamuzu Banda (1896–1997), himself a Chewa, while in all other countries, the language was known as Nyanja. Since the 1990s Nyanja has been harmonized across territorial borders, making it a symbol of African regional cooperation.

Language harmonization

As with many African languages, the first orthographies for Nyanja were developed by missionaries. Different spelling conventions emerged from the different missions, partly reflecting orthographic conventions of the major European contact languages. Further spelling reforms were undertaken by government agencies after independence in 1964. Recently, increased efforts have been made to develop a uniform orthography for Nyanja that can be used in all countries where the language is spoken.

Above *Children from the Tete region of Mozambique, where Nyanja is spoken.*

Above right *A funeral in Malawi.*

KINYARWANDA

9 million speakers

Below *The main countries where Kinyarwanda is spoken.*

Kinyarwanda is the main language of Rwanda and is spoken by about 9 million people throughout the country, as well as in the neighboring Democratic Republic of Congo, Burundi, Uganda, and Tanzania. It is closely related to Kirundi, the national language of Burundi, as well as to Kiha, spoken in Tanzania. Given the close relationship between these three languages, Kinyarwanda is probably understood by about 20 million people. It is a Bantu language of the interlacustrine (Great Lakes) group. There are several dialects, including Ikireera, Igikiga, Oluciga, Ururashi, and Ikinyanduga, on which standard Kinyarwanda is based.

Count to 10

-mwé	1
-biri	2
-tatu	3
-né	4
-taanu	5
-taandátu	6
-riindwi	7
náani	8
icyenda	9
icúmi	10

Kinyarwanda is the language of both the Hutus and the Tutsis, the two groups involved in the 1994 genocide, during which about 1 million Rwandans, mostly from the Tutsi group, lost their lives.

Kinyarwanda is used as a national and official language in Rwanda, and plays an important role in public life and in the media, where it is used in print and radio. It is also broadcast over

Below *School children dance and sing in Kigeyo, western Rwanda.*

the BBC, VOA, and Deutsche Welle. In addition, French and English are used as official languages and they play a role in government, administration, and academia. Although Kinyarwanda is used as a language of instruction in primary education, it is only taught as a subject in secondary and higher education, as the language of instruction shifts to French. A standardized orthography has been in use since the 1940s, although spellings used by Roman Catholic and Protestant missions differ somewhat.

Multiple object marking

As with many other Bantu languages, objects in Kinyarwanda can be expressed by so called object markers. This means that in comparison to English, where pronouns referring to people, objects, or places (e.g. them, us, there) are independent words, in Kinyarwanda they are part of the verb **heera** (to give) represented by **zi**, **tu**, **gu**, and **ha**, respectively, in the example below.

ba-ra-zí-tú-gú-há-hé-er-a

They are giving them to us for you there.

LUBA

7.8 million speakers

Below *The main regions of the Democratic Republic of Congo in which Luba is spoken.*

Luba (also called Luba-Kasai or Tsiluba) is a Bantu language spoken in the Kasai-Occidental, Kasai-Oriental, and Katanga provinces of the southern Democratic Republic of Congo (DRC). There are distinct differences between the eastern and western Kasai region dialects, and between these dialects and the dialect of the Katanga province, which is called Ki-Luba. The Luba originated from the relentless expansion of the Luba Empire (1585–1889), characterized by the idea of a centralized authority vested in a sacred king (Mulopwe), which dates back as far as 1500.

Count to 10

-mwè/mwà	1
-bìdì	2
-sàtù	3
-naayi	4
-taanu	5
sambòmbò(ù)	6
bwandabutekète(a)	7
mwandamukùlù	8
citeema	9
diikùmi	10

The empire only began to diminish in 1870 as Arab slave traders and European invaders challenged notions of Luba supremacy. However, even today local customs and artistic styles continue to reflect a strong Luba influence.

Luba is one of the four national languages of the DRC and is a lingua franca for almost a million second-language speakers. As with the other three national languages (Lingala, Swahili, and Kongo), it is used as a medium of instruction in the first few years of primary education, dating back to the time of the occupation by the Belgians. Despite the large number of speakers, Luba is slightly overshadowed by the more widespread Lingala and Swahili, which many Luba also speak, in addition to French. The Luba people are vigilant in their efforts to retain their language, and those Luba living in areas where other lingua francas dominate usually send their children to private language schools where they can continue to learn Tsiluba. Both State and private media in the DRC use Tsiluba as well as the other national languages. Fortunately, Tsiluba has good language resources that are helpful in promoting the language, including dictionaries and grammars as well as an on-line Tsiluba-French dictionary.

Right *A superb example of a bowl-shaped Luba mask.*

Tonal relative clauses

Tone is used in Luba not only to distinguish words such as **kúbàlá** (to shine) with high-low-high tone from **kúbálá** (to vibrate/tremble) with all high tones, but also grammatically to distinguish sentence types. Thus the difference between the (declarative) sentence in (a) and the (relative) sentence in (b) below is indicated by the difference in tone pattern on the auxiliary verb **uvwa**.

(a)	múntú	ù-vwá	mú-shípà	ntámbwé
	first person	auxiliary	kill	lion
	The man killed the lion			

(b)	múntú	ú-vwá	mú-shípà	ntámbwé...
	first person	auxiliary	kill	lion
	The man who killed the lion...			

XHOSA 👄 **7.2 million speakers**

Xhosa is a tone language in the Nguni group of Bantu, spoken in the Transkei coastal region of South Africa. It is one of the eleven national languages of South Africa, and is taught in primary and secondary schools. Xhosa is most closely related to the other Nguni languages: Zulu, Ndebele, and Swati. It is the second most common home language after Zulu in South Africa. Xhosa is written using a Latin alphabet-based system. It has three basic click sounds represented orthographically by "c" for dental clicks, "x" for lateral clicks, and "q" for alveolar clicks. Tones are not indicated in the written form, despite the fact that they differentiate lexical meaning.

The national anthem

South Africa's national anthem is in Xhosa. The first verse is as follows:

Nkosi, sikelel' iAfrika;
Malupakam'upondo lwayo;
Yiva imithandazo yethu
Usisikelele.

Lord, bless Africa;
May her horn rise high up;
Hear Thou our prayers
And bless us.

The presence of clicks in Xhosa is a reflection of contact with Khoisan languages. It is estimated that 15 percent of Xhosa vocabulary comes from its Khoisan neighbors. Xhosa has also borrowed in recent times from Afrikaans and English. The three basic click sounds can each be produced in five different ways, giving a total of fifteen clicks in the language. The five dental clicks are made with the tongue on the back of the teeth. The five lateral clicks are made by the tongue at the sides of the mouth. The five alveolar clicks are made with the tip of the tongue at the roof of the mouth.

The South African Broadcasting Corporation (SABC) broadcasts in Xhosa on both the radio (Umhlobo Wenene FM) and on the television, while films, plays, and music are also produced in the language. There is an abundance of literary works in Xhosa, including prose and poetry, and newspapers and magazines.

Below *Miriam Makeba is known around the world for her performances of Xhosa songs, recognizable for their numerous click sounds.*

Miriam Makeba's click songs

The best internationally known performer of Xhosa songs is Miriam Makeba (b.1932) whose songs *Qongqothwane* and *Baxabene Oxamu* are known for their large number of click sounds. *Qongqothwane*, "The Knock-Knock Beetle," (known in English as *The Click Song*) is a Xhosa wedding song with the frequent occurrence of clicks:

Igqira lendlela nguqongqothwane
Igqira lendlela kuthwa nguqongqothwane
Sebeqabele gqithapha bathi nguqongqothwane
Sebeqabele gqithapha bathi nguqongqothwane

The diviner of the roadways is the knock-knock beetle
The diviner of the roadways is said to be the knock-knock beetle
It has passed up the steep hill, the knock-knock beetle [repeat]

AFRIKAANS 6 million speakers

In terms of number of speakers, Afrikaans is the third largest language in South Africa, and it is one of the eleven South African national languages. It is also frequently spoken in Namibia. Afrikaans is closely related to Dutch and owes its presence in Southern Africa to the establishment in 1652 of a refreshment station of the Dutch East India Company for the company's shipping route to East Asia. The initially small Dutch community grew, and during the subsequent centuries came into contact with speakers of Khoisan languages; slaves brought from Dutch possessions in India, Indonesia, and Sri Lanka; and speakers of other European languages.

Above Afrikaans owes its origins to Dutch settlements arising from trade routes to East Asia.

Right A dual-language sign is testament to the use of Afrikaans in South Africa.

Due to the heterogeneous linguistic situation during the formation of a distinct African variety of Dutch (Afrikaans means "African" in Dutch), Afrikaans is sometimes thought of as a semi-creole, and it has a number of non-Germanic features, even though the syntax is similar to modern Dutch. Over time Afrikaans speakers developed a strong sense of their own linguistic identity, and following two **Taalbewegings** (language movements) Afrikaans was finally standardized in 1925 and became an official language of South Africa.

Loanwords

The Afrikaans lexicon shows influences from a number of different languages: e.g. **geitjie** (lizard), **dagga** (cannabis), **kierie** (walking stick), and **abba** (carry) from Khoekhoe; **piesing** (banana), **rottang** (cane), and **blatjang** (chutney) from Malay; **milie** (corn/maize) and **kraal** (pen/corral) from Portuguese creole; and **malie** (money), **aikôna** (no), and **hokaai** (stop) from South African Bantu languages.

Double negation of uncertain origin

The syntax of Afrikaans is in many respects similar to Dutch. However, there are some surprising exceptions, for example the use of double negation:

Ek	ken nie daardie	man nie
I	know not that	man not

I don't know that man.

This is quite unlike modern Dutch and indeed other West Germanic languages, and is sometimes seen as evidence for the creole origin of Afrikaans.

During the apartheid era (1948–93), questions of language were highly politicized in South Africa, and Afrikaans became associated with the oppressive regime, highlighted in the 1976 Soweto uprising that originated with school children protesting against the compulsory use of Afrikaans in black schools. Today, it is widely used in South Africa, with Afrikaans newspapers, television, and radio stations, as well as a wealth of Afrikaans creative writing.

KIRUNDI

6 million speakers

Kirundi is spoken in Burundi and is part of the Rwanda-Rundi group of the Bantu languages. There are also large groups of refugee settlements of Kirundi speakers in Uganda and Tanzania. Kirundi is mutually intelligible with neighboring Kinyarwanda, spoken in Rwanda, and it is also related to Ha in Tanzania. Together with French, Kirundi is an official language of Burundi. It is broadcast on radio and television, and there are also newspapers in Kirundi: Ndongozi (pacesetter) founded by the Catholic Church and a weekly government-based newspaper called Ubumwe (unity).

Distinctive tone

Like many tone languages, Kirundi not only shows distinctive vowel length where this results in a difference in meaning, but it also shows tonal distinction where a difference in tone results in different meanings for the same combination of sounds. Consider the example of vowel and tone contrast below (low tone is represented by a falling accent while an acute accent represents a high tone).

Contrastive vowel lengths
-saba	ask
-saaba	shatter
-fuungura	eat
-fuunguura	open

Contrastive tonal melodies
kòròrà	drop
kóròrà	cough
ìntòòrè	garden eggs
ìntóòrè	pieces of dough

The educational and administrative system is conducted in French, although Kirundi is used in the first few years of primary education in Botswana. There has been a standardized Kirundi spelling system in place since the 1940s, but reportedly there are orthographic differences between Catholic and Protestant writings.

The three major groups in Burundi—the Twa, Hutu, and Tutsi—all speak Kirundi, although the Twa have a distinct dialect that is intelligible to the other groups. Descendants of the Pygmies, the Twa are the original inhabitants of present-day Burundi. The Hutu arrived from the west between the seventh and the eleventh centuries. The Tutsi began to appear in the fifteenth and sixteenth centuries, migrating from the Nile region in present-day Sudan and Ethiopia.

The Kirundi people are historically a herding society, and the cow holds a great deal of symbolic power in the national culture and language. For example, a typical Kirundi greeting, **Amashyo**, translates as "May you

Loanword sources

Kirundi has incorporated loanwords from Swahili, German, French, Lingala, and Luganda. This reflects the contact the language has had with these groups of people in the nineteenth and twentieth centuries.

Swahili was introduced in the mid-nineteenth century by ivory and slave traders from Zanzibar; German from a period of colonial rule and from the settlements of the missionary White Fathers from 1898; French from the period of Belgian rule in the First World War; Lingala from Congolese soldiers who occupied the country from 1932 to the late 1950s; and Luganda from the migration of Kirundi countrymen to the Uganda Protectorate from 1920 to 1960.

have herds of cattle." The language is full of references to cattle, which stand for health, happiness, and prosperity.

Above left *The banner reads "Peace in your home, peace to you, peace in Burundi."*

GĨKŨYŨ

Gĩkũyũ (sometimes also Gikuyu or Kikuyu) is a major language of Kenya, spoken in Kirinyaga (The Shining Mountain) in west central Kenya, on the fertile slopes of Mount Kenya just north of Nairobi. Gĩkũyũ is a Central Bantu language closely related to Meru and Kamba. After Swahili (and English), Gĩkũyũ is among the most widely used languages of Kenya, and several Gĩkũyũ newspapers and magazines are available. The Agĩkũyũ people were closely involved in the fight against British colonialism, notably the Mau Mau rebellion (1952–60), and in Kenya's post-independence politics. Gĩkũyũ is particularly known for its modern literature.

Above Ngũgĩ wa Thiong'o, *famous Kenyan author of* Devil on the Cross *and* The River Between.

Below right *The Kirinyaga region of west central Kenya where Gĩkũyũ is spoken.*

A number of Kenyan authors write in **Gĩkũyũ**, including **Mwangi wa Mutahi**, **Gatua wa Mbugwa**, and **Ngũgĩ wa Thiong'o**, one of the giants of African literature whose early works in English such as *Weep Not, Child* (1964) and *The River Between* (1965) have become classics of African literature. In the 1970s **Ngũgĩ** started writing in **Gĩkũyũ** and his latest book in this language, **Mũrogi wa Kagogo** (*Wizard of the Crow*), appeared in 2006.

Several aspects of **Gĩkũyũ** linguistic structure have received special attention from Bantu languages scholars, such as processes of tone spreading and consonant dissimilation in pronunciation, as well as the complex focus-marking system in syntax.

Spelling

The spelling of the name of the language varies from **Gĩkũyũ** to Gikuyu to Kikuyu, the first usually regarded as the correct form. One reason for this is that **Gĩkũyũ** has a seven-vowel system where high and tense mid-vowels are distinguished in the orthography by the use of the tilde (~) to indicate tense mid-vowels. Using "i" and "u" without the tilde would (incorrectly) indicate high vowels. In addition, **Gĩkũyũ** disallows a sequence of two voiceless consonants that is sometimes reflected in the orthography (Gikuyu) and sometimes not (Kikuyu).

Focus marking

Gĩkũyũ has a complex focus-marking system employing a focus marker **nĩ**:

Wambui	nĩ-a-ra-nyu-ir-e	ma-ĩ
Wambui	(focus) (past) drink	water

Wambui drank water

nĩ	ma-ĩ	Wambui	a-ra-nyu-ir-e
(focus)	water	Wambui	(past) drink

Water, Wambui drank (not orange juice)

In the first example, **nĩ** precedes the verb, showing neutral or predicate focus. However, if the object is focused, it is fronted, and now **nĩ** precedes the fronted object rather than the verb. Although many Bantu languages use word order for the expression of focus, a focus marker such as the one found in **Gĩkũyũ** is not found in many other Bantu languages.

99

SWAHILI

5 million speakers

Swahili is a Bantu language spoken by about 5 million first-language speakers, and by an additional 50 million second-language speakers. It is the main language in East Africa, spoken in Tanzania and Kenya, where it is a national language, and parts of Somalia, Uganda, Rwanda, Burundi, the Democratic Republic of Congo, and Mozambique, as well as by expatriates throughout the world. Swahili belongs to the Sabaki group of the Northeast Bantu languages. Swahili has been spoken on the East African coast since about 800 CE, after Bantu-speaking people from the Great Lakes region reached it.

Above *Reading Swahili aloud in a small mosque in Zanzibar, off the coast of Tanzania.*

Below right *A selection of newspapers in East Africa, printed in Swahili and English.*

Due to maritime trading, Swahili became established in settlements along the coast from Mogadishu to Cape Delgado. Through contact with Arab traders, many Swahili people became Muslims, and loanwords from Arabic have entered the language, leading to the mistaken belief that it is a "mixed" language.

In the nineteenth and twentieth centuries, Swahili spread along trade routes beyond the coast, and it was used as a language of administration in the British colonial period. After independence in Tanzania (1961) and Kenya (1963), Swahili became the national language of these countries and shared an official status with English. In Tanzania, and to a lesser extent Kenya, Swahili is widely used today in public administration, (mostly primary) education, and the media. Especially in urban centers, Swahili is increasingly the first language of younger Tanzanians and Kenyans, sometimes sprinkled with English and other African languages. Swahili has a rich literary (especially poetic) heritage. The earliest surviving Swahili manuscripts, written in Arabic script, date to the first half of the eighteenth century. While Standard Swahili is based on the dialect of Zanzibar, the traditional centers for poetry are Lamu, Pate, and Mombasa in Kenya. More recently, literature in Standard Swahili includes fiction and drama, as well as poetry.

Structure

Swahili has many loanwords from other Bantu languages, as well as Arabic, Indian, and European languages. The grammatical structure of the language is very faithful to its Bantu historical roots. Thus, all Swahili nouns belong to one of sixteen noun classes, which differ in semantic meaning, morphology, and syntax. Verb roots can be changed by adding different derivational suffixes, and within sentences a complex agreement system operates.

Loanwords

Some Swahili words are found in English, the most well known probably being **safari** (journey). A number of others have recently entered English through the film (and musical) *The Lion King*: e.g. the characters **simba** (lion) and **rafiki** (friend) are Swahili, as is **hakuna matata** (no problem). The greeting **Jambo**, a simplified version of the Swahili greeting **Hujambo**, to which the reply is **Sijambo**.

SESOTHO

4.8 million speakers

Sesotho (sometimes also called Southern Sotho to distinguish it from Northern Sotho) is a southern Bantu language. It belongs to the Niger-Congo language family, which is spoken in the south of South Africa, and is one of the two national languages of Lesotho. It is also one of the official national languages of South Africa, and can be heard spoken around Johannesburg and Soweto. A unified orthography for Sesotho, Northern Sotho, and Tswana was proposed in 1945 but was never adopted. The first written form was devised by French missionaries of the Paris Evangelical Mission who arrived in Lesotho in 1833.

Tsotsitaal

Sesotho is one of the languages from which Tsotsitaal is derived. Tsotsitaal is an urban variety consisting primarily of a unique vocabulary and a set of idioms used mostly with the grammar and inflexion rules of Sesotho or Zulu. It is a part of the youth culture in most Southern Gauteng townships and is the primary language used in Kwaito music, a genre that emerged in Johannesburg in the early 1990s. *Tsotsi*, as in the title of the 2006 South African Oscar-winning film, translates as "thug," thus **tsotsitaal** (**taal** from Afrikaans "language") translates as "thug-language."

Above *A depiction of Chaka, the Zulu warrior-king.*

Above right *A support group for mothers in Mafeteng, Lesotho, where Sesotho is one of two national languages.*

The dialects of Sesotho include Sekwena, Sephuthi, Setlokwa, and Setaung in the central region, and Sekgolokwe and Serotse in the northeastern region. The dialects are considered to be mutually intelligible and it is often said that Sesotho has very little dialectal variation. It is most closely related to Tswana, Northern Sotho, and Lozi. An interesting feature of Sesotho, in contrast to other Bantu languages, is the nine-vowel system with three different heights in mid-vowels. One of the earliest written works in Sesotho is *Litsomo tsa Basotho* (*Legends of the Basotho*), published in 1909 and 1911. There is an abundance of written literature in Sesotho and the highly acclaimed novel *Chaka*, which relays the notorious life of the Zulu warrior king, was first written in Sesotho by Thomas Mafolo (published in 1925). Sesotho is used as a medium of instruction in Lesotho and can also be studied at the university.

Clicks

Sesotho has a large system of forty consonants, which includes click consonants taken from Khoisan and Nguni languages. The three click sounds are more adequately described as one click that is produced in three different ways, as radical (using the back of the tongue), nasal, or aspirated:

Radical:	**q**eta (finish)	ho **q**o**q**a (to chat)
Nasal:	**nq**alo (place)	ho **nq**osa (to accuse)
Aspirated:	**qh**itsa (drip)	**qh**waya (wave)

TSWANA

4.5 million speakers

Tswana, which is also called Setswana, belongs to the Bantu group of the Niger-Congo languages and is spoken in Botswana (1.1 million speakers) and South Africa (3.3 million speakers), and in some parts of Namibia and Zimbabwe. It is closely related to the languages Sesotho and Northern Sotho. Tswana has a total of eight dialects, and these are as follows: Sekgatla, Sengwaketse, Sengwato, Sehurutshe, Serolong, Setlharo, Sekwena, and Setlhaping. Tswana is, next to English, the official language of Botswana and has a large number of second-language speakers, for whom it is used as a lingua franca.

Above The Tswana-speaking regions of South Africa, Botswana, and Namibia.

Below right Botswanan schoolchildren; Setswana is the language of instruction for the first four years of education.

Dialects

Among the eight Tswana dialects, four different groups can be distinguished on pronunciation grounds. The northern dialect's "t" corresponds to the southern dialect's lateral ł, spelled as "tl," as for example in **tou** versus **tlou** (elephant) or **tala** versus **tlala** (famine). Furthermore, eastern and western dialects can be distinguished by "f" versus "h" respectively: **phefo** versus **pheho** (wind), or **fisa** versus **hisa** (burn).

Standard Setswana incorporates features of all the eight dialects. Representatives from all dialects form the Setswana Language Board, which among other things is responsible for the standardization of the language to be used in schools and in literature. This board has established a standard Setswana for all the dialects, and so no single dialect can claim to have had a greater influence on the standard language.

Setswana is used in Botswana as the language of instruction in the first four years of education. In South Africa, Setswana is one of the eleven official languages that was recognized in the 1996 constitution, and it enjoys legal rights in a number of official contexts. In Botswana a daily newspaper, *Dikgang Tsa Gompieno*, and a monthly newspaper, *Kutlwana*, are published in Tswana. Both the South African Broadcasting Company and Radio Botswana broadcast radio and television programs in Tswana.

Foreign missionaries can be regarded as the heralds of Western education in Botswana through the London Missionary Society, which came to southern Africa in 1817 and translated the Bible into Tswana. However, education, and particularly the teaching of reading and writing in Tswana, is largely due to female missionaries aided by Tswana women, themselves Christian converts. Major figures in this respect are Kolebale and Semane Setlhoko, who are considered pioneers of teaching Tswana, the latter having also tutored the first president of Botswana, Sir Seretse Khama.

KITUBA   4.3 million speakers

Kituba is a Bantu Creole based on Kikongo. It originated in the late fifteenth century as a contact language between speakers of partially mutually intelligible varieties of Kikongo who were involved in trading along the River Congo, prompted by the Portuguese presence on the coast. Kituba's development into a creole was slow and gradual, despite its widespread and regular use. However, the construction of the Brazzaville-Pointe Noire railroad at the beginning of the twentieth century gave the language new life; a grammatically simplified language evolved from railway workers of diverse linguistic backgrounds.

Above *The Brazzaville-Pointe Noire railroad gave Kituba a new lease of life.*

Below right *Gullah-speaking Gospel singers in South Carolina, USA. Kituba is one of the sources of the Gullah language.*

By the 1940s, Kituba had gained a community of native speakers and had also developed a written form. It was spoken by many Africans from the western Central African region who were taken into slavery and sold to the Americas. For this reason, the language is found in the rituals of African-derived religions in Brazil, Jamaica, and Cuba. It is also one of the sources of Gullah spoken in South Carolina and Georgia, and the Palenquero creole in Colombia.

Kituba is now an official language both in the Democratic Republic of Congo (formerly Zaire) and the Republic of Congo. Kituba is also referred to as **Kikongo ya leta** (Kikongo of the state administration) in the DRC and **Kikongo** for short. In the DRC, it is the main lingua franca in the provinces of Kongo Central, Kwango, and Kwilu, and to a lesser extent Kinshasa, Mai-Ndombe, and Kasai. Most speakers of Kituba also speak other lingua francas, as well as French.

Borrowed words

Although the bulk of Kituba words come from Kikongo, other Bantu languages have influenced Kituba as well, including Kimbala, Kisongo, Kiyaka, Kiyansi, Lingala, and Swahili. There are also many borrowed words from French, Portuguese, and English. A few examples are:

Kituba borrowed word		Source language	
sandúku	box	Swahili	sanduku
matáta	trouble	Swahili	matata
letá	state	French	l'état
sodá/solodá	soldier	French	soldat
kilápi	pencil	Portuguese	lápis
mesa	table	Portuguese/Spanish	mesa
katekisimu	catechism	English	catechism
bóyi	boy	English	boy

Left Luo children in Mfangano fishing village, Kenya. The Luo ethnic group is the third largest in Kenya.

NORTHERN SOTHO

4.2 million speakers

Northern Sotho, also known as Sesotho sa Leboa, is a southern Bantu language related to Southern Sotho and Setswana. It is spoken in the Transvaal province of northeastern South Africa. Sepedi is the main dialect on which the standard orthography of Northern Sotho, which consists of up to thirty dialects, is based. The division between Northern Sotho, Southern Sotho, and Setswana is based primarily on historical and social factors, as the three languages are quite mutually intelligible. Northern Sotho is one of the official languages of South Africa and is taught in primary and secondary schools. There is a considerable amount of literature describing the Northern Sotho language, including grammars and dictionaries.

LUO

4 million speakers

Luo is an eastern Sudanic language of the Nilo-Saharan family. It is spoken in southern Sudan, northern Uganda, eastern Democratic Republic of Congo, western Kenya, and the northern tip of Tanzania. The Luo from Luoland in Kenya are the third-largest ethnic group after the Kikuyu and the Luyha, numbering more than 3 million. Luo is taught in primary schools, and Luo speakers usually speak Swahili and English. Song is a popular genre of Luo culture, and most stories are also accompanied by song. *Gidi Gidi Maji-Maji* are a popular hip-hop duo in Kenya, whose song lyrics are mostly in Luo mixed with Swahili and English. The internationally famous *Song of Lawino* was first written in Luo as *Wer pa Lawino* by the Acholi-born Ugandan poet Okot p'Bitek (1931–82).

RUNYAKITARA

4 million speakers

Runyakitara, a language spoken in western Uganda, is remarkable on a sociolinguistic level, because it only developed in the 1980s as a combination of the closely related varieties of Runyankore, Runyoro, Rutooro, and Rukiga. Through standardization, these four previously rather minor languages of Uganda, where more than forty languages are spoken, have consolidated into one of the country's main languages, spoken by a remarkable 20 percent of the population. The name "Runyakitara" comes from the Kitara kingdom of western Uganda, which was a thriving community from the fifteenth century onward, but had declined by the nineteenth century and was then further oppressed under British colonial rule. Runyakitara nowadays is used on radio, and in the print media, as well as for education.

SUKUMA

4 million speakers

Sukuma is a Bantu language spoken on the western and southern shores of Lake Victoria in northwestern Tanzania, a few hundred miles south of the equator. Sukuma is closely related to Nyamwezi. The two languages share close ethnic links and a high lexical similarity of 80 percent. Kiya and Kigwe are the main dialects of Sukuma. Most speakers of Sukuma are bilingual with Swahili. The political influence of Swahili has meant that, despite the large number of Sukuma speakers, there is hardly any written literature in the language. Swahili being the sole official language, Sukuma has no official status in the educational or political sector, and the younger generation increasingly incorporates Swahili loanwords into Sukuma. However, Sukuma culture is rich in oral folklore and narratives that are also expressed in song.

Left The northwestern shore of Lake Victoria, where Luganda is spoken.

Left School children in southern Angola, where Umbundu is spoken by about a third of the population.

TSONGA

4 million speakers

Tsonga is primarily spoken in the Limpopo province of South Africa and in Mozambique. There are also a few speakers in Zimbabwe and Swaziland. Tsonga is a Bantu language. There are various dialects, but the three most distinct ones are Xironga, spoken in Maputo and the surrounding areas in Mozambique; Xitshwa/Chihlengwe, spoken in Zimbabwe and in Mozambique; and Xitsonga, which is spoken in South Africa. All these dialects have been influenced by Zulu, and as a result Tsonga now has click consonants in borrowed words. It has been referred to as a "whistling language" because of its whistling consonants, such as "sw"/"sv," "tsw"/"tsv," and "dzw"/"dzv."

UMBUNDU

4 million speakers

Umbundu is a Bantu language spoken in southern Angola in the provinces of Bié, Huambo, and Benguela. It is the most widespread Bantu language, spoken by about a third of the population. A decree passed by the Portuguese in 1919 required all Africans seeking education to speak Portuguese, reducing spoken Umbundu. The Umbundu have therefore lost much of their traditional culture during 500 years of Portuguese colonialism, twenty-seven years of civil war, and the consequent migration of people to the urban centers. The official language of Angola remains Portuguese, but there are pilot projects currently underway that use Umbundu for instruction in the first years of education.

LUYIA

3.75 million speakers

Luyia is a Bantu language spoken around Lake Victoria in the Western Province of Kenya and in Uganda. Luyia has more than ten dialects representing an even larger number of ethnic groups. The Luyia are the second-largest ethnic group in Kenya. The origins of the Luyia can probably be related to the Bantu migrations out of Cameroon around 1000 BCE, but myth has it that they migrated from the north, coming from as far as Misri in Egypt. Luyia culture revolves around the extended family, and polygamy is allowed if the marriage is conducted under African traditional law or Muslim law.

LUGANDA

3.5 million speakers

Luganda is a tone Bantu language spoken north of the northwestern shore of Lake Victoria in the Buganda province of Uganda. Luganda is a regional language, a lingua franca with a large number of second-language speakers, and it is the official vernacular language of education in many school districts. A standardized orthography was devised in 1947. Television and radio broadcasts are relayed in the language, and the Catholic Church of Uganda publishes a magazine *Musizi* in Luganda. It is the most widely spoken second language next to English. Luganda is closely related to Soga and Gwere.

BEMBA

3.4 million speakers

Bemba is a Bantu language spoken in the Northern, Luapula, and Copperbelt provinces of Zambia. Some Bemba is spoken in the Democratic Republic of Congo and Tanzania. The Bemba originate from the Luba-Lunda empires of the upper Congo basin. Bemba is one of the national languages of Zambia and an important lingua franca in the country. It is the most widely spoken African language in Zambia, with many second-language speakers. There are about eighteen ethnic groups that speak it. Bemba is taught in schools and there is a range of literature in the language. The Bemba are renowned for using proverbs as a form of expression. Popular music in Bemba, usually mixed with other African languages and English, is widespread.

LOMWE

3.3 million speakers

Lomwe is a Bantu language spoken in southeastern Malawi and in the Zambezia province of Mozambique. The Lomwe are originally from what is now Mozambique to the east of Malawi, but today the majority (1.8 million) live in Malawi, having migrated there over a stretch of time before the arrival of missionaries in 1861. A later Lomwe migration to Malawi occurred in the 1930s due to tribal wars in Mozambique. The Lomwe are now one of the four largest ethnic groups in Malawi. However, the dominance of Chichewa in Malawi has radically diminished the use of Lomwe there, which is now spoken only among elders in rural areas. The long period of civil war in Mozambique has also badly affected its rural-dwelling Lomwe.

KIKONGO

3.2 million speakers

Kikongo, or Kongo, is a Bantu language spoken by the Bakongo people living in the tropical forests of the Democratic Republic of Congo, the Republic of Congo, and Angola. It is a tonal language that formed the basis for Kituba, a Bantu creole and lingua franca throughout much of western Central Africa. Kikongo was the earliest Bantu language committed to writing and it also had the earliest dictionary and grammar of any Bantu language. A Kikongo catechism was produced under the authority of Diogo Gomes, a Jesuit born in Kongo of Portuguese parents in 1557, but no version of it exists today. There is some confusion as to the present number of speakers of Kikongo, because the boundary with Kituba is not clear.

KIMBUNDU

3 million speakers

Kimbundu is a Bantu language which is spoken in the provinces of Luanda, Bengo, Malanje, and Cuauza-Norte in central Angola. The Kimbundu have their roots in the Ndongo Kingdom of Chief Ngola (from whom the country derives its name) established around the 1400s. This kingdom was subjugated by Portuguese colonists in 1671 after almost 100 years of resistance. Portuguese is the official language of Angola but Kimbundu is one of six other recently established official languages. Located close to the coast and to Luanda, the Kimbundu are more susceptible to Portuguese influences, and the younger generation usually speak a slang that is a mix of Portuguese and Kimbundu. There are some television programs in Kimbundu but no written literature.

Left *Kinshasa, capital of the Democratic Republic of Congo, where Lingala is spoken.*

Left *Kamba girls pose for a photograph in the Machakos district of Kenya.*

MAKUA

2.5 million speakers

Makua (also written Makuwa or Makhuwa) is a Bantu language spoken in the central belt of Mozambique north of the Zambezi river. It is closely related to Lomwe. The Makua are the largest ethnic group in northern Mozambique, and Makua is the most important indigenous language there. Although there are some grammatical descriptions of Makua, it is not taught in schools. The main reason for this is the dominance of Portuguese as the national language, in addition to the almost three-decade civil war (1975–92), epidemics, scanty economic resources, and natural disasters that have afflicted Mozambique. There is, however, hope in sight, as the teaching of national languages is currently under experiment in several schools of different provinces.

KALENJIN

2.5 million speakers

Kalenjin represents a cluster of closely related dialects, mainly spoken in the Kenyan western highlands and the Rift Valley. Kalenjin is classified as Nilo-Saharan of the Southern Nilotic group. There are about twelve dialects that came to be known collectively as Kalenjin in the 1940s, but the peoples represented can be traced back to about 1500 CE. The main dialects are Keyo, Cherangany, Tugen, Nandi, and Kipsigis, including a few languages of Tanzania and Uganda. Some standardization of the dialects has been attempted but this is yet to be fully completed. The creation of Kalenjin has played a crucial role in the stronger ethnic presence of otherwise small minority tribes and languages, as its people are now Kenya's fourth-largest ethnic group.

KAMBA

2.5 million speakers

Kamba is a Bantu language spoken in the eastern province of Kenya in an area southwest of Nairobi. Kamba has four dialect clusters: Masaku, South Kitui, North Kitui, and Mumoni. It has structural similarities to Gikuyu (see p. 99), which is spoken in close proximity. Kamba is one of the languages broadcast by the Kenya Broadcasting Corporation. The Kamba people moved to their present location from western Tanzania (Unyamwezi), into the Usambara Mountains and eastern Kenya. The Kamba people are known for their fine craft work in basketry and pottery. They perform spectacular dances displaying their athletic agility and acrobatic techniques.

LINGALA

2.1 million speakers

Lingala is spoken in Kinshasa, capital of the Democratic Republic of Congo, as well as in the northwestern province of Equateur and part of the Haut-Congo. Unlike other languages in the area, Lingala does not serve as the basis for a community but is a strong symbol of Congolese identity. There is a pidgin variety in the northeast called Bangala. Lingala spoken in Kinshasa today has incorporated many loanwords from French, while still using the Lingala grammatical structures. It is probably the fastest-spreading language of the four lingua francas of the DRC, since it is the language of the army and of the popular music heard across sub-Saharan Africa.

YAO

2 million speakers

Yao is a Bantu language spoken by about 1 million speakers in southern Malawi, and by about half a million speakers each in northern Mozambique and southern Tanzania. Yao does not have any official status because it is spread across three different countries, with other languages serving in official functions (Nyanja in Malawi, Portuguese in Mozambique, and Swahili in Tanzania). However, Yao is used in the media in Malawi, and as a cross-border language it plays an important role in regional pan-African cooperation. Yao is well known to historians through one of the earliest historiographies of the region, Yohanna B. Abdallah's 1919 *Chiikala Cha Wayao* (*The Yaos*).

SWATI

1.7 million speakers

Swati (also called Siswati or Swazi in Zulu) is a Bantu language of the Nguni group spoken in Swaziland and South Africa. Swati is the national language of Swaziland and one of the official languages of South Africa. The literacy rate in Swati is very high in Swaziland, and the language is taught in all national schools and used in the media. Swati manifests "depressor consonants" that provide an example of consonant-tone interaction, where a low tone is placed on a vowel following a voiced (obstruent) consonant. Depressor consonants in Swati also trigger a number of other pronunciation effects involving tone spreading, tone shifting, and the blocking of tone shift.

GUSII

1.6 million speakers

Gusii is a Bantu language spoken in the Kisii district of western Kenya. Many Gusii speakers are bilingual with Luo. Located just thirty miles from Lake Victoria in the Nyanza province, the Gusii live in a productive agricultural area, making them fairly affluent. They are believed to have settled in this area around the 1800s, originating from the Democratic Republic of Congo. The Gusii have a strong oral tradition and their folklore typically involves prominent figures linked to historical events. Naming is an important part of Gusii culture, and children are usually given names according to the events surrounding their birth.

NDEBELE

1.5 million speakers

Ndebele is spoken in southwestern Zimbabwe around the city of Bulawayo, and also in South Africa. Ndebele belongs to the Nguni language cluster within Bantu. It is closely related to Zulu because the Ndebele were a breakaway group from the Zulu in 1821, at the height of the Shaka Empire (1817–28) led by King Mzilikazi (1790–1868). Ndebele has three click sounds. It is the second-largest African language of Zimbabwe after Shona, and is an official language that is taught in schools in the areas where it is spoken. A distinction can be made between northern Ndebele (of Zimbabwe) and southern Ndebele (of South Africa).

Left *Mount Kilimanjaro, Tanzania. Chaga is spoken on the slopes of this impressive mountain.*

Left *An open-air health clinic in northern Zimbabwe, where Tonga is spoken.*

CHAGA

1.5 million speakers

Chaga is spoken in northern Tanzania, around Moshi and on the slopes of Mount Kilimanjaro. Chaga is primarily an umbrella term referring to a group of people, the Wachaga, who are the third-largest group of Tanzania. Chaga, or Kichaga, is a dialect continuum, including dialects such as Machame, Vunjo, Rwa, Rombo, Mochi, and Kahe, which show considerable differences and are sometimes regarded as individual languages. Wachaga communities are often seen as economically successful (historically based on coffee and banana farming) and well educated, but due to the dominant role of Swahili as a national language of Tanzania, Kichaga is restricted mainly to local use.

TONGA

1.4 million speakers

Tonga is a Bantu language spoken mainly in southern Zambia but also in northern Zimbabwe and in Malawi. In Zambia the Tonga are divided into valley Tonga, who live on the shores of the Zambezi river and the Kariba dam, and the plateau Tonga, who are farmers living on the southern plateau of Zambia, thus creating two distinct but mutually intelligible dialects. Tonga is one of the national languages of Zambia and schooling is conducted in Tonga in the southern province. In Zimbabwe it is spoken in parts of Matebeleland. Tonga is an important lingua franca in the places where it is spoken with speakers from other ethnic groups, particularly the Toka, Ila, and Leya.

TUMBUKA

1.4 million speakers

Tumbuka (or Chitumbuka) is a cross-border language spoken in northern Malawi (1 million speakers) and in the northeast of Zambia's Eastern province (400,000 speakers). During the reign of Kamuzu Banda (c.1896–1997) in Malawi, Chichewa was the only language promoted and used in public discourse, but after Bakili Muluzi became president in 1994 Malawi's language policy was liberalized, and Tumbuka is now found in the media and receives some national recognition. In Zambia, Tumbuka is spoken in the Eastern province, although the main language is Nyanja. Tumbuka and Nyanja are closely related Bantu languages.

WAMBO

1.4 million speakers

Wambo, or Oshiwambo, is the name for a group of language varieties spoken in northern Namibia and southern Angola. These include Oshikwanyama, Oshindonga, and Oshikwambi. The question of language versus dialect for Oshiwambo is not easy to answer. All Oshiwambo "dialects" are mutually intelligible, although there is variation in pronunciation. The Namibian Broadcasting Corporation seems to treat Oshiwambo as one language. On the other hand, there is no standard orthography for Oshiwambo, whereas Oshikwanyama and Oshindonga have (different) standard written forms and are taught in schools.

Left A Makonde artist with his carvings in northern Mozambique.

MAKONDE

1.37 million speakers

Makonde is a central Bantu language spoken in southeastern Tanzania and northern Mozambique. It is closely related to Yao, which is mainly spoken in southern Malawi but also in Tanzania. Many Makonde speakers also speak Swahili and Makua. There is limited information on Makonde, but a grammar of the language has been written. The Makonde are a matrilineal society and are master woodcarvers known throughout East Africa. The revolution that drove the Portuguese out of Mozambique in the 1960s was launched from the Makonde homeland of the Mueda Plateau.

MERU

1.3 million speakers

Meru is a Bantu language spoken around the slopes of Mount Kenya and on the Nyambene ranges in the Eastern Province of Kenya. There are at least eight distinct clans and dialects, including Igembe, Imenti, Tharaka, Igoji, Mwimbi, Muthambi, and Chuka. These dialects are probably due to centuries of migrations from the north. With Swahili and English as the official languages of Kenya used in the entire education system, and Swahili a dominant lingua franca, Meru has more of a local-language status and Meru speakers use Swahili to communicate with other tribes.

NYAMWEZI

1.2 million speakers

Nyamwezi is a Bantu language of northwestern Tanzania, and the name of the second-largest ethnic group after the Sukuma. The word is of Swahili origin and translates as "people of the moon," a name given to the Nyamwezi by the coastal people to indicate that they came from the west. The Nyamwezi are thought to have settled in their current location in the seventeenth century. Speakers are usually bilingual with Swahili, the national language of Tanzania. Nyamwezi has linguistic similarities with Sukuma, Sumbwa, and Nilamba. One of the most important historical figures for the Nyamwezi is King (**mtemi**) Mirambo, who revolutionized long-distance trading and founded a powerful kingdom with an intricate political, economic, and military system in 1870.

CHOKWE

1.6 million speakers

Chokwe is spoken in Angola, the southeastern Democratic Republic of Congo, and the northwestern corner of Zambia. It is a Bantu language in the Chokwe-Luchazi group. The origins of the Chokwe can be traced back to central Angola from the 1600s, as they were one of the clans of the Lunda Empire (c. 1665–1887). They began to move northward from about 1850, in search of fertile lands after a serious epidemic and famine. Chokwe is one of the six national languages in Angola. The Chokwe have been greatly affected by modern conflicts but continue to practice their traditions of strong belief in ancestral spirits in militarized areas of Angola and the DRC, and in refugee camps in Zambia. The Chokwe are widely renowned for their fine sculptures and art objects.

Left *Northern Malawi. The Nyakyusa speakers here were formerly regarded as a distinct group.*

Left *Women carrying water in the Dodoma region of Tanzania, where Gogo is spoken.*

ZANDE

1.14 million speakers

Zande is an Adamawa-Ubangi tone language mainly spoken in northern Democratic Republic of Congo but also in southwestern Sudan and eastern Central African Republic. Its orthography was established at a language conference in 1928. Past materials have not consistently marked vowel quality and nasalization, but present efforts include these, as well as tone on the tense particles. Zande is a local first language but its speakers also use Lingala. Zande has the less common verb-subject-object word order, in addition to the more common subject-verb-object order. There is some literature available in Zande, including a grammar and a dictionary.

GOGO

1 million speakers

Gogo is a Bantu language of Tanzania spoken in the Dodoma region. Gogo is part of a group together with Kagulu, Kihehe, Sangu, and Nilamba, with which it shares some features. Gogo is a major language of the Anglican Church of Tanzania whose commune has been based in Dodoma since 1970. There are three main dialects of Gogo: Nyanmbwa (West Gogo), Nyaugogo (Central Gogo), and Tumba (East Gogo). The prominent Tanzanian musician and highly regarded singer Hukwe Ubi Zawose (1938–2003) is believed to have developed his talent singing on the cattle farms of the Gogo where he grew up.

NYAKYUSA

1 million speakers

Nyakyusa is a Bantu language spoken by just over 1 million speakers in southern Tanzania and northern Malawi. The two speaker groups were formerly regarded as distinct groups divided by the Songwe river, owing to the German East Africa rule in Tanzania and the British in Malawi. There is a myth that Nyakyusa origins trace back to a Nubian queen called Nyanseba who was abducted by warriors. This is still reflected in the importance of the female lineage to date. Like other Tanzanian languages, Nyakyusa suffers from underdevelopment due to the predominance of Swahili. Most Nyakyusa speakers also speak Swahili.

SENA

1 million speakers

Sena is a cross-border language that is spoken on the southeastern border of Malawi and the central provinces of the Zambezi Valley in Mozambique. It is classified as a Bantu language historically situated between the two major centralized kingdoms of the Monomotapa (of Great Zimbabwe) and the Maravi (in today's Malawi). Sena was spoken across Mozambique and Malawi as a result of demarcating the Shire river as their political border. The influence of English and Chichewa on Malawian Sena and of Portuguese on Mozambiquan Sena has made standardization extremely difficult.

SOUTH ASIAN LANGUAGES

SOUTH ASIAN LANGUAGES

In the seven countries that make up South Asia (Bangladesh, Bhutan, India, Maldives, Nepal, Pakistan, and Sri Lanka), altogether some 500 to 1,000 languages are spoken. The tasks of determining the number of languages and the number of speakers of a particular language are difficult ones, because of "dialect continua" (see p. 126), "diglossia" (see p. 117), incomplete census data, and the inconsistent use of language names (both different names for the same language and the same name for different languages). Cases in point are the varieties of mainland Indo-Aryan and modern Tibetan languages.

Most of the South Asian languages belong to one of four major language families: Indo-European (represented by its Indo-Aryan [IA] and Iranian branches and by the Germanic language, English); Dravidian; Sino-Tibetan (the Tibeto-Burman branch); and Austro-Asiatic (both the Munda and Mon-Khmer branches). The Andamanese languages form a small, proposed language family confined to the Andaman Islands. In addition, Burushaski, Nihali, Kusunda, and possibly some others have no known genetic affiliations.

Three-quarters of the population of South Asia speak an Indo-Aryan language as one of their native languages (widespread multilingualism also being a feature of South Asia). Many South Asian languages are spoken in diaspora, in Southeast Asia, Africa, the Persian Gulf States, Europe (particularly the UK), the Indian and Pacific Oceans, the USA, and Australia.

Several hundred different scripts have been and continue to be used throughout South Asia. Modern South Asian writing systems by and large have three different origins. The majority

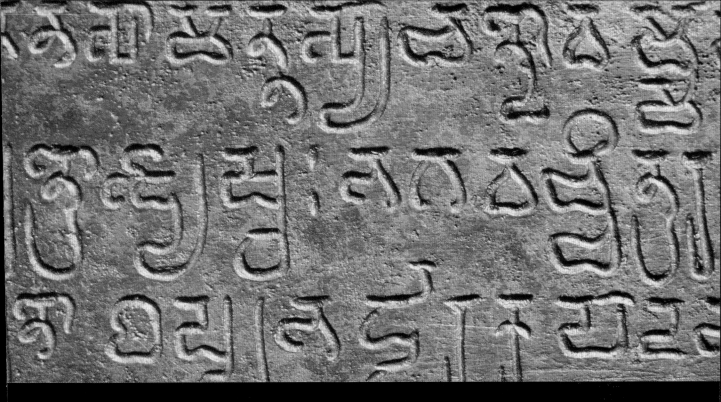

are derived from the ancient Brahmi script (third century BCE). The best-known Brahmi script is probably Devanagari, used for writing Sanskrit and Hindi. The Brahmi scripts tend to be associated with Hinduism, Buddhism, and their offshoots. For this reason, Muslim communities often use variants of the Perso-Arabic script instead. In some rare instances, the Roman script is used. It is not uncommon for the same language to be written in more than one script.

As elsewhere in the world, all languages spoken in South Asia are not equal. Only a select few have official status, as follows: **Bangladesh**—Bengali (IA); **Bhutan**—Dzongkha (Tibeto-Burman); **India**—(2 official languages of the Union) Hindi (IA), English (Germanic); (22 national languages) Assamese (IA), Bengali (IA), Bodo (Tibeto-Burman), Dogri (IA), Gujarati (IA), Hindi (IA), Kannada (Dravidian), Kashmiri (IA), Konkani (IA), Maithili (IA), Malayalam (Dravidian), Marathi (IA), Meitei (Tibeto-Burman), Nepali (IA), Oriya (IA), Punjabi (IA), Sanskrit (IA), Santali (Munda), Sindhi (IA), Tamil (Dravidian), Telugu (Dravidian), Urdu (IA); **Maldives**—Dhivehi (IA); **Nepal**—Nepali (IA); **Pakistan**—Urdu (IA), English (Germanic); **Sri Lanka**—Sinhala (IA), Tamil (Dravidian).

The languages covered in the following pages are (i) feature languages: Assamese, Gujarati, Kannada, Kashmiri, Maithili, Malayalam, Marathi, Nepali, Newar, Oriya, Punjabi, Sindhi, Sinhala, Tamil, Telugu, and Urdu; and (ii) others: Awadhi, Balochi, Bodo, Brahui, Burushaski, Dzongkha, Kinnauri, Konkani, Kurukh, Meitei, Mizo, Santali, Sherpa, Shina, Siraiki, and Tulu.

PUNJABI

93 million speakers

Below *The Punjab region of India, which is centered around the five tributaries of the Indus river.*

Punjabi (Panjabi) is an Indo-Aryan language spoken in Pakistan by more than half the population, and by most of the population in the state of Punjab in the northern part of India, where it is the official language. Punjabi is also spoken in the neighboring Indian states of Haryana, Himachal Pradesh, some parts of Uttarakhand, and in Delhi, as well as in Bangladesh. It is one of the twenty-two national languages of India. Punjabi means "(the language) of Punjab." Punjab in turn derives its name from the (Persian) phrase panj a:b (five waters) referring to the five tributaries of the Indus that run through the area.

Count to 10

ਇਕ (ik)	1
ਦੋ (do)	2
ਤਿਨ (tin)	3
ਚਾਰ (car)	4
ਪੰਜ (pəñj)	5
ਛੇ (cʰe)	6
ਸੱਤ (sətt)	7
ਅੱਠ (əṭʰʰtʰ)	8
ਨੌ (nɔ̃)	9
ਦਸ (dəs)	10

Below *Punjabi script in use at the 1988 Talwand Sabq Sikh convention.*

Punjabi has been used as a literary language since the eleventh century CE. Its history is commonly divided into three distinct stages: Old (tenth to sixteenth century); Medieval (sixteenth to nineteenth century), and Modern (nineteenth century onward).

Adi Granth, the holy scripture of the Sikh community, which constitutes a dominant segment of the Punjabi population in India, is written in Old Punjabi. Three main scripts are used to write Punjabi: the Brahmi-derived Gurmukhi and Devanagari, and a Perso-Arabic script known as Shahmukhi. Gurmukhi means "from the mouth of the Guru" and is mostly associated with the Sikh community. It is also the official script of the state of Punjab. The Devanagari script is occasionally used by Hindu speakers of Punjabi in India, while Shahmukhi is written by Muslims, mainly in Pakistan.

As with many of the Indo-Aryan languages, sources differ as to which language varieties are counted as (dialects of) Punjabi, and which as separate languages. For example, Dogri, Siraiki, Hindko, and Lahnda are names of language varieties that are sometimes considered dialects of Punjabi and sometimes separate languages. The uncertainty is compounded by the fact that, in many areas, Punjabi is a spoken language only, while writing is done in the closely related Urdu or Hindi.

A tonal language

Punjabi is one of a small group of Indo-Aryan languages in northwestern South Asia which display contrastive word tones. This means that some words differ only by their tonal contours, an otherwise rare trait in the Indo-Aryan family. Punjabi has three possible tones on a stressed syllable, for example:

level tone	ꞌkora (whip)	ca (fervor)
falling tone	kòra (leper)	cà (tea)
rising tone	kóra (horse)	cá (peep)

TELUGU  **70 million speakers**

Telugu is a Dravidian language spoken by most of the population in the state of Andhra Pradesh along the southeast coast of India, as well as in the border districts of the neighboring states of Tamil Nadu, Orissa, Karnataka, and Madhya Pradesh. It is the official language of the state of Andhra Pradesh and is one of the twenty-two national languages of India. Telugu is the largest Dravidian language in terms of numbers of speakers and has a long literary tradition. The first extant Telugu inscription is from the sixth century CE and the first literary work from the eleventh century CE .

Above *A painting from the Virabhadra Temple in Andhra Pradesh, showing Shiva riding the bull Nandin. Telugu is spoken by most of the population in this Indian state.*

However, Telugu words and place names appear in inscriptions and texts written in Maharashtri Prakrit (see p. 118) from the centuries around the beginning of the Common Era. With time, the region's rulers progressively used and encouraged the use of the languages of the masses, leading to the waning of Prakrit and the emergence of Telugu as a literary and court language. The golden age of Telugu was in the times of the Vijayanagar rulers (fourteenth to seventeenth century CE).

Until the middle of the twentieth century, Telugu was characterized by "diglossia." This is where the written language adheres to an archaic style very different from the everyday spoken language. The present written standard for Teluga is based on the modern spoken language.

The Telugu and Kannada (see p. 123) scripts are extremely closely related. The original Telugu-Kannada script developed from a southern Brahmi script used between the fifth and seventh centuries CE. By the fourteenth century, this script had developed into two highly distinct forms, which were the precursors of the modern scripts that we see today. Both of these scripts were standardized at the beginning of the nineteenth century. There were official attempts in both the 1950s and the 1960s to unify the two scripts again, in order to simplify printing, but this is an issue that has largely disappeared since the advent of computers. With modern printing methods, it is relatively easy to reproduce both scripts, which in turn means that technology is helping to keep a script in existence that might otherwise have been lost.

The Dravidian languages

The Dravidian languages make up a family of about twenty-five members, subdivided into four branches:

South Dravidian: Badaga, Irula, Kannada, Kodagu, Koraga, Kota, Kurumba, Malayalam, Tamil, Toda, and Tulu

South-Central Dravidian: Gondi, Konda, Kui, Kuvi, Manda, Pengo, and Telugu

Central Dravidian: Gadaba, Kolami, Naiki, Naikri, Ollari, and Parji

North Dravidian: Brahui, Kurukh, and Malto

Kannada, Malayalam, Tamil, and Telugu are major languages with a long literary tradition. Kodagu and Tulu are more recent literary languages, and the remainder are non-literary languages.

MARATHI

68 million speakers

Marathi is an Indo-Aryan language spoken in the state of Maharashtra on the west coast of India, where it is the official language. It is also spoken in Gujarat, Madhya Pradesh, Andhra Pradesh, Goa, Karnataka, and Tamil Nadu. The name Marathi comes from Maharashtri "(the language) of Maharashtra," Maharashtra meaning "the great land." Marathi's ancestor language was Maharashtri Prakrit, which was the Middle Indo-Aryan language used in ancient times by the ruling Satavahanas. According to contemporary grammarians, this was the "best" and most prestigious Prakrit (see panel below)—the literary standard.

Above *The seven states of India where Marathi is currently spoken.*

Stages of Indo-Aryan languages

The history of the Indo-Aryan languages is generally divided into the following stages:

Old Indo-Aryan (OIA; c. 1500–600 BCE): Vedic (the language of the Vedas, the ancient holy books of the Hindus), Sanskrit (the classical language of South Asia).

Middle Indo-Aryan (MIA; c. 600 BCE–1000 CE): Pali (the language of Buddhism), the so-called Prakrits (earlier MIA), and Apabhramshas (later MIA).

New Indo-Aryan (NIA; c. 1000 CE–present): older stages of NIA have often attained a classical, prestigious status in relation to their modern successors.

The relationship between the confirmed OIA and MIA languages is not one of direct descent. Rather, some unconfirmed OIA language must be posited, a bit like the unconfirmed Vulgar Latin dialects supposed to be the ancestors of the modern Romance languages. Nevertheless, it is often possible to trace a NIA language back to some proven MIA.

Maharashtri Prakrit developed via Maharashtri Apabhramsha into Old Marathi, attested by inscriptions from the eleventh century CE, while the earliest literary work in the language is considered to be *Viveksindhu* by Mukundaraja (1199 CE). *Jnaneshwari* (thirteenth century), a commentary on the famous Hindu religious epic poem *Bhagavadgita*, is another important literary work in Marathi.

Marathi is situated between its Indo-Aryan sister languages to the north and (unrelated) Dravidian languages to the south. As elsewhere in South Asia, multilingualism is the rule rather than the exception, which has resulted in neighboring languages of the region influencing each other. Thus Marathi displays both inherited Indo-Aryan and borrowed Dravidian linguistic features. Marathi is written in a script called Balbodhi, a slightly modified version of the Devanagari script, a Brahmi-derived script also used to write Hindi and Sanskrit, among others.

Above *The Balbodhi script as demonstrated by a young schoolboy writing in Marathi.*

TAMIL

66 million speakers

Tamil is a Dravidian language spoken by most of the population in the state of Tamil Nadu in the south of India, where it is the official language, and in the neighboring states of Andhra Pradesh, Karnataka, and Kerala. It is one of the twenty-two national languages of India, and it is also an official language of Sri Lanka and Singapore. Tamil cave inscriptions in the Brahmi script dated to the third to the first century BCE make it the earliest written Dravidian language. Tamil boasts a rich literary tradition, the oldest among the Dravidian languages. The earliest extant work is *Tolkappiyam*, from the third to the first century BCE, which discusses poetics and grammar.

Above *A Tamil woman in Sri Lanka. Tamil is an excellent example of an ancient language that is thriving today.*

Right *As well as being used in newspapers, Tamil is one of the four Dravidian literary languages of India.*

Loanwords

Tamil (or in some cases the closely related Malayalam) is the source of a number of loanwords in English (especially Indian English), mostly denoting specifically local south Indian natural and social phenomena. However, some Tamil/Malayalam loanwords that have gained wider currency in English are: **betel** (Malayalam), **catamaran, cheroot, corundum, curry, mango, orange, pariah, poppadom/ papad,** and **teak** (Malayalam).

The Tamil script evolved from the Brahmi script during the reign of Emperor Ashoka (third century BCE), and later became a variant called Grantha, which was used to write Tamil and Sanskrit.

Tamil has exerted considerable influence in the development of the other three literary Dravidian languages of India, namely, Telugu (p. 117), Malayalam (p. 122), and Kannada (p. 123).

The Tamil language community is characterized by "diglossia," a situation in which radically different language varieties (or even different languages) are used in formal and informal settings. Written standard Tamil is based on a classical language form that was codified in the thirteenth century CE; imagine when writing English that we still had to use the language of Chaucer! This means that classical as well as modern and contemporary literature becomes intelligible only to those who have mastered the written standard. This mastery requires quite a substantial effort because the written standard is so distant from all contemporary spoken varieties. Because of the widening gulf between the written

standard and the spoken varieties, and because of the demands of modern broadcast mass media, a standardized spoken form of Tamil has emerged in modern times. Diglossia has deep roots in South Asia, where a succession of classical language forms have emerged as successively new vernaculars developed over 2,500 years of written history.

URDU

60.5 million speakers

Below *The Urdu-speaking regions of India, Pakistan, Bangladesh, and Nepal.*

Below *The striking scenery of the state of Jammu and Kashmir, where Urdu is the official language.*

Urdu is an Indo-Aryan language of the Indo-Iranian branch, spoken in India, Pakistan and, to a certain extent, Bangladesh and Nepal. In Pakistan, Urdu is the official language and is widely used for personal correspondence and public literature, literary works, and popular media. However, it is spoken natively by less than 8 percent of the population, making it only the fifth-largest language of the country. In India, it is the official language of the state of Jammu and Kashmir in the north, and the second official language of the states of Uttar Pradesh, Bihar, Delhi, and Andhra Pradesh. It is one of the twenty-two national languages of India.

Count to 10

ایک (e:k)	एक	1
دو (do:)	दो	2
تین (ti:n)	तीन	3
چار (ca:r)	चार	4
پانچ (pã:c)	पाँच	5
چھه (cʰɛ:)	छ	6
سات (sa:t)	सात	7
آٹھ (a:ʈʰ)	आठ	8
نو (nɔ:)	नौ	9
دس (das)	दस	10

The name Urdu means "camp"; it reflects the same Turkish word that has given English "horde." It comes from the expression **zaba:n-e-urdu:-e-mu'alla:** "The language of the Exalted Camp (= The Red Fort of Delhi)," and was first used in a late eighteenth-century poem.

Urdu and Hindi have the same roots, in the emerging New Indo-Aryan language varieties spoken in an area centered on Delhi, and especially the variety called Khari Boli, which spread throughout India with the Muslim armies under the Delhi Sultanate (thirteenth to fifteenth century CE). Literary use of Urdu, written in the Perso-Arabic script, started in the seventeenth century, alongside Persian, which was the language of the elite. In the early nineteenth century, the British colonial administration in India chose Khari Boli under the name of Hindustani as their local administrative language, encouraging the use of the Perso-Arabic and Devanagari scripts in parallel. The choice of script and source of learned vocabulary (Persian/Arabic versus Sanskrit) gradually became a sign of religious affiliation, and ultimately resulted in the two standard languages Urdu and Hindi. Even today, the grammatical differences between the two are minimal, and the colloquial spoken varieties share the "v" of their vocabulary (less so the standard languages).

In southern India, in Hyderabad and adjoining regions, there is a distinct Urdu variety called Dakhani, which is greatly influenced by Dravidian languages such as Telugu and Kannada.

GUJARATI

Gujarati is a modern Indo-Aryan language spoken by most of the population in the state of Gujarat in western India, where it is currently the official language, and in the neighboring states of Maharashtra and Rajasthan, as well as in Pakistan and Bangladesh. The Gujarati language is another of the twenty-two national languages of India. The Parsis, who were followers of the Zoroastrian religion and first came to India from Persia in the eighth century CE, settling along the Gujarat coast, also speak Gujarati. Today the vast majority of Parsis live in Mumbai, the capital city of the Indian state of Maharashtra.

Above *The unmistakable figure of Mahatma Gandhi, the leader of the Indian Independence Movement, who both spoke and wrote in Gujarati.*

Below right *A woman stripping paint off a colorful wall in Bhuj, Gujarat. Gujarati is written in a distinct Brahmi script, which is similar to the Devanagari script.*

Count to 10

એક (ek)	1
બે (bɛ)	2
તૂરણ (trəṇ)	3
ચાર (car)	4
પાંચ (pāc)	5
છ (cʰə)	6
સાત (sat)	7
આઠ (atʰ)	8
નવ (nəv)	9
દસ (dəs)	10

Gujarati means "(the language) of Gujarat." Gujarat in turn is derived from a phrase meaning "the land of the Gurjara," a tribe of ancient India who ruled the area during the eighth and ninth centuries CE.

Scholars divide the development of Gujarati language and literature into three phases: Old Gujarati (twelfth to fifteenth century CE), Middle Gujarati (fifteenth to eighteenth century), and Modern Gujarati (eighteenth century onward). The earliest literary work in Gujarati was a so-called **rasa** (didactic narrative) written in 1185. Established in 1822, the Gujarati daily newspaper *Mumbai Samachar* is one of the oldest in Asia. Mahatma Gandhi, the father of the modern Indian nation, was a Gujarati speaker. A prolific writer, most of Gandhi's writings were in Gujarati, in a style that has come to have a strong influence on modern Gujarati prose.

Gujarati is written in a Brahmi script close to that of Sanskrit, and Hindi Devanagari, but there is no horizontal line at the top of the letters, and some of the characters are slightly different. This characteristic script developed gradually out of Devanagari, in which the oldest texts in Gujarati were written. The earliest document with handwritten Gujarati script is dated 1592. The printed script appeared in an advertisement in 1797, but the Gujarati script was used only for accounting and writing letters until the nineteenth century, with literary works being written in Devanagari. The Gujarati script was thus also known as the **sarafi** (banker's), **vaniasi** (merchant's), or **mahajani** (trader's) script.

MALAYALAM

36 million speakers

Malayalam is a Dravidian language spoken by most of the population in the state of Kerala on the southwest coast of India, where it is the official language, and also on the Lakshadweepa islands off the coast of Kerala in the Arabian Sea. It is another of the twenty-two national languages of India. The etymology of the name "Malayalam" is not clear. However, there is general agreement that the first part (mala) means "mountain." There are then three competing plausible explanations for the name, which are: "mountain dweller," "the mountain land," and "the land between the mountains and the ocean."

Above *Conversation and negotiation at a busy market in Kerala state.*

Below right *The state of Kerala and the Lakshadweepa islands, where Malayalam is spoken.*

Malayalam is closely related to Tamil. Originally a west-coast dialect of Tamil (or rather of Proto-Tamil-Malayalam), it emerged as a variety distinct from Tamil in the ninth century CE. The oldest extant Malayalam inscription is dated to around 830 CE. The early development of Malayalam was heavily influenced by Sanskrit and Tamil, which at the time were respectively the languages of the spiritual and the temporal sphere. Malayalam shows considerable Indo-Aryan influence, primarily in the form of loanwords, but also in its grammatical structure.

Malayalam has a long literary tradition, from an early stage that drew upon traditional Tamil and Sanskrit genres as well as native Malayalam genres, to the modern age encompassing a wide range of contemporary genres such as poetry, drama, fiction, and nonfiction.

For writing Malayalam, various Brahmi-derived scripts have been used. The earliest writings are in a south Brahmi script known as **vattezhuthu** (round writing). The present distinctive Malayalam script emerged in the seventeenth century. The script was simplified in the 1970s and 1980s to make it amenable to printing. The language is also written in the Arabic script by Muslim speakers in Singapore and Malaysia.

Malayalam does not exhibit the diglossia of its sister language Tamil (see p. 119). This may have contributed to the literacy rate in the state of Kerala (where 95 percent of the population are Malayalam speakers) being the highest in India at almost 91 percent.

Count to 10

ഒന്നു (onnu)	1
രണ്ടു (raṇtu)	2
മൂന്നു (mu:nnu)	3
നാലു (na:lu)	4
അഞ്ചു (añcu)	5
ആറു (a:ru)	6
ഏഴു (e:ḷu)	7
എട്ടു (eṭṭu)	8
ഒന്പതു (onpatu)	9
പത്തു (pattu)	10

KANNADA

Kannada (Canarese) is a Dravidian language spoken by most of the population in Karnataka, where it is the official language. Kannada is also spoken in the border regions of the adjacent states Tamil Nadu, Andhra Pradesh, Kerala, and Maharashtra. It is one of the twenty-two national languages of India. The etymology of the name "Kannada" is plausibly to be found in the combination kar(u) (black) + naḍu (land), in other words "the land of black soil." The earliest written record is an inscription from the fifth century CE, and the earliest extant literary work is from the ninth century, *Kavirajamarga*, written by King Nriputunga Amoghavarsha I in 850.

Above and right Contrasting images of Bangalore, the capital of Karnataka state in India where Kannada is the predominant language. The Kannada language has managed to adapt to changing times, and borrows from numerous other languages, including English.

This work on grammar is an attempt to standardize the various dialects of Kannada which had been used in earlier literary writings. The history of the language is commonly divided into three distinct stages: Old (fifth to thirteenth century), Medieval (thirteenth to nineteenth century), and Modern (from the nineteenth century onward). Kannada has an old and rich literary tradition, although not many works have been translated.

In sharp opposition to its Dravidian sister language Tamil (but similarly to English), Kannada has been very open to outside linguistic influence as the preferred mode of adapting the language to changing times. Its vocabulary is permeated with elements borrowed or calqued from Sanskrit, Prakrit, Perso-Arabic, and, most recently, English. Calqued means "loan-translated," as in the English phrase "flea market" which comes from the French **marché aux puces**. Sanskrit word-formation devices have become a productive part of the linguistic system of the language (as the Classical Greek ending -ism is used even with native English words, for example, "McCarthyism").

The Kannada and Telugu (see p. 117) scripts are closely related. The Proto-Telugu-Kannada script developed from a southern Brahmi script, which was used between the fifth and seventh centuries CE. By the fourteenth century, this script had developed into two distinct forms, which are both precursors of the modern scripts we see today. Both scripts were then standardized at the beginning of the nineteenth century. The Kannada script is also used for writing other languages, these being Tulu (see p. 133), Kodagu, and Konkani (see p. 132).

Count to 10

ಒಂದು (ondu)	1	
ಎರಡು (eraḍu)	2	
ಮೂರು (mu:ru)	3	
ನಾಲಕ್ (na:ku)	4	
ಐದು (aydu)	5	
ಆರು (a:ru)	6	
ಏಳು (e:ḷu)	7	
ಎಂಟು (eṇṭu)	8	
ಒಂಬತುತ್ (ombattu)	9	
ಹತುತ್ (hattu)	10	

ORIYA

32 million speakers

Oriya is an Indo-Aryan language spoken by most of the population in the state of Orissa on India's southeast coast, where it is the official language, and in the states of Jharkhand, West Bengal, Andhra Pradesh, and, in recent years, in the state of Gujarat, particularly in the city of Surat. It is also spoken in Bangladesh. It is one of the twenty-two national languages of India. The Middle Indo-Aryan precursors of Oriya were Magadhi Prakrit and Magadhi Apabhramsha. Oriya belongs to the eastern group of Indo-Aryan languages, where its closest relatives are considered to be Assamese and Bengali, while Bhojpuri, Magahi, and Maithili are more distantly related.

Above *Women at a malaria prevention project in the Indian state of Orissa.*

Below right *The Jagannath temple at Puri, home to the Palm Leaf Chronicles from the twelfth century CE, written in Oriya.*

Oriya is geographically situated between its Indo-Aryan sister languages to the northwest and Dravidian languages (see p. 117) to the south. Oriya also has a long history of contact with the various Austro-Asiatic languages spoken in the area. As elsewhere in South Asia, multilingualism is the rule rather than the exception, which has resulted in neighboring languages of the region influencing each other. Thus Oriya displays both inherited Indo-Aryan and borrowed Dravidian and Austro-Asiatic linguistic features.

Oriya has a rich literature dating back to the thirteenth century CE. *Madala Panji* (the Palm Leaf Chronicles) of the Jagannath temple at Puri were supposedly written in the twelfth century CE. Some still older texts (e.g. the *Charyapada* Buddhist hymns from the tenth to thirteenth century) claimed to be in Old Oriya are also claimed to be in Old Assamese, Old Bengali, or Old Maithili by scholars of the respective languages.

The modern Oriya script is a descendant of an eastern variant of the Brahmi script. The distinctive curved and rounded appearance of the Oriya script is often attributed to a deliberate redesign by users who wrote on palm leaves. The curved shapes would have been less likely to tear the fragile leaves, as opposed to the straight lines of the original Brahmi or Devanagari script.

Count to 10

ଏକ (e:k)	1
ଦୁଇ (dui)	2
ତିନି (tini)	3
ଛାରି (cʰa:ri)	4
ପାଞ୍ଚ (pa:njcʰ)	5
ଛଅ (cʰɔ)	6
ସାତ (sa:t)	7
ଆଠ (a:tʰ)	8
ନଅ (nɔ)	9
ଦଶ (dɔs)	10

MAITHILI

25 million speakers

Maithili is an Indo-Aryan language spoken in the northeastern part of the state of Bihar in India, and adjacent areas of Nepal. It is the second most-spoken language of Nepal. It is one of the twenty-two national languages of India. Maithili means "of/from Mithila," which was the name of a kingdom once covering a large area in present-day northeast Bihar and southeast Nepal. Although Maithili is recognized as an independent literary language in India, it is also occasionally considered to be a dialect of Bengali or Hindi, or as a dialect of a language called Bihari, supposedly consisting of Bhojpuri and Magahi, in addition to Maithili.

Above *An example of Devanagari script used on a hoarding in Muzaffarpur in the state of Bihar.*

Below right *Areas of India and Nepal where Maithili is spoken.*

A polite language

Possibly because of non-Indo-Aryan influence, Maithili has developed a number of linguistic traits that distinguish it from its neighboring Indo-Aryan sister languages. In its grammar, for example, it has lost the distinction between singular and plural and almost all gender distinctions, but has added a very complex verbal-agreement system. It also has multifarious distinctions of honorificity in its pronouns: in other words, the use of a pronoun is determined by the social distance between the speaker, the listener, and the person(s) discussed.

Maithili is a language with a long literary tradition, dating back to the thirteenth century CE. The earliest extant text in Maithili is from the early sixteenth century.

Some still older texts (e.g. the *Charyapada* Buddhist hymns from the tenth to thirteenth century) said to be in Old Maithili are also said to be in Old Assamese, Old Bengali, or Old Oriya, according to scholars of the respective languages. These two controversies illustrate well the difficulties involved when examining a historically and geographically contiguous language area, such as that of the Indo-Aryan languages (see p. 126).

The Middle Indo-Aryan precursors of Maithili were Magadhi Prakrit and Magadhi Apabhramsha. Maithili was a prestigious language at the court of Nepal from the fourteenth to the eighteenth century, alongside Newar, the Tibeto-Burman language of the rulers (see p. 131). In addition to Tibeto-Burman, Maithili has long been in contact with the Austro-Asiatic language Santali (see p. 133).

The oldest Maithili texts are written in a Brahmi-derived script called Mithilakshara, closely related to the Bengali and Assamese scripts. This script is still occasionally used for decorative purposes. Before the turn of the twentieth century, a script called Kaithi was used for record-keeping during the time of the British Raj (1858–1947) in India. Around 1900, Devanagari started to be used for writing Maithili, and, ever since then, it has been kept as the main script.

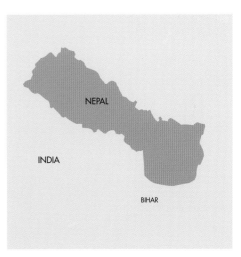

SINDHI

22 million speakers

Sindhi is an Indo-Aryan language spoken mainly in the Sindh province of Pakistan, where the majority of Sindhi-speaking people live, and in India, where Sindhi speakers are to be found largely in the western states of Maharashtra and Gujarat. It is one of the twenty-two national languages of India. The Indus river was known in earlier times as the Sindhu river, and this is where the name of the Sindh region and its language comes from. Sindhi is a language with a long and rich history, dating from at least the ninth century CE, and a translation of the Qur'an into the this language has been dated to 883.

Above *A young Sindhi-speaking girl in the Sindh province of southern Pakistan.*

According to some sources, Sindhi has six major dialects: Siraiki (Seraiki), Vicholi, Lari, Lasi, Thari (Thareli), and Kacchi (Kachchhi). However, other sources consider at least Kacchi to be a separate language. In addition, the name Siraiki is used to describe a different language variety, sometimes listed as a separate language and sometimes as a dialect of Punjabi.

Sindhi and its sister languages Kacchi (if not a dialect of Sindhi), Marwari, and Siraiki (if not a dialect of Punjabi) are unique among the Indo-Aryan languages for having implosive stops. These are sounds that are also generally rare in all languages. Sindhi has four implosive stops —ɓ, ɗ, ʄ, ɠ— which are produced by drawing in instead of expelling the breath, giving the language a unique and memorable vocal tonality.

Several scripts are used for writing Sindhi. The Hindu Sindhis have preferred the Devanagari script, while the Muslim Sindhis use a Perso-Arabic script. The Kacchis in Gujarat, whose language is sometimes considered a dialect of Sindhi, use the Gujarati script.

How many languages are there?

The Indo-Aryan language group illustrates the problem of determining how many languages exist in a vast region without sharp linguistic borders. Here neighboring language varieties differ little, but differences grow with distance so that at least the varieties at the edges of this region will not be mutually intelligible. This is known as a "dialect continuum." In South Asia, there are several dialect continua, the largest being that of Indo-Aryan mainland languages covering most of northern and central South Asia, with the so-called "Hindi belt" at its center. Here there is conflicting information as to (i) whether a named language variety is a language in its own right or a dialect; and, if the latter, (ii) of which language it is a dialect. The issue is also influenced by social and historical factors, aptly summarized by the American linguist Max Weinreich as "A language is a dialect with an army and a navy."

Below *The states where Sindhi is most commonly spoken in Pakistan and India.*

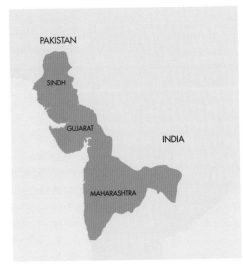

NEPALI

17 million speakers

Nepali is an Indo-Aryan language spoken in Nepal, in the north Indian state of Sikkim and some other parts of India, and in Bhutan and Burma. It is the official language and also the most-spoken native language within Nepal. It is, once again, one of the twenty-two national languages of India. Nepali means "(the language) of Nepal." The name Nepal, originally a name for the Kathmandu Valley region, is of Tibeto-Burman origin, and the original speakers of what is still called Nepal Bhasa, "the Nepal language," a Tibeto-Burman language, are commonly known as Newars (see p. 131).

Count to 10

एक (ek)	1
दुइ (dui)	2
तीन (ti:n)	3
चार (ca:r)	4
पाँच (pã:c)	5
छ (cʰa)	6
सात (sa:t)	7
आठ (a:tʰ)	8
नौ (naw)	9
दश (das)	10

The ancestors of the present-day Nepali speakers had settled in western Nepal by the twelfth century CE, from where they advanced eastward during the following centuries. Eventually, they managed to conquer the kingdom of Nepal in the eighteenth century, after which their language replaced Newar and Maithili (see p. 125) as the official language of the court. At that time, the speakers were known as the Khas, and their language as Khas Kura, Khas Bhasa, or Gorkhali, the latter name coming from the Kingdom of Gorkha in central Nepal, founded by the Khas in the sixteenth century. A better-known variant spelling in English of this name is Gurkha. The Indo-Aryan language of the conquerors started going by the name of Nepali only in the early twentieth century.

The oldest extant Nepali text is a bilingual Khas-Tibetan inscription from the fourteenth century (although scholars dispute whether the language of the inscription is a direct ancestor of modern Nepali, or an indirectly related, older dialect). Literary texts first appeared in the seventeenth century.

Genetically, Nepali is closest to the northern Indo-Aryan languages spoken in the Himalayas in western Nepal and northern India. Nepali has been in close contact with Tibeto-Burman languages for most of its recorded history, but the extent of Tibeto-Burman influence on Nepali is disputed. That Nepali, on the other hand, has influenced many of the Tibeto-Burman languages spoken in Nepal and adjacent areas is beyond dispute and well documented.

In earlier times, Nepali was written in an old indigenous Brahmi-derived script called Bhujimol, but today it is written mostly in Devanagari, the script also used for Sanskrit and Hindi.

Above *Map showing the main areas over which Nepali is spoken.*

Right *Today, Nepali is written using the Devanagari script.*

ASSAMESE  **15 million speakers**

Assamese (Asamiya) is an Indo-Aryan language spoken by most of the population of Assam in northeast India, where it is the official language, and in some pockets in the states of West Bengal, Arunachal Pradesh, and Meghalaya. It is also spoken in Bangladesh and Bhutan. It is one of the twenty-two national languages of India. The Middle Indo-Aryan precursors of Assamese were Magadhi Prakrit and the Magadhi Apabhramsha. Assamese belongs to the eastern group of Indo-Aryan languages, where its closest relatives are Bengali and Oriya (see p. 124), while Bhojpuri, Magahi, and Maithili (see p. 125) are more distantly related.

Above *A stone relief from the state of Assam depicting the Hindu deity Ganesha.*

Below *An Assamese tea garden. Tea is the crop that this region is associated with most.*

In the northeastern corner of South Asia where Assamese is spoken, languages belonging to all four major language families of South Asia are spoken: Indo-Aryan, Dravidian, Tibeto-Burman, and Austro-Asiatic (Khasi, a language of the Mon-Khmer branch, and some scattered pockets of Munda languages). Assamese has long been used in the area as a lingua franca, in other words, a language of wider communication.

Thus, Assamese exhibits certain linguistic characteristics that may be the result of contact with languages of the three other language families spoken in the region. The two separate d-/t-series of stops (called dental and retroflex), otherwise ubiquitous among Indo-Aryan languages, have merged in Assamese into one series of stops with an articulation intermediate between the earlier two series, much like the English "t" and "d" sounds. In the area of grammar, it has developed a series of classifying definite articles that are added as endings to nouns, numerals, and definite pronouns: **manuɦ-zɒn** (the man); **gai-zɒni** (the cow); **kitap-kʰɒn** (the book); **pani-kʰini** (the water); **latʰi-dal** (the stick).

The earliest literary works in Assamese date from the thirteenth to sixteenth century CE, representing mainly original poetry and drama, and translations of classical Sanskrit works. Some even older texts (including the *Charyapada* Buddhist hymns from the tenth to thirteenth century) said to be in Old Assamese, are also claimed to be in Old Bengali, Old Maithili, or Old Oriya by scholars of the respective languages.

Count to 10

এক (ek)	1
দুই (dui)	2
তিনি (tini)	3
চাৰি (sari)	4
পাঁচ (pãs)	5
ছয় (səy)	6
সাত (xat)	7
আঠ (atʰ)	8
ন (nə)	9
দশ (dəx)	10

SINHALA

 **13 million speakers**

Sinhala (Sinhalese) is an Indo-Aryan language spoken by most of the population of Sri Lanka, where it is one of the two official languages of the nation (together with Tamil). The closest relative of Sinhala is Dhivehi (Divehi, Maldivian), the official language of the Maldives. These two languages form a distinct subgroup of Indo-Aryan languages. Buddhist settlers from northeastern India are said to have brought Sinhala to Sri Lanka around the fifth century BCE. The language spoken by the settlers is known as Sinhala Prakrit. This is confirmed in inscriptions from the third century BCE. The earliest literary work in Sinhala is from the ninth century CE.

Above *Books in Sinhala find ready hands at the Colombo International Bookfair in Sri Lanka.*

Below right *A roadside vegetable stand in Sri Lanka. Sinhala is one of two official languages in this country.*

Having developed separately from the other Indo-Aryan languages on the South Asian mainland for over two millennia, Sinhala has become quite distinct from its sister languages, although some scholars consider it somewhat closer to the eastern Indo-Aryan languages (e.g. Assamese, Bengali, Maithili, and Oriya) than the other subgroups. Sinhala was also influenced by the surrounding Dravidian languages, especially Tamil and Malayalam. Even in the earliest records, Sinhala had lost the distinction between aspirated and unaspirated stops so characteristic of Indo-Aryan languages, most likely due to Dravidian influence.

Also attributable to Dravidian influence is the characteristic of Sinhala syntax that modifiers consistently go before the words they modify, to the extent that Sinhala lost its relative pronouns, using instead structures such as the following: **siri gunəpa:latə dunnə potə**, literally "Siri Gunapala-to gave-which book," in other words, "the book that Siri gave to Gunapala"; the parts of the literal translation glossed as "-to" and "-which" are special inflections in Sinhala.

The Sinhala language community is characterized by diglossia (see p. 117). Literary Sinhala differs markedly from all the spoken varieties of the language. For instance, spoken Sinhala lacks verb agreement, while literary Sinhala has an elaborate verb-agreement system involving person, number, and gender.

Sinhala is written in a Brahmi-derived script unique to Sinhala (although, like other Brahmi scripts, it is also used locally to write Pali and Sanskrit).

Count to 10

එක	(ekə)	1
ඩෙක	(dekə)	2
තුන	(tunə)	3
හතර	(hatərə)	4
පහ	(paha)	5
හය	(hayə)	6
හත	(hatə)	7
අට	(aṭə)	8
තුමය	(naməyə)	9
දහය	(dahayə)	10

KASHMIRI

4.5 million speakers

Below *An illustration of shawl weavers from the* Album of Kashmiri Trades, *c. 1850.*

Kashmiri is an Indo-Aryan language spoken in the Kashmir Valley in the state of Jammu and Kashmir in India, and in the neighboring region in Pakistan. The official language of the state of Jammu and Kashmir, however, is Urdu. Kashmiri is one of the twenty-two national languages of India, and belongs to the Dardic group, a non-genetic term that covers about two dozen Indo-Aryan languages spoken in the geographically isolated, mountainous northwestern part of South Asia, which includes eastern Afghanistan and northern Pakistan. In 1919, George Grierson wrote that "Kashmiri is one of the only Dardic languages that has a literature."

Below right *The main Kashmiri-speaking regions of South Asia.*

A V2 language in the Himalayas

A peculiarity of Kashmiri grammar, making it unique among the Indo-Aryan languages, is that it is a so-called verb-second (V2) language, a trait found mostly in some Germanic languages (German, Dutch, Yiddish, and the Scandinavian languages). A finite verb must stand in the second position in the clause (except in relative clauses). In English, this becomes most noticeable when something other than the subject occupies the first position of a clause. The word order "Yesterday the town celebrated" is ungrammatical in a V2 language; it has to be "Yesterday celebrated the town" (as in German).

Kashmiri literature dates from the twelfth century CE and consists largely of Sufi- and folklore-based poetry. Its first great poet was a woman called Lal Dad who wrote *Lalleshvari*, a mystic poem from the fourteenth century. Love poetry, mostly by women—among them Habba Khatoon (1551–1600) and Aarnimal (late eighteenth century)—was also very popular. Mehmood Gani and Walliullah Mattu (both mid-nineteenth century) wrote poetry in Kashmiri that shows considerable influence from Persian literature. Prose and drama writing in Kashmiri began only around the turn of the twentieth century.

Kashmiri has a large number of dialects of which major ones include the standard Kashmiri spoken in the city of Srinagar and its neighborhood, and Kashtwari, or Kishtwari, used in the Kishtwar Valley in southeastern Kashmir. Other widespread dialects are Poguli, Saraji, Rambani, and Bhunjwali. There is also some variation in the language according to the class and religion of the speakers. Hindu Kashmiris use more Sanskrit-derived vocabulary, while the Muslim Kashmiris use more words of Persian and Arabic origin.

The oldest script of Kashmiri was the Brahmi-derived Sharda script, which was developed in the tenth centuryand is still in restricted use by Hindu priests nowadays. Kashmiri has been and still is written today by Hindu Kashmiris in a variant of Devanagari. The officially recognized script for Kashmiri in the state of Jammu and Kashmir is a modified form of Perso-Arabic script, which, however, still lacks standardization.

NEWAR  **800,000 speakers**

Newar (Nepal Bhasha, Newari; the latter is increasingly felt to be derogatory) is a Tibeto-Burman language spoken by an ethnic group called Newars, who inhabit an area centered on the Kathmandu Valley in Nepal. It is also spoken in India. The names "Newar" and "Nepal" have the same origin, but there are several proposed explanations for the etymology of the word. The name "Nepal" originally referred to the Newar homeland in Kathmandu Valley. It is not known how long the Newars have occupied this territory. The oldest extant writings in Newar are from the twelfth century CE, being inscriptions and administrative documents.

Count to 10

गच्छिग	1
गच्छिस	2
गस्छुग	3
नेली	4
ध्या	5
खुछुग	6
नद्छुन	7
बर्खुछुन	8
द्गुष्	9
बछुष्म	10

Although a Tibeto-Burman people, the Newars have adopted both a Sanskrit literary tradition and the Indo-Aryan caste system. Against this background, it comes as no surprise that Newar has been strongly influenced by Indo-Aryan languages, in particular Sanskrit, Maithili, and, in modern times, Nepali. It has been estimated that about half the vocabulary of Newar is of Indo-Aryan origin. Its phonology and grammar have also been profoundly influenced by Indo-Aryan languages.

Newar was the dominant language in the kingdoms of the Kathmandu Valley at least from the twelfth century, and the official language of the court of Nepal from the fifteenth century until the end of the eighteenth century. At this time Indo-Aryan speakers from the Gorkha kingdom conquered the valley, and their language, later to be called Nepali, became dominant, Newar being actively repressed in Nepal until about the mid-twentieth century. The literary language used until the beginning of the twentieth century is referred to as Classical Newar. The Gorkha conquest led to a break in continuity with the

written tradition, resulting in a gap developing between the classical written language and spoken Newar, so that the classical language is no longer intelligible to a modern Newar speaker.

A number of different Brahmi-derived scripts for writing Newar have been used throughout its history. At present, however, the language is almost exclusively written in the Devanagari script that is also used for writing Nepali, the national language of Nepal, Hindi, Sanskrit, and some other Indo-Aryan languages.

Above *A young Newar girl walks to a local shrine in Kathmandu, Nepal, at the end of the Barha ceremony.*

Right *Newar men c.1865. Their language was actively repressed in Nepal until the mid-twentieth century.*

Left *The Sibi region of Balochistan, Pakistan, where the Balochi language is spoken.*

AWADHI

21 million speakers

Awadhi is an Indo-Aryan language spoken in the Awadh (Oudh) region around Lucknow in the state of Uttar Pradesh in India, and in Nepal. It is the language in which a popular literary work of India, the *Ramcharitamaanas* of Tulasidas was written in the sixteenth century CE. Although a language with an old literary tradition, ever since Hindi emerged as a literary standard from the early nineteenth century onward, Awadhi has tended to be included in the so-called Hindi belt as a dialect of Hindi. Awadhi is written mostly in the Devanagari script, but sometimes also in another script called Kaithi.

SIRAIKI

14 million speakers

Siraiki is an Indo-Aryan language spoken in Punjab, Balochistan, the northwest province of Pakistan, and also in India. It shows strong traces of non-Indo-Aryan influence. About 60 percent of the vocabulary is Dravidian and Munda in origin, and the phonetic system of the language differs from that of its Indo-Aryan sister languages. Siraiki is sometimes classified as a dialect of Punjabi (see p. 116). Like many other non-major South Asian languages, Siraiki is only sporadically written (in the Arabic script), due to literacy among its speakers being either in another language or nonexistent.

KONKANI

7.6 million speakers

Konkani is an Indo-Aryan language spoken on the west coast of India, the Konkan coast. Konkani is spoken by most people in Goa, where it is the official language. It is one of the twenty-two national languages of India. Konkani is sometimes classified as a dialect of Marathi (see p. 118). It is written in many scripts: Devanagari, Kannada, Malayalam, Roman, or Arabic, depending on the original region or religion of the speakers. It has borrowed extensively from Kannada and Portuguese. Among the modern Indo-Aryan languages, Konkani boasts the earliest grammars and dictionaries, written by Portuguese missionaries to Goa.

BALOCHI

7 million speakers

Balochi is an Iranian language spoken in Pakistan, Afghanistan, Iran, Turkmenistan, and the Persian Gulf States. It is related to Kurdish, Persian, Pashto, Dari, Tajik, and Ossetian. Balochi has been influenced by neighboring South Asian languages, borrowing vocabulary from Sindhi (Indo-Aryan) and Brahui (Dravidian). Like many other non-major South Asian languages, Balochi is only sporadically written (in the Arabic script), literacy among its speakers being either in another language or nonexistent. Since 1959 there has been a Balochi Academy in Pakistan, which supports the Balochi language and publishes Balochi literature.

SANTALI

6 million speakers

Santali is a member of the Munda subgroup of the Austro-Asiatic languages spoken in the states of Jharkhand, Bihar, Orissa, West Bengal, Assam, and Tripura in India, and in Bangladesh, Nepal, and Bhutan. It is one of the twenty-two national languages of India. Santali and its North Munda sister languages are morphologically complex. Santali has been written using Roman, Bengali, or Devanagari. A distinct alphabetic script to suit the language, the Ol Chiki script, was developed in 1925 by combining the Indic and the Roman scripts. This script is used for writing Santali alongside the Bengali, Devanagari, and Roman scripts.

BRAHUI

2.2 million speakers

Brahui is a Dravidian language spoken far from the main present-day, Dravidian-speaking area of the south of India. It is spoken mainly in the Balochistan province of Pakistan and some parts of Afghanistan and Iran. The language has been strongly influenced by its linguistic environment, especially in Iran. Brahui and the other northern Dravidian languages are thought to be remnants of an extensive pre-Indo-Aryan Dravidian presence in the north, indicated by early loanwords in Sanskrit. According to one theory, people of the Indus Valley civilization (c. 3000 BCE, just east of the present-day Brahui-speaking area) were Dravidian speakers.

KURUKH

2.1 million speakers

Kurukh (Kurux) is a Dravidian language spoken in the states of Jharkhand, Bihar, Orissa, Chattisgarh, and West Bengal of India, and also in Bangladesh and Nepal. Kurukh, the closely related Malto, and the more distant Brahui together make up the North Dravidian branch of Dravidian, isolated from the main body of Dravidian in southern India. The main dialects of Kurukh are Kisan, Oraon, and Dhangar. The Oraon variety is being standardized. Like many other non-major South Asian languages, Kurukh is only sporadically written (in the Devanagari script), literacy among its speakers being either in another language or nonexistent.

TULU

2 million speakers

Tulu is a Dravidian language spoken in India along the coast of the southern state of Karnataka and in the northern parts of Kerala, an area commonly referred to as Tulu Nadu. It is written using a script close to that of Malayalam, which is the main language of Kerala. The Kannada script is also used to write Tulu. Some original early literary works written in Tulu have survived, such as the *Tulu Mahabharata*, which was written in the fifteenth century CE along with a prose rendition called *Tulu Devimahatme*, and some epic poems which were written in the thirteenth century CE.

Left *Two Meitei women dress up for "Daughters Fest Day," a celebration of all Meitei women.*

MEITEI

1.3 million speakers

Meitei (Meitei-lon, Manipuri) is a Tibeto-Burman language spoken by most of the population in the state of Manipur in India, where it is the official language. It is also spoken in the states of Assam and Tripura, and in Bangladesh and Burma (Myanmar). Under the name of Manipuri, Meitei is one of the twenty-two official national languages recognized in the Constitution of India. It is written in the Bengali script, but efforts are being made to revive its traditional script, the Meitei-mayek script, which was in use until the eighteenth century.

SHINA

1.1 million speakers

Shina is an Indo-Aryan language spoken in the northern areas of Pakistan, and also in the Kargil and Ladakh areas of the state of Jammu and Kashmir in India. Estimates of the number of speakers vary wildly, from 300,000 to 3 million. Shina is one of a small group of Indo-Aryan languages in the northwest part of South Asia that displays contrastive word tones, a rarity in the Indo-Aryan language family as a whole. Shina is only sporadically written (in the Arabic script), and literacy among its speakers is either in another language or nonexistent.

BODO

600,000 speakers

Bodo is a Tibeto-Burman language spoken in the state of Assam in northeastern India, where it is an official language, and also in the neighboring part of Nepal. Bodo is one of the twenty-two official national languages recognized in the Constitution of India. It has a rich literary tradition with a considerable output of poetry, prose, plays, literary criticism, travelogues, biographies, children's books, etc. Bodo is written in the Devanagari script, but the Roman script too has been used for writing the language. There are efforts to revive its original script, which was called Deodhai.

MIZO

500,000 speakers

Mizo (Lushai, Duhlian) is a Tibeto-Burman language spoken by most of the population in the state of Mizoram in India, where it is the official language, and in the states of Tripura, Assam, and Manipur, and also in Bangladesh and Burma (Myanmar). Mizo belongs to the Kuki-Chin-Naga dialect continuum that encompasses some seventy to eighty named varieties, but where language boundaries are often difficult to establish. Mizo is written in the Roman script, in an alphabet developed by Christian missionaries. The literacy level in Mizoram is the second highest among Indian states (after Kerala).

SHERPA

151,000 speakers

Sherpa is a Tibeto-Burman language spoken mainly in the upper reaches of the Himalayas in Nepal by a small ethnic group frequently engaged as guides and also as carriers of supplies for mountaineering expeditions in the Himalayas. It is also spoken in China and India. Linguistically, Sherpa belongs to the Tibetan dialect continuum with some thirty to forty named varieties, but where language boundaries are often difficult to establish. Like many other non-major South Asian languages, Sherpa is only sporadically written (in the Tibetan or Devanagari script), due to literacy among its speakers being either in another language or nonexistent.

DZONGKHA

133,000 speakers

Dzongkha is a Tibeto-Burman language spoken in Bhutan and by a small number of people in India and Nepal. It is the official language of the Kingdom of Bhutan. Linguistically, Dzongkha belongs to the Tibetan dialect continuum that encompasses some thirty to forty named varieties (including modern Tibetan), but where language boundaries are often difficult to establish. **Dzong-kha** literally means "monastery language," in other words the language used in the Buddhist monasteries of Bhutan founded in the seventeenth century. Dzongkha is written using distinct Bhutanese varieties (called Joyi and Joshum) of the Tibetan script, one of the South Asian Brahmi scripts.

BURUSHASKI

90,000 speakers

Burushaski is a language isolate (in other words, a language having no known relatives) spoken in two river valleys in the Karakoram mountain range of northern Pakistan. There are also a small number of speakers in India. Burushaski is sporadically written using a Perso-Arabic script, but this is a recent development; there are no older (pre-twentieth-century) texts in the language. Many attempts have been made over the years to demonstrate a genetic connection between Burushaski and a number of other languages and language families all over Eurasia and even North America, but so far no such proposal has gained general acceptance.

KINNAURI

50,000 speakers

Kinnauri (Kanauri) is a Tibeto-Burman language spoken in the Kinnaur district in the state of Himachal Pradesh, northern India. Kinnauri is the dominant language locally, with some Indo-Aryan and other languages spoken alongside it. The local religious practices show a mixture of Hindu, Buddhist, and Animist elements. Because of the rugged geography, Kinnauri shows great dialectal variation, but there is also a lingua franca variety called Hamskad. As with Sherpa, Kinnauri is only sporadically written (in the Tibetan or Devanagari script), literacy among its speakers being either in another language or nonexistent.

CENTRAL, WESTERN, AND NORTHERN ASIAN LANGUAGES

CENTRAL, WESTERN, AND NORTHERN ASIAN LANGUAGES

The vast Eurasian landmass is home to hundreds of languages, divided into more than ten language families. Most of the languages of Central, Western, and Northern Asia belong to four main families: Indo-European, Altaic, Uralic, and Paleo-Asiatic, although Dravidian, Caucasian, and Semitic languages also occur.

The Indo-European family is represented by Indo-Iranian languages. These languages tend to have a subject-object-verb word order. They may or may not have a noun case system, either no gender or three genders, and they may be partially ergative (verbs can agree with objects rather than subjects), depending on the language. Grammars in this group are diverse, with mutual intelligibility varying from perfect (Persian—or Farsi—is similar to Dari in Afghanistan and Tajik in Tajikistan and Uzbekistan) to almost none (Persian and Pashto). The predominant alphabets are based on Arabic, with the exception of Cyrillic Tajik. These languages display easily recognizable cognates derived from Indo-European languages such as English, French, Russian, German, or Hindi (e.g. Persian: madar, "mother," padar, "father," kamiz, "shirt").

The Altaic family is represented by the Turkic and Mongolic sub-families. Languages within each sub-family are usually mutually intelligible, with notable exceptions.

Right *Two Uyghur children play in the snow. Uyghur is a Southeastern Turkic language spoken in China in the Xinjiang Uyghur Autonomous Region.*

Above right *Hebrew posters in Me'a She'arim, Jerusalem, act as community newspapers for the founding Orthodox Jews from eastern and central Europe.*

The Altaic languages have vowel harmony (words contain one type of vowel at a time), subject-object-verb word order, do not use gender, have noun cases, and are agglutinative. Meaning is rendered by the accumulation of suffixes at the end of a word, for example, in Uzbek: uy (house); uylar (houses); uyim (my house); uylarim (my houses); uyimda (in my house); uyimdagilar, (those who are in my house); uylarimdagilar (those who are in my houses).

Altaic languages use attributive clauses instead of relative clauses, for example, in Uzbek: Kecha kelgan kishining bugun ketganini ko'rding mi? (yesterday-having-come-person's today-having-gone did you see for yourself?). In a plain English relative clause this would be, "Did you see that the person who came yesterday has left today?".

Altaic languages use verbal evidentiality, in other words, a verb form expresses the degree of certainty of a person describing an event. For example, in Kazak: keldi (he came and I saw it); kelgen (he came and I heard about it); kelgen eken (he came and I heard about it but I'm not sure that it is true).

Also included in this chapter are Finno-Ugrian languages and Northern Caucasian languages, which have small numbers of speakers, and Hebrew, an ancient Afro-Asiatic (Semitic) language of the Middle East. Not included are Brahui, the lone Dravidian language north of the Indian subcontinent, the Pamiri languages of the Afghan pan-handle, China and Pakistan, or the Tungusic languages of East-Central Asia.

Among the languages surveyed, those of the former Soviet Union have absorbed Euro-Russian loanwords such as mashina (car), bugalter (accountant), galstuk (necktie), and straf (punishment), while those associated with Muslim populations also have large numbers of Arabo-Persian words.

The languages covered in the following pages are: (i) feature languages: Persian, Pashto, Uzbek, Azeri, Kazak, Uyghur, Tatar, Turkmen, Mongolian, Hebrew, Kyrgyz, and Tajik; and (ii) others: Kurdish, Balochi, Gilaki and Mazanderani, North Caucasic Cluster, Chuvash, Bashkir, Crimean and Caucasus Turkic, Siberian Turkic Cluster, and West Siberian Uralic Cluster.

PERSIAN

60 million speakers

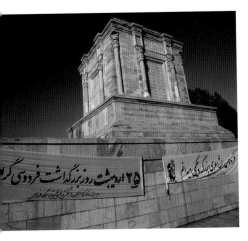

Persian (Fārsi), the official language of modern-day Iran, is an Indo-European, Southwestern Iranian language, very similar to Dari (Afghanistan) and Tajik (Tajikistan, Uzbekistan), and related to Tati and Luri, and more distantly to Kurdish and Balochi. Persian communities exist all over the world. Persian descends from Old Persian, which originated in southwestern Iran in the province of Fars (ancient Parsa), the original homeland of the Persian people. It was written in cuneiform during the Achaemenid Persian Empire (sixth century BCE). The first known inscription dates from the reign of Darius I (522–486 BCE).

Count to 10

yek	1
do	2
se	3
chahar	4
panj	5
shesh	6
haft	7
hasht	8
noh	9
dah	10

Old Persian had eight noun cases, three genders, and two plurals. Middle Persian, or Parsig (fourth to eighth centuries BCE), is a simpler form of the language, closer to the vernacular of the time, and was later associated with the Sassanid era (third to seventh centuries CE). The Sassanids adopted the writing system of the northeast Iranian Parthians, called Pahlavi.

New Persian appeared after the ninth century CE following the conversion to Islam, and used the Arabic script. It was a courtly language for dynasties such as the Samanids, and the Turkic Moghuls, Ilkhans, Timurids, Ghaznavids, Seljuqs, Safavids, and Ottomans. It was also a language of poetry, which influenced the literary traditions of the Islamic world, including those of other Indo-Iranian origins and various Turkic peoples. In turn, New Persian borrowed vocabulary from Arabic, Turkic, and Mongolian. Modern Persian has also borrowed vocabulary from some European languages.

Indo-European links

The selection of words below shows the similarity between Persian (on the right) and some other Indo-European languages such as English, French, and German (on the left):

brother	berader
sister	xwahar
mother	mader
father	padar
shirt	kamiz
water	ab
to grab	gereften

Loanwords

Persian vocabulary can be found in Urdu, Hindi, Armenian, Georgian, Turkic languages, and even Malay, Mongolian, and English, for example:

cummerbund	**kamarband** (belt)
bazaar	**bazaar** (market)
candy	**qand** (sugar)
chess	**shah** (king)

Descending from New Persian, modern-day Persian uses subject-object-verb syntax, numerous suffixes and prefixes, relative clauses, and has no gender. As in German, compound words can be formed via agglutination (for example, **havapeyma-ye-bomendoz**, bomber aircraft).

Dialects spoken in Iran include Luri, Tati, Talyshi, and Gabri. Persian and Dari use a modified Arabic alphabet with four additional letters (**peh, cheh, jeh, gaf**), while Tajik uses Cyrillic. There are also Romanized versions of Persian in use, such as UniPers, Parsik (an international Persian alphabet), and Penglish, which is used in emails and on the Internet.

PASHTO

30–50 million speakers

Pashto (Päshto) is a Southeastern Iranian language spoken mainly in Afghanistan and Pakistan, and in Iran and India. Related languages include Sarikoli, Wakhi, Munji, Shughni, and more distantly, Persian, Baluchi, Kurdish, Gilaki, and Ossetic. Census figures on the exact number of Pashto speakers vary, but the majority of speakers are in Pakistan (perhaps 26 million) and in Afghanistan (perhaps 15 million), where it is an official language along with Dari. It is the language of the Pashtuns, an ethnicity spread over Afghanistan, Pakistan, India, and parts of Iran. The Pashtuns, also known as Pathans, are famous for their martial valor.

Count to 10

ya:	1
dwa	2
dre	3
chalor	4
pinja	5
shpaj	6
o:va	7
ata	8
na:	9
las	10

Pashto has many loanwords from Arabic, Persian, and Turkic. The earliest surviving written Pashto dates to the sixteenth century. Since Islam was introduced in South Central Asia, Pashto has used a modified Perso-Arabic script, with letters representing retroflex consonants (made by curling the tongue backwards in the mouth) and certain vowels absent in other Iranian languages. Until the spelling system was standardized in the late eighteenth century, the representation of these consonants varied greatly. The script styles include the Persian **nastaliq** and the Arabic **naskh**, the latter predominating in modern times. Orthography was standardized when Pashto became a national language in Afghanistan in 1936.

The Pashto literary tradition includes many Pashtun poets, the most famous of whom is Khosal Khan Khattak (1613–90), the "Afghan Warrior Poet" who wrote in the time of the Moghul emperors. Pashtun folk literature includes folktales sung in epic form and folk poems by female poets. Modern Pashtun writers are prolific in literary forms such as the short story. Pashto has four mutually intelligible dialects, based on the pronunciation of four consonants: Southwest (Kandahar), Southeast (Quetta), Northwest (Paktia), and Northeast (Kabul, Jalalabad). The Kandahar dialect has more prestige, and is considered the standard written version of Pashto.

Pashto has subject-object-verb syntax, and is ergative, meaning, in the past tense, transitive verbs can agree with the object of the sentence rather than the subject. It has grammatical gender, noun case declensions, and a complex verbal system, as well as relative clauses.

Vocabulary

The selection of words below shows the similarity between Pashto and other Indo-European languages such as Persian, and provides a glimpse of some of the Arabo-Persian greetings that are used in Pashto.

hello	As salam aleikum	mother	mo:r (English: mother)
good-bye	Da khoday-pe-aman	sister	kho:r (Persian: xwahar)
please	Lutfan	night	shpa (Persian: shab)
thanks	Tashakor	black	to:r (Persian: tar)
excuse me	Abhaka	red	sur (Persian: sor-)
month	mya:sht (Persian: mah)	yellow	zhar' (Persian: zard)
new	nävay (Persian: nau)	wolf	lewa (Spanish: lobo)

UZBEK

25 million speakers

Uzbek (O'zbek tili, O'zbekcha) is spoken in Uzbekistan (22 million), and by minority populations in Tajikistan (1.2 million), Afghanistan (1 million), Kyrghyzstan (551,000), Kazakhstan (333,000), Turkmenistan (318,000), and Xinjiang, China (5,000). It is a Southeastern, or Qarluq Turkic language, like Uyghur. Uzbek is based on the Chagatai literary language, used in Central Asia from the fourteenth to nineteenth centuries, and on Turkic vernaculars spoken during that period. The national poet Ali Sher Navoi wrote in Chagatai. This language derived from the Qarluq Turkic of the Qarakhanids (ninth to twelfth centuries).

Above Schools and the public sector use the new Latin alphabet introduced after 1995 for written Uzbek, but the Cyrillic alphabet is in diminishing concurrent use.

Count to 10

bir	1
ikki	2
uch	3
to'rt	4
besh	5
olti	6
yetti	7
sakkiz	8
to'qqiz	9
o'n	10

The Qarluqs converted to Islam in the ninth century, adopting Arabic and Persian loanwords. Much of that vocabulary exists in contemporary Uzbek.

Uzbekistan's incorporation into the Soviet Union meant that European loanwords were introduced via Russian. Before the establishment of the Uzbek Soviet Socialist Republic, the language of the Turkic population in its territory was known as Turki (Persian for "Turkish"). The name Uzbek derives from the **Özbeg**, who arrived in the sixteenth century, speaking Qypchaq Turkic. They mixed with older Qarluq-speaking Turkic populations in the Ferghana Valley, and also with Oghuz Turkic speakers in Khorezm. Uzbek thus has various mutually intelligible regional dialects.

Uzbek has subject-object-verb syntax, agglutinative morphology, and noun cases, but no gender. Verb moods, aspects, and tenses enable fine distinctions in registers of speech (plain, honorific, deferential), and evidentiality. One can form Persian-style relative clauses and Turkic attributive clauses, add Persian affixes to Turkic words (or vice versa), and draw from numerous Turkic,

Vocabulary

Below are a few culturally significant vocabulary items, which highlight the similarity between the Turkic languages in this chapter while giving a taste of the phonological flavor of Uzbek.

bread	non
water	suv
father	ota, dada
mother	ona, oyi
meat	go'sht, et
milk	shir, sut
sun	kuyash, kun
moon	oy
language	til
person	odam, kishi
work	ish
to work	ishla-

Persian, and Arabic synonyms. Most Uzbeks are also proficient in Russian.

Prior to 1924, "pre-Uzbek" was written in Arabic script. From 1924–40, a Turkic Latin script was used, then Cyrillic was enforced under Stalin. After 1995, a new Latin alphabet (resembling the English alphabet) was introduced.

AZERI  24 million speakers

Azeri is a Southwestern Turkic language, closely related to Turkish and Turkmen, spoken in the Republic of Azerbaijan (8.3 million), western Iran (16.3 million), Dagestan, Georgia, Iraq, Armenia, and Turkey. There are twice as many Azeri speakers in Iran than in Azerbaijan. Azeri is based on Oghuz Turkic, which was used in Central Asia by the Oghuz Confederation by the seventh century CE, and later in Transoxiana, Iran, and Anatolia by the Seljuq Turks in the eleventh to thirteenth centuries. Azeri emerged as a literary language in the fourteenth century, as illustrated by the works of the poets Nesimi, Fuzuli, and Hatayi.

Count to 10

bir	1
iki	2
üç	3
dörd	4
beş	5
altı	6
yeddi	7
sekkiz	8
doqquz	9
on	10

Above *The main regions where Azeri is spoken.*

Right *Young boys in the old quarter of Baku, the capital of Azerbaijan. Azeri is the official language of Azerbaijan. The Shirvani dialect, also known as Azärbaycan dili, is spoken here.*

The nineteenth-century Russian conquest of the Caucasus split the Azeri language community into Northern (Azerbaijan, Shirvani dialect) and Southern (Iran, Tabrizi dialect) regions. In Azerbaijan, Azeri is called **Azärbaycan dili**; in Iran, **Turki**. There are numerous mutually intelligible dialects of Azeri. It is easy for Azeri speakers to understand Turkish. Post-Soviet Azerbaijani contains Euro-Russian loanwords, while Iranian Azeri uses more Persian and Arabic loanwords. In both countries, it is stylistically better to avoid using loanwords to excess, Turkic vocabulary being preferable.

Azeri was written in Arabic script until 1929, when the Republic of Azerbaijan became the first Turkic nation to adopt the Latin alphabet. This lasted until 1938, when Cyrillic was imposed. Then, in 1991, Azerbaijan returned to a different version of the Latin alphabet, similar to the Turkish one. In Iran, the Arabic script is still used for written Azeri.

Azeri has subject-object-verb syntax, agglutinative morphology, vowel harmony, noun cases, and no gender. It shares the same basic grammar as Turkish, with minor differences in some verb tenses. In terms of vocabulary Azeri is also very similar to Turkish, with some differences in usage, pronunciation, and spelling. It uses more Persian terms than Turkish, and Russian words are more common in the Northern region. Azeri and Turkish speakers are in close geographical contact, and the mutual reception of both radio and television broadcasts during the last two decades may have influenced both languages.

KAZAK  **16 million speakers**

Native speakers of Kazak (Qazaq tili) live in Kazakhstan (9.5 million), Uzbekistan (2.2 million), China (Xinjiang, 2.2 million), Russia (1.3 million), Turkmenistan, Mongolia, Afghanistan, Kyrgyzstan, and as immigrants in Turkey and Germany. The name "Qazaq," meaning "free," is the self-given ethnonym of a group of Qypchak-speaking Turks who broke away from the Özbeg Khanate and founded their own state, the Kazak Khanate, in the sixteenth century. Kazak then emerged from Qypchaq Turkic as a distinct language. Despite the spread of Kazak territory, Kazak displays no significant difference in dialect.

Count to 10

bir	1
(y)eki	2
üsh	3
tört	4
bes	5
altï	6
jeti	7
segiz	8
toghïz	9
on	10

The ancestors of the Kazaks used the Old Turkic runiform alphabet, but preferred to transmit their culture orally. Since a person's word was sacred, no written contracts were needed. Kazaks value the spontaneous creation of poetry, and consider eloquence an essential quality. Kazak has a rich oral epic tradition, kept alive by bards. Since the nineteenth century, Kazaks have produced written literature, among them the academic writings of a man who was an army officer, a scientist, artist and ethnographer, Chokan Valikhanov (1835–65) and the work of the novelist and playwright Mukhtar Auezov (1897–1961).

Kazak is ungendered, uses subject-object-verb syntax, agglutination of suffixes, seven noun cases, and a system of verbal evidentiality. Despite conversion to Islam, Kazak uses few Arabic or Persian loanwords. Most of its vocabulary is based on Old Turkic and this is a source of pride for the Kazaks. Euro-Russian loanwords entered the language after the nineteenth century. The majority of Kazaks in Kazakhstan are proficient in Russian, while those in China can usually speak Uyghur and Chinese.

Vocabulary

Here are a few culturally significant vocabulary items, which highlight the similarity between the Turkic languages in this chapter while giving a taste of the phonological flavor of Kazak.

horse	at, jïlqï
water	su
father	ata, äké
mother	ana, shéshé
meat	(y)et
milk	süt
sun	kün
moon	ay

Old Turkic, the ancestor of Kazak, used a runiform alphabet by the fifth century CE, then the Uyghur script from the ninth century. The Arabic script was used for Turkic dialects after the conversion to Islam in the eleventh and twelfth centuries until the early twentieth century. Between 1924 and 1940 a Latin script was used, until a modified Cyrillic alphabet was introduced. In 1995, a new Latin alphabet was adopted. Due to the cost of infrastructural change, Cyrillic still predominates, but there is a plan to phase it out.

Above The Baikonur Cosmodrome in Kazakhstan. Built in 1955, it is the oldest and largest operational space-launch facility in the world. Most speakers of the Kazak language live in Kazakhstan.

UYGHUR

Below *Uyghur in the Arabic script in the Id Kah Mosque in Kashgar, Xinjiang Province.*

Below right *A sign in Chinese and Arabic script in the Xinjiang Uyghur Autonomous Region, where most Uyghur speakers live.*

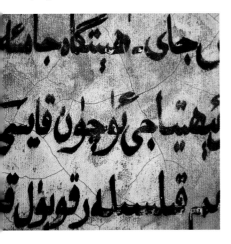

Uyghur is a Southeastern (Qarluq) Turkic language spoken in the Xinjiang Uyghur Autonomous Region in China (10–25 million, disputed), Kazakhstan (0.3 million), Uzbekistan, Afghanistan, Turkey, and elsewhere in Europe and Asia. It is closely related to Uzbek. Modern Uyghur was called Eastern Turki until the Communist takeover in the 1940s. Old Uyghurs, who spoke a form of Old Turkic, ruled a large empire in Central Asia between the eighth and tenth centuries, then a constellation of city-states. They used the Old Turkic alphabet, later devising a cursive script based on Sogdian, which they taught to their Mongol successors.

Count to 10

bir	1
ikki	2
üch	3
tö:t	4
bäsh	5
altı	6
yättä	7
säkkiz	8
toqquz	9
on	10

Vowels

Uyghur has vowel harmony, and shares the other features common to Turkic languages. It also has unique features, such as vowel reduction, where a suffix can influence a root word, for example:

ata   father
-im   my
ata + im = etim my father.

The extensive literature of the Old Uyghurs includes poetry, epics, and philosophical treatises. Another group, the Qarluq Turks, established the Qarakhanid Confederation in the ninth century, accepted Islam, and are ancestors to the modern Uyghurs. A famous work in Qarluq Turkic is the *Qutadghu Bilig* (1069) by Yusuf of Balasaghun. During the thirteenth to nineteenth centuries, the region came under the influence of the Chagatai lingua franca, and Eastern Turki acquired Persian and Arabic loanwords. Modern Uyghur preserves this basic vocabulary, and more recently it has acquired Euro-Russian and Chinese loanwords.

Eastern Turki used an Arabic script from the tenth century, known as the Chagatai or Old Script (**Könä Yeziq**), although the Old Uyghur script persisted in places until the eighteenth century. In 1969 the Chinese introduced a new Latin-based alphabet (**Yengi Yeziq**). In 1983 a simplified Arabic script was introduced, and is in use today. A Cyrillic version of Uyghur is used in the former Soviet Union where Uyghurs are present, and a Turkish-style Latin script is used by Uyghur émigrés in Turkey and on electronic media.

Uyghur tends to drop the final "r" sound in words, elongating instead the vowel which precedes the "r." For example, **adamlar** (people) is often pronounced **adamlaa**.

Almost every Uyghur locality has its own dialect, such as Ili, Kashgar, Hotan, and Lop. Uyghur is one of fifty-six recognized minority languages in China, and benefits from a large number of printed and audiovisual media. Most Uyghur are also fluent in Mandarin Chinese.

TATAR

10 million speakers

Tatar (Tatar tele, Tatarça) is a Northwest Turkic (Bolghar-Qypchaq) language spoken in the Republic of Tatarstan and elsewhere in the Russian Federation (8 million), the former Soviet Union, Afghanistan, China, Estonia, Finland, Japan, Latvia, Lithuania, Moldova, Poland, and Turkey. "Tatar" refers to Volga or Kazan Tatar spoken in Tatarstan, and by Tatars in Eurasia. Crimean Tatar is a distinct but related language. Members of other ethnic groups living near the Tatars also use the Tatar language (for example, the Mari and Chuvash) and its influence is apparent in most Caucasion, Slavic and Finno-Ugric languages of the Volga river region.

Above *The Qol Sharif Mosque in the Tatarstan capital, Kazan. The mosque stands on the site where the original mosque stood during the Russian conquest of Kazan in 1552. It is named for Qol Sharif, the poet, diplomat, and religious leader who devoted his life to the freedom of his people.*

Below right *The Russian Republic of Tatarstan, and some of the other countries where Tatar is spoken.*

Count to 10

ber	1
ike	2
öch	3
dürt	4
bish	5
altï	6
jide	7
sigez	8
tughïz	9
un	10

Between the eighth and thirteenth centuries, Tatarstan was home to the Bolghars, who spoke Oguric or "r-Turkic," used the Old Turkic alphabet, and wrote in Arabic script after converting to Islam in the ninth century. When "z-Turkic"-speaking Qumans, Qypchaqs, and Pechenegs settled the area in the eleventh to fourteenth century, a new language evolved, combining elements of Bolghar and Qypchaq. This was Old Tatar, ancestor of Kazan Tatar. Written in the Arabic alphabet, it was the literary language of the Golden Horde and the Kazan Khanate.

Tatar was one of four medieval Turkic literary languages, along with Chagatai, Azeri, and Ottoman. It has a rich literature. A famous literary work in Old Tatar is the poem *Qyssa-i-Yosif*, by Qol Ghali, a twelfth-century Bolghar Turk.

Kazan was conquered by Russia in 1552 and Tatar lost its official status, not regaining it until 1917. In the Soviet period, Tatar absorbed Euro-Russian loanwords. It in turn influenced Russian and other surrounding languages. Turkic vocabulary in Russian is usually from Tatar, e.g.

the Russian word **utyug** (an iron) comes from **ütüg**; and **uzyum** (raisin) comes from **üzim**. Tatar used the Latin alphabet in 1927, then switched to Cyrillic in 1938, which it uses in official contexts, but a new Latin alphabet has existed since 1995. Tatars in Turkey, Finland, Poland, and Japan use the Latin alphabet. Public signs in Tatarstan are bilingual in Tatar and Russian. There are three main dialects of Tatar: Western (Mishar), Middle (Qazan), and Siberian.

TURKMEN

9 million speakers

Below Map of Turkmenistan,
where Turkmen is the
official language.

Below left The majority of Turkmenistan's
5 million population. are Turkmen-speaking.
As many as eleven dialects are identified.

Turkmen (Türkmen dili) is a Southwestern (Oghuz) Turkic language spoken in Turkmenistan (3.5 million), where it is the official language. Other similar languages also called Turkmen are spoken in northern Iraq, Iran (Khorasan region), Afghanistan, and Turkey. Turkmen is closely related to Turkish and Azerbaijani, and more distantly to Salar (China), and Crimean Tatar. Turkmen descends from the Oghuz Turkic spoken in Central Asia since the middle of the first millennium CE. The Seljuq Turks, who ruled an empire in Central Asia, and eventually settled in Anatolia, speaking what became modern Turkish, were ancestors of the Turkmen.

Count to 10

bir	1
iki	2
üç	3
dört	4
beş	5
altı	6
yedi	7
sekiz	8
doquz	9
on	10

The term **Türkmen** was first used to distinguish Oghuz who converted to Islam from those Oghuz who retained the Old Turkic religion. **Türkmen** literally means, "I am a Turk" in Oghuz Turkic.

Turkmen literature shares a rich epic heritage common to Oghuz Turkic speakers, including the epics of **Dede Gorqut** and **Köroğly**. In addition, the medieval Chagatai literature of Central Asia also influenced Turkmen, which emerged as a distinct literary language by the eighteenth century. It came to life most prominently in the work of the Turkmen national poet known as Mahtumquli (*Magtymguly*).

Oghuz Turkic was probably first written in the Old Turkic runiform alphabet, and later in the Uyghur script. It was written in the Arabic script after contact with Islam around the tenth century. Turkmen, deriving from Oghuz Turkic, used the Arabic script until 1929, when it received a Latin alphabet, then a Cyrillic script in 1938. Since 1991, Turkmen has used a new Latin alphabet. Most Turkmen in Turkmenistan are fluent in Russian. Turkmen in Iran, Iraq, and Afghanistan know Persian, Arabic, and Dari respectively.

Turkmen has vowel harmony, is agglutinative, uses a subject-object-verb syntax and a noun case system, and also has no gender. Turkmen features phonemic vowel length, which can change the meaning of a word, for example, **at**, (name), versus **a:t**, (horse). Turkmen in Turkmenistan has three main dialects: Yomud, Gökleng, and Teke. Standard written Turkmen is mostly based on Yomud.

MONGOLIAN

6 million speakers

Mongolian (Mongol khel, Khalkha Mongol) is a Central Mongolic language spoken by almost 80 percent of the population of the Mongolian People's Republic (2.5 million), Inner Mongolia (Chahar dialect, 3 million), and in adjacent regions of China and Russia. It is related to other main Mongolic languages, Kalmyk and Buryat, and to minority languages in China (Daur, Oyrad, Barghu) and Afghanistan. Early Mongols were nomadic hunting-gathering herdsmen who moved into Mongolia from the northeast, mingling with earlier Turkic populations. Mongolian thus contains several Old Turkic loanwords.

Above *A fourteenth-century Persian illumination of Chinggis Khan, the "emperor of all emperors," and brilliant military strategist who was also the product of a rich cultural and artistic heritage, including a fine Mongolian literature.*

Mongols were animists and later converted to Buddhism, with the result that many Tibetan and Sanskrit loanwords were also adopted. Mongolian has a rich oral literature, particularly in heroic epics such as *Gesar* and *Jangyr,* believed to be at least 1,000 years old. During Chinggis Khan's Mongol Empire (thirteenth century), Uyghur scribes introduced writing in 1208 and more Turkic and Sanskrit vocabulary. A written Mongolian literature later developed, which used the Uyghur script. The first work is the *Secret History of the Mongols* (thirteenth century). The *Altan Tobchi* ("Golden History" in Mongolian) is a famous seventeenth-century piece of literature. Over the centuries, Mongolian has absorbed Chinese, and more recently Euro-Russian and English loanwords.

Mongolian grammar is somewhat similar to Turkic, although there are distinctly Mongol features, such as the use of the question particle **ve/be?** in sentences already containing an interrogative pronoun (**xen**) or the possessive suffix **tei/tai: Ta xen ve?** (Who are you?) Mongolian phonology is distinctive, with its lateral fricative "-l-," which is reminiscent of the Welsh "ll-." Versions of the Uyghur script are still used in Inner Mongolia, and in Xinjiang, China. In Mongolia, the Communists introduced the Latin alphabet in 1931, then Cyrillic in 1937, with the traditional script being eliminated in 1941. Neo-traditionalists attempted to reintroduce it in the 1990s. Mongolian orthography often reflects Classical Mongolian spelling, while the modern pronunciations may differ.

Vocabulary

Here are some vocabulary items that are of great cultural significance for Mongols. The reader may note the similarities and differences between Mongolian and neighboring Turkic languages.

mother	eje, eej
father	ava, aav
water	uus
milk	süd
meat	makh
horse	mör
yellow	shara, shar
white	tsaagan
black	khara, khar

Count to 10

Classical		Modern
nigen	1	neg
khoyar	2	khoyor
ghurban	3	gurav
dörben	4	dorov
tabun	5	tav
jirghughan	6	zurgaa
dolughan	7	dolo
nayman	8	naym
yisün	9	es
arban	10	arav

HEBREW  8 million speakers

Below *An example of modern Hebrew script, which developed from a script known as Proto-Hebrew or Early Aramaic.*

Below left *The Stele of Mesha, more commonly called the Moabite Stone, contains inscriptions in Moabite and Hebrew dating from the ninth century BCE.*

Hebrew (Ivrit) is a Semitic language spoken in Israel (7 million) and in Jewish communities around the world. It is the sole surviving Canaanite language and is related to Aramaic, and more distantly to Arabic. The first written Hebrew is the Gezer calendar, from the tenth century BCE, written in an old script possibly derived from Egyptian hieroglyphs. Other inscriptions include the famous Moabite Stone. Classical Hebrew is categorized as Archaic Biblical, Biblical, Late Biblical, Dead Sea Scroll, and Mishnaic. Modern Hebrew is based on Biblical Hebrew (sixth century BCE), which Jews refer to as the "Holy Language" (Leshon Ha-Kodesh).

Count to 10

ahat	1
shtayim	2
shalosh	3
arba	4
hamesh	5
sesh	6
sheva	7
shmone	8
tesha	9
eser	10

Hebrew flourished from the tenth century BCE onward, then was gradually replaced by Aramaic. After the second century CE, Hebrew was used as a written language only, for poetry, philosophy, science, commerce, letters, and liturgy, and it featured some famous philosophers, poets, and grammarians of the "Golden Age" of medieval Jewish culture such as Maimonides (1135–1204), Judah ha-Levi (1408–1508), Solomon ben-Gabirol, and Judah ben-David (both c. 945–1000.)

Hebrew remained only a written language until the Jewish activist Eliezer ben-Yehuda revived it as a spoken language in the nineteenth century. During this revival, intellectuals modernized Biblical Hebrew, borrowing words from Aramaic, Arabic, and European languages. Hebrew became an official language along with Arabic in Palestine in 1921, and in Israel in 1948. Hebrew was also used as an international language of communication among Jews.

Several dialects of Hebrew are used in religious services. These are Ashkenazi Hebrew, used by

Yiddish-speaking Jews; Sephardic Hebrew, used by formerly Ottoman Jews; and Mizrahi Hebrew, used by Jews in the Muslim world. Revived Hebrew follows Mishnaic spelling, and was originally used by native Yiddish speakers, but Modern Israeli Hebrew is also influenced by the pronunciation of Sephardic Hebrew, and Ladino (also known as Judeo-Espanyol, the original language of the Sephardic Jewish citizens of Turkey). This leads to a variety of accents. For example, more than half the population pronounces "r" in a glottal way as in French, whereas the remainder trill it as in Spanish. Hebrew has vocabulary from Yiddish, European languages, and Arabic, and has influenced other languages spoken by Jews, such as Ladino, Yiddish, Karaim, Aramaic, and Arabic.

Hebrew grammar is analytic, uses prefixes and suffixes, and a system of consonant roots from which one derives vocabulary. Hebrew is written from right to left. Each letter of the alphabet has a numerical value, which forms the foundation of Kabbalistic Numerology, an aspect of the Jewish mystical belief system.

KYRGYZ  **5 million speakers**

Kyrgyz (Kïrgïz tili) is a Central Turkic (Noghai-Qypchaq) language, spoken in Kyrgyzstan where it is an official language, and in China, Afghanistan, Kazakhstan, Turkey, Uzbekistan, Pakistan, and Russia. It is related to Kazak, and is a bridge between Central and Northeastern Turkic languages. The Kyrgyz are an ancient people who were vassals of the Kök-Türks (fourth to eighth centuries CE). Originally from the Yenisey area in Southern Siberia, the Kyrgyz conquered the Uyghur Empire in 840 CE, then migrated to their present location in the seventeenth century. The Kyrgyz were vassals of the Khanate of Kokand until conquest by Russia in 1876.

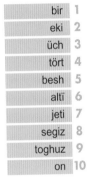

The Russians called the Kyrgyz "Kara-Kyrgyz," to distinguish them from the Kazaks whom they called "Kyrgyz." Some Turkic-speaking neighbors referred to them as Buruts, a name also used in Mongolian folklore.

The Kyrgyz place great premium on eloquence and the ability to compose poetry spontaneously. Kyrgyz literature is best known for oral epics. Also of international acclaim is the Kyrgyz novelist Chingiz Aitmatov (b. 1928).

Vocabulary

Here are a few culturally significant vocabulary items, which highlight the similarity between the Turkic languages in this chapter while giving a taste of the phonological flavor of Kyrgyz.

horse	aat, jïlqï
water	suu
father	ata
mother	ene
meat	et
milk	süt
sun	kün
moon	ay

Count to 10

bir	1
eki	2
üch	3
tört	4
besh	5
altï	6
jeti	7
segiz	8
toghuz	9
on	10

Kyrgyz maintains a South-Siberian (Northeast Turkic) substratum, while being greatly influenced by Qypchaq Turkic (Kazak and Noghai). Kyrgyz absorbed limited Arabo-Persian vocabulary during conversion to Islam and exposure to sedentarized Muslims. Its vocabulary is mainly Turkic, with some recent Euro-Russian loanwords.

The Kyrgyz first wrote in the Old Turkic runiform alphabet and later used the Arabic alphabet, but the Arabic orthography of the language was not standardized until 1923. The Kyrgyz adopted a Latin alphabet in 1928, which was changed to Cyrillic in 1940. In 1995, scholars decided to adopt a Latin-based alphabet, but this change has not yet been implemented in Kyrgyzstan. The Kyrgyz minority in Qizilsu district, Xinjiang, China, uses the Arabic script and the Chinese-implemented Latin alphabet, while Kyrgyz in Turkey use the Turkish Latin alphabet. This is also used on the Internet.

TAJIK

5 million speakers

Tajik is a Southwestern Iranian language similar to Persian, spoken as the official language in Tajikistan (3.5 million), and by minority populations in Uzbekistan (Samarqand and Bukhara), and Afghanistan (Kabul, Herat). Other Iranian languages called "Tajik" are spoken in China and Afghanistan. Before the spread of Muslim culture into Central Asia in the eighth and ninth centuries CE, Eastern Iranian languages such as Sogdian were spoken there. With the rise of New Persian, these languages were assimilated. Tajik and Dari (spoken in Afghanistan) are forms of New Persian. In the region where they are both spoken, Tajik and Dari are difficult to distinguish.

Below The main countries and regions where Tajik is spoken.

Count to 10

yak	1
du	2
se	3
chor	4
panj	5
shäsh	6
haft	7
hasht	8
nuh	9
dah	10

During the ninth-century Samanid rule over Central Asia, New Persian flourished in the urban centers of Herat, Bukhara, Samarqand, and Merv. When Turkic peoples arrived, New Persian took second place to Chagatai and absorbed Turkic elements.

New Persian speakers of Central Asia developed a rich literature including lyric and heroic epics (*Tohir-u-Zuhro*, *Farhod-u-Shirin*, *Shahnameh*), and poetry. Local scholars also authored academic works in the medieval period, in Arabic. The term "Tajik" is of Arabic origin, and referred to Muslim Persian speakers in medieval Central Asia. In 1929, Tajik became an official language of the Tajik Soviet Socialist Republic. On Tajikistan's independence (1991), linguistic revival led to the introduction of native terminology to replace loanwords, sometimes diverging from Persian and Dari; conversely, media contact with Iran and Afghanistan is growing.

Tajik has a subject-object-verb word order, relative clauses, and numerous prefixes, prepositions, and postpositions. It retains some older features lost in Persian and Dari. Its vocabulary contains many Arabic loanwords, as well as some Euro-Russian vocabulary. The four main dialects are Northern, Central, Southern, and Eastern. Standard Tajik is based on the Northern dialect, reflecting some influences from Turkic languages (mainly Uzbek).

While New Persian was written in the Perso-Arabic script, a Latin script was adopted for Tajik in 1928, followed by the Cyrillic script in 1938, which is still in use. The Afghan Tajiki-Dari speakers use the Persian script.

Right The Saman Khuda monument in Tajikistan's capital Dushanbe. In Tajikistan today, Khuda is considered to be the father of the Tajik nation.

KURDISH

24 million speakers

Kurdish (**Kurdî**) is a Northwestern Iranian language of Iran, Iraq, Syria, Turkey, and the former Soviet Union (FSU). It is related to Balochi, and more distantly to Persian. It is an official language in the Northern Iraqi Kurdish region. Its dialects are Qurmanji and Sorani, and some consider Zaza-Gorani to be a Kurdish dialect. It is written in Latin script in Turkey, in Arabic script in Iraq and Iran, and in Cyrillic in the FSU. Starting in the thirteenth century, Kurdish poets developed a literary language and a rich oral literature. Kurdish is accessible via satellite television and the Internet.

BALOCHI

7–8 million speakers

Balochi (**Baluci**, **Baloci**) is a Northwestern Iranian language spoken by the Baloch in Pakistan, Iran, and Afghanistan, in the region of Balochistan. It is one of nine official languages of Pakistan, and is closely related to other Northwestern Iranian languages, such as Kurdish. Balochi was spoken at the Baloch courts, but was first written in the nineteenth century, first in Latin script by British linguists, then in Nastaliq Arabic script by Baloch scholars, and in Pashto-Arabic script in Afghanistan. Balochi has between three and six main dialects: East, South, and West, or Rakhshani, Saravani, Lashari, Kechi, Coastal, and Eastern Hill.

GILAKI-MAZANDERANI

5–9 million speakers

Gilaki (**Gilehki**, 2–4 million) and Mazanderani (3–5 million) are closely related Northwestern Iranian languages spoken in the Gilan, Mazanderan, and Golestan provinces of Iran. Their dialects are Western, Eastern, and Galeshi for Gilaki, and Gorgani, Ghadikolahi, and Palani for Mazanderani. They are related to Zazaki (Turkey) but differ grammatically from Persian, with which mutual intelligibility is low. They have fewer loanwords from Arabic or Turkic. Due to Mazanderan's period of independence in the Middle Ages, Mazanderani has a literary tradition dating back to the tenth century CE, which includes the work *Marzban Nameh* and the poetry of Amir Pazevari.

NORTH CAUCASIC CLUSTER

10 million speakers

The North Caucasic languages are a diverse group of distantly related languages, spoken in the area of the Caucasus Mountains, between the Black Sea and Caspian Sea in the Russian Federation, and in Turkey. The two families are Northwest Caucasian (Circassian, including Abkhaz, Adyge, and Kabardin, 3 million), and Northeast Caucasian (including Chechen, Ingush, Lak, Lezgin, 3 million). These languages share features such as a great number of distinct consonants (eighty-four in Ubykh!), ergativity (the verb can agree with the object rather than the subject), and agglutinative morphology. They use various types of Cyrillic script.

Left A painter uses Chuvash motifs in Cheboxary, Russia.

Left Bison in Russian Siberia. They have recently been re-introduced to restore parts of Siberia to how it was 10,000 years ago.

CHUVASH

2 million speakers

Chuvash (**Chavashla**) is an isolated Turkic language of European Russia. It is the only Oguric ("r-Turkic") language, and is related to medieval Volga Bolghar, Khazarian, and Hunnic. It differs phonologically from other Turkic languages, which are all "z-Turkic." For example, words ending in "z" in common Turkic end in "r" in Chuvash, and words beginning with "y" in common Turkic begin with "s" in Chuvash; **so yüz**, (one hundred), becomes **ser**. Chuvash also maintains ancient Proto-Turkic vocabulary. It is an official language of the Chuvash people in the Chuvash Republic. It uses a modified Cyrillic alphabet.

BASHKIR, CRIMEAN, CAUCASUS TURKIC

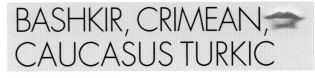

3 million speakers

Bashkir (**Bashqort tele**, 1.5 million) is a Bolgar-Qypchaq Turkic language primarily spoken in the Bashkir Republic in the Ural Mountains, and is closely related to Tatar. It was a spoken language only, as Bashkirs wrote in Kazan Tatar until the Soviet era. Crimean Tatar (500,000) is an Oghuz-Qypchaq language, spoken in Crimea (Ukraine), and by exiles in Central Asia and Turkey. Its speakers were deported by Stalin, but are now returning home. All Western or Southern Qypchaq, the Caucasus Turkic languages include Qumuq (300,000), Karachai-Balkar (300,000), Urum, Krymchak, and Karaim (5,000), and Noghai (200,000).

SIBERIAN TURKIC CLUSTER

1 million speakers

These are the Northeast Turkic languages of Russian Siberia: Sakha, Tuvan, Altai (Tuba, Qumandy, Teleut, Telingit, Qu, Khakas, Chulym, Dolgan, Tofa, Shor, and Fuyu Girgis (China). They are conservative Turkic languages, unaffected by Persian or Arabic, which influenced other Turkic languages. They preserve Ancient Turkic vocabulary, but also include Mongolic, Tungusic, and Euro-Russian loanwords. They are usually mutually intelligible, except for Sakha (Yakut), which is an isolated Turkic language. They are written in the Cyrillic script, and while some are endangered (Tofa, Chulym, Shor), others are witnessing a linguistic revival (Sakha, Tuvan, Altai).

WEST SIBERIAN URALIC

3–5 million speakers

This cluster of languages of western Siberia includes Ob-Ugric (Khanty, Mansi, Udmurt), and Finno-Permian languages (Komi, Mari, Mordva), most of which are distantly related to Hungarian, Finnish, and Estonian via the Finno-Ugric family. They are agglutinative, subject-object-verb languages without gender, with a large number of noun cases (up to twenty-seven for Komi), and vowel harmony. Their degree of mutual intelligibility varies regionally, but is usually low. Many of them have been influenced by Turkic languages (Tatar) and Russian, and are written in Cyrillic.

EAST AND SOUTHEAST ASIAN LANGUAGES

EAST AND SOUTHEAST ASIAN LANGUAGES

This section discusses the languages of East and mainland Southeast Asia, other than Mandarin Chinese and Japanese (see World Languages—pp. 14–15 and 34–35). East Asia comprises China, Mongolia, Korea, and Japan, which form a region of long and extensive cultural contact and influence.

South of China is southeast Asia, divided into mainland (from Burma to Vietnam, Thailand, and west Malaysia) and island (Indonesia, Singapore, east Malaysia, and Philippines). This region is home to 600 million people and marked by social, cultural, and linguistic diversity. Southeast Asia has historically seen massive migrations and movement of peoples, resulting in the complex linguistic situation found today.

Six major language families are represented: (1) Sino-Tibetan with ten Sinitic (Chinese) languages and about 150 Tibeto-Burman languages; (2) Mon-Khmer, about 100 languages; (3) Tai, about fifty Thai-Kadai languages; (4) Miao-Yao languages; (5) Austronesian languages with the Chumic group; (6) Altaic languages. Some officially recognized composite groups speak several languages and have multiple written varieties: Zhuang/Buyi, Miao, Karen, Yi, Shan, Yao, Hani/Akha, and Wa. Some with a long written history use distinct literary and spoken varieties for different purposes, such as Burmese and Tibetan.

Left Vietnamese woman in the city of Hoi An. Vietnamese belongs to the Mon-Khmer language family and is the first language of 66 million people in Vietnam

Above right Tibetan monks engage in worship. The Tibetan language uses a South Asian script, while other languages of the area use Chinese characters

Many languages were first written using Chinese characters, including Japanese, Korean, Vietnamese, Zhuang/Buyi, and Bai. Other languages are written with South Asian scripts, including Khmer and Tibetan. Khmer script was borrowed by Mon, and then by Burmese and Shan, and separately by Thai, Lao, and Myang.

All Mon-Khmer and Dai languages in this region place the verb before the object, as do the Sinitic languages and the Tibeto-Burman Karen and Bai languages. All other Tibeto-Burman languages, along with the Altaic languages, place the verb after the object. All Sinitic, Tibeto-Burman, Dai, and Mon-Khmer languages in East and Southeast Asia have what are known as numeral classifiers, which must follow a numeral and are semantically determined by the noun; for example, in the Thai language máa sìi tua means "horse three (animal)." Altaic and some Mon-Khmer languages have

fairly complex words, but other languages from this region have a considerably simpler word structure and many of them contain phonological tones.

The twelve major languages discussed in this chapter include the national languages of Vietnam, North and South Korea, Thailand, Burma, Laos, and Cambodia. The languages included are Min, Vietnamese, Korean, Thai, Burmese, Lao, Zhuang/Buyi, Kmer, Tibetan, Miao, Karen, and Yi. Other languages that are discussed more briefly include one of the main languages of Hong Kong, Cantonese (Yue), and two languages that are closely related to Thai—Myang and Shan. Nine languages from more than 300 minority languages in the region, many of which are currently endangered, are also included. These are Hani/Akha, Yao, Dong, Bai, Lisu, Wa, Mon, Lahu, and Gong.

MIN 👄 100 million speakers

Below *A girl in traditional costume in Fujian province, China, where Min is widely spoken. The language is written using Chinese characters.*

Like Mandarin Chinese and Cantonese speakers, Min speakers regard themselves as Chinese and write with Chinese characters. Those in Taiwan and overseas use traditional characters; since 1958, those on the mainland use simplified characters. Some Min speakers in Taiwan regard themselves as distinct, though still culturally Chinese. Min has diverged from the rest of Chinese for two millennia; it was the earliest group to separate from Sinitic, before the 601 CE *Qieyun*, a book representing the sounds of Chinese at that time, from which Mandarin, Cantonese and other Sinitic languages can be derived.

Count to 10

Taiwanese		Cantonese
၃က၁	1	၀�က၁
၁၁၃၂	2	၁၁ၟၟၐ
၂၆	3	၂၆
၂၆	4	၂ၟ၆
၂၀	5	ၟ၁
၂၉	6	၂ၟ
၃က၁	7	၁ၟက
၀ၟ	8	၀ၐက
၁ၐ၁	9	၁ၐ၁
၂ၐ၁	10	၂ၐ၁

Compare the numbers in Taiwanese Min to those for Cantonese and the Mandarin numerals on page 14. The Cantonese numerals are similar to old Chinese numerals, and the Sino-Korean and Sino-Japanese numerals. The Mandarin numerals have undergone greater changes in their pronunciation, while the Min numerals show various changes as contrasted with the rest of the Sinitic languages.

The Min language is widely spoken on the coast in the province of Fujian (pronounced "Hokkien" in Min), along with northeastern Guangdong, eastern Hainan, and Taiwan; many overseas Chinese migrations into Southeast Asia came from here. The main variety of Chinese spoken in Thailand is Teochiu, a Southern Min subvariety, whereas the dominant Chinese lingua franca of Singapore until 1979 was another Southern Min subvariety, there called just Hokkien. Min speakers also predominate in many towns in the Philippines, Malaysia, and in Indonesia.

Southern Min, which has about 80 million speakers, is the largest subgroup within Min. One subvariety is the home language of about 85 percent of the population of Taiwan, and is sometimes also called **Taiyu** in Chinese and Taiwanese in English. Taiwanese Min is now spreading into wider use in the media, public life, and even schools, as it represents a symbol of Taiwanese separateness from China.

Min is phonologically very distinct from other Chinese language groups. A good example of this is to compare the Min word **Teochiu** and its Mandarin pronunciation, which is **Chaozhou**: this is the same word, and it is written with the same characters, but it is clearly pronounced quite differently between these two groups. There are also major vocabulary differences and extensive tone sandhi in the Min language, whereby the tones of the syllables combined within a word differ from the tones of those syllables when spoken alone.

Left *A busy street in Taiwan—where the majority of the population speak Min.*

VIETNAMESE  **78 million speakers**

Vietnamese is the national language of Vietnam and the first language of over 66 million people there. Outside Vietnam, the large minorities in Cambodia, Laos, and Thailand, the small Jing group in Guangxi, China, and, after reunification in 1975, over a million refugees in Western countries, overall total at least 2 million. Vietnamese is spoken as a second language by over 10 million members of the minority ethnic groups of Vietnam. Over 80 percent of Vietnam's people are ethnic-majority Vietnamese; fifty-three other minority ethnic groups are recognized; thirty-four were only in the former north and eighteen only in the former south.

Above *Young tour guides in the Tam Coc river complex, north-central Vietnam. The Míuíong language spoken in this area is a close relative of Vietnamese.*

Below right *The primary areas where Vietnamese is spoken as a first or second language.*

One group known as Van Kiêu in the north and Bruu in the south was on both sides of the former border; it is now called Bruu-Van Kiêu. Of the other fifty-two groups, 1.1 million Míuíong in the uplands of north-central Vietnam speak a language closely related to Vietnamese. Very similar to Míuíong are the seven languages of the Chíut ethnic group of Vietnam and the Arem (formerly Bo) ethnic group of Laos, all with very small speaker populations. Many of the other minority groups speak more distinct Mon-Khmer languages; there are some Austronesian languages in the south, and some Thai and Tibeto-Burman languages in the north.

In Vietnamese, the word for ethnic Vietnamese people is **Kinh**; this is also the source of the Chinese term **Jing. Việt** is the traditional name for the country; **nam** (south) is one of a very large number of Chinese loanwords in Vietnamese; northern Vietnam was part of China until 939 CE. The traditional **chữ nôm** "southern language" script used Chinese characters to represent Vietnamese, but in 1910 during the French colonial period (1862–1954) this was replaced by the **quốc-ngữ** "national-language" romanization, devised by the Jesuit Alexandre de Rhodes in the early seventeenth century. The standard dialect of Hanoi has six tones, written with diacritics in the romanized orthography, but some are not differentiated in southern dialects. Much of the grammar and learned vocabulary is borrowed from Chinese. French and now English loanwords are also numerous. However, the Vietnamese numbers to five show that Vietnamese is a Mon-Khmer language.

Count to 10

một	1
hai	2
ba	3
bốn	4
năm	5
sáu	6
bẩy	7
tám	8
chín	9
mười	10

KOREAN

75 million speakers

Korean is the national language of the Democratic People's Republic of Korea (North Korea, 21.4 million people) and the Republic of Korea (South Korea, 48.4 million people); the Koreas are ethnically uniform, with no indigenous minorities. Korean is also the spoken language of nearly 2 million Koreans in northeastern China, many of about 1.8 million Koreans in urban areas of Japan, several hundred thousand in Central Asia and eastern Russia, and a similar number in Western countries, mainly the United States, with a worldwide total of 75 million speakers. Some additional overseas ethnic Koreans, especially in Central Asia, do not speak Korean.

Above *The Nong-ak dance, one of the oldest dance forms in Korea, is performed at Yongin in South Korea.*

Below right *Shoppers in the South Korean capital of Seoul. Due to trade and Westernization, the South Korean language is inundated with English loanwords.*

Until 1446, Korean was written using Chinese characters, but then King Sejeul devised the Han'geul system, which now uses combinations of twenty-four symbols to write the syllables in a box approximately the size and shape of a Chinese character: initial consonant at the top left or on top, vowel at the top right or in the middle, and final consonant, if any, at the bottom. For example, ˚Û is **sang**; the inverted "v" at the top left is "s," the vertical line with a short horizontal crossbar is "a," and the circle underneath is final "ng."

Chinese characters, known as Hanja in Korean, continue to be used in South Korea to represent the very numerous Chinese loanwords, but such words can also be written in normal Han'geul. North Korea abolished the use of Hanja in 1949, but has recently permitted some reintroduction in scholarly contexts. There is also a standard romanization of Korean in South Korea, slightly revised in 2000, used to show the pronunciation of Korean words there. Korean has an unusual three-way contrast between voiceless unaspirated, voiceless tense and weakly aspirated, and voiceless strongly aspirated stop consonants.

There is a very large stratum of old Chinese borrowed vocabulary, including many basic words. Japanese colonial rule from 1910 to 1945 left only a small residue of loanwords, but Korean in South Korea is now inundated with recent English borrowings. Fifty years of partition have also led to substantial vocabulary differences between North and South. Korean, like Japanese, has two sets of numbers: original Korean and Sino-Korean.

Count to 10

Korean		Sino-Korean
hana	1	il
dul	2	i
set	3	sam
net	4	sa
dasět	5	o
yěsět	6	yuk
ilgop	7	chil
yěděl	8	pal
ahop	9	gu
yěl.	10	sip

THAI

Thai is the national language of Thailand, the mother tongue of 26 million people in central Thailand. It is spoken fluently by nearly 40 million other Thai citizens, including the speakers of Lao in the northeast, Myang in the north, and Pak Tai (southern Thai) in the south, all of which are closely related to Thai, as well as the numerous Khmer, Malay, and other minorities around the borders. It is also easily understood by the majority of Lao in Laos and by many Shan in Burma. Thai belongs to the Tai family and is related to languages such as Zhuang, which is spoken in China.

Above A street vendor sells newspapers to car drivers in Bangkok. The Thai language is written in a script derived from Khmer.

Below right A priceless statuette of the Buddha in royal attire, dating from the seventeenth century. Khmer script is still used for some religious purposes.

The Thais entered what is now Thailand from the north, and gradually conquered existing Mon kingdoms and parts of the Khmer kingdom over the last millennium. Thai was first written in the Ramkhamhaeng pillar inscription of 1283, named after the famous king of Sukhothai, whose laws it embodied. It uses a script derived from Khmer, later somewhat modified. Khmer script is still used to write Thai in some religious amulets and horoscopes. Thai was the language of the Ayudhya kingdom up to 1767, and of the Rattanakosin Dynasty at Bangkok since then.

The oldest stratum of loanwords in Thai, dating from when the Thai were still in southwestern China more than a millennium ago, is from old Chinese; this includes some basic material such as numbers above one, and many other words such as **máa** (horse). Thai also has a large number of Khmer and Pali loanwords, often spelled in archaic ways unlike their modern pronunciation; for example, **tamruát** (police) is from Khmer "harem attendant" and is still spelled **tamruac**. The most recent stratum is English loanwords, such as **kùkkîi** (cookie/biscuit).

Since 1933, Thailand has had a Royal Institute responsible for standardizing the Thai language. It has produced a standard dictionary and is now drafting a national language policy. There are regional dialects, such as the western dialect of Kanchanaburi, Suphanburi, and Ratburi provinces, in which the rising tone merges into the falling tone. Extensive social differences are seen, as in the replacement of the "r" sound with "l" or its deletion, and a newer trend in Bangkok to change "s" into a sound like English "th" in "thin"; such changes are stigmatized and strongly resisted by the education system.

Count to 10

nɣ̀ng	1	Note the similarity to Lao (p. 163) and Zhuang (p. 164) numerals all except for 1 are borrowed from old Chinese.
sɔ̌ɔng	2	
sǎam	3	
sìi	4	
hâa	5	
hòk	6	
cèt	7	
pὲɛt	8	
kâw	9	
síp	10	

BURMESE 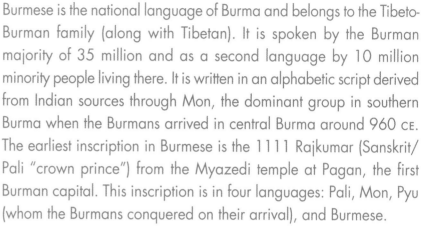 **45 million speakers**

Burmese is the national language of Burma and belongs to the Tibeto-Burman family (along with Tibetan). It is spoken by the Burman majority of 35 million and as a second language by 10 million minority people living there. It is written in an alphabetic script derived from Indian sources through Mon, the dominant group in southern Burma when the Burmans arrived in central Burma around 960 CE. The earliest inscription in Burmese is the 1111 Rajkumar (Sanskrit/Pali "crown prince") from the Myazedi temple at Pagan, the first Burman capital. This inscription is in four languages: Pali, Mon, Pyu (whom the Burmans conquered on their arrival), and Burmese.

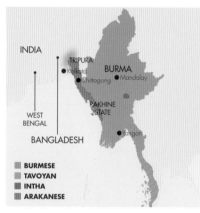

Much of the formal vocabulary of Burmese comes from Pali, adjusted to Burmese pronunciation. For example, "nirvana" is **nibbana** in Pali, written thus but pronounced **nei'ban** in Burmese.

Burmese is still spelled according to the pronunciation of the late Pagan Dynasty c. 1250, with minor reforms in the 1880s and 1970s. The literary language is based on old Burmese,

with some Pali influence. The spoken language has changed greatly. One example is the name of the country: in literary Burmese "Myanmar" and in spoken Burmese "Burma" (until 1990, when the military government changed place names to the literary forms). Nearly every grammatical element and many other frequent words have two different forms: "this" is **i** in literary and **di** in spoken Burmese. Literary Burmese is taught in schools and used in most written and formal spoken contexts; spoken Burmese is used in informal writing, such as comic books, and in most everyday speech. During British rule between 1885 and 1948, many English loanwords entered the language.

Some groups speaking regional varieties of Burmese are recognized as separate ethnic groups: 2 million Arakanese or Rakhine in the west; 400,000 Tavoyans or Dawe in the southeast; and 90,000 Intha around Lake Inle in the northeast. They preserve some conservative pronunciations, such as "r" in Arakanese, pronounced as "y" in Burmese. Arakanese is also spoken in Bangladesh and India.

Top A young monk engaged in study at the Bagaya monastery, Burma. The liturgical language for the Theravada Buddhists is Pali.

Above The spread of some of the regional varieties of Burmese.

Count to 10

Burmese numeral		Burmese script	Spoken pronunciation
၁	1	တစ်	ti'
၂	2	နှစ်	hni'
၃	3	သုံး	thòun
၄	4	လေး	lè
၅	5	ငါး	ngà
၆	6	ခြောက်	chau'
၇	7	ခုနစ်	hkuni'
၈	8	ရှစ်	shi'
၉	9	ကိုး	kòu
၁၀	10	ဆယ်	hseh

LAO

Lao is the national language of Laos, a landlocked country, bordered by Burma, China, Vietnam, Cambodia, and Thailand. It is also the regional language of Isan in northeastern Thailand, with nearly 3 million speakers in Laos and 27 million in Thailand. About 2 million additional members of forty-eight recognized, ethnic-minority groups in Laos also speak Lao in addition to their own languages. There are a few Lao in northeastern Cambodia and northwestern Vietnam. Many but not all of more than 100,000 post-1975 refugees from Laos in western countries are ethnic minorities. The Lao language is closely related to Thai (see p. 161).

Above *A farmer gathering crops in the Isan region of northeastern Thailand, where Lao is the regional language.*

Right *Buddhist cloisters in the Wat Mai temple in Luang Phrabang, the old royal capital of Laos. Due to spelling reformations, the city name is now written "Luang Phabang."*

Lao has five main regional subvarieties with quite different tone systems: Savannakhet in southern Laos; Vientiane (in Lao, Wiang chan, "moon city" or "sandalwood city") in central Laos and much of northeastern Thailand; Luang Phabang in northern Laos; a northeastern Laos variety; and Korat in the southwestern part of northeastern Thailand; these are readily mutually intelligible. There are also many villages of various of these subvarieties of Lao scattered across the central plain of Thailand, due to eighteenth- and nineteenth-century forced relocations of captured populations brought back by Thai kings from what is now Laos. These groups often call themselves Lao plus some specifier, such as Lao Wiang for the Lao from the Vientiane area, Lao Dan for those from the southern border area, and so on.

The Lao script used in Laos is like Thai script but it is more rounded; it is also derived from the Khmer script. After 1975, written Lao was reformed to make spelling conform closely to speech. For example, Luang Phrabang, the old royal capital, is now written Luang Phabang with the unpronounced medial "r" omitted. As in Thai,

there is a Lao Tham script much more similar to Khmer, and it is used to write Lao for some religious and astrological purposes (such as reading horoscopes).

All Lao in Thailand are bilingual in Thai and Lao, and write in Thai rather than Lao. Thai media is intelligible to all Lao speakers, even in Laos; but most Thai speakers have difficulty understanding Lao due to lack of exposure.

Count to 10

nyng	1	Note the very close similarity to Thai numerals (p. 161) and the similarity to Zhuang numerals (p. 164).
sŏɔng	2	
săam	3	
sii	4	
hàa	5	
hók	6	
cét	7	
pὲὲt	8	
kâw	9	
sip	10	

ZHUANG/BUYI 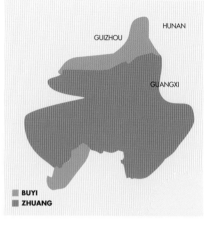 **22 million speakers**

Members of the officially recognized ethnic groups of Zhuang (16 million people, most in Guangxi, some in southeastern Yunnan, and half a million in western Guangzhou, China), Buyi or Bouyei (3 million people, mainly in Guizhou, China, and a few thousand in Vietnam), Nung (1 million people), and Tay (2 million people) in northeastern Vietnam, speak a cluster of related Central and Northern Tai languages. Tai was also formerly known as Thô. Some ethnic Zhuang and Buyi speak only Chinese. A few people classified as Buyi actually speak one of several languages related to Dong (see p. 172).

Count to 10

it	1	The Zhuang numbers are all old Chinese loanwords. Note the similarity to the Thai and Lao numerals from 3 to 10 (see pp. 161 and 163).
nyi	2	
sam	3	
seiq	4	
haj	5	
roeq	6	
caet	7	
bet	8	
gouj	9	
cib	10	

Top *The spread of the Northern Tai languages Zhuang and Buyi in China and Vietnam.*

Right *A Zhuang girl in Longji, in the Guangxi province of China, contemplates a series of stunning terraced rice paddies.*

Many members of other ethnic groups in Zhuang-majority areas also speak Zhuang as a second language. Zhuang has the largest population of any minority group in China, whereas Buyi has the tenth largest. The main linguistic boundary between Northern Tai and Central Tai speech varieties within Zhuang is across southwestern Guangxi; all Buyi and about two thirds of the Zhuang in northwestern Guangxi, including the Wuming standard dialect speak Northern Tai varieties, and about a third of the Zhuang in southwestern Guangxi and southeastern Yunnan speak Southern Zhuang, similar to Nung and Tay. Altogether, there are about 12.5 million speakers of Northern Tai varieties and about 7 million speakers of Central Tai varieties. Zhuang languages are fairly closely related to Southwestern Tai languages including Thai, Lao, Myang, and Shan, and structurally similar, too.

Like Vietnamese, these languages were formerly written using adapted Chinese characters, but since the 1950s there have also been romanizations. The romanization for standard Northern Zhuang, as seen on older Chinese currency notes, was based on the dialect of Wuming and used additional Cyrillic letters for tones, but the Cyrillic letters were replaced in 1981. The Zhuang and Buyi romanizations represent similar Northern Tai languages. However, the romanization for Southern Zhuang used in Yunnan represents a Central Tai language similar to Nung and Tay. Since 1954, a single romanization has been used for both Nung and Tay in Vietnam; this was made official in 1961.

KHMER

10 million speakers

Khmer is the national language of Cambodia and of large Khmer minorities in the Mekong delta of Vietnam, along the southern border of northeastern Thailand, and is spoken by post-1975 refugees in the West. Most of the people of Cambodia are ethnic Khmer; there are small Austronesian-speaking groups in the northeast, an urban Chinese minority, many Vietnamese in the southeast, and some smaller minorities speaking Mon-Khmer languages closely related to Khmer. All are bilingual in Khmer. Many ethnic Khmer were resettled to central Thailand after Thai invasions in the early nineteenth century.

Above *The Wat Phnom pagoda in Phnom Penh, Cambodia. Built in 1373, it is the tallest religious structure in the city.*

Right *An example of Khmer script from the Preah Ko temple near Angkor, Cambodia. The script represents the pronunciation of the Angkor period between the seventh and fifteenth centuries.*

Khmer has been written since 609 CE in a nearly unchanged script representing the pronunciation of the Angkor period (seventh to fifteenth century CE). Modern speech has undergone radical sound changes; the same original written symbol for a vowel may now be pronounced completely differently, depending on the type of consonant that precedes it. The consonants first produced a difference of voice quality, breathy versus normal; the voice-quality difference then caused changes in most vowels. The voice-quality differences are still found in some regional varieties of Khmer but are now absent from the standard speech of the capital, Phnom Penh.

Count to 10

muy	1	The Khmer
pii	2	and
bei	3	Vietnamese
buan	4	numbers up to 5 are related
bram	5	Mon-Khmer
bram muy	6	words; from 6
bram pii	7	to 9, Khmer combines 5
bram bei	8	with 1 to 4.
bram buan	9	
dawp	10	

Standard Khmer has a rich vowel system: beginning from the written system with nine long and short vowels, and three long and short vowel sequences, it has nine short and ten long vowels, and thirteen vowel sequences, including contrasts of five vowel heights of front vowels, as in the English language—"beat," "bit," "bate," "bet," "bat,"—but ten different vowel sounds, long and short. There is also a great deal of regional variation.

Khmer has basic Mon-Khmer vocabulary, and extensive earlier Sanskrit and later Pali loanword strata. During nearly a century of French rule, the Khmer elite learned French and many French loanwords entered the language. From 1975 to 1978, the ruling political party, the Khmer Rouge, discarded much of the formal vocabulary, but some has been brought back since. Most recently, some English loanwords have started to enter Khmer as well.

TIBETAN

6 million speakers

There are more than 6 million Tibetan speakers and the range of spoken varieties, many not mutually intelligible, is enormous. Variants are spoken in northeastern Kashmir, across historical Tibet, including the so-called Tibetan Autonomous Region, in Qinghai, western Sichuan, northwestern Yunnan, and the southwestern Gansu provinces in China, as well as in northern Nepal, Sikkim, and Bhutan. There are three main linguistic divisions within the Tibetan language, and these are: Central, Northeastern (also known as Amdo), and Southeastern (also known as Kham).

Count to 10

གཅིག /g.cig/cî	1
གཉིས /g.nyis/nyi	2
གསུམ /g.sum/súm	3
བཞི /b.zhi/shi	4
ལྔ /l.nga/ngá	5
དྲུག /drug/chù	6
བདུན /b.dun/týn	7
བརྒྱད /br.gyad/cèh	8
དགུ /d.gu/kǔ	9
བཅུ /b.cu/cú	10

The Tibetan numerals are given in written Tibetan, transliteration, and modern spoken Lhasa form; this illustrates some of the changes within Tibetan over the last twelve centuries.

Above A beautiful example of the Indic script: Tibetan prayers written on "Mani" stones.

Central Tibetan includes four subgroups: dBus varieties around Lhasa, the traditional capital; gTsang varieties to the southwest; Southern varieties in western Bhutan, Sikkim, and nearby in Tibet; and Western varieties in Ngari Prefecture of far western Tibet, and Ladakhi, Purik, and Balti in northeastern Kashmir. Virtually every valley has its own speech variety, often not intelligible to other Tibetans, but the speech of Lhasa is widely used as a spoken lingua franca. Kham Tibetan is also used as a lingua franca in the southeast and among Tibetan herdsmen.

Sherpa (meaning "eastern people") of the Mount Everest area of northeastern Nepal is a gTsang variety, like most of the languages of the northernmost valleys in Nepal (see p. 135).

There are also various groups speaking related but quite distinct Tibeto-Burman languages in central Nepal, Bhutan, northeastern India, southeastern Tibet, Sichuan, and Yunnan. Many Mongols, who follow Tibetan Buddhism, use literary Tibetan as a liturgical language.

Tibetan (written **Bod**, spoken Lhasa Bö) has been written for thirteen centuries in an Indic script. Literary Tibetan has been stable for more than a millennium, and is still used in Tibetan Buddhism. Most still use the Indic Tibetan script, though the Moslem Balti and Purik in northern Kashmir use Arabic script, with many Arabic, Persian, and Urdu loanwords.

Since 1959, more than 150,000 Tibetans, including the Dalai Lama, have left Tibet and resettled in India, Nepal, and many Western countries; the capital of the Dalai Lama's government in exile is at Dharmsala in northwestern India.

Dzongkha (see p. 135), the national language of Bhutan, is one of the southern subvarieties of Central Tibetan, as is Danjong, the former court language of Sikkim State in India, and still an official language there.

MIAO

5.3 million speakers

Miao, Meo, and Maew are, respectively, Chinese, Vietnamese, and Thai/Lao names for a composite nationality or ethnic group, more than half of whose members speak one of twelve languages. Of 9 million in the Miao nationality of China, nearly 5 million speak only Chinese. Altogether, there are 5.3 million speakers of Miao languages: more than 4 million in southwestern China, 787,000 in Vietnam, 230,000 in Laos, 125,000 in Thailand, and about 100,000 from Laos who became refugees in the United States, France, Australia, and so on after 1975. Miao languages belong to the Miao-Yao family, along with Yao languages.

Above *Long Horn Miao girls in traditional costume celebrating the flower dance festival in Guizhou Province, China.*

Below right *Map showing the spread of Miao languages, of which there are 5.3 million speakers.*

The twelve mutually unintelligible languages form three groups: Western (seven languages originating in western Guizhou and spreading over many hundreds of years into nearly every part of Yunnan, parts of southwestern Sichuan, and much of northern Southeast Asia); Central (three languages with substantial internal diversity in central Guizhou); and Eastern, or Qoxiong (two languages in northeastern Guizhou and southwestern Hunan). About 3 million speak western Miao languages and call themselves Ahmau, Hmong, or Mong; about 1.5 million speak various Hmo or Central Miao languages, and about 800,000 speak Qoxiong languages.

Starting in China in 1905, the missionary Samuel Pollard and his colleagues devised several related scripts for various Miao and other languages, combining letters, some Pitman shorthand symbols, and various modifications. In the 1950s, various romanizations based on the principles of Chinese pinyin were devised by Chinese and Miao linguists. Several of these are still in use—some Pollard scripts among Miao Christians, and romanizations in some

government primary schools in Miao areas. Hmong Daw of Laos is a typical Miao language, with six tones, eleven vowels, and a very complex array of initial consonants and consonant clusters. Final "b" represents a high tone, final "m" represents a low short tone, and final "j" represents a falling tone; with no final consonant, the tone is mid. A double vowel represents a nasalized vowel, and "xy" represents a sound like "ch" in German "ich."

Count to 10

Hmong Daw	
ib	1
ob	2
peb	3
plaub	4
tsib	5
rau	6
xyaa	7
yim	8
cuaj	9
kaum	10

KAREN

5.1 million speakers

BELOW *The distribution of Karen languages in Burma and Thailand.*

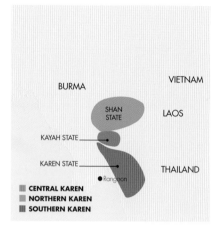

Members of the composite Karen ethnic group speak various related languages, which can be divided into Southern, Central, and Northern language clusters. Altogether, there are at least 5.1 million speakers, more than 90 percent in Burma and nearly half a million along the western border of Thailand. There may be as many as 10 million ethnic Karen. The speakers of the Southern-cluster languages Pho and Sgaw live mainly in the Karen State of Burma, and across the border in western Thailand. Pho is furthest south; Pa-O (formerly known as Taungthu) is mostly spoken further north in the southern Shan state.

Count to 10

Sgaw Karen	
ta	1
khi	2
tha	3
lwî	4
yêh	5
chy	6
nwi	7
cho'	8
khwi	9
chi	10

The Central cluster includes various Bwe varieties, also known as Kayah in Burmese, whose speakers live mainly in and around the Kayah State of Burma. Other Central-cluster languages include Blimaw, Bre, Geba, and Yintale. Speakers of Northern-cluster languages live in the southern Shan State of Burma; languages include Kayan (formerly known as Padaung, whose women traditionally wear metal neck and leg rings), Gekhu, and various smaller groups, such as Yinbaw (autonym Kangan) and Zayein (Latha).

Many of the Karen were converted to Christianity during British rule in Burma, and many Pho and especially Sgaw Karen moved into the delta region west of the Irrawaddy river, which may now have 2 million ethnic Karen, though many no longer speak a Karen language.

Starting in the early nineteenth century, foreign Christian missionaries devised writing systems for Pho and Sgaw, using Burmese letters with some additions and modifications. Often the letters have very different values from the corresponding symbols in Burmese. There are also more recent

romanizations for some Northern and Central Karen languages, as well as indigenous writing for Sgaw, a more recent indigenous Kayah script, and some orthography employing Thai letters for use in Thailand.

Karen languages are all verb-medial, but otherwise show Tibeto-Burman grammatical patterns. Apart from vocabulary that is clearly related, there is also some non-Tibeto-Burman vocabulary in Karen, such as the word "person," **Sgaw pra**, **Pho he**, **Bwe bwe**, and so on.

Right *Padaung women of the Kayah state in Burma, wearing traditional leg and neck rings.*

The Yi nationality, an officially recognized, composite ethnic group known before 1950 as Lolo, has 8 million members in southwestern China and a few thousand in Vietnam and Laos. More than half speak one of three very closely related languages: Nuosu (2.3 million, also known as Northern Yi), Nasu (1.1 million, Eastern Yi) and Nisu (800,000, Southern Yi); all three names mean "black people." Each dialect has its own logographic script, mainly used by Yi traditional priests prior to 1950, and distinct from Chinese characters, though based on the same principle. From a language point of view, Yi is a member of the Tibeto-Burman family.

Above *The dramatic scenery surrounding the River Li in southwestern China, where more than 8 million members of the Yi ethnic group live.*

At least fifty other distinct but related languages are spoken by other members of the Yi nationality. One of these is Sani (120,000 speakers) in Shilin County, Yunnan, which has another logographic script. Other larger Yi languages without traditional orthographies include Lalo (600,000 speakers in western Yunnan); Lolo (500,000 speakers in north central Yunnan); Pula (various distinct languages including Pula, Powa, and Muji totalling 250,000 speakers in southeastern Yunnan), and Axi (also sometimes referred to as Ahi or Ahsi, about 100,000 speakers just south of Sani in Mile County), among numerous others.

Many of these languages, even some with many speakers, are contracting or disappearing, with younger people only able to speak Chinese. For example, the Sanie language just west of Kunming City, the capital of Yunnan, has only 8,000 speakers out of about 17,300 ethnic Sanie; it is nearly extinct in the villages closest to Kunming, and in decline even in more remote areas.

A syllabic script for Nuosu based on the Shengza dialect as spoken in Xide County was developed in the 1970s and approved for official use from 1978. Among the Nuosu in Sichuan this is a great success, with widespread literacy and publishing. In the 1980s, a logographic version of Nasu was standardized in Guizhou, and Yunnan Reformed Yi, a composite logographic script with Nasu, Nisu, Sani, and Nuosu characters, was created in Yunnan. Nasu, Nisu, and Sani characters are also used in a very limited way in some Nasu, Nisu, and Sani areas.

Count to 10

Nuosu		Nasu	Nisu	Sani
tshɿ	1	thà	thì	thì
nyì	2	nyí	nì	ǹ
sɔ	3	sa	sá	séu
l	4	hli	hlí	hlɿ
ngeu	5	ngu	ngo	ngá
fú	6	chɤ	chù'	khù'
shɿ	7	shí	shɿ	sɿ
hi	8	hí	xi'	hè'
gu	9	keu	kéu	kéu
tshi	10	tshì	tshèu	tshi

CANTONESE 👄

63 million speakers

Cantonese, like Min (see p. 158), is a Chinese variety unintelligible to Mandarin speakers (see p. 14). Canton is an anglicization of Chinese Guangdong, the province whose capital, Guangzhou, was the main trading port of southeastern China before Hong Kong (established 1841). In Chinese, the speech of this area is called Yue. There are more than 63 million speakers: 44 million in Guangdong, Hainan, and eastern Guangxi provinces, 7 million in Hong Kong, and about 12 million overseas, especially in Vietnam, Cambodia, and some towns in Malaysia. Until about twenty years ago, Cantonese was the main Chinese variety in English-speaking countries. The speech of Guangzhou City is the most prestigious dialect, very similar to that of Hong Kong.

The official language of the Hong Kong Special Administrative Region, returned to China on 1 July 1997, is Cantonese written in traditional Chinese characters, with Mandarin and English as supplementary languages. Cantonese is widely used in the media in Hong Kong and increasingly in Guangdong.

Literary Cantonese is more archaic. Cantonese differs from Mandarin and some other Chinese varieties in being conservative with final consonants, as in **yat** (one)—compare Mandarin **yi**—and having more tones, up to eight.

MYANG 👄

8 million speakers

Myang (city), Kham Myang (city language), Yuan, Nyuan or Northern Thai is a distinct language with its own script, closely related to Thai (see p. 161) and sometimes considered a dialect of Thai for political reasons. Since 1292, the Myang kingdom called Lanna (million rice fields) had its capital at Chiangmai, with an earlier kingdom at Chiangsaen, and various other Myang kingdoms including Chiangrai. This area was contested between the Burmese and various central Thai dynasties between 1338 and 1727, and has been part of Thailand since 1776. All Myang speakers are bilingual; they write in Thai and speak Thai as the official language. There is a small-scale folkloristic revival of the Myang script, which is rather different from Thai and Lao but also derived from Khmer script.

Nearly all Myang speakers live in northern Thailand, with a few thousand in northwestern Laos. There are substantial dialect differences, mainly in the tones, between the eastern areas including Chiangrai and Nan versus the western area around Chiangmai. Myang has some similarities in vocabulary with Lao (see p. 163); Thai words are also widely borrowed. However, speakers cherish the vocabulary of Myang and may use it even within Thai, such as Myang **lam** instead of Thai **aroy** (delicious).

Left *Pearl River and the heart of Guangzhou, the capital of Guangdong province. Cantonese is the Chinese variety spoken here.*

SHAN

2.6 million speakers

Shan is related to Thai (see p. 161) and Zhuang (see p. 164) in the Tai language family. This group's own name is Tai; others call them Tai Yay (big Tai). They live mainly in northeastern Burma and nearby in China, Thailand, and India. Their language, with various dialects, has a total of 2.6 million speakers. Shan is the modern Burmese ethnic name for the group; Siam, the former name of Thailand, is also related. Lik Tai (Tai writing) is similar to Burmese script; a reformed version is used in China, and another has been used in Burma since 1970.

In China, Shan and other related languages are grouped together in the Dai nationality, with 1.2 million people, including Tai Lue, and other groups with distinct languages and scripts. Most Shan in China live in Dehong Prefecture; they are called Tai Mao from their dialect name, or De Dai in Chinese. There are several groups in northeastern India who write with versions of Lik Tai, including Ahom, former rulers of the upper Assam plains, who no longer speak Shan, other small groups such as the Aiton and Phake who are losing it, and the Hkamti (gold place) who still speak it. The Khyn of the eastern Shan State in Burma have a distinct language and a script similar to that of Myang.

HANI/AKHA

1.5 million speakers

Hani is an official ethnic group of China and Vietnam; Akha is an ethnic group of Laos, Burma and Thailand. 760,000 of the Hani in south central Yunnan Province and northern Vietnam along the Honghe (Red River) speak Hani, and 565,000 Akha further west and in Laos, Burma, and Thailand speak Akha, a very similar language; 140,000 Hani north of the main Hani concentration in central Yunnan Province up to and beyond the capital, Kunming, speak divergent Haoni. Over 300,000 other ethnic Hani in China speak different but closely related languages, including Biyue and Kaduo; the Mpi language of Thailand is similar to these languages.

There are three main romanized orthographies: Catholic and Baptist for Akha, and pinyin Chinese for Hani. The Akha migrated southwestward about 400 years ago, later reaching Laos, Burma, and Thailand. Hani and Akha genealogies diverged twenty-four generations ago, reflecting this split; and in ritual language, the Akha call themselves Zani, related to the Hani name for themselves.

Hani and Akha are very closely related to Yi (see p. 169), Lisu and Lahu and fairly closely to Burmese (see p. 162). Comparing numerals, 1 is **chi'** in Hani, **ti'** in Akha, **te** in Lahu and **thi** in Lisu; compare also Yi and Burmese.

YAO

1.65 million speakers

The Yao language cluster has six languages and is related to Miao in the same family (see p. 167). Over 700,000 speakers of eight Bunu languages and Thai-Kadai Lajia are also included in the 2.6 million Yao ethnic group in China; many other ethnic Yao speak only Chinese. There are 620,538 Yao in Vietnam, 18,000 in Laos, 48,000 in Thailand, and 25,000 in Western countries. Of them, 85 percent speak Western Yao languages (Iu Mien and Kim Mun). Yao men traditionally used written Chinese for liturgical purposes. Various romanizations were developed from the 1930s, and in 1984 a unified worldwide Iu Mien romanization was agreed.

DONG

1.4 million speakers

Dong, or Kam, is a national minority of China and the major language of the ten Kam-Sui Thai-Kadai languages. Of 3.1 million Dong, about 1.4 million can speak the language. Of them, more than half live in southeastern Guizhou, especially in southeast Guizhou Dong and Miao Autonomous Prefecture; 29 percent live in southwestern Hunan; 10 percent live in northeastern Guangxi; 2 percent live in northwestern Guangdong. The language has two major varieties and various further subdialects. Its most notable feature is that it has ten distinct tones. It is written in a romanization devised in the 1950s, based on the principles of Chinese pinyin.

BAI

1.1 million speakers

There are about 2 million members of the Bai ethnic group, but only about 1.1 million can speak Bai. The Bai ethnic territory centers on Lake Erhai in northwestern Yunnan, formerly the Nanzhao kingdom. The Bai language retains some Tibeto-Burman vocabulary and grammatical characteristics, but has been heavily influenced by Chinese over two millennia, borrowing 85 percent of its basic vocabulary and some of its grammar. There is a new romanization based on Northern Bai of Jianchuan County, but most speakers use Chinese characters if they write Bai. Dialect differences are substantial, with some outlying groups in other areas of Yunnan.

LISU

948,000 speakers

Lisu is spoken in northwestern Yunnan (about 600,000 speakers), northeastern Burma (nearly 300,000), northern Thailand (45,000) and northeastern India (2,700). Some of the 250,000 Lipo in north-central Yunnan, whose language is closely related, are classified as Lisu nationality in China. Lisu has two romanizations: a missionary orthography devised in 1914 and a 1958 orthography based on Chinese pinyin; there is another missionary script for Lipo, sometimes called "Eastern Lisu." Lisu is also used as a lingua franca by several groups in northwestern Yunnan and far northern Burma, and is replacing some of them, among them Anong and Laemae.

Left The Gong language is now restricted to around 100 speakers in the Kwai river basin in Thailand.

Left Minority ethnic Mon children at a ceremony held to urge the release of the Burmese opposition leader.

WA

900,000 speakers

Wa (own name Paraok) has about 400,000 speakers in China (mostly in the Wa nationality, population about 1 million) and 500,000 in the northeastern Shan State of Burma; there are many dialects, some not completely mutually intelligible. The closely related Rianglang language, also known as Riang, Yanglam, or Black Karen, and Yang Sek, has a further 70,000 speakers, mostly in Burma. The term Paraok is also used to refer to the "standard" dialect, which is a medium of literacy. There are missionary romanizations for Wa and Rianglang, and a 1950s' Chinese romanization. Structurally, Wa is a typical Mon-Khmer language.

MON

800,000 speakers

The Mon ruled various ancient kingdoms of central Thailand and lower Burma; Mon has been written in an Indic script for more than a millennium. After conquests by others, the Mon gradually contracted, leaving the vestigial Nyahkur population speaking a language derived from Mon in the northeast of central Thailand, and the Mon community in the Mon State of southeastern Burma. Some Mon remigrated from Burma into the Bangkok area after 1780. About 800,000 speakers of Mon are in Burma and a few in Thailand, as well as the 10,000 remaining Nyahkur speakers. The ethnic Mon population of these areas is much larger.

LAHU

723,600 speakers

There are 453,705 Lahu in southwestern Yunnan Province, China, 200,000 in northeastern Burma, 60,000 in northern Thailand, 8,700 in northwestern Laos, and 1,200 refugees from Laos in the United States. The Lahu are recognized as an ethnic group of China, Vietnam, Laos, Thailand, and Burma. The main dialect difference is between Black Lahu (Lahu Na) and Yellow Lahu (Lahu Shi); there are extensive differences within each of these. The Kucong speak a closely related language and joined the Lahu nationality in China in 1989; they are scattered, with over 40,000 in south central Yunnan Province, and 6,874 nearby in Vietnam.

GONG

100 speakers

The Gong were formerly widespread in the Kwai river basin of west central Thailand; most Gong speak only Thai, and the language is endangered. Of 400 Gong in two villages, about fifty people over the age of fifty speak the language well; some younger people have limited knowledge. Because of rapid structural change within Gong, the two remaining villages speak rather different dialects, both very different from traditional Gong as spoken elsewhere up to about 1980. Gong is verb-final, unlike Thai but like related Tibeto-Burman languages, and closely related to Burmese. Many other small groups in this area are also losing their traditional languages.

AUSTRALIA-PACIFIC
LANGUAGES

AUSTRALIA-PACIFIC LANGUAGES

The vast geographic area that includes Australia, Papua New Guinea (PNG), New Zealand, and the islands of the Pacific Ocean contains somewhere around one-third of the world's languages, with upward of 2,000 different languages spoken there. Many of these languages are spoken by small remote communities and are currently undocumented. Most of the languages of this region do not have indigenous writing systems, but are now written due to missionary activity in the nineteenth and twentieth centuries.

There are three major language groupings identified in this region: Australian, Papuan, and Austronesian. Some scholars believe that all indigenous languages of Australia belong to a single family, with the exception of Meryam Mir (see below), and the Tasmanian language, which has not been shown to be related to other languages, due in part to the very little information that was recorded about it before it ceased to be spoken. Other researchers are not convinced that a single family group can be demonstrated, and believe rather that there are twenty-six different groupings that occupied the continent.

It is well established that Australia has been occupied for at least 50,000 years. The largest indigenous language group is known as Pama-Nyungan, which covers the majority of the continent except for parts of the north and northwest, in which around twenty-five other groups are represented. These languages are collectively known as non-Pama-Nyungan.

Left *The large stone statues* (moai) *on Rapanui (Easter Island). The widespread Austronesian language family spreads across the Pacific to Easter Island.*

Austronesian is a very widespread family of languages, extending from Rapanui (Easter Island) in the east of the Pacific, through Indonesia and the Philippines, north to Taiwan, and west to Madagascar. These languages appear to have spread into Papua New Guinea perhaps as far back as 4,000 years ago, but did not move out into the Pacific (to become what are known as Oceanic languages) until around 3,500 years ago.

The term "Papuan" is used to refer to the languages spoken in Papua New Guinea, some parts of the Solomon Islands, and in parts of East Timor and the neighboring islands of eastern Indonesia that do not belong to the Austronesian family. Papuan is not a language family, as no relationship between all of these languages has yet been established. They are very diverse, and may consist of as many as forty different language groups.

Above Aboriginal art from Alice Springs in Australia. This country has been occupied by man for at least 50,000 years, and possibly as long as 176,000 years.

The languages covered in the following pages are as follows:

(i) Featured languages: Bislama, Maori, Motu/Hiri Motu, South Efate, Warlpiri, Mian, Murrinh-Patha, and Pitjantjatjara.

(ii) Other languages: (Australia) Arrernte, Kriol, Kunwinjku, Kuuk Thaayorre, Mawng, Meryam Mir, Yolngu Matha; (Papua New Guinea) I'saka, Saliba, Yimas; (Pacific) Anejo, Cèmuhî, Fijian, Hawai'ian, Kokota, and Mokilese.

Comparison of words from Austronesian languages across the region

English	Mokilese	Hawai'ian	Cèmuhî	Saliba
sky	loang	lani	miidèn	yada
fire	oai	ahi	miu	kaiwa
eye	maj	maka	mii-	mata
road	al	ala	pwaaden	keda
five	limoaw	lima	nim	haligigi
die	mahdi	make	met	mate
coconut	ni	niu	pii-nu	niu
bird	mahn	manu	meni	manuwa

BISLAMA

200,000 speakers

Melanesia displays an extraordinary diversity of languages totaling more than 1,100 in number. Communication between speakers of these languages has been facilitated by the use of Melanesian Pidgin, known as Tok Pisin in Papua New Guinea, Pijin in the Solomon Islands, and Bislama in Vanuatu. The word Bislama comes from the French word for sea slug, bêche-de-mer, which was traded by Europeans and Melanesians and still continues to be traded today. This enterprise was part of the early trade of sandalwood and whale meat between the two regions, and it led to the development of a pidgin language.

Above Map showing the location of Vanuatu in the South Pacific Ocean. Bislama, a Melanesian creole, is one of the official languages of Vanuatu.

Below A sign in Bislama in Port Vila, Vanuatu, reads: "If you want the ferry to come, strike the gong."

Melanesians recruited to work in the Queensland sugarcane fields in the 1800s used pidgin to communicate with each other, and, on their return to their homes they took this variety with them, finding it useful when talking to their compatriots. After Vanuatu gained independence in 1980, Bislama became the national language of the island and is spoken by most of the population.

It is the first language of 20,000 people (mainly urban youths), as well as being used on national radio and television. The Bible has been translated into Bislama.

The grammar of Bislama draws mainly on Melanesian languages, while much of the vocabulary is taken from English and French, as well as from local languages. Thus, in the following sentence, the subject of the verb **wantem** is marked by the third-person singular pronoun "i," just as it is for example in South Efate (see p. 181). Similarly, as in many

Bislama words from French

loto	(from l'auto)	car, truck
saie	(from ça y est)	that's it
sora	(from les oreilles)	ears
lameri	(from la mairie)	town hall

Indigenous words in Bislama

nakaemas	magic
nakamal	meeting house, kava bar
nasama	canoe outrigger

Melanesian languages, verbs take a suffix to show that they are transitive. In this case it is -m usually with a vowel, as in **want-em**. The word **yumi** is something like "us" in English, but is more specific, referring to both the hearer and the speaker and others. For example: **From wanem nao man i stap wantem kakae bitim yumi?** (Why does the man want to eat more than us?)

The word that would be used to refer only to the speaker and others (and not the hearer) would be **mifala**. Again, this is a distinction made in many local languages.

MAORI  70,000–160,000 speakers

Below A Māori *man with a traditional Moku tatoo, North Island, New Zealand.*

Māori is the indigenous language spoken with some variation throughout New Zealand (*Aotearoa*), where it is also an official language and is increasingly being used at official events, on signage, and in the media. In part, this attention is due to the Treaty of Waitangi (1840), which accorded certain rights to the Māori—which it was the responsibility of the New Zealand government to enforce—as found by the Waitangi Tribunal in 1986. Consequently, Māori was recognized in 1987 as an official language and the Māori Language Commission was established to promote the use of Māori as a living language.

Count to 10

tahi	1
rua	2
toru	3
wha	4
rima	5
ono	6
whitu	7
waru	8
iwa	9
tekau	10

Right *A Māori language lesson takes place at a school on New Zealand's North Island.*

The **Māori** are Polynesians who arrived in Aotearoa between 800 and 1,000 years ago. Their language is closely related to eastern Polynesian languages such as Tahitian, and is part of the widespread Austronesian family.

Māori was first written by missionaries, and today the spelling system includes several letters not found in the Roman alphabet: "ng" is used for the sound English expresses in "sing," and "wh" is used for a sound like English "f." Long vowels are marked with a macron, as can be seen in the spelling of the language name.

Following the European invasion, **Māori** continued to be spoken as a first language, but it began to decline after the Second World War. In the 1980s it was clear that, while many **Māori** speak some **Māori** language, very few could speak it fluently. Recently there has been a revival of interest in

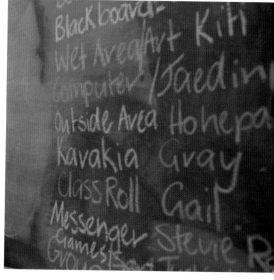

Maori literacy

From early in the colonial period the **Māori** language had achieved high status (compared to the status of indigenous languages in other parts of the Pacific, or in Australia). By the late 1850s half the adult **Māori** population could read their own language, equaling the literacy level in England at the time. In the 1890s the Kotahitanga parliament used only **Māori**. Many **Māori** took to literacy and produced Maori newspapers (in print in one form or another for more than 100 years) and literature, such as Apirana Ngata's two-volume work *Nga Moteatea*, published in 1929.

and use of the **Māori** languages, including the famous **kōhanga reo**, or language nests, in which kindergarten children spend time with old people and speak only in **Māori**. It has some regional variation, but **Māori** is the one language throughout Aotearoa and so is in a stronger position to endure than some of the many languages of Melanesia or Australia.

MOTU/HIRI MOTU 👄 14,000–150,000 speakers

Motu (which is sometimes called Pure Motu or True Motu to distinguish it from Hiri Motu, see below), is the Austronesian language that is spoken by some 14,000 people in twelve villages around Port Moresby in Papua New Guinea (PNG). The area in which Motu is spoken extends some 70 miles (113 km) along the coast. Papua New Guinea is one of the most diverse countries on earth. It is famous for having a remarkable 830 indigenous languages from both the Austronesian and non-Austronesian (which is commonly known as Papuan) families, despite having a population of fewer than 6 million people.

Above The village of Hanuabada, near Port Moresby (visible in the distance), where Motu is spoken.

The London Missionary Society produced the first book in Motu in 1877. Motu then became the language of Christian missionaries across a large area outside of traditional Motu territory, and was accepted among a widespread group of neighboring peoples as the language of the Church. Motu was a major language of education until 1955, when a change of administration policy led to English becoming the preferred language in schools.

The Motu traditionally traded on expeditions called **hiri** 200-miles (322 km) to the Gulf of Papua in the west, where they encountered speakers of non-Austronesian languages, and also their Austronesian-speaking neighbors.

Motu was thus a common means of communication in a trading network before the arrival of Europeans. It was taken up by the colonial police force and became known both as "Police Motu" and also "Hiri Motu." By 1962 Police Motu was spoken throughout Papua, with the exception of some areas where the administration was not established or where the local Church language was already strongly entrenched (e.g., Milne Bay).

Together with English and Tok Pisin (the variety of Melanesian pidgin spoken in Papua New Guinea), Motu is one of the three official languages of PNG. In 1971 Motu had around 150,000 speakers, making it the largest PNG language after Tok Pisin.

Hiri Motu has different varieties, partly dependent on whether the speakers have a first language that is Papuan or Austronesian. So, for example, central Hiri Motu marks possession in the same way as Motu, as seen below left, while non-central Hiri Motu marks it in a way more similar to Papuan languages. True Motu was used as a Church language throughout Central Papua, so maintaining a pressure to retain the Austronesian features in that variety.

Count to 10

ta	1
rua	2
toi	3
hani	4
ima	5
tauratoi	6
hitu	7
taurahani	8
taurahani ta	9
gwanta	10

Dialect variations

Motu	Central Hiri Motu	Non-central Hiri Motu
tama-gu (my father)	tama-gu/lau-egu tamana	lau-egu tamana

SOUTH EFATE

6,000 speakers

South Efate is a Melanesian language spoken on the island of Efate in central Vanuatu in the southwestern Pacific Ocean. This island and neighboring islands have only been inhabited for some 3,500 years. South Efate is part of the widespread Austronesian family, of which some 110 other languages were or are spoken in Vanuatu, in addition to the national language Bislama and the colonial languages, French and English. As there is no indigenous name for the language, it is generally known as South Efate. Speakers of South Efate originally lived in an area that now includes the capital of Vanuatu, Port Vila, and villages around the southern and eastern coast of Efate.

These include the villages of Erakor, Eratap, and Eton, where speakers continue to live today. Place names on Efate typically begin with "e-," which is a prefix meaning "place," so the capital city, Vila, is **Efil**.

South Efate was first written by missionaries and used in schools in the late 1800s. The writing system today is mainly used for Christian hymns and sermons, but schoolwork is now written in English or French. Children continue to learn South Efate in the home and use it every day.

South Efate uses mainly subject-verb-object word order and avoids case marking. The sound system includes two sounds that involve closing both the back of the mouth and the lips at the same time, as if saying "kp" or "ngm," written as p̃ and m̃. The word for "brother" is p̃al and "house" is **nasum̃**. South Efate deletes vowels at the end, and often in the middle of words, so that "village" is **natokona** in a neighboring language but **natkon** in South Efate. This means that there are words like **kraksmanr** (meaning "to miss when throwing") with the unusual consonant cluster "ksm." South Efate has borrowed words from the neighboring Polynesian language, Atara Imere (**faftai**, "thank you" and **taaloof**, "shake hands"), and also some words from Bislama (**mas**, "must" and **traem**, "try"). Negation in South Efate uses two parts (similar to French **ne … pas**) with **ta** occurring before the verb and **mau** occurring after, as in the following example:

P̃a	ta	fes	mau!
You	not	talk	not

(Don't you talk!)

Count to 10

iskei	1
inru	2
itol	3
ipat	4
ilim	5
ilates	6
ilaru	7
ilatol	8
ilfot	9
ralim iskei	10

Above
An islander in Port Vila, the capital of Efate, where South Efate is spoken.

Pronouns in South Efate

There are three sets of pronouns, the choice of which depends on whether the action to which they relate—or the aspect—is occurring, will occur, or has occurred. Every sentence needs to include a pronoun, so the aspect has to be expressed. In the following examples the pronoun meaning "I" is underlined:

<u>Ka</u> fo pak talm̃at pa.	<u>A</u> pak talm̃at pa.	<u>Kai</u> pe pak talm̃at pan.
I will go to the garden	I go to the garden	I went to the garden

WARLPIRI

4,000 speakers

Warlpiri is spoken by about 3,000 people as their first language, and by another 1,000 as a second or third language across a large area of Central Australia, northwest of Alice Springs, Northern Territory. The main Warlpiri-speaking communities are Yuendumu, Lajamanu, Nyirrpi, and Willowra. Warlpiri belongs to the Yapa subgroup of the large Pama-Nyungan family, which includes the majority of Australian languages, and is one of the largest Australian indigenous languages by numbers of speakers. The Warlpiri sound system is fairly typical for a Pama-Nyungan language, and contains a number of sounds that are not found in English.

Word order

Warlpiri is a "free word order" language, which means that the nouns and verbs can come in any order in the sentence, without changing the meaning. Case suffixes are used at the ends of nouns to indicate who is doing what to whom. In the following sentence, the suffix **-ngku** after **ngarrka** (man) tells us that the man is the subject, irrespective of the order of the words.

Ngarrka-ngku ka wawirri pantirni
The man is spearing the kangaroo

Pantirni ka ngarrka-ngku wawirri
The man is spearing the kangaroo

Wawirri ka pantirni ngarrka-ngku
The man is spearing the kangaroo

Walpiri has a series of "retroflex" sounds that are made by curling the tongue tip back and touching the roof of the mouth with the underside of the tongue (producing an "r"-like quality to the sound). These sounds are written with a preceding "r": **pirli** (stone, hill) versus **pili** (wooden dish); **karna** (I am) versus **kana** (digging stick); **mirta** (shield) versus **mata** (tired). Like most Australian languages, Warlpiri has no fricative sounds ("s," "z," "f," and "v") and no contrast between voiced stops ("b," "d," "g") and voiceless stops ("p," "t," "k"). The sound written "t" will sometimes sound more like a "d" (for example, after an "n," as in **kanta** (bush coconut)), but without changing the meaning of the word. (Compare English "bit" and "bid," where the change from "t" to "d" signals a new word.)

There are different ways of using Warlpiri. As well as regional dialectal variation, there is a distinctive baby-talk style for addressing children, an "avoidance" register for particular kin relations (for example, between son-in-law and mother-in-law), a sign language, and secret languages used by groups of initiated men. In addressing kin relations, adults do not normally refer to their opposite sex siblings by name. Rather, men refer to their sisters as **kari-pardu** (the other), while women refer to their brothers as **yakuri** (the sweaty). Men and women use different terms to refer to other kin relations: a woman refers to her parents as **ngati** (mother) and **kirdana** (father), while a man refers to his parents as **murturna** (old woman) and **purlka** (old man).

MIAN

3,500 speakers

Below *The Sandaun Province in the northwest of Papua New Guinea, where Mian is spoken.*

Mian (also known as Mianmin) is a Papuan language of the Ok family, from the Sandaun Province of Papua New Guinea. "Mian" is not a Mian word, but means "dog" in the related languages of Faiwol, Bimin, and Oksapmin. This name was acquired by the Mianmin people in the 1930s, during a government survey. Their neighbors referred to them as "Mian," possibly because the Mianmin had a reputation as fierce warriors. It subsequently became the standard administrative name for the people and their language, and was later adopted by the Mianmin themselves.

Below right *A young boy from the Sandaun Province in Papua New Guinea.*

In Mian, the word for "language" is **wěng**, and so the Mianmin refer to their own language as **Mian wěng**. While still the language of daily communication in the Mianmin region (including the villages of Yapsiei, Gubil, Fiak, and Hotmin), Mian is under constant threat and influence from English and Tok Pisin (an official language of Papua New Guinea). Mian speakers are conscious of the potentially destructive influence of these languages on their own language, and regularly identify words and constructions taken from Tok Pisin and English as **wan weng fúnin** (bird language thinking) and **tablasebwáli weng fúnin** (white man language thinking) respectively.

Mian has fifteen consonants and six vowels (as well as four diphthongs). In addition to having the two velar consonants "k" and "g," it has a second set of labialized velar consonants "kʷ" and "gʷ," which are pronounced with rounded lips, as if saying "g" and "w" together in the one sound. For example, **gi** is the verb stem meaning "laugh," while **gwi** is the verb stem meaning "poison." Mian also has a tonal system, by which words are associated with one of five tones. These tones often distinguish between words that are otherwise pronounced the same. **Mén** in a high tone means "child" and **měn** in a low-rising tone means "string bag." Tone in verbs can also be used to distinguish tenses.

Body counting system

The Ok languages (including Mianmin) are known for their "body-tally" system, whereby the parts of the body are used systematically for counting. Counting in the Mian tally system starts with the left thumb, followed by the fingers of the left hand, then up the left side of the body (wrist, forearm, elbow, shoulder joint, shoulder top, cheek, ear, eye, nose), each time adding a number so that one reaches the number 14 at the nose. From there, one proceeds down the right-hand side, reaching the number 27. Examples are:

tumin	shoulder joint	9
kwing-dim	shoulder -top	10
tam-dim	side of face	11
klon-dim	on the ear	12
kin-dim	on the eye	13
munung-dim	on the nose	14
kin milim	eye other side	15
klon milim	each other side	16
tam milim	side of face other side	17
kwing milim	shoulder top other side	18
tum milim	shoulder joint other side	19

MURRINH-PATHA

2,500 speakers

Murrinh-Patha is spoken in and around the community of Wadeye (Port Keats mission) in the Northern Territory of Australia. Wadeye is situated 261 miles (420 km) southwest of the city of Darwin and is home to approximately 2,000 people. Murrinh-Patha is the dominant language of the area, and is used in all daily activities by the whole community (although government services and facilities are delivered in English). Although it is apparently related to other Australian languages, Murrinh-Patha's detailed genetic relationship with them has not yet been well established.

Verbs

Murrinh-Patha has extremely complicated verbs, which can carry large amounts of information corresponding to what would be a whole sentence in English:

Perremnunggumangime
Those few people gave things to each other

Wurdamnawalthidamatha
He was laughing at him so hard his sides were aching

Thurdingayithmaningintha
You two women should tell me the story

Above *Players relax after an AFL football game in Wadeye.*

Right *Part of the Northern Territory, Australia, showing the location of the community of Wadeye, where Murrinh-Patha is the dominant language.*

Murrinh-Patha, meaning "good language," (**murrinh** "language" + **patha** "good"), is still being acquired by children (and therefore as a language it is not immediately endangered). It has become a lingua franca for the Wadeye region (replacing the traditional languages of other language groups in the area, such as Magati Ke, Marri Ngarr, and Marri Djebin). Consequently, it is one of the few Australian indigenous languages whose speakers have increased in numbers over the last generation.

There is no traditional writing system for the language. However, a writing system did develop in the 1970s and is well established in the community. This system uses English letters, but combines them in different ways to capture sounds that exist in Murrinh-Patha but not in English. For example, Murrinh-Patha has three "t" sounds: one similar to the English "t" (written "t"), another produced with the tip of the tongue between the teeth (written "th"), and a third produced with the tip of the tongue curled back in the mouth (written "rt"). Whereas European languages divide nouns into two or three

genders, Murrinh-Patha nouns are divided into ten meaning-based classes. Every time a noun is used, it must be preceded by the appropriate class marker. These classes give us some insight into the ways in which Murrinh-Patha speakers categorize the world around them: **kardu** (Aboriginal people); **ku** (non-Aboriginal people, animals); **kura** (water, liquids); **thamul** (spears); **thu** (other offensive weapons, thunder, lightening); **thungku** (fire); **da** (places, times); **murrinh** (language, song); **nanthi** (everything else).

PITJANTJATJARA

2,500 speakers

Below *The distribution of the four main dialects of the Western Desert in Australia.*

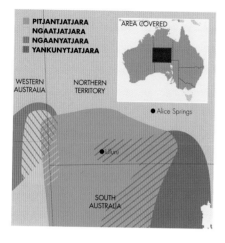

- PITJANTJATJARA
- NGAATJATJARA
- NGAANYATJARA
- YANKUNYTJATJARA

AREA COVERED

WESTERN AUSTRALIA

NORTHERN TERRITORY

● Alice Springs

● Uluru

SOUTH AUSTRALIA

Pitjantjatjara is the best-known dialect of the Western Desert language, which spans the arid western central interior of Australia. In fast speech, the middle -tja- syllable is deleted, so that the language name is pronounced Pitjantjara. The various dialects of the Western Desert language are mutually intelligible, although they each have their own distinctive features, and are considered to be distinct varieties (with their own names) by the speakers themselves. The Western Desert language is a fairly typical member of the Pama-Nyungan language family, which encompasses approximately 90 percent of the Australian continent.

Numbers

As in many Australian indigenous languages, Pitjantjatjara has very few words for numbers. The basic terms are: **kutju** (one), **kutjara** (two), **mankurpa** (three), and **tjuta** (many). Additional terms can be added by combining these, as in **kutjara kutjara** (four), **mankur-kutjara** (five), and **mankur-mankurpa** (six), but usually the more general **tjuta** (many) is used.

Place names

The longest official place name in Australia is a Pitjantjatjara word, "Mamungkukumpurangkuntjunya Hill" in South Australia.

Right Kata Tjuta, formerly known as "the Olgas," which is sacred to the Pitjantjatjara people.

The Pitjantjatjara dialect is spoken by around 2,500 people living mainly in the Pitjantjatjara freehold lands in northwestern South Australia. It is one of the strongest Australian languages as well as being one of the best known by non-indigenous people, and it is still being acquired by children. One of its distinctive features is that words cannot end in a consonant. Words that end in consonants in the other dialects are given a **-pa** ending in Pitjantjatjara. For example, **nguwan** (almost, kind of) and **watjil** (lonesome, homesick) in the Yankunytjatjara dialect have the form **nguwanpa** and **watjilpa** respectively in Pitjantjatjara. Another distinctive feature is reflected in the dialect name itself, which is comprised of **pitjantja** (meaning come/go) and **-tjara** (having) as a suffix, so that **pitjantjatjara** (**pitjantja**-having) means the variety with the word **pitjantja**. This is opposed to the Yankunytjatjara dialect, which uses the word **yankunytja** (for come/go), hence Yankunytjatjara (**yankunytja**-having).

The Pitjantjatjara people refer to themselves as **Anangu**, and are the traditional owners of the area that includes Uluru (Ayers Rock) and Kata

Tjuta (the Olgas). These sacred sites are extremely important to the Anangu, and were eventually handed back to their ownership by the federal government in 1985.

Pitjantjatjara has been written with the Roman alphabet since the 1940s, and has been used in educational, religious, and other material. It is also one of the few indigenous languages to be taught at university level (for example, at the University of South Australia).

Left *Hawai'ian street signs in Honolulu, the capital city.*

MOKILESE

1,200 speakers

Mokilese is spoken on Mokil Atoll in the Eastern Caroline Islands in Micronesia in the western Pacific. Mokilese has twelve consonants, including fricatives (consonants where the air is not stopped completely like "s" and "v") and velarized labials, written as "pw" and "mw" (made by drawing the tongue back in the mouth) so the word **pa**, "to weave," is different from the word **pwa**, "to say"), and seven vowels. However, there is no tradition of writing Mokilese; most written communication uses English or the neighboring language, Pohnpeian. Hundreds of words from Japanese and English have been adopted into Mokilese, for example, **iakiu** (baseball) and **kainpis** (canvas) respectively.

MAWNG

300 speakers

Mawng is spoken in the northwest of Arnhem Land in Australia's Northern Territory, primarily on South Goulburn Island (known as Warruwi). Despite its few speakers, Mawng is the language of daily communication in the community, although all Mawng speakers also speak English. One of the many complex features of Mawng grammar is the system of gender of nouns. All nouns belong to one of five semantically based genders: masculine, feminine, vegetation, edible (includes non-meat foods and household possessions), and land (includes the land, liquids, and the abstract domains of culture and custom). The noun's gender must be marked on all elements in the sentence that refer to the noun (e.g. adjectives), including the verb, which shows gender agreement with the subject and object.

KOKOTA

500 speakers

Kokota is an Oceanic language spoken on Santa Isabel in the Solomon Islands. It has twenty-two consonants and five vowels. Like many Oceanic languages, Kokota distinguishes between various kinds of possession: inalienable (typically body parts and products), alienable, and consumable. Each of these is marked by a suffix on the possessed noun, for example: **totogale-ḡu ara ine** (this photo of me) versus **no-ḡu totogal ara ine** (this my photo [which I own but it may not be of me]). As is also found in many Oceanic languages, Kokota can allow a noun to be incorporated into a verb when the noun is non-specific. For example, **ara mala flalo vaka-flalo** (I-fly ship-fly/I fly planes), contrasted with the form in which the object occurs and is a specific plane: **ara n-a flalo-i vaka-flalo ine** (I I-fly-it ship-fly this/I'm flying this plane).

HAWAI'IAN

2,000 speakers

Hawai'ian is an eastern Polynesian language closely related to Tahitian. It is now an official language of the U.S. state of Hawai'i. The spelling system used for Hawai'ian is similar to that used for **Māori**, and includes the use of the apostrophe for the glottal stop, a sound made by closing the vocal cords. Thus **mai** means "from," but **ma'i** means "ill." There has been a great deal of writing in Hawai'ian over the past century, including newspapers recording current events. The number of speakers dropped to around 1,000 at its lowest, but the use of **Nā Pūnana Leo** (language nests), based on the Maori experience (see p. 179) to bring children and speakers together has contributed to a renewed use of Hawai'ian; in the recent past a student has completed a PhD dissertation written entirely in Hawai'ian.

Left Malolo Island, one of the 100 islands that make up the Fijian nation.

Left Children reading at a bush school in Arnhem Land, Australia, where Yolngu Matha is spoken.

FIJIAN

350,000–550,000 speakers

Fijian is an Oceanic language. The 100 Fijian islands are home to several varieties of Fijian languages, including Bauan (also known as Standard Fijian), Lau, Nadrogā, and Boumaa. Fijian was only made an official language of Fiji in 1997 (together with English and Hindustani). The writing system was developed by missionaries and is still current. The consonants "b," "d," and "g" are all preceded by a nasal sound ("mb," "nd," "ng"). Some letters that need explaining are: "c" as in "this," "g" as in "sing," "q" as in "finger; "nr" is made by trilling the "r" sound after the "n." Fijian (like Anejom̃) puts the verb before the object and then the subject follows.

ANEJOM̃

600 speakers

Anejom̃ is an Oceanic language spoken on the southernmost inhabited island in Vanuatu. Despite a dramatic depopulation since European settlement (down to 182 people on the island in 1930), the language continues to be spoken. Missionaries first wrote the language in the late 1840s, and schooling was mainly conducted in the Anejom̃ language in the 1850s. Anejom̃ is unique in Vanuatu in having the object occur before the subject. The Anejom̃ counting system is quinary, with numbers above six formed by compounds:
1—ithii, 2—erou, 3—esej, 4—emanohowan,
5—nijman, 6—meled, 7—meled-erou, 8—meled-esej,
9—meled-emanohowan, 10—nijman-(n)ijman.

ARRERNTE

4,500 speakers

Arrernte (also sometimes spelled Aranda) is spoken in Central Australia, including in and around Alice Springs, in the Northern Territory. There are a number of different dialects of Arrernte, including Eastern Arrernte, Mparntwe (Central) Arrernte (the dialect of Alice Springs), Anmatyerr, Alyawarr, and Kaytetye. In total, there are around 4,500 speakers of the Arrernte varieties. Arrernte speakers are known for having a sophisticated ancillary sign language, which is used when speech is not appropriate (when silence is required for practical or cultural reasons). It is possible for speakers to hold detailed and lengthy conversations using only this system of hand signs.

YOLNGU MATHA

5,000 speakers

Yolngu Matha is the name of a group of dialects spoken by Yolngu people from northeast Arnhem Land. The name derives from **yolngu** (people) and **matha** (tongue). The term **yolngu** refers to Aboriginal people only. The Yolngu Matha word for "white person"— **balanda**—comes from "Hollander," and was borrowed from Indonesian Macassan fishermen with whom the Yolngu have traded for hundreds of years. Only since 1935 have the Yolngu had sustained contact with the **balanda** in Australia, when a Methodist mission was opened in Arnhem Land. Yolngu Matha is the language of the 2006 movie *Ten Canoes*—the first full-length feature film to be made in an Australian indigenous language.

Left *The Ngarrag (Mardayin) ceremony in Arnhem Land, where Kunwinjku is spoken.*

KUNWINJKU

2,000 speakers

Kunwinjku (Gunwinggu) is one member of a dialect chain (known as Mayali or Bininj Gun-Wok) that is spoken across the western Arnhem Land region of Australia's Northern Territory. The language has served as a lingua franca throughout the region for the last century, making it particularly useful for missionary work. Early biblical translations into Kunwinjku exist from the 1930s (published by the Bible Society). The dialect name consists of the neuter gender prefix **kun-** combined with the nominal root **winjku** (freshwater), and draws an opposition between the inland-dwelling (freshwater) Kunwinjku and the saltwater communities to the north (for example, Mawng and Iwaidja).

CÈMUHÎ

3,300 speakers

Cèmuhî is an Oceanic language spoken in New Caledonia in the southwestern Pacific Ocean. Cèmuhî has nineteen consonants and twenty-three vowels, and is one of a small group of languages in New Caledonia to use tone to distinguish meaning, for example: **té** (high tone)—heavy, sad; **tē** (mid tone)—to stagger, lose one's balance; **tè** (low tone)—to fly. Like many Oceanic languages, Cèmuhî has serial verbs, that is, it combines verbs to create new meanings. Numbers in Cèmuhî are in a quinary system, that is, they count to five and then use compounding to count higher: 1—**cḗiú**, 2—**áló**, 3—**cié**, 4—**páa**, 5—**nim**, 6—**nim bwɔ mú cḗiu pwón**, 10—**pàjilù**.

KRIOL

24,000 speakers

Kriol is the name given to a number of linguistic varieties spoken throughout northern Australia by Aboriginal people. These varieties developed out of the need for Aboriginal people to communicate with speakers of other languages, including other Aboriginal languages and English (somewhat like Bislama, see p. 178). There are differences between the varieties, partly due to the different source languages from which they adapt grammatical and lexical information. Best documented are Fitzroy Valley (Kimberley), Barunga and Roper river (southeastern Arnhem Land), and Torres Strait Broken or Yumpala Tok (Torres Strait Islands). A translation of the Bible begun in 1978 resulted in the publication of the Kriol Bible for the Katherine region in May 2007.

KUUK THAAYORRE

250 speakers

Kuuk Thaayorre is a language of Western Cape York Peninsula, in Northern Queensland, Australia. It belongs to the larger Pama-Nyungan family, which includes approximately 90 percent of the languages spoken on the Australian continent. It is one of the few Australian indigenous languages still being acquired by children. It is the language (**kuuk**) spoken by the Thaayorre people, hence the name Kuuk Thaayorre. Kuuk Thaayorre is distinctive in allowing words to contain unusual sequences of consonants. For example, like many Australian languages, it has two "r" sounds: one like the English "r" (written **r**), and another more like a rolled Scottish "r" (written **rr**). Unusually, Kuuk Thaayorre allows these two to follow each other in a single syllable (written **rr_r**), as in **parr_r** (kid).

Left The sun sets over the Arafundi river, where the two Yimas-speaking villages are located.

Left An outrigger canoe near Kiriwina Island, Milne Bay, in Papua New Guinea.

YIMAS

250 speakers

Yimas is one of six member languages of the Lower Sepik family of New Guinea. The other members include Karawari (1,500 speakers), Angoram (7,000 speakers), Chambri (1,200 speakers), Murik (1,500 speakers), and Kopar (250 speakers). It is spoken in two villages along the lower reaches of the Arafundi river in the Sepik river-basin area of Papua New Guinea. Lower Sepik languages have complicated verbal structures with multiple prefixes and suffixes. In many cases a single Yimas verb can express the meaning of a whole sentence in a language such as English. For example, **ya-mpu-yamal-wat** (they usually carve them) and **impa-mpu-yakal-irm-tay-cut** (they stood watching them both).

I'SAKA

400 speakers

I'saka (also called Krisa) is spoken in the village of Krisa (Sandaun Province), in the extreme northwest of Papua New Guinea. I'saka has four tones, as well as contrasting nasalized and non-nasalized syllables. For example, **paj** (pronounced like English "pie") means "arrow" while **pãj** (pronounced as if with a heavily blocked nose) means "sling." The language name is pronounced with a high tone on the first syllable (indicated by ') and low tones on the remaining syllables. Counting in I'saka is based on the following system of numbers: **kaipa**—one, **sie**—two, **dou**—hand (five). For example, **sie kaipa** (two-one)—three, **sie sie** (two-two)—four, **dou sie** (hand-two)—ten.

SALIBA

1,000 speakers

Saliba is an Oceanic language spoken in the Milne Bay Province of Papua New Guinea. There is no tradition of writing Saliba and missionary work promoted written material in the neighboring language of Suau. Like other Oceanic languages, pronouns attached to the verb are the usual way of encoding who is doing the action and who or what is the object of the action. It is rare to have nouns in addition to the pronouns with the same reference in the same sentence—see below, in which "he" occurs as **ye-**, attached to the verb **deula**. Tense is not grammatically marked in Saliba, with the time of an event being marked by words such as **malaitom** (tomorrow), **wau** (now), or **lahi** (yesterday). Like its neighboring Papuan languages, Saliba puts objects before the verb: **Koya ye-deula-i-ø** (garden he-terrace-it/He terraced the garden).

MERYAM MIR

300–400 speakers

Meryam Mir is one of two indigenous languages of the Torres Strait Islands, which lie between the northern tip of Australia and Papua New Guinea. Meryam Mir is related to the Papuan languages of the Fly River district of Papua New Guinea (Eastern Trans Fly family) and the speakers are ethnically and culturally Melanesian. Kala Lagaw Ya, the other indigenous language of the Torres Strait Islands, is related to the Pama-Nyungan languages of Australia. Meryam Mir is therefore the only non-Australian indigenous language within Australian political boundaries. Meryam Mir speakers are all also fluent speakers of Torres Strait Creole, but Meryam Mir is no longer being acquired by children. The language name derives from "mir" (word, language) and "meryam," which is the name for one of the clans living on Mer (Murray Island), where the language is spoken.

LANGUAGES OF
THE AMERICAS

LANGUAGES OF THE AMERICAS

The languages discussed in this chapter are all survivors. They represent indigenous American peoples who coexisted with European settlers, and then with their successors, independent American nations governed in European languages. Only one language of the Americas, Guaraní in Paraguay, has been allowed a leading role nationally, although today, at last, some languages are gaining official status regionally. Speaker populations of American languages have never been large, but all too many language communities in this region are now close to extinction.

In North America the 312 languages once known have diminished to 188 today. The main language of the Arctic is spoken by the Inuit, who spread eastward from northern Alaska to Greenland after *c.* 1000 CE. By contrast, the languages of southern Canada (Cree and Ojibwe) moved westward with the European fur trade. These extend further west to Blackfoot, and Dakota/Lakota. Other populous groups include Cherokee and Choctaw/Chickasaw, once southeastern tribes that largely moved westward in the nineteenth century to Oklahoma. In the arid southwest, there are Keres (a Pueblo Indian group) in New Mexico, O'odham in southern Arizona, and the (currently) largest group in North America, Navajo.

Linguistic vitality is greater in Mesoamerica, with more than 300 languages still spoken. The three most important language families in this area are Maya, Otomanguean, and Uto-Aztecan.

Left An Inuit elder from Nunavut, Canada. Inuit is now the official language of Nunavut, and, with Danish, of Greenland.

Above right A stunning yarn painting of the Huichol people of western Mexico. Their language belongs to the Uto-Aztecan family.

Of the thirty Maya languages, more than twenty are spoken in Guatemala and Belize, and the remainder in Mexico. Most Uto-Aztecan languages are spoken in Mexico, but north of the border there are many more, including O'odham, Comanche, Shoshone, Ute, Luiseño, and Hopi. In this chapter, Nahuatl and its close relatives the Nahuat languages are discussed, as well as Raramuri and Huichol.

The Otomanguean family, mostly located in the state of Oaxaca, has contributed much to linguistic diversity in Mexico, including languages such as Zapotec and Mixtec, themselves divided into almost fifty varieties. Three unrelated languages, Purepecha, Huave, and Kickapoo (an Algonquian language) are covered at the end of the chapter.

In South America, some 500 languages survive. The Caribbean coast is home to Warao and Guajiro; Emberá extends around the isthmus of Darien to the Pacific. Further south, in the Andes, are Páez, Awa Pit, and the Jivaroan languages. In the plains to the east is Guahibo; then further south in Amazonia are Ticuna, Shipibo-Conibo, and the Campa languages. Two of the most widespread South American languages, Quechua and Aymara, are associated with the Inca Empire. Guaraní and its kin were once widespread across Brazil's river systems. The Gran Chaco region, extending through Bolivia, Paraguay, Chile, and Argentina, is home to Chiquitano, Nivaclé, Wichí Lhamtés, and Toba. The largest remaining language from southeast Brazil is Kaingáng, and Mapadungun, in central Chile, is a language community that stayed independent until the nineteenth century.

NAVAJO

120,000 speakers

Below *Sand paintings form an important part of Navajo religious and healing ceremonies.*

Navajo (pronounced "Navaho") is spoken on a large reservation in the Four Corners region of southwestern North America. With over 115,000 speakers of all ages, it is the largest surviving indigenous language community in North America. The language has such a reputation for impenetrability that the American military recruited Navajos during the Second World War to use a version of it as "code talk" in the Pacific. Navajo and its cousins—half a dozen forms of Apache—are at the southeastern extreme of the Athabaskan family, which includes some forty other languages spoken across northern California, western Canada, and Alaska.

Religion and way of life

The Navajo religion and way of life are based on the cultivation of **hózhó** (beauty), as created by art or ritual (e.g. sand paintings) rather than perceived in nature. Language is seen to play a central role in creation, and long verbal chants (**hatáál**) are central to religious practices.

It appears that the Navajo moved into the southwest from the Great Slave Lake in Canada between the eleventh and thirteenth centuries CE. It has been proposed that all these languages are related to Ket, spoken in central Siberia, although this grouping remains controversial.

The name Navajo was given by the Spanish around 1620, derived from **navajuu**, a Tewa (Pueblo Indian) word meaning "valley with planted fields." However, the first Navajo grammars and dictionaries had to wait until the Franciscan mission, which came in 1898. Its speakers call the language **diné bizaad**, meaning "people their-language." Navajo is phonetically challenging to foreign learners. It uses plain, aspirated, and ejective consonants, and nasalization (marked with an under-hook) and tone (high tone is marked with an acute accent) distinctive on its vowels. Words

are polysyllabic, particularly so the highly inflected verb forms, which, beside tense and person, distinguish twenty-two different aspects and a variety of classes of shape and substance in their objects. Although most speakers are now bilingual in English, little vocabulary is borrowed. Most of the Navajo are literate and employ the language every day, but use appears recently to be in decline: school-age Navajo children on the reservation who spoke only English have increased from 12 percent of the population in 1980 to 28 percent in 1990, and 43 percent in 2000.

Count to 10

łáa'ii	1
naaki	2
táá'	3
dį́į'	4
ashdla'	5
hastą́ą́h	6
tsosts'id	7
tseebíí	8
náhást'éí	9
neeznáá	10

Navajo has a fully developed decimal-based number system. Multiples of ten terminate in **diin**, hundreds in **neeznádiin** (ten tens), and thousands in (the Spanish-loan) **mííl**; for example: **ashdladiin** (50); **ashdladi neeznádiin** (500); **ashdladi mííl** (5,000).

Right *The Four Corners region of southwestern North America where Navajo is spoken.*

INUIT

90,000 speakers

Above *The regions of Alaska, northernmost Canada, and Greenland, where the Inuit language is spoken.*

The Inuit language is spoken in the extreme north of North America, from Alaska, across Canada, and into Greenland. The language was spread from the west by the Thule people, with their dogs, drills, and archery, who supplanted the Tuniit ("Dorset" culture) between the tenth and fourteenth centuries CE. With various national names, Inuit is now the official language in Nunavut—the northernmost territory of Canada—and in Greenland, which is affiliated with Denmark. "Inuit," the plural of "inuk," is strictly the name of a people, speakers of a language mostly called Inuktitut, literally "like an Inuk."

The language has other names, however: Greenlandic, or Kalaalisut, in Greenland (48,000 speakers); Inupiatun in Alaska (7,500 speakers); and there are sections of the Inuit who call their language Inuinnaqtun in Nunavut and Inuvialuktun in the Northwest Territories (18,840 speakers in Canada). In practice, those who accept the name "Inuktitut" are those who use the Inuktitut syllabary (derived from, and largely identical to, the Cree syllabary), which is strong in Nunavut ("our home"), and northern Quebec (**Nunavik**, "place to live"). Inuktitut is also used in Nunatsaviat since 2005 an autonomous region of Labrador on the southeastern coast of Canada. Another 9,000 speakers now live in Denmark.

Inuit are not generally considered "First Nations" or Amerindians. Their language is closely related to the Yupik of southern Alaska and Siberia, and more distantly to the Aleut of the Aleutian Islands.

Count to 10

INUIT				YUPIK		
Greenlandic	West Canadian	North Alaskan		Central Alaskan	Chaplino
ataaseq	atausiq	atautseq	1	atauciq	atasuq
marluk	malRuk	matleruk	2	malRuk	malRuk
pingasut	piŋasut	pingayun	3	piŋayun	piŋayut
sisamat	sitamat	stauman	4	cetaman	stamat
tallimat	tallimat	tatliman	5	taliman	talimat
arfinillit	aRvinilik	aravinligin	6	aRvinleghen	aRvinlik
arfineq marluk	aypak	matlerunligin	7	malRunleghen	maRraRvinlik
arfineq pingasut	piŋasunik	pingayunligin	8	piŋŋayunleghen	pingayuniŋiŋlyalik
qulingiluat	quliŋiluat	qulingúneritāran	9	qulŋunRitaRaan	stama niŋiŋlyalik
qulit	qulit	qulin	10	qula	qulya

This chart shows some representative forms of Inuktitut (Inuit) and, for contrast, two branches of Yupik.

Related languages

The Yupik language has been spoken in western and south central Alaska (12,000 speakers) and northeastern Siberia (500 speakers) from the time of the Inuit migration westward across the Arctic zone of North America, i.e., the eleventh century CE. It also has multiple dialects, principally Central Yupik, Čupik, and Alutiik in Alaska, and Central Siberian, Chaplino, Naukan, and (now extinct) Sireniksky in Siberia.

CREE

80,000 speakers

Cree is the name for a group of Algonquian languages that are spoken over a vast area, across almost the width of Canada in the middle latitudes, from Alberta to Labrador. There is a great deal of linguistic diversity in a continuum from the west to the east. Although speakers of Cree are few, particularly in the east, its use is extremely vigorous, even without strong institutional support. The language is also notable for its use of the Cree syllabary (see below). There are two creole languages that include elements from Cree, these being Michif, the language of the Métis people, and Bungee (see below).

Above *A tri-lingual traffic sign in Quebec, Canada, written in English, Cree, and French.*

The name "Cree" is originally a corruption (through French) of the word "Kiristino," the first group of speakers to be encountered in the 1620s in the Swampy Cree area.

There is great variation in pronunciation across the Cree language group. This is demonstrated by the phrase for "native language" (in other words "Cree") in some representative varieties, here listed from west to east: Plains Cree (**Nēhiyawēwin**); Woods Cree (**Nīhithawīwin**); Swampy Cree (**Ininīmowin**); Moose Cree (Ililīmowin); Innu Cree (**Īnū Ayimūn**); and Naskapi (**Īyiyū Ayimūn**). The easterly varieties (the latter two here) are often known as **Montagnais** (French for "mountaineers").

Frequent intermarriages between French fur trappers and Plains Cree women led, in the seventeenth and eighteenth centuries, to the creation of a **métis** (mixed) community, with a distinctive creole named Michif, still spoken by fewer than 1,000 in Saskatchewan and North Dakota: formally, it is characterized by French nouns and Cree verbs. Bungee was another creole, this time with Scots Gaelic, which evolved in Manitoba in the nineteenth and twentieth centuries.

The Cree syllabary is a system of approximately ten symbols for consonants, in which the vowels that follow (only four are in use) are indicated by the orientation of the symbol. This syllabary was invented by the Wesleyan missionary James Evans in 1840. Versions of the syllabary are now widely used to write Cree, Ojibwe, and Inuktitut.

Count to 10

Plains	Woods		Innu	Naskapi
peyak	pēyak	1	peikw	pāikw
nisho	nīso	2	nishw	nīsu
nisto	nisto	3	nishtw	nistu
newaw	nēw, nēwo, nēyo	4	neu	nāw
niyalan	niyānan	5	patetat	pitātāhch
nikotwas	nikotwāsik, kotwāsik	6	kutuasht	āsutāhch
niswas	tēpakohp	7	nishuasht	nīswāutāhch
niyananew	ayinānew, ēnānēw	8	nishuaush	yānāw
shank	kēkāc mitātaht	9	peikushteu	pāikustāw
mita	mitātah, mitāyaht	10	peikunnu	pāikuyuw

OJIBWE

43,000 speakers

Ojibwe—also known as Chippewa, Ojibwa, or Ojibway in English, and Anishinabe or Anishinaabemowin to its own speakers—is a language in the Algonquian family, spoken by some 43,000 people in southern Canada and the northern United States. Numbers of Ojibwe speakers are growing as the language is passed on to the next generation. It has several dialects. From west to east they are Western or Plains Ojibwe (also known as Saulteaux), Central Ojibwe, Northern Ojibwe (Severn Ojibwe, verging into Oji-Cree), Minnesota Ojibwe or Chippewa spoken in the USA, and Eastern Ojibwe with Ottawa (Odawa or Odaawa) spoken in Ontario and Michigan.

Above *A student at the Ojibwe Immersion School, Hayward, Wisconsin. Here, pupils are taught the Chippewa language.*

These dialects are mutually intelligible. Another, more divergent, dialect is Algonquian (spoken northwest of Ottawa), which is itself split between the northern dialect and Nipissing. Oji-Cree is heavily influenced by Cree (a closely related language), and often written in the Cree syllabary rather than the Roman alphabet.

Fur trading with the French made the Ojibwe language the main trade language of the Great Lakes region from the mid-seventeenth century to the late nineteenth century, replacing the (now extinct) Wyandot language as the lingua franca there. Its use spread to non-Ojibwe peoples, as well as others beyond—ultimately to an area bounded by the Ohio river valley in the south, James Bay in the north, the Ottawa river in the east, and the Rocky Mountains in the west. It also gave rise to a pidgin language known as "Broken Ojibwe."

Ojibwe has influenced neighboring related languages, such as Menomini and Potawatomi on either side of Lake Michigan.

Cultural concepts

Hiawatha, whose story is told by Henry Wadsworth Longfellow (1807–82), is in fact an Onondaga (Iroquois tribe) character (*Hayowentha*, "he who combs"). But most of the indigenous words quoted in Wadsworth's poem are Ojibwe, for example:

Gitche Manito, the mighty, the creator of the nations
Gichi-manidoo (Great spirit)

Honor be to Mudjekeewis!
majiikiwis (first-born)

Smote the mighty Mishe-Mokwa
mishi-makwa (great bear)

Count to 10

Western Ojibwe	Algonquian		Menomini	Potawatomi
bezhig	pegik	1	nekot	ngot
niizh	ninch	2	nīs	nish
niswi	nissoue	3	neqniw	nswɛ
niiwin	neou	4	nīw	nyaw
naanan	narau	5	nianan	nyanĭn
(n)ingodwaaswi	ningoutouassou	6	nekūtuasetah	ngotwatso
niizhwaaswi	ninchouassou	7	nōhekan	nowak
(n)ishwaaswi	nissouassou	8	suasek	shwatso
zhaangaswi	changassou	9	sakew	shak
midaaswi	mitassou	10	metātah	mdatso

MODERN NAHUATL

1.5–2 million speakers

Below *The main Nahuatl-speaking states in Mexico.*

This group of languages is spoken by roughly 1.5 to 2 million people throughout Mexico, with at least a dozen separate languages. The Nahuatl area includes the states of Durango and San Luis Potosi, through Jalisco, Michoacán, and Mexico City, reaching Tlaxcala, Morelos, Guerrero, Veracruz, and Oaxaca southward. Due to migration, the Nahuatl map also covers an area ranging from enclaves around the United States–Canada border, through Chicago to southern Arizona, California, and Texas. Nahuatl is the name given to this set of languages in English and Spanish, but speakers give it different names, depending on the region in question.

Below right *Aztec ruins of the Templo Mayor, Mexico City. Nahuatl was the language of the Aztecs.*

Nahuatl traits

Nahuatl is polysynthetic, i.e., it can create very long words by fusing words together, as in **tsiintsinkiriantsiintsoonk-waakwaa**, which simply means "scissors."

Metaphors in Nahuatl

Metaphors are used profusely in Nahuatl. For example, body parts indicate spatial or numerical relations:

Macuilli (five): **ma** (hand) + the root of the verb—**cui**— (to hold)

ixtetl (eye): **ix** (face) + **tetl** (stone)

Mexicano is the most common alternative name, as pronounced in Spanish. Derived from Nahuatl **Mexicah** (more widely known as Aztec), it was appropriated by Nahuatl speakers during the nineteenth century. **Mexicanero** is used in the state of Durango and **Macehualcopa** was spoken in Tepoztlán, Morelos, but is now extinct. Classical Nahuatl, **Nahuatlatolli**, is still spoken in the Milpa Alta region by some adults and elders, and a revival movement has recently been initiated in the region.

There are different degrees of Nahuatl retention and shift, from extinct and moribund (dying) varieties to high degrees of vitality in some regions.

An example of the diversity found between Nahuatl languages is the following sentence, which means, "He is not at home": **x-aak** (Balsas, Guerrero); **amo-hka** (Tezcoco, State of Mexico); **am-iga** (Hueyapan, Morelos); **amo yetok** (Puebla Sierra); and **mach nikaan kah** (Rafael Delgado, Veracruz).

NAHUAT LANGUAGES

500,000 speakers

Pipil is an Uto-Aztecan language still spoken in enclaves in El Salvador by a few elders, mainly in the towns of Izalco, Nahuizalco, Santo Domingo de Guzmán, and Cuisnahuat. It is the most southern of the Uto-Aztecan languages, and the first to be recognized as a separate Nahuat language by scholars. Its split from Nahuatl languages dates back to the decline of Teotihuacan, Mexico, in around 800 CE, from where the Pipil group migrated southward through the Gulf of Mexico, later establishing themselves in Guatemala, Nicaragua, and finally El Salvador. It is likely that Pipil will die out within a few decades.

Numeral system

Mesoamerican languages have twentieth-based numeral systems, **pohualli**, meaning "twenty" in Nahuatl. The count up to ten "twenties" is as follows:

20	cempoalli
40	ompoalli
60	yeipohualli
80	nauhpohualli
100	macuilpohualli
120	chicuacempohualli
140	chicompohualli
160	chicueypohualli
180	chicunauhpohualli
200	matlacpohualli

Other ways of counting depend on the form of the object. For example, round-like objects take the classifier **tetl** (stone), as in **centetl pantzin** (a piece of bread).

Today's dramatic decline of Pipil is due mainly to the massacre of many indigenous people during a revolt in the twentieth century in El Salvador, and a prohibition by local authorities of speaking Pipil, which prevented indigenous people from presenting themselves with a distinct identity.

Other Nahuat languages include the closest relative to Pipil, Pochutec (still spoken in the Oaxaca Isthmus at the beginning of the twentieth century, now extinct), the Sierra Norte de Puebla Nahuat, which presents high degrees of language retention, and Veracruz Nahuat, which has one of the largest number of speakers of languages in the Nahuatl group.

A language feature unique to Pipil and the Nahuat languages most closely related to it is the voicing and velarization of the unvoiced phoneme /k/. This feature is not shared by any other language in the Nahuatl group.

Endangerment and extinction

Some indigenous languages have become extinct, or nearly extinct, due to intense pressures on their speakers, including genocide and forced assimilation. Pipil and two other unrelated neighboring languages, Lenca and Cacapoera, were obliterated after the suppression of their communities' revolt for territorial rights and justice, meaning that few speakers learnt Pipil after the 1930s. Ironically, today, the same agencies that forbade the use of Pipil are trying to reintroduce it.

Right *The Pico de Orizaba volcano in the state of Veracruz, Mexico, where Veracruz Nahuat is spoken.*

OTOMANGUEAN

2 million speakers

Below A page from the Mixtec Codex Fejeváry-Mayer. Mixtec is an Otomanguean language.

The Otomanguean language family illustrates the complexity of linguistic diversification in Mexico. The family consists of twenty different named languages, most of which show extreme internal variation, and could themselves be termed separate language groups. This is especially the case for Zapotec (which has at least forty local varieties), and Mixtec (with a similar number). Other Otomanguean languages include Amuzgo, Chatino, Chichimec, Chinantec, Chocho, Chontal, Cuicatec, Ixcatec, Matlazinca, Mazahua, Mazatec, Ocuiltec, Otomi, Pame, Popoloca, Tlapanec, and Triqui.

Count to 10

Ñuu Savi	
i'in	1
ui	2
uni	3
kumi	4
u'un	5
iñu	6
ucha	7
una	8
iin	9
uchi	10

The most widely spoken of the Otomanguean languages are Zapotec and Mixtec, with more than 400,000 speakers each, followed by Otomi and Mazatec, with nearly 300,000 each. All of these languages were originally spoken in the state of Oaxaca, Mexico.

Due to migration, speakers of several of these languages can be found in urban areas in Mexico and the United States, notably in Mexico City, Los Angeles, Tucson, and Houston.

In certain cases migration is so high that entire communities in Mexico are known to be left only with elders, women, and children, while most men work abroad. Many speakers living and working in the United States have reinforced their sense of belonging to an indigenous community, creating associations of indigenous people while away from their communities.

Otomanguean languages are tonal, with at least three basic tones, and present very elaborate sound systems. Some of them have developed whistled speech, which follows the intonational patterns of specific languages such as Chinantec. Speakers of this language dwell in a fairly inaccessible semi-jungle region of Oaxaca, which explains the genesis of the whistling system of communication. A similar case is that of Mazatec.

Mixtec is spoken in two main regional areas of Oaxaca: the coast and the Sierra. The original name of Mixtec is Ñuu Savi, "the language of the rain" (Mixtec of the coast). Mixtec equates body parts with locatives, thus a form such as **nuu** meaning "face" also means "in front of."

Right A Zapotec urn in the shape of a goddess. Zapotec is one of the most widely spoken of the Otomanguean languages.

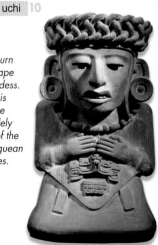

A Riddle in Ñuu Savi (Mixtec of the coast)

Yu'u kuu in soko ñavi ñivi kui
Ta xini kua'achi ta io cha'a kuaanchi
Ta sa' mayu kuii chi.

(Ri Kutora)

I'm a talkative one, I just love to chat.
You'll know me by my tall red hat.
Still at the height of elegance,
My bright green has no pants!

(The Parrot)

YUCATEC MAYA

1 million speakers

Yucatec Maya has more than 1 million speakers. It is an extremely compact language, and has low internal differentiation, even across the different Mexican states that constitute the Yucatec Peninsula (Campeche, Yucatán, Quintana Roo). A good example of this is the opening of a popular riddle, which runs: Na'at le ba'ala' paalen... Between Yucatán and Quintana Roo, the only change is from an "a" to an "o," as seen here in the complete riddle and its solution: Na'at le ba'alo' paalen, U paache' u táan, u táane' u paach: k'aan. The riddle is: "Don't lose track, its front is its back." And the answer is: "A hammock."

Above *A codex dating from c. 1200 CE showing Mayan hieroglyphic writing.*

Unlike the Western perception, riddles are not thought of as an exclusive children's genre. In addition to being a powerful way of socializing children in the native culture, riddles are also commonly used by adults at specific events, such as wakes, or while working in the field.

The high degree of awareness of cultural and linguistic unity within Yucatec Mayan communities allows for a high retention of the indigenous language and culture. This also enables communication in Maya with other neighboring languages, such as its Itzá offspring in Belize, and even with speakers of Mopán, a Maya language also spoken in Guatemala and

Belize, with up to over 80 percent of mutual comprehensibility. The same is the case with Lacandon, spoken in the rainforest in the state of Chiapas, southern Mexico. The high degree of loyalty to and pride in Yucatec Maya reflects a strong demographic presence on the peninsula (about half of the total population), and the fact that the Maya were the last group to be conquered by the Spaniards.

The Yucatec Maya are famous for using zero as early as 350 BCE for precise ritual, as well as for agronomical calendars and hieroglyphic writing, which can be seen on numerous monuments in the Yucatán peninsula.

Language games in Yucatec Maya

Language games are a long-established way of asserting a Maya identity. A good example of this is the language of the **Zuyua**, in which the **Dzules**, or Maya nobles, were initiated in pre-Hispanic times. The language was a type of code, which included riddles for the initiates (**Chilam Balam**, or jaguar-priests). For example, they would be asked to bring "a firefly by night that has been licked by a jaguar" (in other words a burning cigar).

The Popul Vuh

The *Popol Vuh*, also known as *The Book of Counsel*, the sacred book of the Kiché Maya, is the oldest written source for the Maya language family. Based on a lost Maya hieroglyphic codex, it was written around the middle of the sixteenth century and transcribed into the roman script in the seventeenth century. It is about the origin of the Kiché people, the creation of man in different forms and materials, and the adventures of two brothers in the war of the gods.

QUECHUA

9 million speakers

Quechua is the largest surviving indigenous language of the Americas, centered on southern Peru and spoken in six countries extending through the Andean region from southern Colombia to the northern borders of Argentina. Dialects are diverse. Quechua has occasionally been granted official status in Peru, but it mainly survives in rural areas. The name "Quechua" (also Quichua in Ecuador) is a Spanish spelling of qhišwa, meaning "valley" or "temperate zone" intermediate between coast and highlands. From the Spanish conquest of Peru in 1532, the language was associated with the Inca capital at Cuzco (qusqu meaning "navel").

Above *The regions of South America where Quechua is spoken.*

Below right *Quechua now has official status, which means that literacy levels, even in remote Andean regions, are improving.*

Cords as symbols

Central to Inca administration was the **qhipu** (spelled **quipu** in Spanish), bundles of knotted cords with symbolic meaning. They were evidently used for accounting, but may also have served other purposes, e.g., to support narratives.

Quechua had, however, originally been the language of the coast around Lima, particularly used by the Chincha peoples but spreading northward through trade in the first millennium CE. The Inca empire, at the time largely Aymara-speaking, expanded northward from the Cuzco region, and coalesced through marriage with the Chincha realm in the mid-fifteenth century, adopting Quechua as a common language. Inca aggression expanded the empire northward to Quito, and south into Chile.

The Incas actively spread Quechua, inviting noble youths in conquered regions to be educated in Cuzco, and sending out substantial colonies (**mitmaq**, meaning "transplants") into the new domains. Later adopted as a **lengua general** (common tongue) by the Spanish, Quechua spread further, into the mines of Potosí in Bolivia, the settlements in Tucumán, northern Argentina, and Christian missions in Paraguay and Brazil.

Quechua written literature flowered immediately after the Spanish conquest, with plays such as *Ollantay* and *The Tragedy of the End of*

Atahuallpa, symbolic of resistance struggles occurring as late as 1780. The language was widely adopted by the **criollo** landowners in order to distance themselves from the urban elite in Lima. It achieved little official recognition in the liberation wars of the early nineteenth century, and the speaking population was considerably weakened in the twentieth century by widespread drift to the cities. Despite this, Quechua was declared a joint official language of Peru from 1975 to 1979, and now has official status in Peru and Bolivia. As a result, the level of literacy is at last increasing in these countries.

GUARANÍ

5 million speakers

Along with Spanish, Guaraní is the joint official language of Paraguay. Among the few indigenous languages of the Americas with official status (others being Quechua and Aymara), it is the only one with a domestic role equal to Spanish. It is represented equally in the constitution and in state-produced textbooks. The name Guaraní supposedly derives from guaryny, meaning "war." The Tupi-Guaraní languages had spread widely through the river systems of eastern South America (the Amazon and Rio de la Plata) long before the arrival of Europeans in the early sixteenth century.

Above *Schoolchildren in Mato Grosso do Sul, Brazil, where the Mbyá variety of Guaraní is spoken.*

Count to 5

Guaraní		Tupinambá
petẽi	1	oiepé
mokõi	2	mukúi
mbohapy	3	mosapýre
irundy	4	irundy(k)
po	5	ãmbo, xepó

Po literally means "hand," as **pó** does in Tupinambá. **Oiepé** in Guaraní means "all together." In modern Guaraní a further set of digits built on **po** represents 6–10: **pote, pokõi, poapy, porundy, pa**. Numbers above 4 or 5 are usually borrowed from Spanish.

Tupinambá, the northern form of Guarani, was adopted as a **língua geral** (contact language) by the Portuguese in Brazil, and promoted by the Jesuit missionaries. Guaraní, to the south, in the zone of the Spanish Conquest, is closely related, and remained mutually intelligible with Tupinambá. In Paraguay, the speakers of Guaraní contracted military and marital alliances with the Spaniards. Jesuit missionaries were even more influential here than in Brazil. They were, however, expelled by royal decrees from Portuguese territories (1759) and Spanish territories (1767), and use of the indigenous contact languages was banned; Tupinambá succumbed, but in Paraguay Guaraní persisted.

Paraguay, unlike other American colonies, did not have a Spanish-speaking elite, rather a mixed (**mestizo**) community with bilingual families. This continued after independence in 1813. Guaraní, typically acquired in the home, has a rustic, "folksy" image, contrasting with Spanish, which is seen as a metropolitan, business-oriented medium.

Guaraní has six vowels, spelled "a," "e," "i," "o," "u," and "y." The last is a low central vowel as in English "duh." The language has nasal harmony: in general, if a word contains a nasal sound, it cannot contain a non-nasal sound. Affixes, too, come in nasal and non-nasal varieties, selected to match the word root, for example, **pe-ike-pa** (you-enter-all) but **pe-sẽ-mba** (you-exit-all). However, there are irregularities, and pre-nasalized stops—"mb," "nt," "nd," and "ngg"—count as non-nasal within a word stem.

Varieties of Guaraní include the Paraguayan standard, **Avañẽ'ẽ**, meaning "plainsmen's language," spoken by some 484,000 people, more than 80 percent of the Paraguayan population. Around the capital, Asunción, most speak Guaraní mixed with Spanish as **jopará**, meaning "mixture." There is also Mbyá, spoken to the northeast and in Brazil (8,000 speakers) and Paraguay (8,000 speakers); and Guarayo/Chiriguano to the southwest (49,000 speakers, perhaps 300 in Paraguay, but 70 percent in Bolivia and 30 percent in Argentina).

AYMARA

2.2 million speakers

Aymara (Aymará) is a major language of central South America, now spoken in eastern Bolivia (1.6 million speakers), southern Peru (420,000 speakers), and northern Chile (15,000 speakers). Most of its speakers are workers on the land, the staple crop being potatoes. The language has recently gained official status in Bolivia and Peru, but not as a national language on a par with Spanish. The Aymara area now bisects the Quechua-speaking zone (see map on p. 202), but it seems once to have been spoken more widely in northern Peru. For example, Cajamarca, a town in Peru, is an Aymara name—q'aja marca (valley-town).

Above *Flag-bearers at an Aymara religious ceremony in Tiwanaku, Bolivia. Most speakers of the Aymara language live in Bolivia.*

Aymara is the largest member of the language family named Jaqi (a person) or Aru (a speech), whose other members are the closely related Jaqaru (2,000 speakers) and Kawki (possibly just eleven speakers), spoken southeast of Lima.

Aymara was the language of the Incas until their fusion with the Chincha in the fourteenth century. However, the marked structural similarity between Aymara and Quechua (with complex verb forms built on the same pattern) suggests that speakers of these languages have been in close contact, often bilingual, for more than a millennium. (Some scholars believe that the two languages belong to a single family.)

The Aymara (known to the Incas and Spaniards as Colla, from **k'ullu** meaning "hard") had little to do with the Spanish conquest of Peru, but were Christianized soon afterward. In current use, their language contains many loanwords from Spanish, extending even to surviving elements of their traditional religion; for example, **wirjina**, from Spanish **virgen**, represents the Earth Mother. Although Aymara was soon accepted as

a **lengua general** in its region—the first grammar being written in 1603 by Fra Ludovico Bertonio—it has continued to lose speakers to Spanish and Quechua until very recently. A new orthography was devised by Juan de Dios Yapita in 1968.

Like Quechua, Aymara has only three distinctive vowels: "a," "i," and "u." But in the context of the uvular consonant "q," both "i" and "u" sound like "e" and "o." Aymara is also highly agglutinative, as is Quechua. Its nouns and, especially, verbs are made up of strings of short parts in a determinate order, each part having a transparent meaning. For example: **aruskip-t'a-si-p-xa-ña-naka-sa-ki-puni-rakï-spa-wa**, which translates as "We really must communicate with one another."

Aymara distinguishes future tense (indeterminate) from present/past (determinate), and personal knowledge from hearsay. These properties, as well as the productive and easily interpretable word structure, prompted Guzmán de Rojas in 1969 to suggest its use as an ideal link language for computer translation.

Count to 10

Aymara		Quechua
maya	1	huk
paya	2	iskay
kimsa	3	kimsa
pusi	4	tawa
p'isqa	5	pichqa
suxta	6	suqta
paqallqu	7	qanchis
kimsaqallqu	8	pusaq
llatunka	9	isqun
tunka	10	chunka

MAPUDUNGUN

Mapudungun, meaning "land-speech," is the language of the Mapuche, or "land-people," indigenous to central Chile. It is also known as Araucanian, after the town of Arauco on the Pacific coast. Still spoken in Chile, Mapudungun also has about half as many speakers in Argentina. The communities there are fairly new, due to Mapuche domination in the eighteenth and nineteenth centuries over other groups who spoke unrelated languages. Despite fierce resistance, the Mapuche had yielded their northern regions in Chile to Inca conquest in the early fifteenth century, including the present-day capital, Santiago.

Above *The flag of the Mapuche Nation, held aloft at a march in Santiago, Chile.*

Related languages

Mapudungun, although spoken over a wide area in Chile and Argentina, is fairly uniform. The most divergent variety is Huilliche (south-people) spoken by a few thousand people south of the main Araucanian region in Valdivia, Chile, and on Chiloe Island off the Chilean coast. This variety is called **ce-suŋun**, meaning "people-speech," corresponding to **če-θuŋun** in the standard variety.

The Mapuche accepted with pride the Incas' name for them: **purumawqa**, which means "uncivilized enemies." They were also known to the Spanish as **promaucaes** or simply **auca**. In the mid-sixteenth century they successfully resisted Spanish invasion and settlement, establishing an independent zone in the present-day provinces of Arauco, Biobío, Malleco, and Cautín, with Spanish colonies to the north and south. During this period, the Mapuche assimilated by force or colonization other groups, notably the Pehuenche (Araucaria-pine people) in the eastern Andes, the Ranquelche (reed people) in the north of Argentina near Córdoba, the Puelche (eastern people) in the Argentinian Pampas, and the Tehuelche (valiant people) in the south of Chile and Argentina. All these names are Mapudungun.

The Chilean government finally suppressed the independence of the Mapuche in 1882, at about the same time as the Argentinian government destroyed their cousins' communities (1879–81). In Chile the Mapuche were confined to discontinuous **reducciones** in the southern part of their region, within Malleco and Cautín; they were further dispossessed during the Pinochet regime, 1973–89. It is now estimated that only 30 percent of the 928,000 ethnic Mapuche speak their language; more than 100,000 Mapuche are now resident in Santiago.

The first grammar of Mapudungun was written by Luis de Valdivia (1560–1642) in 1606. The Mapudungun sound system has six vowels, "a," "e," "i," "o," "u," and a back unrounded vowel, here written "ü." It is a suffixing language, with a complex system of agglutinative verb-endings, typologically similar to Quechua and Aymara.

Count to 10

kiñe	1
epu	2
küla	3
meli	4
kechu	5
kayu	6
regle	7
pura	8
aylla	9
mari	10

Higher numbers are constructed from these items (20 is **epu** (2) + **mari** (10). But 100 (**pataka**) and 1000 (**waranqa**) are borrowed through Aymara from Quechua (**pachaq**, **waranqa**).

DAKOTA

26,000 speakers

Dakota means "people" in the language of the Sioux. They were Plains Indians, originally from the upper Mississippi, who moved west in the seventeenth and eighteenth centuries, their livelihood revolutionized by the **shunke wakan** ("dog-holy," in other words, horse). Different phonetic forms of the word refer to different groups: "Dakota" to the Santee and Sisseton in the east (**Isanti**, "knife," for a local lake); "Nakota" to the Yankton and Yanktonai in the central plains (**ihanktowan**, "village at the end"); and "Lakota" to the Teton of the west. In fact, Nakota represents better the language of two groups further north, the Assiniboine and the Stoney Sioux, both now mostly in Canada. The Lakota were involved in sustained armed resistance to the U.S. Army between 1865 and 1890. Crazy Horse and Sitting Bull were Lakota chiefs, and The Little Big Horn and Wounded Knee battles that they respectively won and lost.

Dakota is notable for its sentence-final particles that determine the force of what has been said—for example, assertion (**kšt**), question (**hųwo**), command (**yo**). Females typically use variants heard as milder (**kšto, hųwe, ye**). The standard greeting to a stranger is **hau**, or **hau kola**: hence the movie convention of "How."

CHOCTAW-CHICKASAW

10,000 speakers

Choctaw (9,211 speakers, perhaps 8 percent of the tribe) and its close relative Chickasaw (1,000 speakers, 3 percent) make up the western branch of the Muskogean languages of the U.S. southeast, with Creek and Seminole as major languages of the west. Originally from the mid-Mississippi area, the Chickasaw later moved east and the Choctaw south. Both groups resisted Hernando de Soto's (c. 1496–1542) Spanish incursion in 1540. In the early eighteenth century, the Choctaw and Chickasaw maintained peaceable relations with the French, and, after 1763, with settlers, the four major Muskogean tribes (along with the Cherokee) becoming known as the Five Civilized Tribes. A pidgin of Choctaw-Chickasaw, "Mobile Trade Language" (**Yamá**), became the lingua franca of the southeast in the eighteenth century. Since Andrew Jackson's (1767–1845) great Indian removal of 1830–35, most of the Choctaw and Chickasaw have lived in Oklahoma, though smaller groups stayed in Mississippi and Louisiana. Choctaw speakers worked as code-talkers in both World Wars. Their language is known as **chahta anumpa** in Choctaw.

Left *Cherokees in North Carolina, 1939, from a group who escaped the move to Oklahoma.*

Left *A pottery workshop in Acoma Pueblo, New Mexico, where Keres is spoken.*

CHEROKEE

12,000 speakers

Cherokee is an Iroquoian language, originally spoken in North Carolina and Georgia, but related to languages such as Oneida, Seneca, Mohawk, and Tuscarora far to the north. For their peaceable relations with white settlers the Cherokee were counted among the Five Civilized Tribes. They also developed their own literacy, the syllabary invented in 1809 by the (previously illiterate) Sequoyah. Nevertheless, in 1838–39, they were illegally forced to move to Oklahoma. Oklahoma Cherokee now live separately from North Carolina Cherokee, descendants of those who escaped the "Trail of Tears." The name "Cherokee" is from the Creek language, meaning "people with another language." The Cherokee self-name is unpronounceable in Cherokee and has been adapted as **Tsalagi**.

O'ODHAM

12,000 speakers

O'odham is spoken in southern Arizona in the United States and in Sonora, Mexico. It has two main dialects, Tohono O'odham, meaning "desert people," and Akimel O'odham, meaning "river people"; previously these were called Papago and Pima. It is an Uto-Aztecan language, related to Shoshone, Comanche, and Hopi to the north and east, but also (distantly) to Nahuatl, the Aztec language in the south. Plurals are usually formed with a reduplicated infix: **ceoj** (boy), **cecoj** (boys); **gogs** (dog), **gogogs** (dogs); **ko:ji** (brand; verb singular), **kokji** (brand; verb plural). However, transitive verbs agree with their object, not subject: **cecoj 'o g ko:ji ceposid**, means "the boys are branding the pig"; **ceoj 'o g kokji ha-cecposid**, means "the boy is branding the pigs."

BLACKFOOT

7,000 speakers

Blackfoot is an Algonquian language spoken on both sides of the United States–Canadian border. There are four dialects: Blackfeet (South Piegan) spoken in Montana; and Siksika (literally "black-foot," named for this people's moccasins), Kainaa (blood), and Apatohsopiikani (or Piegan) spoken in Alberta. Fewer than half the 15,000 Blackfoot population speak the language, very few of them in the United States. Blackfoot is currently undergoing a major shift, with a distinct young people's dialect emerging. Traditionally the Algonquian were a powerful tribe, subsisting on buffalo, but by 1900 the buffalo were extinct. A typical insult in Blackfoot is: **máipaxkóxsinisikápokmipúminàs** (your lice have a very bad death-dirty taste).

KERES

8,000 speakers

Keres is a group of dialects spoken in the Pueblos of New Mexico: to the east, Cochiti, San Felipe, Santa Ana, Santo Domingo, and Zia; and to the west, Acoma and Laguna. Keres is unrelated to other Pueblos languages, of which there are over a dozen. Acoma Keres has a system of prefixes, jointly marking subject (S) and object (O), for example, **s'-** (I [S], him/her [O]); **sk'u-** (he/she [S], me [O]). Hence, **s'îita** (I stepped on him/her) and **sk'ûita** (He/She stepped on me). Some prefixes are used as possession markers: **sk'ad^{y}ñuuni** (my pottery) and **s'ad^{y}á** (my pet). The "pet" word is obligatory when referring to owned animals—**kawâawu s'ad^{y}á** (my horse; literally, horse my-pet)—a pervasive feature of languages in southwestern U.S.A.

Left *Lake Patzcuaro, Mexico, where one of the main dialects of Purepecha is spoken.*

HUAVE

20,000 speakers

Huave is an isolate language, not related to any other language. The people, whose culture is based on fishing, dwell on the southeastern coast of the Tehuantepec isthmus in Oaxaca, Mexico. They call themselves **Ikoots**, meaning "we" in Huave, and **mareños** in local Spanish, derived from one of the towns they live in, San Mateo del Mar. They also live in the towns of San Dionisio and San Francisco del Mar. Their language is called Ombeayiuts, meaning "our mouth" in Huave.

The history of the Huave is one of intense contact and conflict with neighboring groups. About a century before the Spanish conquest (1519–21), the Huave occupied an area near Mixe Zoque and Chontal lands, but Zapotec expansion forced them to move to their current territory. In the past the Huave learned Zapotec, and currently learn Spanish, to exchange products in the local markets, which the Zapotecs dominate, but Zapotecs never learn Ombeayiuts.

Although Ombeayiuts experiences language shift in San Francisco del Mar, there have been a number of efforts to protect the language, including the production of songs played on the local radio, and the work of Huave writers with a strong sense of loyalty to, and pride in, their language. Contrary to some claims, Ombeayiuts is a single language, with high levels of mutual intelligibility among its different communities.

PUREPECHA

150,000 speakers

The word Purepecha derives from **P'urhe** (person) plus the plural **echa** (persons). The term and its variants, P'urhepecha and P'urhempe, refer to the people and their language, most commonly known as Tarascan (from the Purepecha word **Tarascue** meaning "father-in-law, son-in-law").

Purepecha is spoken in central Michoacán, Mexico, on the lakeside, and in the **cañada** (gully), swamp, and Sierra areas, corresponding to its four main dialects and occupying about 6 percent of the Michoacán territory. It has no proven genetic relationship to any other language.

The longstanding history of retention of the Purepecha language and culture stems back to pre-Hispanic times, when Purepecha territory was never conquered. Some indications of this high sense of autonomy are the status of Purepecha as a lingua franca before Spanish invasion, plus the widespread prevalence of Purepecha toponyms in their territory, such as Tzintzuntzan, the center of their political power in pre-Columbian times.

As part of a movement to reinforce the present-day use of the language, threatened as it is by global forces, such as high rates of migration and urbanization, some initiatives have been undertaken, including an Academy of the Purepecha language.

Left *The Purepecha Day of the Dead celebrations are famous throughout Mexico.*

Left *The Kickapoo Red Earth Festival in Oklahoma.*

Right *Tarahumara farmland in Chihuahua, Mexico.*

RARAMURI

100,000 speakers

Raramuri has the second-largest number of speakers in the Uto-Aztecan language family. It is commonly known as Tarahumara, a name adapted into Spanish from another ethnic group, the Tepehuas (Tarúmare). Its population inhabits the vast territory of the Sierra de Chihuahua in the north of Mexico, the largest Mexican state. The word "Raramuri" (or the names of its dialects Raromari, Raramari) derives from **rara** (foot) and **muri** (runner), an allusion to the people's great capacity for traveling enormous distances by foot. Raramuri has many loanwords from Spanish, for example, **riosi** (gods, from **dioses**), **gurusi** (cross, from **cruz**), **geso** (cheese, from **queso**), and **asukari** (sugar, from **azucár**). Counting to ten is as follows: 1—**bire**, 2—**okwa**, 3—**biekia**, 4—**nao**, 5—**mari**, 6—**ushani**, 7—**kitzao**, 8—**osa nao**, 9—**kimakoi**, 10—**makoi**.

HUICHOL

40,000 speakers

Huichol (usually known as Wirrakira by the Huichol people) has the third-largest number of speakers in the Uto-Aztecan language family. The language is known as Vixaritari Vaniuki in the states of Jalisco and Nayarit, western Mexico. The Huichol have experienced a growth in population, and there are still some monolingual speakers of the language. The vitality of these communities is related to the maintenance of their own religion, blended with Catholic practices (and associated with the peyote cactus, a powerful hallucinogenic), together with their isolation and the prestige of the **Marakame**, or shaman. As an expression of cultural and linguistic encroachment, the Huichol people still refer to the **mestizos** of Guadalajara, Jalisco, as "the Spanish from Guadalajara."

KICKAPOO

250 speakers

Kickapoo belongs to the Algonquian language family and has around 250 speakers, mostly in Mexico. In the United States, the language is now nearly extinct. The people were originally from the northern Great Lakes region in the United States, but as a result of forced migration they were moved south to reservations in Oklahoma and Kansas. In the mid-nineteenth century, some Kickapoo migrated to El Nacimiento Kikapú, in Coahuila, Mexico.

In Mexico young Kickapoos are trilingual: Kickapú-Spanish-English. They have relative wealth, when compared with poorer Mexican farmers. Until recently, Mexican Kickapoos still used the "whistling" language of courtship, **onowechikepi**, mimicking the intonational contour, pitch, vowel length, and cluster vowel groups of the spoken language. Originally a system based on playing a flute, and practiced by young male Kickapoos, it has since been abandoned.

In the 1980s Mexican Kickapoos still maintained part of their ancestral religion, which included prayers to the deer, their sacred animal, and a clearcut sexual division of labor, men collecting the raw material, **tulle** to build their tepees.

WAYUU/GUAJIRO

305,000 speakers

Wayuunaiki, language of the Wayuu, is the most populous indigenous language in Colombia and Venezuela, and one of the most vigorous. In Colombia, to the west, it has about 135,000 speakers, while in Venezuela another 170,000 people speak it. It is spoken in the northernmost peninsula of the two countries, Guajira, eastward into the northwest of Zulia. The language and people are known in Spanish as **Guajiro**, but for the Wayuu this term means "settlers." Their word for person is **wayuu**, specifically of the Wayuu people, contrasting with two kinds of foreigner, **kusina** (indigenous) and **alihuna** (non-indigenous, civilized). Most speakers are monolingual, especially in Colombia.

It is a Maipurean (or Arawakan) language, of the family most widespread in South America and (once) the Caribbean. Its closest relative is **Anyuu**, or **Paraujano**, a language (now with fewer than twenty speakers) spoken on the western shore of Lake Maracaibo, Venezuela. Since Spanish contact (1499), the Wayuu have kept apart, farming with cattle, sheep, and goats. A settlement is a **miichipala**, meaning "place of houses," with up to 100 people living in nuclear families.

PÁEZ

75,000 speakers

Páez is known to its speakers as **Nasa Yuwe**, meaning "human speech," and is spoken in an area of peasant farmers, near Popayán in Cauca, south central Colombia. Only half of the Páez still speak their language, but of those who do about half are monolingual. Nowadays, Páez is taught in schools, and the low prestige associated with using it is gradually diminishing. The **Consejo Regional Indígena del Cauca** (CRIC) is active in its defense.

The prehistory of Páez is unknown, although past theories associated it with the Chibcha language to its north and the Barbacoan languages to its south, such as Awa Pit and Tsafiki (Colorado) in Ecuador. The documented history of the Páez people relates bitter struggles with the Spanish until the eighteenth century, when they largely accepted Christianity. Currently, the Páez live close to a center of insurgency and government counter-insurgency.

Left *The landscape of the Cauca region of Colombia, where Páez is spoken.*

Left *The Eastern Andes, Peru, where speakers of the Jivaroan languages live.*

Left *A young Emberá boy in Ipeti village, Panama.*

JIVAROAN LANGUAGES

100,000 speakers

The four closely related Jivaroan languages, spoken in the eastern Andes, all have substantial speaker communities: Shuar/Jívaro (47,000 speakers) in southern Ecuador; Aguaruna/Awajun (38,000 speakers); Huambisa (9,000 speakers); and Achuar/Achual/Shiwiar (5,000 speakers) in northern Peru. **Shuar** means "people" and **achuar** "people of the swamp palm (**achu**)." The Aguaruna successfully resisted Inca conquest. Invaded by the Spanish from 1534, the Jívaro and Aguaruna rebelled in 1599 and remained largely independent until 1816. The Aguaruna rebelled against the Jesuits in 1886. Now reconciled to the **apach** (Spanish-speaking) governments, and able to speak their own language (and Quechua), their independence continues.

EMBERÁ

80,000 speakers

Emberá, meaning "people," is a Chocoan language, now spoken on both sides of the Panama–Colombia border, with a lesser population on the Panamanian side (10,000 speakers). (It is spoken in the same areas as the related Woun-Meo language, which has 6,000 speakers between the two countries.) This may be the result of a historic spread of the community from a previous concentration in the Chocó, on the northern Pacific coast of modern Colombia. Currently, the community extends south to Cauca, and north into Córdoba. There is great phonetic variation within Emberá, to the extent that one southern dialect pronounces this word for the language as "Epena."

WICHÍ LHAMTÉS

45,000 speakers

The Wichí, until recently nomadic, are indigenous to the Chaco of Argentina and Bolivia, near the Pilcomayo and Bermejo rivers, currently under pressure from the spread of cattle ranching and soya-bean agriculture. They call their language Wichí Lhamtés, rejecting another commonly used name, Mataco. It has four major dialects, of different sizes: Vejoz (25,000 speakers) in the city of Embarcación (Salta); Guisnay (15,000 speakers) in eastern Salta (Mosconi, Tartagal, and Misión La Paz) and western Formosa (Ramón Lista county); Teuco (3,000 speakers) further south on the Bermejo (or Teuco) river in Salta (Rivadavia county) and Chaco; and Noctén (2,000 speakers) in Bolivia.

CAMPA LANGUAGES

50,000 speakers

The Campa (or pre-Andean) group of the Maipurean languages is found in the region of the Apurímac, Ene, Perené, and Tambo rivers, tributaries of the Ucayali, as well as the Urubamba, in the eastern foothills of the Peruvian Andes. The family includes several closely related languages: Asháninka, Ashéninka, Axaninca, Machigenga, Nomatsigenga, Gran Pajonal Campa, and Caquinta. Having rebuffed the Franciscans' attempts at Christian proselytism in the late eighteenth century, they largely resisted European interference until the expansion of the railways under the (British) Peruvian Corporation from 1886. Most cultural development now involves US Protestant missionaries. Bilingualism in Spanish and Quechua is increasing.

Left *Ticuna villagers on the Amazon. The Ticuna language is an isolate, with no known relations.*

TICUNA

41,000 speakers

The Ticuna (or Tukuna) language community live on the upper Amazon around the Colombian city of Leticia, divided between Brazil (25,000 speakers), Peru (8,000 speakers), and Colombia (8,000 speakers). As a language, it is an isolate and has no known relations. It has three levels of tones, but most word roots exceed one syllable, creating a pattern of pitch contours. Historically, the Ticuna people seem to have previously lived up-country, but they moved into the Amazon after their traditional enemies, the Omagua, succumbed to Spanish colonization and Portuguese slavers. Nowadays, language use is stronger in more remote villages than in Leticia.

SHIPIBO-CONIBO

30,000 speakers

Shipibo-Conibo is a Panoan language. The Tacana-Panoan languages are all found within lowland Amazonia, to the north, east, and south, down into Bolivia. It is spoken on the Ucayali river in Peru, north of the area inhabited by the Campa. Other subgroups speaking this language are the Piskibo and Shetebo, **-bo** being a plural marker in this language. They appear to have come to this region in the eighth century, and then defended it against all enemies, including the Spaniards, from 1657 until the late eighteenth century. Recovering from the devastating effects of the early twentieth-century rubber boom, they are now embracing literacy in their language.

AWA PIT

21,000 speakers

The Awa Pit language, also known as Cuaiquer, is spoken in Nariño, southwestern Colombia, and (since the early twentieth century) in Carchi, northwestern Ecuador. It is a Barbacoan language, hence a relative of Guambiano to its north, and Tsafiki (Colorado) to its south (in Ecuador). Awa Pit appears to have been influenced in its grammar by Quechua, owing to Inca imperial forays northward in the fourteenth century: the location ending **-ta** (for example, **Pastu-ta**, meaning "to Pasto") and the possession marker **-p** or **-pa** after vowels and consonants respectively (e.g. **a-p** meaning "my," **Santos-pa** meaning "of Santos"). Quechua is still spoken nearby, and is called **Inga/Ingano** (from "Inca").

KAINGÁNG

21,000 speakers

Kaingáng (originally known as Guaianá, and later as Coroado) is spoken in four contiguous states in the extreme south of Brazil, namely São Paulo, Paraná, Santa Catarina, and Río Grande do Sul. Its speakers now live in a patchwork of thirty scattered settlements in this extended area, traditionally of pine forests, which they dominated before the start of Portuguese infiltration in 1812. Kaingáng—with its eastern neighbor and close relative Xokleng (Chocrén), now comprising 250 speakers—is the southernmost member of the Jê, or Gê, family, which extends throughout Brazil. In fact, Kaingáng alone now makes up 50 percent of the speakers of this family.

GUAHIBO

24,000 speakers

The Guahibo (also known as Sikuani, though they reject the name) live in the eastern plains of Colombia, verging into Venezuela (2,000 speakers). The language is related to its close neighbors (Cuiba, Playero, Macaguán [Hitnú], and Guayabero), but not to others. It has, however, been influenced by neighboring Maipurean languages (Achagua and Piapoca to the west and south). All these communities are traditionally hunter-gatherers, whom the Jesuits never succeeded in congregating in settlements. The Guahibo, the most numerous of the communities, took advantage of the Jesuits' expulsion in 1767 to settle and dominate the river system. This has been contested in the nineteenth and twentieth centuries by the spread of cattle ranches eastward.

CHIQUITANO

20,000 speakers

Chiquitano (also Tarapecosi) is spoken in the plains of eastern Bolivia. Ethnic Chiquitanos number some 47,000 (2,000 in Brazil's Mato Grosso), but only a minority speak the language. Different indigenous groups were brought together by Jesuit missionaries in the seventeenth century, and Chiquitano was designated the lingua franca. Although the Jesuits were expelled in 1767, others stepped in to keep the Chiquitano together. A Chiquitano standard language was documented: one feature was a style used only by males, with masculine gender assigned to many nouns. During the Chaco War (1928–35) Bolivia used Chiquitano speakers for coded messages; but Spanish has become universal, and diverse dialects have replaced the standard.

WARAO

20,000 speakers

The Warao (a self-designation from either **waja**, "sandbank" or **wa**, "boat," and **arao**, "people") live in the Orinoco delta in the east of Venezuela, extending into Guyana and Surinam. The language is most vigorous in Venezuela. Literally "little Venice," Venezuela was given its name by the explorer Alonso de Ojeda (c. 1465–1515) in 1499 after his first sighting of Warao houses built on stilts over the water. The Orinoco, too, has a Warao etymology: **wiri-noko**, "rowing-place." This language is agglutinative, that is, sentences can be made up of strings of affixes, each affix making a clear contribution to the complete meaning of the sentence. Warao is an isolate and has no known relatives.

NIVACLÉ & TOBA

18,000 speakers/20,000 speakers

The Nivaclé (meaning "human") live in a community on the southern edge of Filadelfia in the Chaco region of Paraguay. They have also been known as Ashlushlay and Chulupí, but they reject the latter as it is considered derogatory. Their language belongs to the Matácoan family, like Wichí Lhamtés. Somewhat more distantly related is the Guaycuruan language of the Toba in Argentina, a neighboring traditional enemy. (Their name is from Guaraní **tobá**, meaning "forehead," since they shave the front of their heads in mourning.) They call themselves **Qom-lik**, meaning "people." Both groups have suffered from the devastation of Chaco through the Gran Chaco War (1928–35), and subsequent exploitative tree-felling, ranching, and agriculture.

ENDANGERED LANGUAGES

ENDANGERED LANGUAGES

An estimated 6,800 languages are spoken in the world today. By the end of this century, as many as 90 percent of these languages will have disappeared entirely, replaced by more widely used (national and/or global) languages. A language is said to be endangered when it is threatened with total extinction, the loss of all its speakers. This typically occurs through destructive contact with another language, where one language goes on to replace the other. In "language shift," speakers abandon the language of their parents in favor of another language.

Other causes of endangerment, such as massive population loss due to disease, warfare, or natural disaster, are far less common. UNESCO has established a set of criteria for determining when languages are likely to be endangered: (1) Is the language being passed on to the next generation? (2) What is its absolute number of speakers? (3) What proportion of the indigenous community still speaks the language? (4) Is the use of the language diminishing as it loses domains of use (e.g., in print or in the workplace/home)? (5) How does the language respond to new domains (e.g., mass media and the Internet)? (6) What materials are available for language education and literacy? (7) What are governmental and institutional attitudes and policies, including official status and use of the language? (8) What are community attitudes toward the language? (9) What amount and quality of documentation of the language is available? The first of these,

Left *Linguistic diversity in the South Asia region is seriously threatened.*

ntergenerational transmission, is the most critical factor n a language's vitality: for a language to remain healthy, t must be spoken by children.

Causes of language shift vary considerably, but several overarching factors emerge: urbanization, globalization, and social and cultural dislocation. These reflect imbalances n prestige and power between speakers of the majority anguage and culture and the minority language community. Socioeconomic improvement is usually perceived as tied to knowledge of the dominant language, and to renunciation and abandonment of the minority language and culture.

One commonly used way to assess language vitality is to measure knowledge of a language in each generation. Since he overall life of a language depends not just on the number of current speakers, but also on the promise of future speakers

knowing and using the language, intergenerational transmission is considered to be the most significant factor in determining the future of a language. A fine-grained scale of language vitality was established by the linguist Michael Krauss (1997): (1) the language is spoken by all generations, including all, or nearly all, children; (2) the language is learned by all or most children; (3) the language is spoken by all adults, parental age and up, but learned by few or no children; (4) the language is spoken by adults in their thirties and older but not by younger parents; (5) the language is spoken only by adults in their forties and older; (6) all speakers in their fifties and older; (7) all speakers in their sixties and older; (8) all speakers in their seventies and older; (9) all speakers in their seventies and older, and fewer than ten speakers; (10) extinct, no speakers.

EUROPE

Europe is home to an estimated 239 languages, accounting for only 3.5 percent of the world's total. Approximately 100 or more of them are considered endangered. As elsewhere, determining the exact number of languages and actual speakers is complicated. Some experts believe that Catalan, with 6 million speakers, is the only European language without statewide official status that should not be considered endangered. The linguistic scene in Europe is dominated by a relatively small number of national languages that have absolute supremacy. Many of these, such as English, Spanish, and French also represent (present and past) colonial powers.

Above *Young children being taught at Ireland's only "all Gaelic" school in Lahinch, County Clare. All subjects other than math are taught in Gaelic.*

Thus these languages are globally dominant as well (see Chapter 1). In addition, a large number of European minority languages are related to these national languages, and their marginalized status is further reinforced by being identified as dialects of the majority and official language. France provides an illustrative example. In addition to the sole official language (French), a number of smaller Romance languages are spoken. These include Picard, which is spoken in Picardie and Nord-Pas-de-Calais, and in Belgium. It is considered a distinct language by linguists, the Belgian government, and the European Bureau for Lesser Used Languages. The French government, however, officially views it as a **patois**, or dialect, of French. The total number of speakers is unclear, but experts consider it seriously endangered, with all speakers aged fifty or older.

Speakers of European minority languages are highly organized relative to minority communities elsewhere in the world, and this organization has in some cases led to greater political recognition and even autonomy. North Saami stands out in this regard, having gained semi-autonomy in northern Finland, and general political recognition in Sweden and Norway. In Eastern Europe and, in particular, in Russia, this is less the case. In the regions of the former Soviet Union, there has been a steady decline in the use of indigenous languages since the Second World War, which has accelerated since the Soviet break-up. Although majority languages (such as Belarusian and Ukrainian) have received some autonomy, the minority languages are endangered to varying degrees. Tatar, a Turkic language, is the only one with several million speakers and no official status. Other Turkic varieties (Chuvash, Bashkir, Crimean Tatar, Nogai, to name a few) are all endangered. For some, the situation is extreme: Karaim has only 200 to 300 speakers in Lithuania, all of whom are middle-aged or older.

Official status does not guarantee vitality. Irish is the first official language in Ireland, English is the second official language, but the majority of the population speaks only English. Irish is one of the surviving varieties of Celtic spoken today. It is closely related to two other Celtic languages,

Manx and Scottish Gaelic. The last speaker of Manx died in 1974, although there have been recent attempts to revive the language. Irish has been in decline for more than a century. In 1893, it was spoken by slightly more than 15 percent of the population of Ireland; today it is estimated that only 5 percent use it on a regular basis. However, knowledge of Irish is clearly associated with national and cultural identity, and there is very strong support for Irish language education. The decline of Scottish Gaelic is even more marked. By the 1981 census, only 1.64 percent of the national population above the age of three had knowledge of Gaelic. Since then, language shift has accelerated. Although historically the Presbyterian Church was a stronghold of Gaelic usage, English has been increasingly on the rise, even for worship and Sunday school in recent decades.

There are a handful of languages in Europe that have broad geographic distribution and are spoken across several different geopolitical regions. This includes Romani (more commonly known as the "gypsy" language), a term that actually encompasses a number of different groups, whose linguistic differences are in many cases more language-like than dialect-like. Romani live in small and often nomadic groups, stretching throughout Eastern Europe and beyond into Russia, spreading from Finland in the north, Turkey in the south, and Wales in the west. The total number of speakers of Romani is difficult to assess due to unreliable statistics, but there are probably several million. Although children do continue to learn some varieties of Romani, European governments are generally hostile to Romani language and culture, resulting in policies and attitudes that increase language shift. Some varieties (such as Welsh Romani in Wales, and Finnish Romani in Finland) have very few speakers.

The Vlakh Romani dialects developed during the 500- to 600-year period when gypsies were kept as slaves in parts of Wallachia and Moldova (both part of modern-day Romania). The Vlakh dialects spread throughout Europe in the mid nineteenth century with the end of gypsy slavery, and dialect groups can also be found in the Americas, Australia, and parts of Asia and Africa.

Above *The language of the Romani people is subject to ongoing shift because of European governments' hostility toward its use.*

Count to 10

Vlakh Romani	
jekh	1
duj	2
trin	3
štar	4
pandž	5
šov	6
efta	7
oxto	8
inja	9
deš	10

NORTH AND WEST AFRICA

More than 2,000 languages, or about 30 percent of all the world's languages, are spoken in Africa by just less than 12 percent of the world's total population. The average number of speakers per language is 323,082, and the median is 25,391. Surveys report that 300 or more African languages are seriously endangered, and another 200 nearly extinct or extinct. We do not have accurate sociolinguistic data for most African languages, and so the number of endangered languages is certainly higher than this estimate. Language endangerment in the African continent differs from the situation in the rest of the world.

Above *Nigeria has the greatest number of endangered languages in Africa.*

Yangkam

Yangkam, a Niger-Congo language of the Bashwara ethnic group, is close to being lost completely. The Yangkam are considered to be the original inhabitants of the Wase area in Nigeria. Speakers today are all more than fifty years old and are bilingual in Hausa. We lack the most basic information on Yangkam.

Speakers of one African language rarely shift to speak a European language (such as English, French, German, or Spanish); the shift is most often in the direction of another African language, such as Swahili in East Africa.

Indigenous languages in North Africa are threatened by Arabic, which is the official language of the governments in this region. The indigenous peoples and their languages here are generally known as Berber (historically meaning "barbarian"), although they themselves prefer the ethnonym Amazigh, which means "free people." There is less language diversity in North Africa than in other parts of the continent, where a wider variety of languages are spoken by very small communities. It is difficult to provide an accurate count of the Amazigh languages, as the speakers themselves, in efforts to underscore their unity, assert that they speak a single unified language. Linguists agree that there are many distinct Amazigh languages, with some estimates as high as 100. A more conservative estimate puts the total in the vicinity of twenty-five. Be that as it may, only two languages are fully robust,

with all children learning the language: Tarifit in Morocco (1.5 million speakers) and Siwi in Egypt (10,000 speakers). All others are experiencing some level of shift, and some are seriously endangered. Fully 70 percent of the Amazigh inhabitants of North Africa speak no Amazigh at all, and have fully shifted to Arabic. Both Amazigh language use and sense of identity are in flux.

Languages are endangered across North Africa. Of the eighteen indigenous languages spoken in Algeria, four are highly endangered, and seven less endangered. Morocco has nine indigenous languages, with five endangered, and two nearly extinct. Judeo-Arabic presents a particularly striking case of endangerment. At one time a number of varieties of Judeo-Arabic were widely spoken across the region. Judeo-Arabic evolved from contact between Arabic spoken in the region, and Hebrew spoken by Jewish communities of North Africa; prior to the twelfth century, Judeo-Berber was pervasive instead among these communities. (The latter is still spoken by some 2,000 elderly people now living in Israel, and is seriously endangered.)

Judeo-Arabic is heavily influenced by Hebrew. Historically it was spoken by Jewish communities in southern Morocco, and parts of Algeria and Tunisia, and was even used along with Hebrew in traditional ceremonies. Varieties of Judeo-Arabic spread throughout North Africa. When members of these communities emigrated to Israel in the middle of the twentieth century, they encountered hostile attitudes toward their language and strong pressure to shift to Hebrew.

Languages of the Niger-Congo family make up 85 percent of the languages of West Africa, which is defined here as encompassing fifteen countries, extending to North Africa and bordered by, but not including, Cameroon and Chad. These countries are: Benin, Burkina Faso, Gambia, Guinea, Guinea-Bissau, Ivory Coast, Liberia, Mali, Mauritania, Niger, Nigeria, Senegal, Sierra Leone, and Togo. In all, 1,075 languages are spoken in this region, with 553 of them spoken in Nigeria alone, which arguably has the greatest number of endangered languages in Africa.

Of the total number of languages, 155 have fewer than 3,000 speakers, and so their small size alone makes them vulnerable. The region is dominated by the use of African languages as lingua francas, including first and foremost Hausa, Yoruba, Efik, Akan, and Wolof. Thus Efik, for example, which has a reported first-language speaker population of 200,000 in Nigeria, is spoken by 2 million people there as a second language, although its use in this capacity is declining. In contrast, use of Hausa is increasing. Kiong is giving way to Efik and is close to extinction, but most other endangered Nigerian languages are being replaced by Hausa. Bade, for example, an Afro-Asiatic language with an ethnic population of 250,000 people, still has a relatively large speaker base, but they are rapidly shifting to Hausa, and the Shirawa dialect is already extinct. Such is the case with a number of languages, while some already have very small numbers of remaining speakers: Dyarim and Mvanip have about 100 each, while others, such as Luri and Sambe, have only two.

Below *In North Africa there is a strong shift toward Arabic over the indigenous languages.*

CENTRAL, EAST, AND SOUTHERN AFRICA

Approximately 800 languages are spoken in Central Africa, representing three major language families: Afro-Asiatic, Niger-Congo, and Nilo-Saharan. Afro-Asiatic languages are found primarily in Chad and northern Cameroon. Niger-Congo represents the largest of these, with just fewer than 600 languages spoken throughout Central Africa. At least sixty languages in Central Africa are endangered or have fewer than 1,000 speakers. There is little information available about languages in some regions, and so the actual number of endangered languages is likely to be higher.

Above *Of the 284 languages spoken in Cameroon, thirty-one are endangered and six of these are nearly extinct.*

In some countries, such as Congo, some languages are giving way to Lingala, the local lingua franca, and others to French, the official language of government, education, and organized religion. For example, Bonjo (a Bantu language with 2,000 to 3,000 speakers) is being replaced by Lingala, and even languages with large numbers of speakers, such as Mbosi (with 200,000 speakers), show a shift to Lingala, Teke, and French. Language endangerment is most acute in Cameroon, which is second only to Nigeria in terms of overall number of languages in Africa. (For number of languages in relation to population, Cameroon outranks Nigeria.) Current reports indicate that Cameroon has thirty-one endangered languages with fewer than 1,000 speakers each; six of these languages are nearly extinct. These include Njerep, with only four speakers, the youngest of whom is over the age of sixty, and Baldamu, a Chadic language with at most three speakers. Of the 284 languages known to be spoken in Cameroon, there is no information available for fifty-four of them.

Southern Africa is home to many cultures and peoples, including the Zulu, Xhosa, Ndebele, Tswana, Pedi, Venda, Sotho, San, Tsonga, Afrikaners, and Shona. Colonization and settling since the nineteenth century have resulted in significant populations of European and Indian descent in the region. The indigenous people here most probably originally spoke Khoisan, a family of languages best known today for its inventory of click sounds. Many Khoisan languages have already become extinct, and those that are still spoken are either seriously

Nama clicks (Source: Peter Ladefoged)

	Dental	Alveolar	Palatal	Alveolar Lateral
Voiceless unaspirated	k|oa put into	k!oas hollow	k‡ais calling	k||aros writing
Voiceless aspirated	k|^{h}o play music	k!^{h}o belt	k ^{h}aris small one	k||aor strike
Voiceless nasal	ŋ|^{h}o push into	ŋ!^{h}oas narrating	ŋ‡ ^{h}ais baboon's rear	ŋ||^{h}aos cooking place
Voiced nasal	ŋ|o measure	ŋ!oras pluck maize	ŋ‡ais turtle dove	ŋ||aes pointing
Glottal closure	k|ʔoa sound	k!ʔoas meeting	k‡ʔais gold	k||ʔoas reject a present

endangered, or on the verge of extinction. The languages of the !Ui branch were once spoken throughout the interior of South Africa, but now only one of them, Nǀu, remains, with fewer than twenty speakers. ǂHua, which appears to be a separate Khoisan language, has fewer than 200 speakers in Botswana. Khoekhoegowab, a central Khoisan language with more than 175,000 speakers in Namibia, is probably the only Khoisan language that is *not* endangered today. That said, recent surveys of language-attitudes show that the primary speakers of Khoekhoegowab, the Damara and Nama peoples, have adopted a negative stance toward the language, reflecting the attitudes of the majority population about their culture. Thus, many are even reluctant to send their children to schools where Khoekhoegowab is the language of instruction. So it too may soon be endangered.

The remaining Khoisan languages still spoken today are all endangered to varying degrees. Naro, with an estimated 9,000 speakers living primarily in Botswana and Khwe, with a total of 5,000 speakers in Botswana, Namibia, and South Africa, are the most stable. Khwe is still learned by children in Namibia, who grow up speaking it as their first language.

Eastern Africa is home to some seventy indigenous languages, which are all endangered to varying degrees. Children still learn fewer than twenty of these, and only two (Alagwa, spoken in Tanzania, and Bongo, in Sudan) are spoken by groups of more than a few thousand. Most have relatively small population bases, although there are exceptions: there are an estimated 170,000 ethnic K'emant in Ethiopia, but only 1,500 speakers, all of whom are elderly. Many

languages are represented by only a handful of speakers. Such is the case of Nyang'i in Uganda, or 'Ongota/Birale in Ethiopia, to name just two. Amharic, Setswana, and Swahili, major languages of East Africa (see Chapter 4), are in competition with English as national and transnational languages, and may grow at the expense of the local indigenous languages. In the Republic of Tanzania, Swahili threatens an estimated 130 languages, such as Akie (fifty speakers in Tanzania and Kenya combined), or Gweno, (with only a handful of remaining speakers). Nyang'i in Uganda is spoken by fewer than ten people today. In general, however, small indigenous languages are more likely to be replaced by one of the neighboring languages than by one of the national African languages.

Below *Khoisan languages, as spoken by this fisherman in Botswana, are rapidly dying out in southern Africa.*

SOUTH ASIA

South Asia is home to a number of different language families, including Austro-Asiatic, Dravidian, Tibeto-Burman, and Indo-European, as well as some unclassified languages. There are 415 languages spoken in India alone. However, the incredible linguistic diversity of the South Asia region is seriously threatened by a number of larger languages of wider communication, which are steadily replacing vast numbers of indigenous languages. These are, first and foremost, English, Hindi, and Urdu, but other Indo-European languages are beginning to take over as well, a good example being Nepali, in Nepal.

Above *Use of the Nepali language is growing in dominance in Nepal.*

Historical importance

Languages that are endangered are of significance for a wide range of reasons. **Dumākī**, for example, is seriously endangered, being spoken by fewer than 600 older people. Historically it was spoken by blacksmith and minstrel castes in areas of modern-day northern Pakistan. It is an Indo-Aryan language of great scientific interest because there is some evidence that it is related to Romani, the "gypsy" language, but further investigation is needed.

English is assuming ever greater dominance in the region. The factors that are advancing language shift in other parts of the world are at work here as well, including language and education policies that promote languages of wider communication over others, along with growing urbanization. Bhutan offers an illustrative example of anglicization in South Asia: English is so well established as the language of education, government, and even daily life, that the official national language, Dzongkha, a Tibeto-Burman language, is threatened.

India is a prime example of the multilingual complexity of the region. It has two national or official languages (English and Hindi), as well as an additional twenty-two official "scheduled" languages. Multilingualism is the norm. Slightly more than 20 percent of the population speaks a Dravidian language as their primary tongue (primarily Tamil, Teluga, Kannada, and Malayalam; 1 percent Austro-Asiatic (including Mundari and Santali), and 1 percent a Tibeto-Burman language (such as Singpho). Seventy-five percent (all in the north) speak an Indo-Aryan

language (such as Punjabi, Bengali, or Oriya). There are endangered languages in each of these families, as speakers shift to one of the main dominant languages, and language surveys probably underestimate the amount of shift. Only four of the 200 or so Austro-Asiatic languages are robust and not endangered. These are Khmer (with more than 12 million speakers in Cambodia), Vietnamese, Khasi (865 speakers in India), and Santali (approximately 6 million speakers in India and another 100,000 to 200,000 elsewhere).

Languages of the Munda subgroup of Austro-Asiatic are spoken throughout India, and all but Santali are endangered, despite the fact that some communities have relatively large numbers of speakers. Bilingualism is widespread and this, coupled with tremendous socio-economic pressure to change to the more prestigious majority languages, means that few, if any, of these languages will survive. Sora, for example, is spoken by approximately 300,000 people in south Orissa and Andhra Pradesh, but is giving way to pressure from local Indo-Aryan languages. Sora place names are more widespread,

suggesting that the people themselves ranged further historically. They have survived as a separate group only in the interior of India, and either assimilated elsewhere or were forced to resettle. Still, at present, only about half of the population speaks Sora, suggesting that assimilation is continuing rapidly. The languages of smaller Munda groups are even more endangered, as is the case of the Birhor, a semi-nomadic group of approximately 2,000 whose language is in terminal decline.

There are four major Dravidian languages: Kannada (see p. 123), Tamil (see p. 119), Malayalam (South Dravidian, see p. 122), and Telugu (Central Dravidian, see p. 117), all of which are robust. All the remaining two dozen or so Dravidian languages of India are considered by some experts to be threatened or endangered; they tend to be spoken by small communities, and most do not have written records. Koraga, the language of a group of Dalits (i.e. from the traditionally downtrodden "scheduled castes") is spoken by about 1,000 people who are all bilingual in Kannada.

Language diversity in Nepal provides a similar picture. The official language, Nepali, is one of the Indo-Iranian languages, a major branch of Indo-European. With a population of slightly more than 27 million, there are 126 living languages in Nepal. Fewer than 2.5 million people are speakers of a Tibeto-Burman language, but many are bilingual in Nepali. Nepal Bhasa (also called Newar) is a prime example. It is spoken in the Kathmandu Valley, where it is the prestige dialect, and in towns and bigger villages throughout Nepal, and in parts of India. With inscriptions dating from at least the ninth century, Nepal Bhasi has an ancient literary tradition; the oldest known book (*Guhya Kali Puja Bidhi*) dates to 1280 CE. Despite its historical dominance as the lingua franca of the region, currently more educated people are those less likely to know Nepal Bhasa. Though many still speak it, shift has been rapid, and is well advanced. Nepal census data from 1991 put shift as high as 79 percent in some regions, and it has been suggested that no children are currently being raised in Nepal Bhasa. Sadly, many consider the language as lost, beyond any hope of return.

Above *Women sort red peppers in Orissa, India, where about half the population speak Sora.*

CENTRAL, WEST, AND NORTH ASIA

Central Asia is dominated by the Turkic language-dialect continuum, that has spread south as far as Turkey, through Central Asia from western China. The exception is Tajikistan, where Tajik, the major and official language, is Indo-European. Years of pressure to adopt Russian during the Soviet regime had little effect on the majority languages, but these pressures did increase language shift among the minority languages, a shift that has only intensified since the break-up of the former Soviet Union. Russian is a lingua franca even today throughout the region, as is Mandarin Chinese in Inner Mongolia, Qinghai, and Xinjiang.

Above *The Inner Mongolian grasslands, which are inhabited by thirty-six ethnic groups.*

Some Indo-Iranian languages were once widespread in central, west, and north Asia, but are now unfortunately extinct. Such is the case with the language of Sogdian, which was once spoken in modern Uzbekistan and Tajikistan, and whose speakers played an important role in the trade taking place on the inland Silk Road.

In northern and East Asia, all of the forty or so minority languages are endangered to varying degrees, and shift is in the direction of Russian. This group includes a number of isolates, such as Itelmen, Nivkh, and Yukagir, which are not known to be related to any other language, and were once spoken by small communities in the Russian Far East. All three are seriously endangered, with only older speakers remaining.

Tofa

Tofa, an endangered Turkic language spoken in southern Siberia, had several lunar calendars based on activities such as hunting and gathering. These are now only partially remembered by elder speakers. Records from the 1850s show names such as the following:

Approximate equivalent	Recorded in 1850s	Current (remembered by elders)
January	great cold	great white month
February	chasing animals on skis	small white month
April	hunting with dogs	tree bud month
May	greenery	hunting in taiga month
July	Saranki flower blooms	hay cutting month
September	nut gathering	preparing skins month
October	round-up (of deer)	rounding-up male deer month
December	short days	cold month

The Turkic language-dialect continuum spans across Central Asia into Siberia, and although some Turkic languages in Siberia are safe (such as Yakut, or Tyvan), four are not. Dolgan and Shor both have relatively small speaker populations, and are not being learned by all children; Tofa and Chulym are no longer learned by children at all. Sociolinguistic surveys have shown that speaking Ket is now considered unusual to the point of being "unnatural," and parents no longer teach it to their children. A number of Uralic languages are also seriously endangered. This group includes Khanty, once spoken in northern Siberia. It is one of the few known languages where a handful of older speakers remember a now ancient and nearly extinct counting system, often called "overcounting." Concepts and ways of thinking are lost as languages are lost. The only minority indigenous language that experts currently consider to be relatively safe is Tundra Nenets, whose people have managed to maintain a traditional lifestyle due to their isolation. Both factors support the ongoing vitality of the language.

The Tungusic languages are spoken in an expanse stretching from northern China into northern Siberia, and as far north as the Arctic Circle. Some of these languages, such as Orok, Oroch, and Negidal, are severely endangered. Evenki has approximately 9,000 speakers, and is robust in isolated villages of 200 or so in the Amur Basin, and in southern Sakha. Elsewhere, in the region around Lake Baikal for example, shift is nearly complete, and there are few remaining speakers of Evenki. Thus vitality can vary with geographic distribution. That said, it is unlikely that Evenki will survive beyond a generation or two, as fewer and fewer children learn the language, and all speak Russian.

The Caucasus is characterized by rich linguistic diversity, and at least two dozen languages spoken here are endangered. The only one of these that does not belong to the Caucasian language group is Tat, an Iranian language spoken in Daghestan, where shift is toward Russian, and in Azerbaijan, where shift is to Azeri. The Caucasian group comprises three families: Kartvelian, of which Svan is endangered and shifting to Georgian, West Caucasian, and Northeast Caucasian. This group includes many endangered languages: in the Daghestanian branch, fully twenty-one of twenty-six languages are endangered. In the other branch, the Nakh branch, Bats is endangered, with speakers shifting to Georgian, the language of education. Chechen and Ingush, the two remaining Nakh languages, are generally classified as safe, but recently some experts have questioned whether Chechen will survive the many years of raging warfare in the area.

Multilingualism was the norm historically for much of this region, and did not result in language shift. Since Soviet times, however, there has been increasing pressure to learn Russian, and bi- or multilingualism in the former Soviet Union and Russia has, with rare exceptions, been a one-way process, with non-Russians learning Russian but few Russians learning the local languages.

Below *There are only a few speakers of Evenki left in the Lake Baikal region.*

Endangered Languages

EAST AND SOUTHEAST ASIA

There are 145 or so languages that have been identified as endangered in Southeast Asia, China, Taiwan, and Japan. Slightly more than a third of these are Mon-Khmer languages, and another third are Tibeto-Burman. The remaining languages of the region represent a range of language families: Altaic, Austronesian, Indo-European-based creoles, and Ainu, an isolate. Many of the languages spoken in the region are little known outside, with speakers living in isolated locations; in some cases access to foreign researchers may be denied, as with languages in Burma, where foreign linguists are rarely granted permission to conduct fieldwork.

Above *The Marimo festival taking place on Hokkaido Island. Ainu is still spoken here but is now in terminal decline.*

Ainu, which was once spoken in the far east of Siberia on Sakhalin Island, is now spoken only on Hokkaido Island in northern Japan, and is close to extinction. It has not been identified as related to any other language. It is currently remembered only by elderly speakers, who are all bilingual in Japanese. Research is presently underway to collect folklore and linguistic information on the Ainu, and there are moves to revitalize the language. There are fifty seriously endangered Mon-Khmer languages in the region. Of all the Mon-Khmer languages, only Cambodian, Vietnamese, and Khasi (spoken in northeast India) are clearly safe; all others face some level of endangerment. In many cases, populations are divided across geopolitical boundaries, often isolated from one another. Mang provides a striking example. There are about 500 Mang speakers in Yunnan, near its southern border, and another 500 in Vietnam. In the latter case they are recognized as a separate ethnic group, but not in China. The case of Mlabri is broadly similar. The Mlabri are a small group of hunter-gatherers, with about 125 in Thailand and another twenty-four in Laos. Although the number of speakers may well be undercounted, Mlabri is quite definitely endangered, and speakers are shifting to Hmong (see p. 167), Thai (see p. 161), or Lao (see p. 163).

Approximately fifty-five Tibeto-Burman languages are known to be endangered, and specialists estimate that there are at least an additional fifty unreported in China, in Yunnan and Sichuan Provinces. These include a wide variety of languages in multiple countries. Although there is some variation by region, factors such as urbanization and the dominance of one or more official, national languages are important nearly everywhere. For example, a number of Burmese languages (for example, Danu, Intha, and Taroyan) are shifting to Standard Burmese (see p. 162). Throughout China, the influence of Mandarin is pervasive, and a large number of languages are giving way to it, or to some other variety of Chinese (see p. 14). In Yunnan Province alone there are at least eight endangered Tibeto-Burman languages: Baima, Choyo, Ersu,

Guichong, Muya, Namuyi, Shizing, and Zaba. Kadai and Kam-Thai, two subgroups of languages from a very different family, the Austro-Thai languages, also have endangered varieties. Of the five Kadai languages in China—Qaw (in southern Sichuan) and Aqaw, Hagei, A-uo, and Duoluo Gelao—three are highly endangered.

The Gazhuo people of China (Xingmeng township) provide an interesting case. Their language is endangered, as children and younger people do not speak it. They are descended from a Mongol army that invaded approximately 700 years ago. The soldiers married the local women, and their descendants now speak a Northern Loloish language, again Tibeto-Burman, without a trace of Mongol influence, but they are classified ethnically as Mongol.

Manchu represents another interesting case. It is probably the best known of the Tungusic languages, which extend from northern China into Inner Mongolia and Siberia, as far north as the Arctic Circle. The entire Tungusic family is endangered, and will likely disappear in this century. Manchu is moribund, spoken by only a very few. Language shift among the Manchu began long ago: it was the primary language of the Qing, or Manchu Dynasty (1644–1911), but, by the nineteenth century, the court had shifted and lost fluency in Manchu. By the end of the Qing Dynasty, all court documents were already written in both Mandarin and Manchu. A written form of Manchu was adopted in 1599, and the Manchu archived their records even prior to their conquest of China, although less than 40 percent of all Manchu records have been translated. There are virtually no remaining speakers of Manchu living in Manchuria today.

Above *The golden roof of the Tagong Buddhist college, China. The influence of Mandarin is pervasive throughout the country.*

Manchu sequencing

Manchu uses a sequencing system, the way Westerners use the alphabet to organize lists, based on color terms:

A	niowanggiyan	green
B	niohon	greenish
C	fulgiyan	red
D	fulahûn	reddish
E	suwayan	yellow
F	sohon	yellowish
G	šanyan	white
H	šahûn	whitish
I	sahaliyan	black
J	sahahûn	blackish

AUSTRALIA AND THE PACIFIC

Altogether, the Pacific region has more than 1,300 languages (19 percent of the world total) and just 0.1 percent of the population, so that the mean number of speakers per language is 4,675, and the median 800. Thus it has the highest language density in the world, although the overall distribution of languages is very uneven. Of all regions in the Pacific, Papua New Guinea can be distinguished as having the highest language density in the world. There are 820 living and ten extinct languages recorded for this small region. In contrast, New Zealand has only one indigenous language, Māori, although some immigrant languages are now spoken there.

Above *While Aboriginal art flourishes, the majority of indigenous languages in Australia have fewer than 100 speakers.*

Right *Highland tribeswomen participate in the Sing Sing festival, Papua New Guinea.*

The region can be divided into four basic areas, which differ in terms of language endangerment. Australia and New Zealand represent particular cases. The remainder of the Pacific region includes Melanesia on the one hand versus Polynesia and Micronesia on the other. Polynesian and Micronesian societies are organized in relatively large social groups, with a single language dominating a state or an island, and as a result there is little language endangerment.

In contrast, Melanesia has around 1,000 languages, which are distributed across small communities or clusters of communities, ranging in size from a few hundred to a few thousand in some cases. These communities tend to be fiercely proud of their individual language or dialect and this fact, coupled with relative geographic isolation and inter-group hostility, has historically meant that these languages remain relatively robust, despite their small speaker numbers. More recently, however, this has been changing, as the spread of languages of wider communication, such as Tok Pisin in Papua New Guinea, has threatened the vitality of indigenous languages.

Tok Pisin is an English-based creole, which has about 50,000 first-language speakers, but a total of at least 4 million people use it as a second language, at the expense of local languages that were formerly used in contact situations. Bi- and trilingualism in Tok Pisin and English is spreading extremely rapidly. According to a 1980 survey, the Wom language had 2,500 speakers living in five villages, but even then, most speakers

regarded Tok Pisin as the language of economic advancement, and parents reported speaking only Tok Pisin to their children. Another survey around the same time reported all speakers of Yahang (1,116), and Beli (1,400) to be bilingual in the native language and Tok Pisin, with the latter gaining ground as the main and sometimes only language.

New Zealand stands in marked contrast to Papua New Guinea in having a single indigenous language, **Māori**. **Māori** is also relatively unique in that it has official status, and is technically used on a par with English. This language is discussed in more detail on page 179.

The many and varied indigenous languages of Australia are virtually all in varying stages of endangerment. There are more than 600 languages used in the country, and yet only twenty-five of them have more than 1,000 speakers. Significantly, and sadly, the overwhelming majority of languages in Australia have fewer than 100 speakers, or are now extinct.

Nearly half of the hundred or so languages spoken in the Republic of Vanuatu, an island nation in the South Pacific, are endangered to some extent. Many are spoken by extremely small groups of speakers, and as a result are extremely vulnerable to extinction. Baki, for example, has an ethnic population of only 200. Despite a positive language attitude, only 30 percent of the children speak Baki.

Above *Tribal teams compete at cricket in New Caledonia, Melanesia, a region with a huge diversity of languages.*

Avoidance languages

One of the striking characteristics of a number of endangered Australian languages is the use of the so-called "mother-in-law" or "avoidance" languages. For example, in Dyribal there is the "normal," everyday speech style, called Guwal. Guwal is used for speaking to all groups, except in-laws (including children and cross-cousins) of the opposite sex. In speaking to opposite-sex parents or children-in-law, one uses what is called Jalnguy, which substitutes a significant part of Guwal vocabulary with different words. Typically, the mother-in-law variety (here Jalnguy) has fewer total words than the everyday language (Guwal), and so each individual word is used with a broader range of meanings.

THE AMERICAS 👄

The Americas are home to approximately 1,000 indigenous languages, accounting for 14.5 percent of the world's languages, although less than 1 percent of the world's population speak them. Language shift is well underway in all of the Americas, with indigenous languages giving way to English in North America, and to Spanish and Portuguese in South America. In the Americas, the use of language is closely tied to identity, and language revitalization movements are often linked to other movements for greater sovereignty, or at least official recognition of indigenous rights. In North America, rapid language attrition is well advanced.

Above *While Greenlandic is robust in Greenland, the Inuit language is endangered in Alaska, with few speakers younger than forty.*

Experts estimate that at least a third of the indigenous languages that were spoken at the time of European contact, beginning in 1492, have disappeared, and a quarter are remembered only by elderly speakers. Of the more than 300 indigenous languages currently spoken in North America, only forty-six have significant numbers of children learning them today. Thus there is broad agreement that nearly all these languages will disappear by the end of this century. The situation differs only marginally in Canada versus the United States. Presently, there are thirty-six languages with varying degrees of vitality in Canada, down from about sixty in the sixteenth century. In the United States there were an estimated 250 native languages at the time of contact. Only Navajo has a speaker population of more than 25,000. Although the relatively large number of 115,000 Navajo speakers meant that the language was perceived to be safe, recent studies have shown that Navajo children are no longer learning it: only 30 percent of the children know it as a first language.

The situation for Alaskan native languages is especially bleak. Although nineteen of the twenty known Alaskan languages are still spoken (the last fluent speaker of Eyak having passed away in 2008), they are all endangered. Gwich'in, for example, has at most 400 speakers, and Tlingit only 700 in Alaska, and another 145 in Canada. "Eskimo," a term familiar to outsiders but considered derogatory by many insiders, refers to what linguists and native Alaskans call Inuit and Yupik. Although one variety of Inuit, Greenlandic, is robust in Greenland, it is seriously endangered in Alaska, where almost all speakers are above the age of forty.

South America is a place of remarkable linguistic diversity. Prior to European contact, there were as many as 1,200 indigenous groups in South America, representing at least ninety different linguistic stocks. In South America, indigenous languages are giving way to Spanish, and to Portuguese in Brazil. In Paraguay, we see a shift to Spanish or to Paraguayan Guaraní, as both are national languages. Brazil is the prime example of linguistic diversity, as it is home to 188 different

Whistle speech

A number of languages in the Americas, such as Nahuatl, Totonac, Kickapoo, and Zapotec in Mexico, are known to use "whistle" speech, whereby the language is "whistled" rather than spoken. This whistling allows hunters and trappers to communicate without alerting their prey. It is also used by shepherds and herders to communicate over distances where regular speech would not be heard. Each sound of the language has a whistled equivalent, but there is still a fair amount of ambiguity in the sentences, and so the whistlers tend to use relatively simple sentences. They are used only in specific contexts, and the context helps disambiguate meaning. Whistle speech is found in many parts of the world and with different languages, but its use is linked to subsistence lifestyles of hunting and herding.

living languages and forty-seven known extinct languages. Yet the population of more than 184 million includes only an estimated 155,000 speakers of indigenous languages. (More than 163 million speak Portuguese.) Thus the overwhelming majority of native languages have very small speaker bases, from just a handful to a few hundred or, in exceptional cases, a few thousand. This makes them very vulnerable to language shift. Although some groups such as the Ave-Canoeiro (a Tupi-Guarani language) are reported to be solidly monolingual, there are only fifty-six known speakers. A few, such as the Mapidian (fifty speakers), are shifting to another local language; in this case, it is Waiwai, as they live together with Waiwai speakers. But in most cases the shift is to Portuguese, with shift more rapid in urban areas, and isolated groups maintaining their language more robustly.

In Mexico and other parts of Central America, a shift to Spanish is taking place rapidly and the loss of many languages from this area seems almost inevitable.

LANGUAGES OF THE NORTH

Of the seventy-five or so indigenous languages still spoken in the far north, almost all are endangered to some degree. Notable exceptions include Greenlandic Inuit, and arguably some varieties of Saami in northern Scandinavia. Languages of the Eskimo-Aleut family are spread across the north, from the coast of Siberia, all across Alaska and northern Canada, and on to Greenland. The Saami languages, which belong to the Uralic family, are spoken in Scandinavia, Finland, and Russia, and the Athabaskan-Eyak-Tlingit family of languages is spoken in Alaska and Canada.

Above A Nenets woman tends her reindeer. The Nenets live in the far north of Russia and have their own indigenous language, called Nenets.

Other Uralic languages, notably Nenets and Nganasan, are spoken further east in Siberia, as well as the Turkic language Yakut.

The total population of people living in the north is slightly less than 400,000. Of them, an estimated 52 percent speak an indigenous language. Greenland is in a class by itself, with nearly 100 percent of the population speaking the indigenous language (Greenlandic). It is somewhat more difficult to assess language use and vitality in Sweden, Norway, and Finland, with different varieties of Saami recorded as varying greatly in terms of vitality. Thus Northern Saami in Norway and Sweden has a relatively large speaker population of 21,000, and children continue to learn and use the language. But other varieties of Saami are endangered, including Pite and Ume Saami, both spoken primarily in Sweden, and Inari and Skolt Saami in Finland.

In general, the northern languages in Russia are in the advanced stages of attrition, with Ter Saami and Akkala-Babinsk Saami as illustrative

examples, each with no more than a half dozen elderly speakers. It is probably safe to say that the northern languages in Russia are, on the whole, in worse shape than those in Canada, and those in Alaska represent an extreme situation of attrition and loss. It is also important to keep in mind that the northern cultures are currently in an unstable situation due to accelerated climate change, which has already had a significant impact on indigenous lifestyles.

The Inuit languages spread across the far north, stretching from Siberia to Alaska, across Canada to Greenland (see pp. 195 and 232). Of these the most vital and robust is Greenlandic, the first language of the population of Greenland, with an estimated 47,000 speakers. It is the language of education through high school, local media, and of the Home Rule government, and is the only indigenous language with status of this degree. Children in Canada still grow up speaking Inuit (between 24,000 and 30,000 speakers), while in Alaska it is endangered, and in Russia close to extinction.

Right *Two young Saami women in traditional dress trudge through the snows of Lapland. Some forms of Saami are under threat.*

People of the far north have adapted their lifestyle to live in the northern climate. To this day many still live a subsistence way of life, and survive by hunting, fishing, and herding reindeer. The lexicons of their languages reflect how they lives and many have extensive vocabularies for the activities that are central to survival. The Evenki, a Tungusic people of the north, are traditionally reindeer herders and hunters, and so have a well-developed vocabulary to enable them to talk about reindeer herding. Thus they have separate words for a one-year-old male reindeer (**avlakan**), versus a two-year old (**ektana**), versus a one-year-old female (**sachari**), and so on, with more than thirty words to distinguish different types of caribou. As elsewhere, the Evenki language is maintained by those who live a traditional lifestyle. As the lifestyle is lost, so is the language, unless active measures are taken to preserve it. Populations have always been sparse in the far north, but early extractive economies, which revolved around fur trapping, at least required the survival of local peoples to gather the furs. Modern exploitation, focused above all on oil, finds the inhabitants irrelevant.

Evenki words for "reindeer"

Here are some more examples:

reindeer	oron
reindeer harnessed on left-hand side of a sledge team	kostur
reserve reindeer	delemin
wild reindeer	bagadakaa
reindeer with a spot on muzzle	kokchavar, kokchakacha
reindeer that cannot be trained	mullikan

EXTINCT LANGUAGES

EXTINCT LANGUAGES

Language extinction occurs in a great deal of ways, but the immediate cause is always the same: a failure to pass the language on to the next generation. This means that some major stress must have disrupted the community's social traditions. Throughout history, this has often been due to a foreign military invasion; but in the last few centuries the disruption has increasingly come from the influence of world economic markets, government imposition of a common education system, or—most recently—even direct access to mass media in foreign languages.

The extinct languages reviewed here all lack any modern native speakers, but in some cases the language has retained some use—above all, in religious practices. Highly standardized languages may be considered extinct simply because the living tradition has left them behind and adopted a new written form: always, though, there has been some disruptive break in the tradition. In the case of Latin, the disruption happened first when Germanic invaders in the fifth century CE broke the unity of Rome's Latin-speaking domain; then, when widespread literacy finally returned, Latin's unitary standard was ignored. Likewise the replacement of Egypt's ancient religion with Christianity, followed by Arabic conquest in the seventh century CE, left Coptic as a barely understood liturgical language, and its ancient hieroglyphic writing a mystery.

Left The stunningly beautiful columns of the Temple of Khnum at Esna, Egypt, begun by Tuthmosis III and completed by the Romans. Inscriptions spanning hundreds of years adorn the temple walls.

The extinct languages featured in this chapter are drawn from every continent. We have some idea of what each one was like, either from inscriptions or (since 1500) from documentation by colonial linguists. In this respect, these languages are not typical, for even today most languages have no written form in everyday use. But in fact many of the extinct languages here were the original models of literacy to their neighbors: Sumerian and Akkadian in the Middle East, Etruscan within Italy, Ethiopic in East Africa, Sanskrit in India and Southeast Asia, and Sogdian in Central Asia. Some languages (such as Tangut, Hittite, and Gaulish) were just dominant in large regions of military conflict. Once highly influential, all these languages have ultimately been replaced by a neighboring language. At the opposite extreme, the languages of smaller communities (for example, Ubykh,

Sydney, Siraya, and Massachusett) have always been especially vulnerable to imperial aggression, and only recently have they been allowed any record.

Given enough time, perhaps most (if not all) languages that we now know will, like the majority, become extinct. As many examples here show, a period of supremacy, by the standards of the age, is no guarantee of permanence or ultimate survival.

The following languages are covered in this chapter: (Europe) Latin, Etruscan, Gaulish; (West and North Africa) Egyptian; (Central, East, and Southern Africa) Ethiopic; (South Asia) Sanskrit; (Central, Western, and Northern Asia) Hittite, Sumerian, Akkadian, Sogdian, Ubykh; (East and Southeast Asia) Tangut, Siraya; (Pacific and Australasia) Sydney; (South America) Chibcha; and (North America) Massachusett.

Above *The traditional landowners of Sydney, Australia, the Cadigal people. The Sydney language is now extinct.*

LATIN

Until 7th century CE

Right *The title page of* The Consolation of Philosophy, *a work by Boethius, c. 1493.*

Western European countries have used Latin as a common language, especially for government, religion, and literature, ever since they were ruled by the Roman Empire. Latin had originally been confined to the district of Latium, but Rome's political dominance, and its policy of settling ex-soldiers as farmers in conquered territories, spread the language as a vernacular across Italy from the fourth to first centuries BCE, and then into Gaul, Britain, Iberia, the Balkans, and North Africa. A written standard for Latin was established, on the principles of Greek grammar, in the first centuries CE, and it has not changed since, having passed down through about eighty generations.

Count to 10

I	1	ūnum
II	2	duō
III	3	tria
IIII, IV	4	quattuor
V	5	quinque
VI	6	sex
VII	7	septem
VIII	8	octō
IX	9	novem
X	10	decem

Alphabets and scripts

The Roman alphabet was derived from Greek (through contacts with Rome's Etruscan neighbors) from the sixth to fourth centuries BCE. Because of the imperial conquests by Rome and, later, European countries, use of the Roman alphabet spread until it became the most widely used in the world. During two millennia of early use, its letter forms changed (e.g. from **unum duo tria** to **vnum duo tria**); but Renaissance printers restored "roman" and "italic" norms, based on ancient inscriptions and early medieval manuscripts.

The classical literature of Latin was centered on writers of this period, especially the orator and philosopher Cicero (106–43 BCE) and the epic poet Virgil (70–19 BCE). The comedies, too, of Plautus (c. 250–184 BCE) and Terence (c. 190–159 BCE) remained especially popular down the ages.

The decline of the western Roman Empire in the fifth century CE shattered the single-speech community, and spoken Latin evolved into various Romance languages; but the written standard lived on in the Catholic Church. Christian missionaries took it across northern and central Europe as far as Ireland, Norway, Poland, and Hungary. Everywhere Latin remained the main language of education and administration.

In literature during the early Middle Ages, Church fathers, such as the philosopher Boethius (c. 480–524 CE) and the historian Orosius (385–420 CE) came to equal the Ancient Roman authors in prestige, but they had been eclipsed by the fifteenth century. The abandonment of Latin began in the sixteenth century, moving eastward from France and England, as numerous alternative vernaculars were increasingly written and published.

Right *The Roman Empire at its height, showing the spread of Latin across Europe, Asia, and North Africa.*

AKKADIAN  **Until 2nd century CE**

Akkadian was the official language of the Babylonian and Assyrian empires, and as such dominated the Middle East from the twenty-fourth to the ninth centuries BCE. These empires were founded in the valleys of the Euphrates and Tigris rivers, but the language spread northward, and eastward into Syria, from roots in south central Iraq, then known as the lands of Sumer and Akkad. It is named for Agade, the capital of King Sargon the Great (c. 2333–2279 BCE), in Akkadian Šarru-kinu, "the true king," the first Babylonian conqueror. The city was probably located on the west bank of the Euphrates, but its precise location is still unknown.

Count to 10

Aramaic c. 6th BCE		Akkadian c. 24th–6th BCE	Arabic c. 6th–21st CE
ḥad	1	ištēn	wāḥid
trēn	2	šina	iθnāyn
təlātā	3	šalaš	θalāθa
'arbaʕā	4	erba	'arbaʕa
ḥamiša	5	ḥamiš	xamsa
šittā	6	šešš	sitta
šabʕā	7	sebe	sabʕa
təmāniyā	8	samāne	θamāniya
tišʕā	9	tiše	tisʕa
asrā	10	ešer	ʕašra

This table shows how little change there has been in counting in Iraq over 4,500 years, and hence how easy linguistic changes in the Middle East have been. Note that this table is 66 percent identical to that in Ethiopic (see p. 245).

Above *A fragment from the Babylonian* Epic of Gilgamesh, *written in cuneiform, the Sumerian writing system, which was also used to write Akkadian.*

Akkadian was a written language, using an adaptation of the Sumerian writing system (cuneiform logograms on clay), and with this advantage (together with the aggressive policies of its kings and merchants) it had become the diplomatic lingua franca for all developed states, from Egypt and Hatti (modern Turkey) to Elam (modern western Persia) by the fourteenth century BCE. Nonetheless, in the ninth century BCE it was supplanted as the official language of Assyria–Babylon by Aramaic. (Aramaic's advantages were that its alphabetic script was easier to learn and it ranged widely, its speakers having been scattered by Assyrian clearances.)

Despite this, the Assyrian empire lasted another 300 years, and Akkadian was still being written, at least on monuments (by Persian and Greek invaders), from the sixth to third centuries BCE. Its use finally died out, even in Babylon, in the second century CE.

All knowledge of Akkadian was then lost until the 1850s when—stimulated by the 1849 discovery at Nineveh, near Mosul (northern Iraq), of the library of King Ashurbanipal (669–627 BCE)—the Irish clergyman Edward Hincks and the British political agent Henry Rawlinson finally deciphered and identified it as a Semitic language, closely related to Aramaic and Arabic.

By a useful irony, a clay library, once burnt, has been rendered permanent. Scribal school texts from the late period were particularly useful in preserving literary classics, such as the quest for immortality as related in the *Epic of Gilgamesh*. This is an epic poem and among the earliest works of literary fiction, thought to be a compilation of several Sumerian legends and poems into a single work.

UBYKH  Until 7 October, 1992

The Ubykh language, with a remarkable eighty-three distinct consonants, was a leading contender for the language with the most complex known sound system. It is also significant in that its last speaker with full competence was a highly literate man, Tevfiq Esenç, who died in 1992 in the full glare of publicity after some decades during which he had worked with foreign linguists, such as the Frenchman Georges Dumézil, to document the language. As a result, Ubykh became an important symbol of language endangerment and extinction in the late twentieth century.

Characteristics

Typically of the northern Caucasus, Ubykh has many consonants but very few vowels—just [ə] and [a], as the two vowels in English "begun." The variety of consonants comes from secondary configurations of the vocal tract, indicated in these spellings:

. pharyngealized (constricted throat);
' glottalized (catch in throat);
´ alveolarized (tongue tip retracted);
° labialized (lip rounded);
˜ palatalized (tongue pressing hard on palate); and
. retroflex (tongue bent back).

Top *The Caucasus mountains, Russia. Ubykh was a member of the Northwest Caucasian language group.*

Right *Sochi, on the Black Sea coast of Russia, where Ubykh was spoken until 1864.*

Ubykh was a language of the Caucasus, traditionally spoken around Sochi on the Black Sea coast. It was a member of the North west Caucasian or Circassian group, hence related to Adyghe, Abkhaz, and Kabardian, all of which survive in situ around the northern shores of the Black Sea and the northern borders of Georgia. Chechen, Ingush, and Avar, further to the east, are more distant living relatives. The Russian invasion of Circassia after a century of warfare led, in 1864, to the clearance of the 50,000 Ubykh speakers, among many other Caucasians, the survivors moving into the lands of the Ottoman empire. The Ubykh ultimately settled some villages by the Sea of Marmara, Haci Osman, Kirkpinar, Masukiye, and Haci Yakup, not far south of Istanbul in Turkey.

Tevfiq Esenç, the great informant on the language, had learnt it from his grandparents. He died on 7 October 1992, at the age of eighty-eight. Through him, much of the oral literature was transcribed, which revealed the ancient mythology of the Narts, legendary heroes of the Caucasus, who bore striking similarities both to the Greek Prometheus (chained to a high rock in the Caucasus while an eagle feasted on his liver) and the Arthurian knights (e.g., in the ritual of a sword that must be returned to the water on its bearer's death).

Ubykh is highly agglutinative, creating long words that have the value of sentences: for example, **šək'aajəfanamət** (we shall not be able to go back). There is a special second-person pronoun prefix "you," which is used exclusively in reference to women (χa-).

CHICHA

Chibcha was once spoken in the plateau of Cundinamarca, and northward into Boyacá and Santander, in the central highlands of Colombia. The civilization that spoke it had three centers, Muyquyta, "plain of the fields" (modern Bogotá), Funza (modern Tunja), and Sugamuxi (modern Sogamoso). In Chibcha, words are basically spelt as in Spanish: hence "qu" represents "k," "z" "ts," and "y" "ə." The zipa (king) of Muyquyta was famous as El Dorado (Spanish for "the gilded one"), being covered in gold dust for his inauguration. The indigenous regimes were destroyed by Jiménez de Quesada of Spain in 1536.

Count to 10

Chibcha		U'wa
ata	1	ubistia
boza	2	bukaya
mica	3	baya
mhuyzca	4	bakaya
hyzca	5	esíya
ta	6	téraya
cuhupqua	7	kukuya
suzha	8	ábia
aca	9	estária
hubchihica	10	ukásia

The modern U'wa words (see panel) are here for comparison.

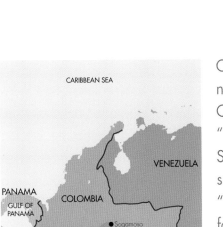

Top *The areas in which Chibcha was spoken.*

Above right *An example of Chibcha golden filigree work, for which these people were renowned.*

After the foundation of "New Granada" in 1538, Chibcha was adopted as a **lengua general** (official lingua franca); and it was taught at various colleges in Bogotá. Grammars therefore survive, and some Christian liturgy. But as the Archbishop of Bogotá wrote to the king on 12 February 1577: "In this Kingdom every valley or province has its own language different from the others." Chibcha had never been used as widely as other languages adopted as **lenguas generales**, and did not spread further under Spanish rule. It died out at about the time that indigenous languages in the Spanish Empire were being proscribed by the royal decree of 1770.

Chibcha is now attested mainly in place names of the region, for example, **Chia** (moon), **Subachoque** (good sun), **Nemocón** (cougar roar), **Gachancipa** (wounded king), and some dialectal loan words in Colombian Spanish, e.g., **guapucha** (minnow), **pinche** (urchin).

Chibcha is a verb-final language with copious prefixes and suffixes, for example, **chi-fun ba chi-hucu a-m-ny-squa** (he gives us our bread today). Here the **chi** prefix expresses our/us; the **a** prefix the implicit "he," subject of the verb; **m** shows that the verb **ny** (give) takes an object (here **fun**, "bread") and the **squa** shows the time aspect is continuing, not complete.

Related languages

In 1888, the German archeologist Max Uhle recognized Chibcha as related to many languages in northern Colombia, Panamá, and Costa Rica: together they are now known as the Chibchan family. Chibcha's closest living relative is U'wa or Tunebo, spoken by some 7,500 people, who practice traditional farming in the neighboring zone toward the northeast, on the slopes of Sierra Nevada del Cocuy, by the Venezuelan border.

EGYPTIAN

Until 14th century CE

Egyptian, later known as Coptic, is the language of Egypt's indigenous civilization, spoken exclusively in the valley and delta of the River Nile. It has the longest written tradition of any language, from the thirty-first century BCE to the fourteenth century CE. It is an Afro-Asiatic language, related—but only distantly—to Cushitic in the south, Semitic to the east and Berber to the west. It suffered incursions from all these groups during its history, but remained unaffected until the advent of Arabic in the seventh century CE. Even then it took another 800 years for the spoken language finally to disappear.

Count to 10

Egyptian (BCE)		Coptic (CE)
wuʃuw	1	wua
sinuway	2	snaw
χamtaw	3	šomt
yifdaw	4	ftou
dīyaw	5	tiu
sa'aw	6	sou
safχaw	7	sašf
χamānaw	8	šmun
pisījaw	9	psit
mūjaw	10	mēt

Above *A new kingdom stela clearly showing Egyptian hieroglyphs.*

Right *The Rosetta Stone, written in hieroglyphic, demotic, and classical Greek, was instrumental in advancing understanding of hieroglyphic writing.*

An original hieroglyphic system of pictures phonetically interpreted was used consistently for three and a half millennia, though it had variants called hieratic and demotic, used for purposes other than writing on monuments. (Hieratic was a system of essentially the same glyphs, written cursively; demotic was a radically simplified system of outlines, but was only in use from the seventh century BCE to the fifth century CE). Hieroglyphic writing was replaced in the fourth century CE by a phonetic system using Greek (Coptic) letters, just as the indigenous Egyptian religion was replaced by Christianity. The texts of the last centuries hint at the decline of the ancient writing: more and more symbols were invented, to be used with esoteric symbolism, rather than as a straightforward representation of a text in Egyptian.

Egyptian written language, known as **maduww nāt^sar** (words of god), was deemed the gift of the ibis-headed god Thoth, and to have played a key role in creation. Many of the linguistic changes inevitable in the 4,500 years of continuous use were cloaked (for the first 3,500 years) by hieroglyphic writing, not least because vowels were not marked. Nevertheless, a noticeable shift toward a more analytic style (presumably closer to the colloquial) emerged under the pharaoh Akhenaten (1353–1336 BCE), who also introduced religious reforms and a personalized "family man" image for himself as the pharaoh. For example, the equivalent of "the brother heard" changes from **sjmn-f sn** (literally, "heard-he brother") to **p-son a-f sōtm** (literally, "the-brother did-he hearing").

ETHIOPIC  **Until 10th century CE**

Ethiopic is currently the liturgical language of the Orthodox (Tewahedo) Christian Church in Ethiopia and Eritrea. It had ceased to be spoken by the tenth century CE, but interestingly continued as Ethiopia's principal written language until the late nineteenth century, separate from the majority spoken languages, for example, Amharic, Tigre, and Tigrinya. By origin, it is likely that it came across the Red Sea from Yemen in the early first millennium BCE as a lingua franca, based on one of the South Arabian languages, but in contact with the ancient Cushitic languages of Ethiopia.

Above *A stele at Aksum, where Ethiopic became an official language in the second century BCE.*

Still recognizably a Semitic language—with the classically complex system of verb inflexion—Ethiopic was formed in what is now Eritrea and northern Ethiopia no later than the sixth century BCE, when the earliest inscriptions were written. From the second century CE Ethiopic became the official language of the kingdom of Aksum, which dominated the

region until the late first millennium. Conversion to Christianity occurred in the fifth century CE. This had a lasting effect on Ethiopic literature, much of which is translated from Greek and (later) Arabic. Ethiopic, therefore, preserves a record of early Arabic Christianity, from before the conversion to Islam. Later literature includes **Kəbræ Nægæst** (*Glory of Kings*), an epic about King Solomon, the Queen of Sheba, and their son Menelik.

Count to 10

Ge'ez Symbol		Ethiopic	Akkadian	Arabic
፩	1	aḥati	ištēn	wāḥid
፪	2	kəlʔeti	šina	iθnāyn
፫	3	sælas	šalaš	θalāθa
፬	4	arbaʕ	erba	'arbaʕa
፭	5	ḥæms	ḥamiš	xamsa
፮	6	səssu	šešš	sitta
፯	7	šæbʕu	sebe	sabʕa
፰	8	sæmani	samāne	θamāniya
፱	9	təsʕu	tiše	tisʕa
፲	10	ʕæśru	ešer	ʕašra

Here the Akkadian and Arabic indicate the closeness to Semitic roots. The traditional symbols are borrowed Greek letters (Α,Β,Γ,Δ,Ε,Ϝ,Ζ,Η,Θ,Ι), signifying numbers as in Greek and, more directly, neighboring Coptic.

Writing system

Between the second and fifth centuries CE Ethiopic developed its own writing system from South Arabian roots, an "abugida," halfway between an alphabet and a syllabary: the basic form of each consonant shifts rather systematically to reflect the following vowel.

Since this extension of the system to mark vowels coincides with the beginning of Christianity in Aksum (the conversion of King Ezana in the fourth century) and—unlike all other scripts of Africa or Arabia—is functionally very close to the scripts of India, it has been suggested that it was introduced by the Christian tutor of Ezana, Frumentius, a merchant's son said to have spent his youth in India. Called **fidæl**, it is now used to write most languages of Ethiopia, notably the dominant Amharic, and Tigrinya, a descendant of Ethiopic widely spoken in the north.

ETRUSCAN

Etruscan's origins are mysterious. It was isolated in Italy, but the ancient Rhaetic language of Austria may be related to it, as may be two inscriptions on the island of Lemnos in the eastern Mediterranean. Recent DNA studies of cattle and people, as well as ancient legends going back to Herodotus (fifth century BCE), link the language with the coast of Anatolia, perhaps Troy: Etruria (Latin) and Troia (Greek) appear to derive from the same root, Trōsia. It was spoken in northern Italy (Etruria, also known as Tuscany) throughout the first millennium BCE, and from 750 to 500 BCE. Its "Twelve Cities" were culturally and politically dominant in central Italy, too.

Count to 10

I	1	ΥΟ	thu
II	2	JA≠	zal
III	3	I)	ci
IIII	4	ΑΜ	śa
Λ	5	↓ΑΜ	makh
IΛ	6	ΟΥΒ	huth
IIΛ	7	ΦΜƷ⁊	semph
IIIΛ	8	⁊≠Ɔ)	cezp
XI	9	ΦϤΥΠ	nurph
X	10	ϤΑƧ	sar

Roman numerals were derived from Etruscan (as shown in the first column) by rotating them through 180 degrees, so that they were upside-down and left to right. Etruscan was written right to left, as shown in the second column.

Above *An eighteenth-century print of a coin showing the emperor Claudius, the last known scholar of Etruscan.*

Right *The Etruscan civilization and its expansion.*

Etruscan power was limited by Greek cities in southern Italy, only to be broken and destroyed piecemeal in wars with Rome from the fourth century BCE. By the end of the millennium, the Etruscan language had died out, and had been replaced by Latin.

Etruscan was the language of a literate civilization, but is known now only from 9,000 inscriptions, mostly very short, and hardly any bilingual. Its alphabet was derived from a version of Greek, and the Romans, in turn, derived theirs from the Etruscan.

The emperor Claudius (d. 54 CE) is the last known scholar of Etruscan in the ancient world, but the name of at least one dramatist, Volnius, is known. The language was not inflexional like Latin, but based on agglutinating suffixes: for example, **clan** (son), **clan-s** (of a son), **clen-ar** (sons), **clen-ar-as** (of sons).

The Etruscans were highly influential in setting Roman tastes (for example, satire, gladiatorial shows, purple on magistrates' robes), but their language also influenced Latin. For example, the term **persona** (mask, character) is derived from the Etruscan word **phersu-na**; and **satelles** (bodyguard) is derived from **zatlath** (axe-man).

The system of three names characteristic of a Roman gentleman (e.g., Gaius Julius Caesar,) and consisting of a **praenomen** (given name), **nomen** (clan name), and **cognomen** (family line) is derived from Etruscan.

GAULISH

Gaulish, also known as Gallic, was the language spoken across most of western and central Europe in the second half of the first millennium BCE. The classical Greek historian Strabo (first century CE) mentions Gaulish speakers in Dalmatia (modern Croatia), and there were certainly numerous speakers in what are now southern Germany and France. The Gauls were the quintessential Celts, and their artefacts are noted for their beautifully elaborate spirals and swirls, having been identified archeologically at Hallstatt in Austria and La Tène in Switzerland.

Above *A sculpture of a Gallic warrior. Gaulish (or Gallic) was spoken across Europe in the first millennium BCE.*

The spread of Gaulish culture is associated with the technology of working iron (this word, common to Germanic, comes from Gaulish **isarno-**), but they also specialized in the building of roads and wheeled vehicles. The best-known Gauls are those who fought with the Romans and Greeks in warring bands that sacked Rome in 390 BCE and Delphi in 279 BCE; the former band

set up a colony around Ankara in central Anatolia, the Galatians, whose language was still used—according to St. Jerome—in the fourth century CE. The great majority of Gauls were subdued during Julius Caesar's Gallic Wars (59–49 BCE), and the Roman conquest led ultimately to the supplanting of the Gaulish language by Latin.

Gaulish is known from Greek and latterly Roman inscriptions of the third century BCE to the first century CE. Although related to modern Celtic tongues, Gaulish in the first century BCE was much more like Latin or Greek: subject before verb, with highly inflected nouns (six cases, including nominative **-os**, accusative **-on**, genitive **-i**) and no mutations of initial consonants. For example, contrast Gaulish (unchanged) **matrebo nemausicabo** (mothers of Nimes) with the Irish **maith** (good) mutating to **bean mhaith** (good woman). Like all Celtic languages, Gaulish lost the consonant "p": for example, Gaulish **lano-** corresponds to Latin **planum** (plain) and Gaulish **rito-** to Greek **poros** (ford).

Count to 10

Ordinal	Gaulish		Welsh	Latin	Greek
First	cintux	1	cyntaf	prīmus	prōtos
Second	all[os]	2	ail	alter	deuteros
Third	trit[ios]	3	trydydd	tertius	tritos
Fourth	petuar[ios]	4	pedwerydd	quartus	tetartos
Fifth	pinpetos	5	pumed	quintus	pemptos
Sixth	suexos	6	chwechfed	sextus	hektos
Seventh	sextametos	7	seithfed	septimus	hebdomos
Eighth	oxtumeto[s]	8	wythfed	octāvus	ogdōos
Ninth	namet[os]	9	nawfed	nōnus	enatos
Tenth	decometos	10	degfed	decimus	dekatos

Only the ordinal numbers are known, occurring in a potter's kiln record (conveniently fired on clay, and thus rendered permanent) from Graufesenque, near Millau in the south of France. Here they are given (broken edges of the record in square brackets) with equivalents in Welsh (a close relative), and their Latin and Greek counterparts.

HITTITE

Hittite was the language of the kingdom "in the land of Hatti" (modern Turkey) from the eighteenth to the thirteenth century BCE. At its height, this kingdom's power extended across Anatolia to the shores of the Aegean, and southward into central Syria. The Hittites even defeated Ramses II, pharaoh of Egypt, at Qadesh (northern Syria) in 1286 BCE, in what is believed to have been the largest chariot battle ever fought, involving some 5,000 chariots. The resulting peace treaty survives in two copies, one (in Egyptian) inscribed on the temple of Karnak on the River Nile, and another (in Akkadian) in the Hittite state library in Turkey.

Top *Map showing the Hittite Empire at its height in 1340 BCE.*

Above *Hittite relief sculpture showing the god Tarhu and King Warpalawas.*

As monuments to Hittite glory there remain the following: the name of the southeastern Turkish province, Hatay; a dozen references to **H̱itti** in the Old Testament and the Khet people in Egyptian records; and inscriptions and clay tablets. Of the latter, some are in a distinctive hieroglyphic system, but most are in cuneiform, evidently learnt from the Assyrians.

The Hittite language was deciphered in the twentieth century, the major breakthrough being made by a Czech professor, Bedrich Hrozný, in 1915. His research was based on a library of texts written in cuneiform script, which had been discovered at **Boğaz Köy** in central Turkey. It emerged that the Hittite empire had been centered not in Syria but Anatolia, at **Boğaz Köy** (once known as Hattusas). The research also revealed that the language was actually called Nesian (**nešili**) after the southern city of Kanesh, since it had superseded Hittite proper (**hattili**),

Hittite literature

Hittite documents have revealed fascinating aspects of the world that preceded Greek civilization. The principal Hittite god, Teshub the storm god, had to be cut from the belly of his father Kumarbi; he went on to kill the cosmic serpent Illuyanka, but at the cost of the death of his own son (the Hurrian god Sarruma), who was married to the serpent's daughter. Hittite horsemanship (c. 1400 BCE) derives from the training manual of Kikkuli the Mitannian, which is full of technical terms in an Indic language very like Sanskrit. Around 1250 BCE the Hittite king Hattusilis III wrote to the king of Ahhiyawa (Achaea—mainland Greece) as his "brother" **ŠEŠ**.

an unrelated language previously spoken in the land of Hatti. The hieroglyphic inscriptions were in yet another language, Luwian (**luwili**), and, most surprising of all, the court language (which is still called "Hittite") was in actual fact an Indo-European language—the oldest known language in this family—related not to the other languages of the Middle East but to Latin (see p. 240), Greek (see p. 49), Iranian, and Sanskrit (see p. 251).

TANGUT

Tangut is a Mongolian name ("Tang" from Chinese Dǎng(xiàng) + ɣut "collective plural") for a people first known in the fifth century CE in the Kökö Nūr region of northern Tibet, who in the eighth century moved into the northwest of greater China (modern Ningxia, Gansu, and Shaanxi provinces). There they established a Buddhist empire in 1032 CE. It maintained control of the Silk Road trade, and claimed parity of status with China itself, until it was destroyed by Genghis Khan in 1227. The same people were known to the Chinese as Xī-Xià (western Xia), and in their own language as 鞏 尾 隋 歡 (Great State of White and High).

The Huang (Yellow) River in Gansu province, China. The Tangut language was brought here in the eighth century CE by people from northern Tibet.

The language is believed to be Qiangic, within the Tibeto-Burman branch of the Sino-Tibetan family (so its closest relatives are spoken in western Sichuan), and indeed Dangxiang is classified as a Qiang tribe in Chinese histories (Tang period). As part of the state-building process, a script was defined in 1036 by Yeli Renrong at the behest of Emperor Li Yuan-hao. This was a system in Chinese style, with some 6,000 ideograms, although quite distinct from Chinese characters; literacy flourished, and in the next fifty years a printed translation of the complete Buddhist Tripitaka was produced. Chinese Confucian classics and many indigenous texts, including a five-volume encyclopedia, followed over time.

Despite annihilation of the empire in the early thirteenth century, writing in Tangut continued until the sixteenth century. Much literature has survived, most notably an extensive library of 10,000 volumes that was discovered in 1908 in Khara Khoto, the old capital.

The language of Tangut had two distinctive tones. It was a language with subject-verb-object word order, and agreement between verb and subject or object: essentially the verb registered a first- or second-person participant, and for preference (if both are present) the object. Verbal prefixes also expressed direction: **a/na** (up/down), **ki/vie** (in/out) and **ndi/tha** (to/from the speaker).

Count to 10

lew	1	刻
njii	2	悑
so.	3	散
ljiir	4	羽
ŋwə	5	庵
tɕhjiw	6	𦻞
ɕja.	7	寶
jar	8	凤
gjii	9	弸
ɣa.	10	敐

Alphabets and scripts

The Tangut script indicates words rather than sounds or syllables. Its symbols are all complex, formed as square blocks. (See the numerals on the left.) Its phonetics can, however, be reconstructed, from rough equivalences in a Chinese bilingual glossary, some Tibetan transcriptions of Tangut, and a phonetic analysis of Tangut words on traditional Chinese principles, into syllable-initial and rime.

MASSACHUSETT

Massachusett was the language spoken in the area of the New England colony centered on Boston and Cape Cod at the time when the European colonists arrived in the early seventeenth century. As an Algonquian language, it was surrounded by close relatives (such as Pequot, Lenape, Powhatan to the south as far as modern Virginia; and Abenaki and Passamaquoddy to the north up to present-day Maine). Massachusett itself has a number of names, such as Wampanoag, Pokanoket, Natick, Mashpee, and Narragansett, which may have referred to different dialects of the language.

Above *Illustration depicting the English theologian Roger Williams being welcomed to Salem, New England in 1633.*

"Massachusett" translates from Algonquian as "The people who live near the great hill." The language was studied by the English missionary John Eliot, who began preaching in the Massachusett language in 1646. He also translated the complete Bible into Massachusett in 1663, an unprecedented achievement in a native North American language—although the Spanish had been making copious Christian literature available in the languages of Central and South America since 1539. Ever industrious, Eliot also published a comprehensive grammar of the language in 1666.

Eliot's Bible translation became extremely common and literacy spread in the late seventeenth century. Many handwritten documents, especially land transfers and wills, attest to this. However, the Native American tribes were severely disrupted by King Philip's War (1675–76), which was one of the bloodiest conflicts in U.S. history, with nearly seven out of every eight Native Americans and thirty out of every sixty-five English settlers killed. Although the Psalter was translated in 1709, nothing more was attempted after 1720. Native populations declined, and by 1800 they had been absorbed into the English majority.

Count to 10

Nequt	1
Neese	2
Nish	3
Yau	4
Napanna	5
Nequtta	6
Nesausuk	7
Shwosuk	8
Paskoogun	9
Piuk	10

The seventeenth-century missionary John Eliot tells us: "From the Number 5 upward, they adde a word suppletive, which signifyeth nothing, but receiveth the Grammatical variation of the Declension, according to the things numbered, Animate or Inanimate. The additional is **tohsú** or **tahshé**, which is varied **tohsúog, tohsúash** or **tohshinash**." In general in Massachusett, it seems that the forms in **-og** are animate, those in **-ash** inanimate. **Piuk** (10) seems to have its own combined forms **Piukqussuog** and **Piukqussuash**.

Loanwords

Many loanwords were absorbed early into English from Massachusett, and are eloquent of early colonial life: **moose, muskrat, skunk, woodchuck; squash** (the vegetable), **succotash; mugwump, papoose, sachem, squaw; powwow, wampum**. According to John Eliot, **wigwam** is a corruption of the phrase **weekuwomut** (in his house).

Sanskrit (the name literally means "refined" or "perfected") is a very ancient language of India, although it is primarily associated with the north and center of the subcontinent. Its grammar was defined in the fifth century BCE by Pānini, a legendary figure, whose work is so abstract and so elaborate that he is assumed to be the heir to a long tradition of orally based grammarians. The grammatical standard has been stable ever since, although actual usage—even in such classic works as the Mahābhārata and Rāmāyana—has not always reflected this accurately.

Above *A Hindu devotee studies a holy book, which is written in Sanskrit.*

Since **Pānini**, Sanskrit has been learnt only formally, but this learning has continued to the present day: Sanskrit continues to be used as the sacred language of Hindu worship, and its words and phrases are believed to have a mystical resonance.

Hindi and other Aryan languages of northern India (Bengali, Marathi, Gujarati, Sindhi, etc) derive from Sanskrit, or something very like it that was a spoken language in India in the early first millennium BCE. But Sanskrit is a member of the Indo-European family, visibly related to Greek and Latin; and this observation, made in the eighteenth century, led to the discovery of comparative linguistics, which rapidly developed into the wider science of historical linguistics.

There is an irony in Sanskrit's history, in that the oldest inscriptions (in Brahmi script all over India by Emperor Ashoka in the third century BCE) are in Prakrit (meaning "natural"), a language clearly later than Sanskrit though derived from it (for example, Ashoka goes by the name of **piya-dasi**,

"of friendly aspect," which would be **priya-darshin** in Sanskrit). Later inscriptions are written in a more antiquated language. Pali, a fundamental language in the spread of Buddhism to southeast Asia, is a form of Prakrit.

There is also a vast secular literature. This makes ample use of Sanskrit's intricate grammar, in which nouns may have up to twenty-one forms and verbs upward of 150. The vocabulary too is highly ambiguous, with many words having more than a dozen senses.

With the spread of Persian (thirteenth to nineteenth century) and English (eighteenth century to the present), India's practical use of Sanskrit narrowed. However, it is still officially recognized, and it contributes to word formation in Hindi.

Count to 10

एकत् (ēkat)	1
द्वौ (dvau)	2
त्रिणि (trīni)	3
च्वार (čatwāri)	4
पृच (panča)	5
पट (šat)	6
स (sapta)	7
अ (ašta)	8
नव (nava)	9
दश (daśa)	10

SIRAYA

Siraya is the modern name for the language discovered in the seventeenth century to be spoken by the Singang (or Sinkan) community in the Tainan region of southwestern Taiwan, which continued to be spoken until the early decades of the twentieth century. (The name "Siraya" is fairly recent, being the word for "I," and in use only since the end of the nineteenth century.) Like all the indigenous languages of Taiwan, Siraya was an Austronesian language, a member of a linguistic family that has been present in that island for some 6,000 years.

Above *Gray herons in a wildlife reserve in Tainan. Siraya was chosen by the Dutch as a lingua franca in this area in the seventeenth century.*

The Dutch United East India Company (well known by its Dutch initials VOC — Vereenigte Ostindische Compagnie) had established a trading base at Daiyuan (modern Anping) in 1624, and they took control of the southern part of Taiwan, which they held until they were expelled by the Chinese warlord Coxinga in 1661–62. Siraya was sufficiently widespread to be chosen by the Dutch as a lingua franca within their Taiwanese domain.

Missionaries were active in the four decades of Dutch rule and, led by Georgius Candidius (active 1627–29), they learnt the language

sufficiently to write a translation of the Gospel of St. Matthew, effectively making the language literate. This literacy in a Roman alphabet persisted after Coxinga's expulsion of the Dutch (and the reversion of their Christian converts), as is shown by bilingual Siraya-Chinese land contracts, which were being drawn up until the early nineteenth century. As a large, accessible, and urbanized community, the Singang were more susceptible to Chinese influence than many smaller linguistic communities in Taiwan, and by the time of the Japanese occupation in 1895 Siraya was almost extinct, supplanted by Hokkien Chinese. Siraya is now being revived.

Count to 10

saat	1	Reduplication—the repetition of syllables or sounds— was common in Siraya and typically used to express plurality. It also applied to numerals, but in different ways when numbers were used to count humans as against anything else. Thus, referring to humans, numbers reduplicated the first consonant with an **a** vowel: **ra-ruha** (two [men]), **ta-turu ki vual** (three people). But non-human numbers reduplicated the full first syllable: **ru-ruha ki rapal** (two feet), **tu-turu ki wai** (three days).
ruha	2	
turu	3	
apat	4	
rima	5	
anim	6	
pitu	7	
kipa	8	
matouda	9	
kitian	10	

SOGDIAN 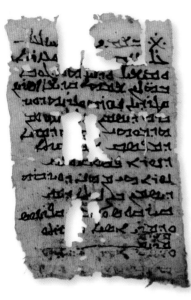 **Until 10th century CE**

Sogdian was the lingua franca of the Silk Road in its heyday (fourth to ninth century CE). It was the native language of a merchant community centered on Samarkand. (Ancient Sogdiana covered an area approximating to present-day southern Uzbekistan and western Tajikistan.) The language was heard as far to the east as China, south into the upper Indus Valley (modern Pakistan), and north into Mongolia's Gobi Desert. But Sogdian itself was related to Persian (see p. 140) and its writing mostly used alphabets derived from Aramaic, which since 522 BCE had been the administrative language of the Persian Empire.

Above *A document written in the Syriac script. This was the script used by Christians for writing Sogdian.*

Surviving records in Sogdian—preserved in the deserts of central Asia—are written in four scripts, selected by religion: Brahmi for Hindus; Manichean for Manicheans (adherents of a faith from Sassanid Persia that spread widely across Eurasia in the fourth and fifth centuries CE); Syriac for Christians; and Sogdian's own alphabet for Buddhists. This shows the wide variety of faiths to which merchants were exposed: Sogdian translators carried their sacred texts northward and eastward into China, as well as back into Sogdiana.

Sogdian is first known from coins of the second century CE. But the bride of Alexander the Great (356–323 BCE) was a Sogdian too: the name Roxane is a Greek conversion of the Sogdian **rukhshan** (bright).

Sogdian's decline began with the Muslim inroads made between 650 and 750 CE. Traditional society was disrupted; Sogdian was supplanted by Persian from the west, brought by Muslim militias, and by Turkic

from the east. Sogdian's last documents, written by Manicheans in northwestern China, date from the fourteenth century. Yaghnobi, spoken by some 2,000 people in Tajikistan, is Sogdian's only modern remnant.

Related languages

Sogdian was one of many eastern Persian languages, including Ossetian in the north Caucasus, Khwarasmian to its west, Bactrian to the south, and Khotanese to the east. Ultimately, these reflect the widespread populations of Persian nomads who ranged across the steppes of central Eurasia in the first millennium BCE, and periodically gave rise to more settled cultures to the south. Of these languages, only Ossetian survives today.

Alphabets and scripts

Sogdian was more influential in spreading writing systems than words. Sogdian script was picked up by the Uyghur (see p. 145) to the east to write their Turkic language, but it was turned through ninety degrees to be written and read vertically; this was then adopted by the Mongolians.

Count to 10

ēw	1
(ə)δwa	2
əθrē, šē	3
čətfār	4
panǰ	5
xušu	6
əβda	7
əšta	8
nəwa	9
δəsa	10

SUMERIAN

Until 13th century BCE

Sumerian, spoken at least since the late fourth millennium BCE but by 1600 BCE purely a written language, provides the world's earliest surviving written record. It was the speech of Šumer—the Biblical "land of Shin'ar," then the name of what is now southern Iraq—a language used by a number of city-states in the region with names such as Ur, Uruk, Nippur, and Eridu. These were conquered in the twenty-fourth century BCE by King Sargon of Akkad. Thereafter Sumerian, which has no known relative, coexisted with Akkadian (an unrelated Semitic language, but the common speech of Babylon and Assyria), and became a classical language.

Count to 10

aš, diš	1	𒁹
min	2	𒐺
eš	3	𒐻
limmu	4	𒐼
ia	5	𒐽
aš	6	𒐾
imin	7	𒐀
issu	8	𒑂
ilimmu	9	𒑄
u	10	𒌋

Numbers 6 to 9 can be interpreted as sums of 5 + 1 to 4.

Sumerian is largely known through the school texts of the Babylonians and Assyrians, written on clay tablets. It is not clear exactly when the language ceased to be spoken, but its great works, such as the *Epic of Gilgamesh* (which deals with lost immortality), hymns to supreme Enlil and the love goddess Inanna, and the exploits of the goddess Ninurta in conquests to the west) remained for more than 2,000 years central to the Mesopotamian education given to students in the **edubba** (the tablet house). Love songs and lullabies were also written in Sumerian, often composed by women (e.g., Sargon's daughter Enheduanna).

It is also striking, and unusual, that Sumerian has a literary dialect called **emesal**, "the fine speech" (contrasted with **emegir**, "the princely speech"), which in dialogue was used exclusively among goddesses. When Akkadian became extinct in the late first millennium BCE, all knowledge of Sumerian vanished with it. The language was only rediscovered, and then painstakingly relearned, by archeologists during the nineteenth century.

Above *King Ur-Nammu, who founded the Sumerian third dynasty of Ur.*

Right *An Assyrian tablet in cuneiform inscribed with a letter from merchants demanding payment.*

Alphabets and scripts

Cuneiform script (based on wedge-shaped incisions in clay) was devised originally for Sumerian in the late fourth millennium BCE. Originally it only offered iconic symbols for particular words, but these were extended to represent the sounds in these words and so created a universal system. All later uses of the script—to write half a dozen other languages, notably Akkadian and Hittite—are extensions of this Sumerian system.

What is called "the Sydney language" first became known to outsiders shortly after 26 January 1788, when the first British group of settlers to Australia, now usually known as "The First Fleet," sailed into Sydney Cove (named for the then Home Secretary Lord Sydney) to found a British penal colony. The settlers, under the command of Captain Arthur Phillip, soon encountered the local inhabitants, but they discovered that the language notes made by Captain James Cook's party in Cape York in 1770 (which famously included the word "kangaroo") were unfortunately of no use in communicating with them.

Loanwords

As Australia's first language to sustain prolonged contact with British settlers, Sydney is the source for many of the best known Aboriginal words in English. "Boomerang" is from **bumarang**, but this was a boomerang used as a weapon for hand-to-hand fighting. "Dingo" represents **dingu** (dog), although this meant a domestic dog. "Koala" is apparently a shortening of **gulaman**, and "wallaby" represents **wulaba**. The "wombat" from **wumbat** is supposed to have been a Dharuk word from inland.

Above Sydney Cove today. The Sydney language became known to the outside world when the first British settlers arrived here in 1788.

Right A prison colony church at Paramatta, now a western suburb of Sydney.

The names that the British gave to this linguistic community were **Iyora** (the local word for "people") and **Dharruk** or **Dharug** (dh as the "th" in English "the"), now evidently revealed as the word for "language." It belongs to the Pama-Nyungan family of languages (which extends over most of Australia); many of these languages have words pronounced **dhāruk** or **jaru**, meaning "word" or "speech."

The best contemporary sources of Sydney are the 1790–92 notebooks of Captain Phillip's officers, although there are later wordlists made in 1875, when "very few of the tribe speaking this language are left," and 1903. (Words quoted here use the rationalization of the sound system and spelling inferred by Jakelin Troy in 1994.) It had a suffixing agglutinative verb system: **yan-muni** (go not); **biyal na-buni biyal** (nowise see not nowise, in other words, "you cannot see it"); **nanga-dyi-niya** (we all slept); **nanga-dya-ngun** (we two slept). The language was not widely used as a lingua franca between Aboriginals and the British; instead, it contributed to New South Wales pidgin until English itself became universal.

Related languages

An expedition in 1791 discovered that Sydney was not spoken on the Hawkesbury river to the north. It was only spoken in the town of Sydney, and (in a related dialect) west of Paramatta to the Blue Mountains. It was surrounded by the languages of Darkinung to the north, Dharawal to the south, Gundungurra to the southwest, and Wiradjuri beyond the Blue Mountains, all distinct but related languages. This discovery was a first sign of the vast multilingualism which was to be revealed in Australia.

MAPS

WORLD

Map guide

This map shows the spread of English, Spanish, French, Portuguese, Arabic, and Russian across the world, to the countries where they are spoken as a first language, or have official status. The speaker populations of the remaining world languages—Mandarin, Hindi, Bengali, German, and Japanese—have grown to enormous numbers within and from a permanent heartland.

Map key

- MANDARIN
- ENGLISH
- SPANISH
- ARABIC
- HINDI
- RUSSIAN
- BENGALI
- PORTUGUESE
- FRENCH
- GERMAN
- JAPANESE

259

EUROPE

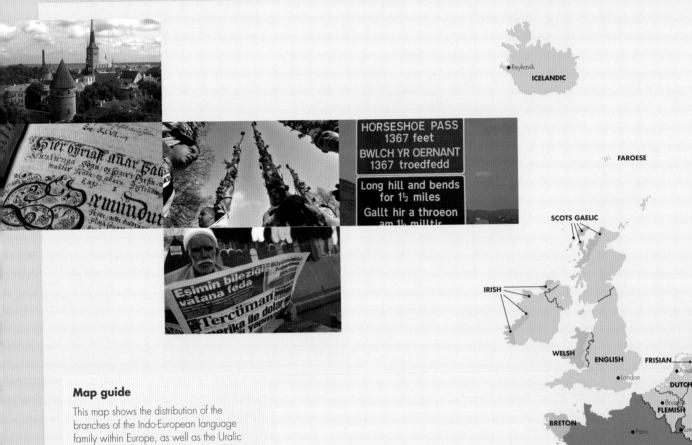

Map guide

This map shows the distribution of the branches of the Indo-European language family within Europe, as well as the Uralic and Altaic language families. Most of the indigenous languages of Europe belong to the Indo-European family. The exceptions are: Finnish, Estonian, Hungarian, and Sámi, which are all Uralic languages; Turkish, an Altaic language; and Basque, which is an isolated language with no known relatives.

Map key

- CELTIC
- ROMANCE
- GERMANIC
- SLAVIC
- BALTIC
- OTHER INDO-EUROPEAN
- URALIC
- ALTAIC
- ISOLATES

SÁMI

SÁMI

SÁMI

SÁMI

SWEDISH

FINNISH

RWEGIAN

• Oslo

• Helsinki

RUSSIAN

• Stockholm

• Tallinn

ESTONIAN

ANISH

• Copenhagen

LATVIAN

• Moscow

• Riga

LITHUANIAN

RUSSIAN

• Vilnius

CASSUBIAN

• Minsk

BELARUSIAN

RMAN • Berlin

• Warsaw

POLISH

SORBIAN

• Kiev

• Prague

UKRANIAN

CZECH

SLOVAK

• Vienna

RAETO-ROMANCE

• Bratislava

• Budapest

HUNGARIAN

SLOVENIAN

• Zagreb

ROMANIAN

GEORGIAN

• Ljubljana

• Tbilisi

CROATIAN

• Belgrade

• Bucharest

• Yerevan

BOSNIAN

ARMENIAN

• Sarajevo

ALIAN

SERBIAN

BULGARIAN

me

• Sofia

AZERBAIJANI

MACEDONIAN

• Istanbul

ALBANIAN

GREEK

TURKISH

ITALIAN

• Athens

261

NORTH AND WEST AFRICA

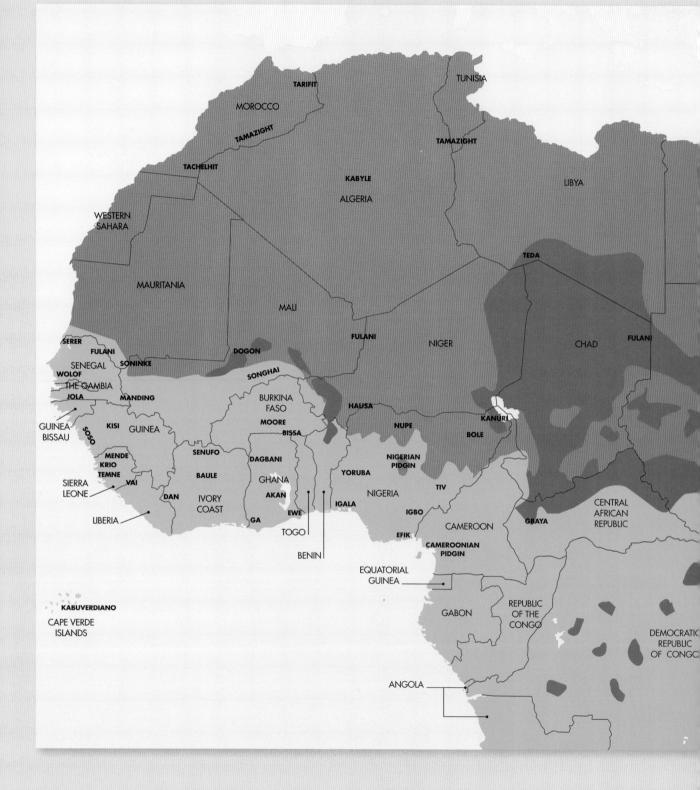

TARIFIT

TUNISIA

MOROCCO

TAMAZIGHT

TAMAZIGHT

TACHELHIT

KABYLE

LIBYA

ALGERIA

WESTERN
SAHARA

TEDA

MAURITANIA

MALI

FULANI

NIGER

CHAD

FULANI

SERER

FULANI

DOGON

SENEGAL

SONINKE

WOLOF

THE GAMBIA

SONGHAI

JOLA

MANDING

BURKINA
FASO

HAUSA

KANURI

GUINEA-
BISSAU

SOSO

KISI

GUINEA

MOORE

NUPE

BOLE

BISSA

MENDE

SENUFO

DAGBANI

NIGERIAN
PIDGIN

KRIO

TEMNE

BAULE

GHANA

YORUBA

TIV

SIERRA
LEONE

VAI

DAN

IVORY
COAST

AKAN

NIGERIA

LIBERIA

GA

EWE

IGALA

IGBO

CAMEROON

GBAYA

CENTRAL
AFRICAN
REPUBLIC

TOGO

EFIK

CAMEROONIAN
PIDGIN

BENIN

EQUATORIAL
GUINEA

KABUVERDIANO

GABON

REPUBLIC
OF THE
CONGO

DEMOCRATIC
REPUBLIC
OF CONGO

CAPE VERDE
ISLANDS

ANGOLA

Map guide

This map shows the distribution of indigenous language families across North and West Africa. The major family to be found in this region is Afro-Asiatic, covering North Africa and the eastern horn of Africa. The map is labeled with the languages that feature in Chapter 3 (see pp. 60–85), corresponding to the main region(s) in which they are spoken.

Map key

- AFRO-ASIATIC
- NILO-SAHARAN
- NIGER-CONGO
- KHOISAN

EGYPT

SUDAN

BEJA

ERITREA

TIGRINYA

AMHARIC

ETHIOPIA

SIDAMO

OROMO

SOMALIA

SOMALI

UGANDA

KENYA

ANDA

URUNDI

TANZANIA

CENTRAL, EAST, SOUTHERN AFRICA

Map guide

This map shows the distribution of language families and subgroups across Central, East, and Southern Africa. The largest language family in Africa is Niger-Congo, containing the Bantu subgroup, to which many of the languages in Chapter 4 belong (see pp. 86–111). The Indo-European family is represented by Afrikaans, a Germanic language. The languages featured are labeled on the map corresponding to the main region(s) in which they are spoken.

Map key

- NIGER-CONGO
- BANTU
- NILO-SAHARAN
- AFRO-ASIATIC
- KHOISAN
- AUSTRONESIAN
- GERMANIC

LINGALA _____

KINYARWANDA _____

SWAHILI, KIRUNDI, AND KINYARWANDA _____

NYAMWEZI _____

ZANDE

ZANDE

LINGALA

LUO
LUO

RUNYAKITARA

KIRUNDI

KITUBA

SWAHILI

LUO
LUYIA

LUGANDA

KALENJIN
GUSII   MERU

KIKONGO

LINGALA

SUKUMA   CHAGA
GIKUYU
KAMBA

SWAHILI

KINYARWANDA

KIKONGO

GOGO

SWAHILI

BEMBA   KIRUNDI

NYAKYUSA

LUBA

MAKONDE

CHOKWE

YAO

KIMBUNDU   CHOKWE   CHOKWE

TUMBUKA

BEMBA

MAKONDE

UMBUNDU

BEMBA

NYANJA

TONGA

LOMWE

YAO

NYANJA   SHONA

WAMBO

TONGA   SHONA   TONGA

SENA

WAMBO

TSWANA

MAKUA

SHONA

NDEBELE

MALAGASY

TSWANA

TSONGA

ZULU   NORTHERN
SOTHO

NDEBELE   ZULU

AFRIKAANS

SWATI   TSONGA
ZULU

SWATI

TSWANA

AFRIKAANS   SESOTHO
ZULU

SESOTHO

XHOSA

265

SOUTH ASIA

BURUSHASKI

SHINA

KASHMIRI

URDU

PAKISTAN

URDU

BRAHUI

PUNJABI

KINNAURI

BALOCHI

SIRAIKI

NEPAL

NEPALI

SHERPA

SINDHI

AWADHI

NEWAR

BHUTAN

DZONGKHA

NEPALI

ASSAMESE

MAITHILI

BODO

GUJARATI

INDIA

KURUKH

URDU

MEITEI

SANTALI

MIZO

KURUKH

SANTALI

BANGLADESH

MARATHI

ORIYA

TELUGU

TELUGU

KANNADA

TULU

KONKANI

TELUGU

MALAYALAM

TAMIL

TAMIL

SRI LANKA

SINHALA

THE MALDIVES

Map guide

This map shows the distribution of indigenous language families across South Asia, including India, Pakistan, Bangladesh, Nepal, Bhutan, and Sri Lanka. The largest language family in this region is Indo-European, represented by the Indo-Aryan and Iranian subgroups. The map is labeled with the languages that feature in Chapter 5 (see pages 112–135), corresponding to the main region(s) in which they are spoken.

Map key

- INDO-EUROPEAN
- DRAVIDIAN
- TIBETO-BURMAN
- AUSTROASIATIC
- ISOLATES

CENTRAL, WEST, NORTH ASIA

RUSSIAN
FEDERATION

WEST SIBERIAN URALIC

CHUVASH

TATAR

BASHKIR

KAZAKHSTAN

KAZAK

CRIMEAN

KYRGYZSTAN

NORTH CAUCASIC
CLUSTER

UZBEKISTAN

CAUCASUS TURKIC

KYRGYZ

UZBEK

TURKEY

AZERI

TURKMENISTAN

UYGHUR

TURKMEN

TAJIK

TAJIKISTAN

KURDISH

GILAKI

MAZANDERANI

HEBREW

PERSIAN

AFGHANISTAN

ISRAEL

IRAN

PASHTO

BALOCHI

PAKISTAN

INDIA

SIBERIAN TURKIC CLUSTER

MONGOLIAN

MONGOLIA

Map guide

This map shows the distribution of language families and subgroups across Central, Western, and Northern Asia. The largest family in this region is Altaic, which covers a vast area, from the Balkan peninsula to northeast Asia. The Afro-Asiatic family is represented by Hebrew, a Semitic language. The map is labeled with the languages that feature in Chapter 6 (see pp. 136–153), corresponding to the main region(s) in which they are spoken.

Map key

- ALTAIC
- INDO-EUROPEAN
- FINNO-UGRIAN
- NORTHERN CAUCASIAN
- AFRO-ASIATIC

EAST AND SOUTHEAST ASIA

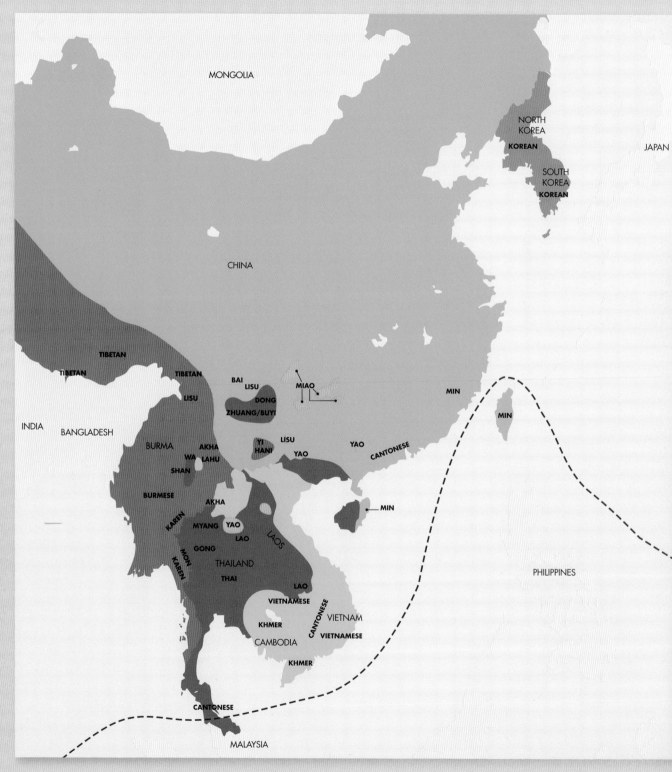

MONGOLIA

NORTH
KOREA
KOREAN

SOUTH
KOREA
KOREAN

JAPAN

CHINA

TIBETAN

TIBETAN

TIBETAN

LISU

BAI
LISU

MIAO

MIN

DONG
ZHUANG/BUYI

MIN

INDIA

BANGLADESH

LISU

YI
HANI

LISU

BURMA

AKHA

YAO

YAO

WA **LAHU**

YAO

CANTONESE

SHAN

BURMESE

AKHA

MIN

KAREN

MYANG **YAO**

GONG

LAO

LAOS

MON
KAREN

THAILAND

THAI

PHILIPPINES

LAO

VIETNAMESE

CANTONESE

KHMER

VIETNAM

VIETNAMESE

CAMBODIA

KHMER

CANTONESE

MALAYSIA

Map guide

This map shows the distribution of language families and subgroups across East and Southeast Asia. The Sino-Tibetan family (which includes the Sinitic and Tibeto-Burman subgroups) has the second largest number of speakers after the Indo-European family. The map is labeled with the languages and language groups that feature in Chapter 7 (see pp. 154–173), corresponding to the main region(s) in which they are spoken.

Map key

- SINITIC
- TIBETO-BURMAN
- TAI
- MON-KHMER
- ALTAIC
- MIAO-YAO
- AUSTRONESIAN

AUSTRALIA–PACIFIC

PHILIPPINES

MOKILESE

EASTERN CAROLINE
ISLANDS

I'SAKA

MIAN

YIMAS

PAPUA NEW
GUINEA

INDONESIA

SOLOMON
ISLANDS

KOKO

MOTU/HIRI MOTU

MERYAM MIR

KRIOL

SALIBA

MAWNG

YOLNGU MATHA

KUNWINJKU

MURRINH-PATHA

KUUK
THAAYORRE

KRIOL

WARLPIRI

ARRERNTE

PITJANTJATJARA

AUSTRALIA

Map guide

This map shows the distribution of indigenous language families and subgroups across Australia and the Pacific. The largest language group in this region is Pama-Nyungan, which covers most of Australia, apart from the north and northwest. The Austronesian family is one of the largest in terms of number of speakers and languages. The map is labeled with the languages that feature in Chapter 8 (see pp. 174–189), corresponding to the main region(s) in which they are spoken.

Map key

- AUSTRALIAN
- AUSTRONESIAN
- PAMA-NYUNGAN
- NON PAMA-NYUNGAN
- PAPUAN

HAWAI'IAN

HAWAI'I
(UNITED STATES)

VANUATU

BISLAMA

SOUTH EFATE

ANEJOM̃

FIJIAN

FIJI

CÈMUHÎ

NEW
CALEDONIA

NEW ZEALAND

MAORI

THE AMERICAS

RUSSIA

GREENLAND

ALASKA
(UNITED STATES)

YUKON
TERRITORY

NORTHWEST
TERRITORIES

BRITISH
COLUMBIA

CANADA

ALBERTA

MANITOBA

QUEBEC

SASKATCHEWAN

ONTARIO

UNITED STATES

MEXICO

BELIZE

HONDURAS

GUATEMALA

NICARAGUA

EL SALVADOR

COSTA RICA

PANAMA

COLOMBIA

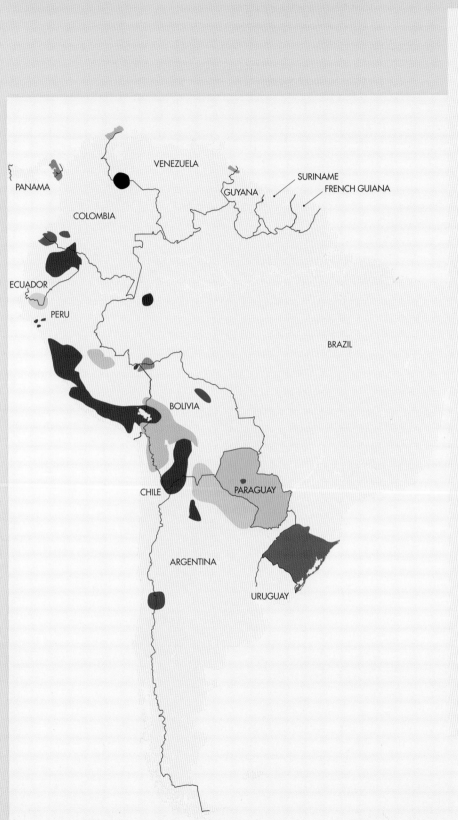

Map guide

This map shows the distribution of the indigenous languages of North, Central, and South America that are discussed in Chapter 9 (see pp. 190–213). Although some of these languages, such as Quechua and Guaraní, still thrive in South and Central America, many other language communities are now close to extinction and in North America many have already been lost.

Map key

- INUIT
- CREE
- OJIBWE
- BLACKFOOT
- DAKOTA/LAKOTA
- NAVAJO
- KICKAPOO
- CHEROKEE/CHOCTAW-CHICKASAW
- KERES
- O'ODHAM
- RARAMURI
- HUICHOL
- PUREPECHA
- NAHUATL
- OTOMANGUEAN
- HUAVE
- YUCATEC MAYA
- PIPIL
- EMBERÁ
- WAYUU
- WARAO
- GUAHIBO
- PAEZ
- AWA PIT
- QUECHUA
- JIVAROAN
- TICUNA
- CAMPA
- SHIPIBO-CONIBO
- CHIQUITANO
- AYMARA
- GUARANÍ
- WICHÍ LHAMTÉS
- NIVACLÉ
- KAINGÁNG
- MAPUDUNGUN

PANAMA

VENEZUELA

GUYANA

SURINAME

FRENCH GUIANA

COLOMBIA

ECUADOR

PERU

BRAZIL

BOLIVIA

PARAGUAY

CHILE

ARGENTINA

URUGUAY

ENDANGERED Language Hotspots

ARCTIC REGION
75 LANGUAGES SPOKEN—ALMOST ALL ENDANGERED

PACIFIC
NORTHWEST

UNITED STATES
SOUTHWEST

THE AMERICAS
**APPROX. 1,000 LANGUAGES SPOKEN
170 LANGUAGES NEARLY EXTINCT**

MEXICO

SOUTH
AMERICA

Map guide

This map shows the regions of the world where languages are most endangered. Areas in which languages are becoming extinct most rapidly include eastern Siberia, Northern Australia, and central South America. It is estimated that by the end of this century, 90 percent of the 6,800 languages of the world will have disappeared.

Map key

■ AREAS WHERE LANGUAGES ARE MOST IN DANGER OF EXTINCTION

(Source: Adapted from Language Hotspots map, Living Tongues Institute for Endangered Languages)

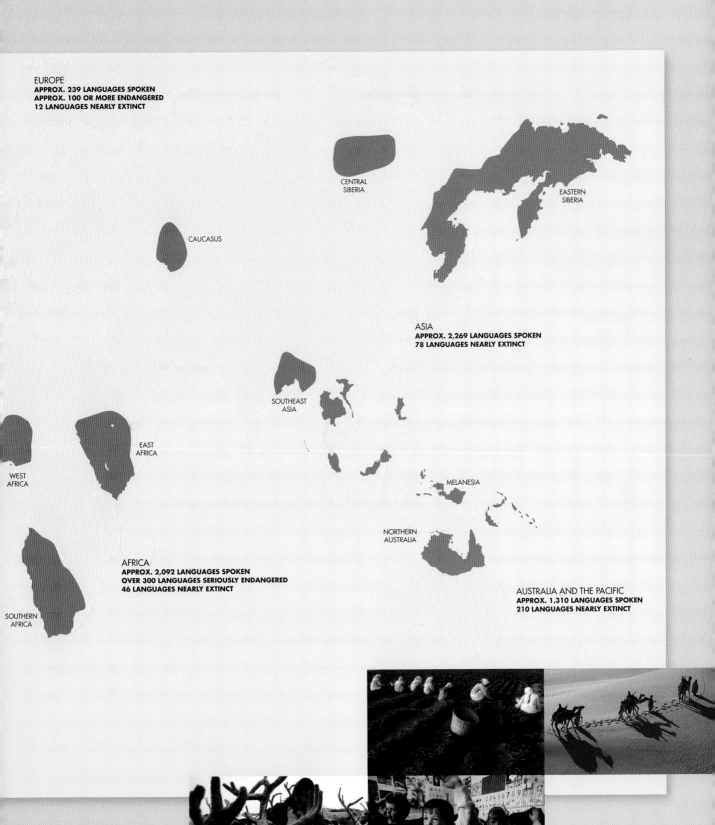

EUROPE
APPROX. 239 LANGUAGES SPOKEN
APPROX. 100 OR MORE ENDANGERED
12 LANGUAGES NEARLY EXTINCT

CENTRAL
SIBERIA

EASTERN
SIBERIA

CAUCASUS

ASIA
APPROX. 2,269 LANGUAGES SPOKEN
78 LANGUAGES NEARLY EXTINCT

SOUTHEAST
ASIA

EAST
AFRICA

WEST
AFRICA

MELANESIA

NORTHERN
AUSTRALIA

AFRICA
APPROX. 2,092 LANGUAGES SPOKEN
OVER 300 LANGUAGES SERIOUSLY ENDANGERED
46 LANGUAGES NEARLY EXTINCT

AUSTRALIA AND THE PACIFIC
APPROX. 1,310 LANGUAGES SPOKEN
210 LANGUAGES NEARLY EXTINCT

SOUTHERN
AFRICA

EXTINCT

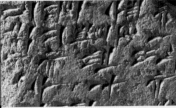

GAULISH
(EXTINCT END 4TH CENTURY CE)

MASSACHUSETT
(EXTINCT EARLY 19TH CENTURY)

ETRUSCAN
(EXTINCT 1ST CENTURY BCE)

EGYPTIAN
(EXTINCT 14TH CENTURY CE)

CHIBCHA
(EXTINCT MID-18TH CENTURY)

Map guide

This map shows the regions in which the extinct languages of Chapter 11 (see pp. 236–255) were spoken across the world. These languages range from Hittite, the language of a great empire, which became extinct in the thirteenth century BCE, to Ubykh, a language of the Caucasus region, whose last speaker died in 1992.

LATIN
(EXTINCT 7TH CENTURY CE)

TANGUT
(EXTINCT 16TH CENTURY CE)

UBYKH
(EXTINCT 1992)

HITTITE
(EXTINCT 13TH CENTURY BCE)

SOGDIAN
(EXTINCT 10TH CENTURY CE)

SILK ROAD

AKKADIAN
(EXTINCT 2ND CENTURY CE)
AND SUMERIAN
(EXTINCT 13TH CENTURY BCE)

SANSKRIT
(EXTINCT 5TH CENTURY BCE)

SIRAYA
(EXTINCT EARLY 20TH CENTURY)

ETHIOPIC
(EXTINCT 10TH CENTURY CE)

SYDNEY
(EXTINCT EARLY 20TH CENTURY)

AGGLUTINATION Combining roots and affixes into complex words with little change in form, e.g., English *un-reason-able-ness*, Japanese *tabe-sase-ta* "eat-cause-past," "caused to eat."

AGREEMENT When two parts of a sentence have the same case, gender, number, or person (e.g., verbs in many languages agree with their subject, or adjectives agree with the noun they modify).

ALVEOLAR Consonant articulated with the tip of the tongue at or near the ridge behind the top teeth, e.g., English *t*, *d*, *n*.

ANTONYM Word or term of opposite meaning to another word or term, e.g., *big* is the antonym of *small*.

ARABIC A Semitic language spoken throughout North Africa and the Middle East; numerals 1, 2, 3, 4 etc. (compare Roman numerals I, II, III, IV etc.).

ASPECT A grammatical category, typically marked on verbs, expressing beginning, duration, termination, repetition, etc.

ASPIRATE Consonant pronounced with a noticeable breath, e.g., English *p*, *k*, *t* at the beginning of a word).

BILABIAL Consonant produced by the closure of the lips, e.g., *b*, *p*, *m*.

CASE A grammatical category, typically marked on nouns, pronouns, or adjectives reflecting the function of that word in the sentence, e.g., nominative case encodes subject, accusative case codes object.

CLASS NOUN A noun with a range of meaning covering membership of a class, e.g., animal, plant.

CLICK Sounds produced with inflow of air into the mouth, used contrastively in some African languages, and non-linguistically in others, e.g., English *tut-tut*.

COGNATE Words with similar form and meaning shared between languages that are related, and originating in a single common root, e.g., English *deer*, German *Tier* (animal), English *fish*, Swedish *fisk*.

COPULA A word that links a subject to a non-verb predicate, e.g., forms of English *be* as in *John is a man*, *The children are sick*.

CREOLE A pidgin language that has developed into a community's native language; descendant of European settlers or black slaves, in the West Indies, Central or South America.

CUNEIFORM Ancient written inscription in the form of wedge-shaped incisions, mostly in clay.

CURSIVE Writing in which the implement is not raised after each character, so giving script a continuous look.

CYRILLIC ALPHABET Family of letters based on Greek and developed by St. Cyril (826–869), apostle to the Slavs, now used to write a range of languages including Russian, Serbian, and Mongolian, e.g. а А б Б b В г Г д Д (compare **GREEK ALPHABET**, **ROMAN ALPHABET**).

DEMOTIC Simplified form of Egyptian hieroglyphic script (see **HIERATIC**); form of modern Greek based on popular speech.

DENTAL Consonant articulated with the tip of the tongue against the back of the top front teeth, e.g., French *t*, *d*, *n*.

DEPRESSOR CONSONANT Consonant that has a lowering effect on the tone of a following vowel.

DIACRITIC Mark added to letters to distinguish a different sound or value of the letter, e.g., é, è, ä, č, ç, ñ etc.

DIALECT Form of language characteristic of a particular location or group of people.

DIALECT CONTINUUM Range of dialects spoken across a geographical area where neighbors can understand each other but speakers far apart cannot.

DIGLOSSIA Regular use of two different varieties of a language in different contexts, one often for administrative or educational purposes and the other for vernacular purposes, e.g., classical and spoken Arabic.

DIPHTHONG Two vowels pronounced together in one syllable, e.g., English *house*.

EJECTIVE Consonant articulated by closing the flow of air and releasing it suddenly.

ERGATIVE A case form used to encode the subject of a transitive verb as distinct from the subject of an intransitive verb (and the object of a transitive verb).

ETHNOLINGUISTICS Branch of linguistics treating the relationship between cultural and linguistic behavior.

ETYMOLOGY Specification of the origins of a word its meaning, and an account of its history.

EVIDENTIALITY Indication of the nature of evidence for a given statement—whether such evidence exists and/or what kind it is, e.g., statement based on visual evidence, statement based on hearsay.

FALLING TONE Pitch, usually associated with a vowel or syllable, which begins high and changes to low.

FOCUS MARKER Sentence marker indicating some prominent or focal element.

FRANCOPHONE French-speaking person or region.

FRANCOPHONIE International organization of French-speaking governments and countries that upholds and encourages the use and influence of the French language.

FRICATIVE Consonant articulated with friction of the airstream within the mouth, e.g., English *s*, *z*, *f*, *v*, *th*.

FRONT VOWEL Vowel produced with the tongue positioned forward in the mouth, e.g., *i*, *e*.

GLOTTAL STOP Consonantal sound produced by the sudden closing of the glottis, the space between the vocal cords, e.g., English *uh-oh*.

GREEK ALPHABET Family of written letters developed by the Greeks from Semitic models, e.g., α Α β Β γ δ Δ etc., frequently used in mathematics and science (see **CYRILLIC ALPHABET**, **ROMAN ALPHABET**).

GUTTURAL Sound formed by the back of the tongue and soft palate.

HIERATIC Style of ancient Egyptian writing used for sacred subjects and made up of shortened forms of hieroglyphics (see **DEMOTIC**).

HIEROGLYPH Character of the ancient Egyptian writing system; figure of an object representing a word, sound, or syllable.

HIGH VOWEL Vowel produced with the tongue elevated close to the palate, e.g., English *i*, *u*, German *ü*.

HIGH TONE High pitch associated with a vowel or syllable.

HOMONYM Two words having the same pronunciation but differing in origin, spelling, and meaning, e.g., *through* and *threw*.

HONORIFIC Form of language expressing respect or honor.

IDEOGRAM (see **IDEOGRAPH**).

IDEOGRAPH Symbol derived from representation of an object, whose form is not linked to the sound structure of the language, e.g., Chinese characters, or numerals like 1, 35, 672.

IDEOPHONE Word whose sound imitates the properties of its referent, e.g., *plop*, *ping*.

IDIOM Written or spoken language of a particular people or area; an expression whose meaning is not equivalent to its parts, e.g., *kick the bucket* meaning "to die."

INDO-EUROPEAN Family of related languages, including most languages of Europe, the northern Indian subcontinent, the Iranian plateau and parts of Central Asia.

INFLECTION Modification of a word by root change, affixation, etc., to express grammatical categories such as case, number, gender, or tense; change of vocal intonation.

INTERNATIONAL PHONETIC ALPHABET Phonetic symbols for international use, formed from Roman and Greek alphabets with added symbols and diacritics, e.g., m, æ, ŋ, χ

ISOLATE Language that cannot be shown to be related to any other language, e.g., Basque.

LABIAL Consonant sound pronounced with complete or partial closure of the lips, e.g., English b, f, m, p, w.

LABIODENTAL Sound formed with lips and teeth, e.g., f, v.

LATERAL Consonantal sound formed by partial closure of the air passage by the tongue, positioned so that breath can flow past one or both sides of the tongue, e.g., English l, Welsh ll.

LATERAL CLICK A click sound produced with airflow past the side of the tongue, contrastive in some African languages.

LEXICAL Pertaining to words or vocabulary.

LINEAR B Later form of Bronze Age writing (the earlier being the undeciphered Linear A) from Greece and Crete, recording a form of Mycenaean Greek.

LINGUA FRANCA (origin: Italian, "Frankish tongue") Language acting as a communication medium between people whose own languages are not the same, e.g., English for international air traffic control.

LOANWORD Word borrowed or adopted from another language.

LOW TONE Low level pitch associated with a vowel or syllable (see **HIGH TONE**, **MID TONE**, **RISING TONE**, **FALLING TONE**).

MACRON Straight horizontal line over a vowel, marking length or stress, e.g., Māori

MID TONE Medial level pitch associated with a vowel or syllable (see **HIGH TONE**, **LOW TONE**, **RISING TONE**, **FALLING TONE**).

MID VOWEL Vowel pronounced with the tongue positioned midway between a high and a low vowel, e.g., e, o.

MORPHOLOGY Structure of words in a language, including their formation, change, and inflection.

MORPHEME Smallest element of words that cannot be analyzed into

NASAL Vowel or consonant produced with airflow through the nose, e.g., m, n, ā.

NEOLOGISM New word or expression; act of coining new word or expression.

NOMINAL Word, compound word, or phrase functioning as a noun.

NOUN CLASS Group of nouns sharing some characteristic in common and usually marked by an affix or other marker, e.g., female human nouns, long thin objects.

OBJECT MARKER An affix or particle indicating a noun functioning as object of a sentence, e.g., Japanese o.

ORTHOGRAPHY System of writing using symbols for sounds or syllables.

PALATAL Sound formed with the tongue near or touching the hard palate, e.g., English ch in church.

PHARYNGEAL CONSONANT Consonantal sound articulated with obstructed airstream at the pharynx, found in Semitic languages.

PHARYNGEAL VOWEL Vowel sound produced by resonance in the pharynx.

PHONEME Unit of sound that cannot be analyzed into smaller units, and that contrasts with other sounds in the expression of the meaning of a word, e.g., English t and m in tan and man.

PHONETIC Written character that represents a sound rather than an object or idea; orthography where each character always signifies the same sound.

PHONOLOGY Systems of sounds in a language.

PIDGIN Language spoken in a simplified or modified form by non-native speakers, usually for trade.

POLYSYNTHETIC Combining several or all sentence components in one word, often by affixation to create one long word.

PREDICATE Word(s) in a sentence or clause expressing what is said of the subject, e.g., walked the dog in Laura walked the dog.

PRONOMINAL Of or pertaining to a pronoun.

RADICAL Pertaining to the root of a word.

REBUS Expression of a word or phrase by pictures, letters, symbols, or objects whose names suggest another word or its syllables, e.g., c u for "see you."

RETROFLEX Sound pronounced by curling the tip of the tongue back and touching the palate with the underneath, producing an r-like sound.

RISING TONE Pitch, usually associated with a vowel or syllable, which begins low and changes to high (see **FALLING TONE**).

ROMAN Plain and upright printed type (as used in Roman manuscripts, on inscriptions), distinct from Italic and Gothic; letter of a Roman font.

ROMAN ALPHABET Family of written letters developed by the Romans from the Etruscan alphabet, e.g., a A b B c C d D etc., the most widely used alphabet in the world today (see **GREEK ALPHABET, CYRILLIC ALPHABET**).

RUNE Letters of (usually) the earliest Germanic alphabet from circa 3rd century CE, Modifications of Greek or Roman letters to enable carving in stone or wood.

SEMANTICS Pertaining to meaning in language.

SEMITIC Pertaining to the family of languages that includes Hebrew and Arabic.

STOP CONSONANT Consonant formed by closing the flow of air through vocal tract and suddenly releasing the breath, e.g., b, d, p, t.

SUBSTRATUM An underlying language structure identified as the relic of, or influenced by, an earlier possibly extinct language.

SYLLABARY System of characters representing syllables rather than individual consonants or vowels, e.g., Japanese kana, Cree syllabary.

SYNONYM Two words with the same or very similar meaning, e.g., cry and weep (see **ANTONYM, HOMONYM**).

SYNTAX The structural principles for putting sentences together from individual words, such as word order, grammatical relations (subject, object, complement) and connections between phrases and clauses (subordination, coordination).

TONE Voice pitch usually associated with a vowel or syllable, often involved in distinguishing between words in Asian or African languages (see **FALLING TONE, HIGH TONE, LOW TONE, MID TONE, RISING TONE**).

TOPONYM Name of place, sometimes derived from a geographical feature of the area, e.g., Bald Mountain, Dead Sea.

TRANSLITERATION Substitution of letters of one alphabet with those of another in order to represent pronunciation, e.g., Cyrillic MOCKBA in Roman, Moskva "Moscow."

UVULAR Consonantal sound produced in the region of the uvula, e.g., French uvular r.

VEDIC Of the Vedas (a Sanskrit word), the sacred literature of Hinduism in four books.

VELAR Sound articulated with the back of the tongue against or near the soft palate, e.g., k, g.

VELARIZED LABIAL Sound articulated by raising the back of the tongue towards the soft palate, e.g., English syllable final (dark) l, as in milk, Polish ł.

VERB-MEDIAL Language in which the verb falls between the subject and object, giving rise to subject-verb-object or object-verb-subject word order.

VERB-SECOND (V2) LANGUAGE Language in which a finite verb must stand in the second position in declarative main clauses (not subordinate clauses), e.g., German Oft gehe ich nach Hause um zehn Uhr, literally "Often go I home at ten o'clock."

VERNACULAR The native language or dialect of a country or region; the distinctive speech of a community of people.

VOICED A sound produced with vibration of the vocal cords, e.g., b, m, z, a, w.

VOICED (OBSTRUENT) CONSONANT Stop or fricative consonant produced with vibration of the vocal chords, e.g., b, z.

VOICELESS A sound produced without vibration of the vocal cords, e.g., p, s, f.

BIBLIOGRAPHY

WORLD LANGUAGES

General

BROWN, KEITH *The Encyclopedia of Language and Linguistics* (Elsevier, 2007)

COMRIE, BERNARD (ed.) *The World's Major Languages* (Oxford University Press, 1990)

CRYSTAL, DAVID *The Cambridge Encyclopedia of Language* (Cambridge University Press, 1997)

GORDON, RAYMOND G. (ed.) *Ethnologue: Languages of the World* (Summer Institute of Linguistics, 2005)

OSTLER, NICHOLAS *Empires of the Word* (HarperCollins, 2005)

Arabic

VERSTEEGH, KEES *The Arabic Language* (Edinburgh University Press, 1997)

Bengali, Hindi

MASICA, COLIN P. *The Indo-Aryan Languages* (Cambridge University Press, 1991)

Chinese (Mandarin)

CRYSTAL, DAVID *English as a Global Language* (Cambridge University Press, 2003)

CRYSTAL, DAVID *The Stories of English* (Overlook TP, 2005)

NORMAN, JERRY *The Chinese Language* (Cambridge University Press, 1988) English

French

NADEAU, JEAN-BENOÎT and JULIE BARLOW *Plus Ça Change: The Story of French from Charlemagne to the Cirque Du Soleil* (Robson, 2006)

German

GLONING, THOMAS and CHRISTOPHER YOUNG *A History of the German Language Through Texts* (Routledge, 2004)

HABERT, WAYNE *The Germanic Languages* (Cambridge University Press, 2006)

Japanese

SHIBATANI, MASAYOSHI *The Languages of Japan* (Cambridge University Press, 1990)

Portuguese

CAMARA, J. MATTOSO *The Portuguese Language* (University of Chicago Press, 1972)

Russian

PRESS, IAN *A History of the Russian Language and its Speakers* (Lincom Europa, 2007)

Spanish

PENNY, RALPH *A History of the Spanish Language* (2nd ed.) (Cambridge University Press, 2002)

EUROPEAN LANGUAGES

PRICE, GLANVILLE (ed.) *Encyclopedia of the Languages of Europe* (Wiley-Blackwell, 2000)

AFRICAN LANGUAGES

CHILDS, G. TUCKER *An Introduction to African Languages* (John Benjamins, 2003)

HEINE, BERND and DEREK NURSE (eds.) *African Languages: An Introduction* (Cambridge University Press, 2000)

NURSE, DEREK and GÉRARD PHILIPPSON (eds.) *The Bantu Languages* (Curzon, 2002)

WEBB, VIC and KEMBO-SURE (eds.) *African Voices: An Introduction to the Languages and Linguistics of Africa* (Oxford University Press, 2000)

SOUTH ASIAN LANGUAGES

CARDONA, GEORGE and DHANESH JAIN *The Indo-Aryan Languages* (Routledge, 2003)

KRISHNAMURTI, BHADRIRAJU *The Dravidian Languages* (Cambridge University Press, 2003)

LAPOLLA, RANDY J. and GRAHAM THURGOOD (eds.) *The Sino-Tibetan Languages* (Routledge, 2002)

MASICA, COLIN P. *The Indo-Aryan Languages* (Cambridge University Press, 1991)

SAXENA, ANJU and LARS BORIN (eds.) *Lesser-Known Languages of South Asia.* (Mouton de Gruyter, 2006)

CENTRAL ASIAN LANGUAGES

JOHANSON, LARS and ÉVA AGNES CSATÓ (eds.) *The Turkic Languages* (Routledge, 1998)

POPPE, NICHOLAS *Grammar of Written Mongolian* (Harrassowitz, 1964)

SIMS-WILLIAMS, NICHOLAS "Iranian languages," in *Encyclopedia Iranica* 7:238–245 (Mazda, 1996)

TOURNADRE, NICOLAS and SANGDA DORJE *Manual of Standard Tibetan* (Snow Lion Publications, 2003)

EAST AND SOUTHEAST ASIAN LANGUAGES

COMRIE, BERNARD (ed.) *The Major Languages of East and South-East Asia* (Routledge, 1987)

GODDARD, CLIFF *The Languages of East and South-East Asia* (Oxford University Press, 2005)

MATISOFF, JAMES "Southeast Asian Languages," in William Bright (ed.) *International Encyclopedia of Linguistics* Vol IV, 44–48 (Oxford University Press, 1992)

MATTHEWS, STEPHEN and VIRGINIA YIP *Cantonese: A Comprehensive Grammar* (Routledge, 1994).

THURGOOD, GRAHAM and RANDY J. LAPOLLA *The Sino-Tibetan Languages* (Routledge, 2003)

AUSTRALIAN AND PACIFIC LANGUAGES

BLAKE, BARRY *Australian Aboriginal Languages* (Angus and Robertson, 1984)

DIXON, R.M.W. *The Languages of Australia* (Cambridge University Press, 1980)

LYNCH, JOHN *Pacific Languages: An Introduction* (University of Hawaii Press, 1998)

LYNCH, JOHN, MALCOLM ROSS and TERRY CROWLEY *The Oceanic Languages* (RoutledgeCurzon, 2001)

AMERICAN LANGUAGES

ADELAAR, WILLEM F. H. and PIETER C. MUYSKEN *The Languages of the Andes* (Cambridge University Press, 2004)

CAMPBELL, LYLE *American Indian Languages: The Historical Linguistics of Native America* (Oxford University Press, 1997)

DIXON, R.M.W. and ALEXANDRA AIKHENVALD *The Amazonian Languages* (Cambridge University Press, 1997)

HINTON, LEANNE *Flutes of Fire: The Indian Languages of California* (Heyday Books, 1993)

MITHUN, MARIANNE *The Languages of Native North America* (Cambridge University Press, 2001)

SHIRLEY, SILVER and WICK R. MILLER *American Indian Languages* (The University of Arizona Press, 1997)

ENDANGERED LANGUAGES

ABLEY, MARK *Spoken Here: Travels Among Threatened Languages* (Mariner Books, 2005)

ANDERSON, GREGORY D. S. and K. DAVID HARRISON (2007) Language Hotspots Map. Living Tongues Institute for Endangered Languages. www.livingtongues.org

BATIBO, HERMAN M. *Language Decline and Death in Africa. Causes, Consequences and Challenges* (Multilingual Matters, 2005)

BRENZINGER, MATTHIAS (ed.) *Endangered Languages in Africa* (Rüdiger Köppe Verlag, 1998)

CRYSTAL, DAVID *Language Death* (Cambridge University Press, 2000)

HARRISON, K. DAVID *When Languages Die. The Extinction of the World's Languages and the Erosion of Human Knowledg* (Oxford University Press, 2007)

MOSELEY, CHRISTOPHER (ed.) *Encyclopaedia of the World's Endangered Languages* (Routledge, 2007)

EXTINCT LANGUAGES

General

HAARMANN, HARALD *Lexikon der Untergegangenen Sprache* (Beck, 2002)

Akkadian

DEUTSCHER, GUY *Syntactic Change in Akkadian* (Oxford University Press, 2000)

Egyptian

LOPRIENO, ANTONIO *Ancient Egyptian* (Cambridge University Press, 1995)

Ethiopic

WENINGER, STEFAN *Ge'ez Grammar* (2nd ed.) (Lincom Europa, 2004)

Etruscan

FACCHETTI, GIULIO M. *L'Enigma Svelato Della Lingua Etrusca* (Newton and Compton, 2000)

Gaulish

LAMBERT, PIERRE-YVES *La language Gauloise* (2nd ed.) (Errance, 2003)

HOFFNER, HARRY J. and H. CRAIG MELCHERT *A Grammar of the Hittite Language* (Eisenbrauns, 2008)

Latin

OSTLER, NICHOLAS *Ad Infinitum, a Biography of Latin* (Walker Books, 2007)

Massachusett

GODDARD, IVES AND KATHLEEN J. BRAGDON (eds.) *Native Writings in Massachusett.* (American Philosophical Society, 1989)

Muisca

ADELAAR, WILLEM F. H. AND PIETER C. MUYSKEN *The Languages of the Andes* (Cambridge University Press, 2004)

Sanskrit

DESPANDE, MADHAV M. *Sanskrit and Prakrit: Sociolinguistic Issues* (Motilal Banarsidass, 1993)

Siraya

ADELAAR, K. ALEXANDER "Grammar notes on Siraya, an extinct Formosan language," in *Oceanic Linguistics* 36/2:164–199, 1997

Sumerian

THOMSEN, MARIE-LOUISE *The Sumerian language: An Introduction to Its History and Grammatical Structure* (Akademisk Forlag, 2001)

Sydney

TROY, JAKELIN *The Sydney Language* (Panther, 1994)

Ubykh

COLARUSSO, JOHN *Nart Sagas from the Caucasus* (Princeton University Press, 2002)

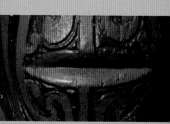

INDEX

Santali 125, 133, 224
Sardinian 38, 40
Saulteaux 197
Scandinavian subgroup 51, 53, 55
Scottish Gaelic 38, 39, 219
Seminole 206
Semitic languages 26, 39, 62, 66, 72, 74, 139, 243, 244
Sena 111
Seneca 207
Senufo linguistic group 79
Serbian 46
Serbo-Croat 38, 46, 50
  dialects 46
Serer 78, 82
Sesotho 101, 102, 104
  dialects 101
Setswana see Tswana
Shahmukhi script 116
Shan 156, 164, 171
  script 171
Sherbro 78
Sherpa 135, 166
Shina 134
Shipibo-Conibo 193, 212
Shona 91
  dialects 91
Shoshone 207
Shor 226
Siberian Turkic Cluster 153
Sidamo 80
Silesian 42, 48
Sindhi 126, 132
  dialects 126
Sinhala (Sinhalese) 129
  script 129
Sinitic languages 156–57, 158,
Sino-Tibetan languages 14, 114, 156
  Tibeto-Burman branch see Tibeto-Burman languages
Siraiki 132
Siraya 239, 252
Siwi 220
Slavic languages 22, 38, 42, 43, 46, 48, 50, 56, 57, 58, 149
  East 43
  South 46, 50, 57, 58
  West 42, 43, 48, 56
Slovak 38, 48, 56
Slovene 38, 46, 50, 57
Soga 105
Sogdian 13, 226, 239, 253
  scripts 251
Somali 70
Songhai (Songhay) language group 77
Soninke 82
Sora 224–25
Sorbian (Wendish, Lusatian) 38, 39, 42, 48

Soso (Susu) 83
Sotho, Northern 101, 102, 104
Sotho, Southern see Sesotho
South Efate 181
Spanish 20–21, 38, 39
Sukuma 104, 110
Sumerian, ancient 239, 254
  scripts 254
Swahili 13, 95, 98, 100
Swati (Siswati) 90, 96, 108
Swedish 38, 51
Sydney 239, 255

T
Tachelhit (Tashelhit) 72
Tahitian 186
Tai language family 156–57, 161, 164, 171
Tajik 132, 138, 140, 151, 226
  dialects/scripts 151
Talishi 38
Tamazight 72
  scripts 72
Tamil 117, 119, 122
Tangut 239, 249
  script 249
Tarahumara 192
Tarifit (Tarafit) 80, 220
Tasmanian languages 176
Tat 38, 227
Tatar 146, 153, 218
  Crimean 146, 153, 218
  dialects/scripts 146
Tati 140
Teda (Tedaga, Teda-Daza) 75, 85
Telugu 117, 119
  script 117
Temne 78
Thai 161, 163, 164, 170, 171
  dialects/script 161
Thai-Kadai languages 156, 172, 228–29
Tibetan 156, 162, 166
  varieties/script 166
Tibetan script 135
Tibeto-Burman languages 114, 127, 128, 131, 134, 135, 156–57, 162, 166, 168, 169, 173, 224, 225, 228–29, 249
  Qiangic subgroup 249
Ticuna (Tukuna) 193, 212
Tigre 74
Tigrinya 67, 74
  dialects/script 74
Tiv 81
Tlapanec 200
Tlingit 232
Toba 193, 213
Tofa 226
Tok Pisin (Melanesian pidgin) 180, 183, 230–31

Tonga 109
Tsafiki (Colorado) 212
Tsiluba see Luba
Tsonga 105
Tswana (Setswana) 101, 102, 104
  dialects 102
Tulu 117, 133
Tumbuka (Chitumbuka) 109
Tungusic languages 227, 229, 235
Tupi 203
Tupi-Guaraní languages 203, 233
Tupinambá 28, 203
Turkic languages 39, 41, 138, 143, 144, 145, 146, 147, 148, 153, 226
  Oghuz group 143, 147
  Qarluq group 145
  Qypchaq group 146, 148, 149, 153
Turkish 39, 41, 143
Turkmen 41, 143, 147
  dialects/script 147
Tuscarora 207
Tuvan 153
Twi 71
  dialects 71

U
Ubykh 239, 242
Udmurt 153
Ugrian/Ugric subgroup 47
Ukrainian 22, 38, 43
Umbundu 105
Uralic languages 39, 227
Urdu 19, 25, 116, 120
Uto-Aztecan language family 192, 199, 207, 209
U'wa (Tunebo) 243
Uyghur 138, 145
  dialects 145
  script 145
Uzbek 139, 142, 145
  script 142

V
Vai 85
Vedic, ancient 118
Veps 54
Vietnamese 156, 159
  scripts 159
  varieties/dialects 159
Vogul see Mansi
Votic 54

W
Wa (Paraok) 156, 173
Waiwai 233
Waiyuunaiki (Guajiro) 193, 210
Wambo (Oshiwambo) 109
Wampanoag see Massachusett
Warao 193, 213
Warlpiri 182

Welsh 38, 39, 59
  in Patagonia 59
West Siberian Uralic 153
Wichí Lhamtés (Mataco) 193, 211
Wolof 78, 82
world languages 12–35
Woun-Meo 211

X
Xhosa 90, 96

Y
Yaghnobi 253
Yalunka (Jalonke) 83
Yangkam 220
Yao 108, 110
Yao Language Cluster 156, 167, 172
Yaqui 192
Yi 156, 169, 171
  linguistic groups 169
  script 169
Yiddish 33, 38, 57
  dialects 57
Yimas 189
Yolngu Matha 187
Yoruba 68, 82
  script 68
Yucatec Maya 201
Yukagir 226
Yupik language/dialects 195, 232

Z
Zaghawa 75
Zande 111
Zapotec 193, 200, 233
Zarma (Djerma) 77
Zhuang/Buyi 156, 161, 164, 171
  dialects/script 164
Zulu (isiZulu) 90, 96, 108

ACKNOWLEDGMENTS

Picture credits

The publisher would like to thank the following organizations and people for their permission to use photographs. Every effort has been made to acknowledge the photographs, however we apologize if there are any unintentional omissions.

Akg Images: 17, 18, 23B, 28, 32, 35R, 35L, 43L, 45B, 47T, 48L, 54, 91T, 97L, 148, 240; Paul Almasy: 103L; Archiv Peter Ruehe: 121L; British Library: 26, 50T; Gerard Degeorge: 165R, 163R; Mark De Fraeye: 146, 224; Daniel Frasnay: 176; Francois Guenet: 15B; Rainer Hackenberg: 58; Marion Kalter: 82; Erich Lessing: 23T, 41T, 55T, 149B, 241;Gilles Mermet: 20; Jean-Louis Nou: 27T, 86TL, 115, 117; Dirk Radzinski: 157; RIA Nowosti: 144; Sambraus: 37MR; Schuetze/Rodemann: 51; Juergen Sorges: 20; Bildarchiv Steffens: 49L, 177; Yvan Travert: 62; Ullstein bild: 90, 92, 220, 249; Ullstein bild/A.S.: 222; Ullstein bild/ P.S.I.BONN: 55B; Ullstein bild/Colourvision: 113MR; Ullstein bild/R. Dietrich: 39; Ullstein bild/Europress: 85L, 219; Ullstein bild/Haag: 143; Ullstein bild/Haeckel: 153R; Ullstein bild/Heike Heller: 5B; Ullstein bild/Ihlow: 165L, 173L, 271B; Ullstein bild/Kanus: 181; Ullstein bild/Mei-ner: 89T; Ullstein bild/Mitterbauer: 171TR; Ullstein bild/Reitz: 99B; Ullstein bild/Rihrbein: 96B. Alamy/Mark Boulton: 106; Mark Bourdillon: 97R; Neil Cooper: 109R; Mike Goldwater: 98; Images of Africa Photobank: 107R, 88, 104, 102; Images&Stories: 93R; Zute Lightfoot: 100B, 110; Craig Lovell/Eagle Visions Photography: 91B; Ross McArthur: 121R; Nordicphotos: 53T; Mark Pearson: 70L, 70R; Neil Setchfield: 42; Charlotte Thege: 111R; Paul Thompson Images: 59. Bridgeman Art Library/British Library Board: 130. Corbis: 12, 206T, 207L; Peter Adams: 25; Steve Allen/Brand X: 169; Paul Almasy: 64T, 105L, 233; Archivo Iconografico, S.A.: 201; Arctic-Images: 59; Jon Arnold/JAI: 29T; Atlantide Phototravel: 40, 56, 73, 83R, 155BML; Patrick Aviolat/epa: 68T; Ricardo Azoury: 203; Kapoor Baldev/ Sygma: 116; Carlos Barria/Reuters: 205; Dave Bartruff: 140; Morton Beebe: 193; Neil Beer: 49R; Remi Benali: 231, 229; Bettmann: 206B, 250, 254L; Nic Bothma/epa: 76, 78, 107L; Bojan Brecelj: 100T; Brooklyn Museum: 244L; Will Burgess/Reuters: 239; John Carnemolla: 7TR; Philippe Caron/Sygma: 5TL; Alvin Chan/Reuters: 5TR; Christie's Images: 95, 254R; Dean Conger: 242L; Ashley Cooper: 187L; Pablo Corral V: 21; Margaret Courtney-Clarke: 71T; Richard Cummins: 154; Gianni Dagli Orti: 200B, 257R; Howard Davies: 67, 124L, 133L; Jay Dickman: 189L; M. ou Me. Desjeux, Bernard: 75; Patrick Durand/Sygma: 93L; Epa: 128B; Michele Falzone/JAI: 120; Bruno Fert: 69; The Gallery Collection: 244R; Gallo Images: 245; Colin Garratt/Milepost 92 ½: 81R; Christel Gerstenberg: 255R; Lynn Goldsmith: 89B; Jose Miguel Gomez/Reuters: 264; Annie Griffiths Belt: 126, 136TL; Justin Guariglia: 138; Louise Gubb/SABA: 105R; Erol Gurian: 127; Peter Guttman: 53B, 57L; 174TR; Antoine Gyori: 142; Blaine Harrington III: 162; Lindsay Hebberd: 134; Chris Hellier: 247, 248; Gavin Hellier/JAI: 135R, 211R, 228; Jon Hicks: 123R, 137MR, 186; Historical Picture Archive: 131R, 246; Jeremy Horner: 24, 156; 191MR; Rob Howard: 6, 66, 27B; Hulton-Deutsch Collection: 57R; Gavriel Jecan: 237MR; Wolfgang Kaehler: 212, 163L; Jens Kalaene/dpa: 94; Sergei Karpukhin/Reuters: 242R; Ed Kashi: 152, 197, 133R; Bob Krist: 33, 61BMR, 77, 214TL; Ludo Kuipers: 175BR, 188, 217; M.A. Pushpa Kumara/epa: 129L; Jacques Langevin/Sygma: 85R, 234; Frans Lanting: 223; Adrees Latif/Reuters: 136 TMR, 141; Floris Leeuwenberg: 225; Danny Lehman: 194, 199R, 207R, 208B; Charles & Josette Lenars: 83L, 174TL, 208T, 232; Yadid Levy/Robert Harding: 129R; Liu Liqun: 170B; Yang Liu: 158B; Anuruddha Lokuhaparachchi/Reuters: 119R; Craig Lovell: 155MR; Frank Lukasseck: 221; Olivier Martel: 63, 71B; Francis G. Mayer: 243; Stephanie Maze: 218; Will & Deni McIntyre: 123L; Colin McPherson: 99T; Gideon Mendel: 125; Gideon Mendel for UNICEF: 101R; Gideon Mendel for The Global Fund: 108; Silvia Morara: 31R; Richard Nebesky/ Robert Harding: 45T; Stoyan Nenov/Reuters: 50B; Kazuyoshi Nomachi: 109L, 202, 211L; Kerim Okten/epa: 41B; Diego Lezama Orezzoli: 210B; Ralph Orlowski/Reuters: 65; Micheline Pelletier/Sygma: 253; Mark Peterson: 196; Fred Prouser/Reuters: 236TL; Carl & Ann Purcell: 136MR, 145R; Ryan Pyle/None: 145L; Jose Fuste Raga: 238, 255L; Steve Raymer: 139; 171BR; Reuters: 7T; David Samuel Robbins: 72; Fulvio Roiter: 79L, 79R; Hans Georg Roth: 124R; Rachel Royse: 47B; Anders Ryman: 131L, 178; Chico Sanchez/epa: 213L; Sangdao Sattra/epa: 170T; Albrecht G. Schaefer: 180, 189R; Alan Schein Photography: 16; Phil Schermeister: 209R; Gregor M. Schmid: 153L; Michel Setboun 235, 236TR; Radu Sigheti/Reuters: 74; Hugh Sitton/zefa: 119L; Smithsonian Institution: 68B; Frédéric Soltan: 19; Paul A. Souders: 179R, 182T; Stapleton Collection: 150T; George Steinmetz: 179L; Studio DL: 216; Keren Su: 164, 166, 167, 175MR, 230R; Chaiwat Subprasom/Reuters: 173R; Rudy Sulgan: 46; Sygma: 38; Tetra Images: 149T; Luca Tettoni: 161R, 172; David Turnley: 136R, 147, 214L; Peter Turnley: 209L; Penny Tweedie: 81L, 174B, 187R, 230L; Harish Tyagi/epa: 251; John Van Hassel: 182B; Robert van der Hilst: 168, 84; Francesco Venturi: 128T; Werner Forman: 200T, 64B; Cathrine Wessel: 103R; Paulo Whitaker/Reuters: 233; Ralph White: 227; Nevada Wier: 150B; Adam Woolfitt: 14; Alison Wright: 135L; Marilyn Angel Wynn/Nativestock Pictures: 192; Corbis/Li Xin/Xinhua Press: 226; Cha Young-Jin/epa: 160L, 160R. Getty Images: 52; AFP: 80, 13, 43R, 161L, 44, 252;

Neil Emmerson/Robert Harding: 122; Jerry Kobalenko/Photographer's Choice: 15T; Adrian Neal/Stone: 31L; Karen Su: 158T, 171TL; Michael S. Yamashita/National Geographic: 14. Sarah Howerd: 159. iStockphoto/Bogdan-Gabriel Postelnicu: 48R. Jupiter Images: 185. Lonely Planet Images/Jonathan Chester: 183. Newspix/News Ltd: 184. Photoshot/Steve Robinson/NHPA: 111L; World Pictures: 151. South American Pictures/Jason P Howe: 199L; Tony Morrison: 213R; Chris Sharp: 29B, 198. Topfoto/HIP: 101L; ImageWorks: 118.

Front cover: Corbis/Matthew McKee/Eye Ubiquitous (BL); Corbis/George Steinmetz (BMR)

Contributors

Professor Peter Austin is Märit Rausing Chair in Field Linguistics, and the Director of the Endangered Languages Academic Program at the School of Oriental and African Studies, University of London.

Professor Nicholas Ostler is Visiting Fellow at the Department of European Studies and Modern Languages, Bath University and Honorary Fellow in Linguistics at Lancaster University, U.K. He is currently chairman of the Foundation for Endangered Languages.

Professor Glanville Price is Emeritus Professor of French at the University of Wales, and was also Visiting Professor, University of California, Berkeley, 1982.

Dr. Friederike Lüpke is a lecturer in language documentation and description at the Department of Linguistics, School of Oriental and African Studies, University of London.

Professor Philip J. Jaggar is Professor of West African Linguistics, School of Oriental and African Studies, University of London.

Dr. Nancy Kula is lecturer in phonology at the Department of Language and Linguistics, University of Essex, U.K.

Dr. Lutz Marten is Senior Lecturer in Southern African Languages at the Department of Linguistics, School of Oriental and African Studies, University of London.

Professor Anju Saxena is Associate Professor at the Department of Linguistics and Philology, Uppsala University, Sweden.

Dr. Kagan Arik is Lecturer in Central Asian Languages and Culture at the Department of Near Eastern Languages and Civilizations at University of Chicago.

Dr. David Bradley is Tenured Reader and Associate Professor in Linguistics at LaTrobe University, Victoria, Australia.

Dr. Nicholas Thieberger is Postdoctoral Fellow in the Department of Linguistics and Applied Linguistics at the University of Melbourne, Australia. He is also the Project Manager for the Pacific and Regional Archive for Digital Sources in Endangered Cultures.

Dr. Rachel Nordlinger is Senior Lecturer at the Department of Linguistics and Applied Linguistics at the University of Melbourne, Australia.

Dr. José Antonio Flores Farfán is a full-time researcher at CIESAS (Centro de Investigaciones y Estudios Superiores en Antropología Social). He has developed research collaboration with a number of international institutions, and has on-going collaborations with the University of Amsterdam, where he is a guest researcher.

Professor Lenore Grenoble is Professor of Russian and Linguistics at Dartmouth College, Hanover.